C000274491

CAR GUIDE
2007

The facts
The figures
The knowledge

© 2006, Uitgeverij de Alk b.v., Alkmaar, The Netherlands

Published as Alle Auto's 2007, by Uitgeverij de Alk b.v., Alkmaar, The Netherlands, in November 2006, This English edition, titled Haynes Car Guide 2007, published by Haynes Publishing, in November 2006

A catalogue record for this book is available from the British Library

ISBN 1 84425 399 6

Library of Congress catalog card no 2006907963

Produced by HSPublicity bv, Bodegraven, The Netherlands Dutch editorial team: Henri Stolwijk, Wim Otten, Niels van der Weiden, Celeste Rooswinkel, Gwenda van Gorkum, Paul Spek, Charissa van Eijk, Ellen de Vos, Kristian Spithout, Alma van Vliet

UK editorial team: Richard Dredge, Derek Smith, James Robertson, Lee Parsons

Published by Haynes Publishing, Sparkford, Yeovil, Somerset BA22 7JJ, UK
Tel: 01963 442030 Fax: 01963 440001
Int.tel: +44 1963 442030 Int.fax: +44 1963 440001
E-mail: sales@haynes.co.uk
Website: www.haynes.co.uk

Haynes North America Inc., 861 Lawrence Drive, Newbury Park, California 91320, USA

Printed and bound in Holland

Contents

Concepts and forthcoming models

At the Mondial de l'Automobile, also known as the Paris Motor Show, the car manufacturers present their own vision of the future. Some of these concept cars we never see again, while others come onto the market as production models almost unchanged. Here are some of the most exciting designs shown in Paris for 2007.

Alfa Romeo 8C Competizione

Alfa Romeo

Partly as a result of pressure from the consumers and politicians, almost all car manufacturers are busy developing environmentally friendly, economical cars. And yet the classic sports car is still not forgotten. Alfa Romeo is breathing new life into its own sporting pedigree with the 8C Competizione. The name derives from a racing car from the 1930s, while the body is inspired by the beautiful 33 Stradale of long ago. The 8C started its career as a concept car but is now being made available in a limited edition of five hundred to (rich) enthusiasts. Alfa Romeo borrowed the technology and the chassis from Maserati, who will help with its market introduction in the United States.

Audi

With Lamborghini under its wing, Audi has a golden advantage. The time to capitalise on this has arrived and thus Audi is bringing the R8 onto the market. Like the Alfa 8C, the R8 derives from a concept car: the Le Mans Quattro. The 4.2 V8 FSI delivers 420hp and gives the R8 a top speed of 188mph (301km/h). This means that Audi is breaking a gentleman's agreement with the German government, which dictates a top speed of 250 km/h (156mph). Immediately following its arrival, there was heated speculation over an even more powerful version (with a V10 engine, for example) but Audi is keeping its lips tightly sealed about this.

Audi R8

Dodge

In 2006, DaimlerChrysler focused on its Dodge brand which, after a long absence, is once again selling cars in Europe. The Caliber seems to be doing well and the compact Nitro will surely turn the compact SUV class on its head at a later stage. In Paris, Dodge showed a proposal for a mid-class car named the Avenger. The Avenger is based on the new Chrysler Sebring that is already in production. DaimlerChrysler have yet to give the Avenger the green light because for the time being it is still classed as a study model. However, it is expected that if the Avenger does indeed go into production (and that is pretty well certain) its appearance will be very little changed.

Dodge Avenger

Ford

The Mondeo is on its last legs, which is why Ford is showing a successor at the Geneva Autosalon in March 2007. To calm everyone down, a concept model for the new Mondeo Wagon was shown in Paris. As in the case of the Dodge Avenger, the production model will differ little from this.

Ford Mondeo

Hyundai Arnejs

Hyundai

Like its sister brand Kia, Hyundai also has a compact mid-class model ready to launch. What this will look like, only the manufacturer knows, but this Arnejs (pronounced Arnez) gives a few useful hints. Like Kia's Golf competitor, this Hyundai will also be developed and built in Europe. Apart from the regular rather tame engine, Hyundai is developing a sport Arnejs that produces more than 220 hp. Count on an estate version too.

Lancia

The exquisite Lancia disappeared into oblivion when the parent company Fiat had no more money to develop new models. That time has passed and we can even expect a new Delta. A concept car with this celebrated name was widely admired at the Paris Motor Show. Of course, details will change, but the main points of the model will be retained. In 2008, the Delta can prove its worth.

Lancia Delta HPE

Landwind

The Chinese Landwind had a short-lived triumph in Europe with a cheap, old-fashioned SUV, but this was ended by rumours about the car's safety record. The brand is fighting back bravely, however, and has announced two new models. One of these is the X-pedition, the successor to the SUV, while the other is called the Fashion. The

Landwind Fashion MPV

Fashion is a seven-seat MPV in the tradition of the Vauxhall Zafira but for the price of a Meriva. We will find out whether Landwind can succeed with these two models in 2007.

Peugeot 207 Epure

Peugeot

The French PSA (Peugeot-Citroën) is gambling heavily on diesel hybrids. These miracles of economy will be gradually introduced onto the market in 2008. However, for the longer term, other solutions to the energy problem are needed, which is why the Peugeot 207 Epure has been developed. This is equipped with a fuel cell that uses hydrogen and therefore emits no harmful substances or CO_2. The model itself is the basis for the new 207 Coupé-Cabriolet.

Renault Twingo

Renault

No fewer than three concept cars featured on the Renault stand, two of which will find their way to dealers in a changed form. After almost fourteen years of faithful service, the Twingo is getting a successor. This was at the Motor Show in a very over-developed version but will be toned down a bit for the premiere of the production model.

Skoda

In a couple of years' time there will be a new Fabia on the market. If you want to know, approximately, what it will look like then, take a good look at the Joyster. The model will not go into production but Skoda will certainly use the lines and design details in a new compact car.

Skoda Joyster

Toyota

After more than forty years, Toyota is bidding farewell to the most successful model name in car history. The successor to the Corolla is called the Auris. The name derives from the Latin word for gold, which is why the concept car was sprayed gold. Apart from a couple of details, this is the car that must replace Toyota's biggest success.

Toyota Auris

Volkswagen Iroc

Volkswagen

The 'Iroc' echoes the name Scirocco and that says a lot about where Volkswagen wants to go with this concept car. The two-door coupé from the 1970s and 1980s is getting a successor whose appearance will be based strongly on this mean street machine. The technology derives from the Golf, as was the case with the old Scirocco.

Haynes books

From classic cars to learning to drive, you can trust Haynes to have it covered.

By Robert Davies
£12.99 PAPERBACK

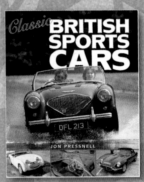

By Jon Pressnell
£15.99 HARDBACK

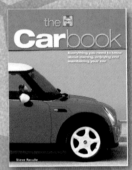

By Steve Rendle
£17.99 HARDBACK

By Paul Guinness
£19.99 HARDBACK

By Martin Buckley
£19.99 HARDBACK

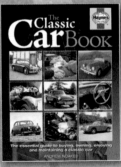

By Andrew Noakes
£17.99 HARDBACK

By Giles Chapman
£7.99 HARDBACK

By Stephen Vokins
£14.99 HARDBACK

By Karl Ludvigsen
£40.00 HARDBACK

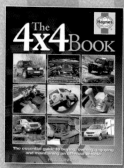

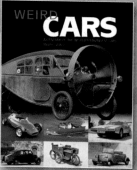

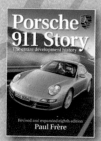

By Paul Guinness
£17.99 HARDBACK

By Stephen Vokins
£14.99 HARDBACK

By Paul Frère
£25.00 HARDBACK

Explanation of the catalogue listings

Make and model designation

The model names are at the top of the tables. In most cases two engine types are stated, separated by a slash. Usually the descriptions are limited to the basic versions with manual gearboxes. For hatchbacks, these are the three-door versions. In most cases we have chosen not to describe all available engines separately, but to spread them over several pages. Diesel engines, for example, are described with the estate cars.

Engine type

This is described as petrol or diesel, followed by the number of cylinders and the construction method. The standard construction method on the European market is the four-cylinder, in-line engine, so called because four cylinders are placed in a single line on the crankshaft. This arrangement is also used for three, five and six cylinders. Another popular configuration is the V with two separate banks of cylinders that are placed at an angle to each other on the crankshaft. Volkswagen has a sort of combined line and V engine in which the cylinders are at so small an angle that they fit under one cylinder head. The Volkswagen W engines even have four banks of cylinders in a compact arrangement. The boxer engine (Porsche and Subaru) is an arrangement with two cylinder banks mounted horizontally opposite each other. Finally, there is a car on the market with a rotary engine, the Mazda RX-8. This concept, with a fixed housing and a rotating piston, will no longer be used in the future.

Maximum output

The correct output specification is in kilowatts. For those who are used to hp it is difficult to switch to kilowatts, and indeed 400 hp sounds a lot better than 294 kW. For this reason, we have used both. One hp is 0.735 kW, so one kW is 1.36 hp.

Maximum torque

Torque, expressed in Newton metres (Nm), represents the 'turning force' a motor can produce when the crankshaft turns. In simple terms, torque x rpm = power output. An engine with a lot of torque does not have to make so many revolutions to move the car. This makes cars quieter and more pleasant to drive. Another way of expressing it is that power output produces the top speed, while torque provides acceleration without having to change gear.

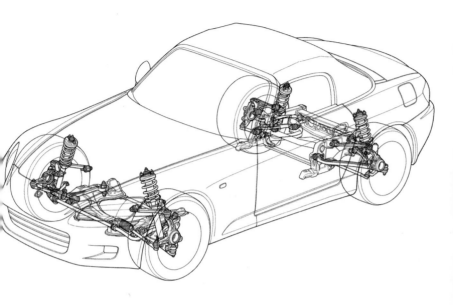

Gears

The number of gears is stated. There is constant pressure to make cars more economical and the gearbox plays a major role in this: a transmission with more gears means that the engine does not have to run as fast and therefore operates more economically. Noise reduction is also a consideration. The six-speed gearbox is gradually replacing the five-speed gearbox, just like the five-speed replaced the four-speed in the 1980s.

Automatic

In the case of the automatic, we are no longer just talking about an automatic with torque converter. Often the automatic has five ratios too and even six in the case of Mercedes-Benz. In addition, there is an increasing number of manual gearboxes with a clutch operated by a hydraulic pump. The continuous variable transmission is gradually gaining ground and Volkswagen has its own system, DSG, which in fact consists of two half gearboxes, each with its own clutch so that the electronics can get the next gear 'ready' in advance.

Drive

Front-wheel drive is the norm for compact cars but has difficulty in handling outputs higher than 250 hp. This is why large cars are fitted with rear-wheel or four-wheel drive. The latter is not just for off-road cars because the advantages also apply in winter. More and more manufacturers are supplying four-wheel drive and offering it as standard.

Brakes F/R (front/rear)

Most, if not all, cars have a power-assisted braking system with disc brakes at the front. Often the rear brakes are solid discs and, in the case of smaller cars, sometimes old-fashioned drum brakes. Ventilated or perforated discs have channels to conduct the heat to the air quicker.

Kerb weight

Most manufacturers give the kerb weight according to the European directive. This represents the car including all fluids, with a 90 per cent full tank and 75kg of load. However, the weight is only an indication because it also depends on the version. Optional wheels, air-conditioning or roof rails add weight. The vehicle registration weight will always differ from the manufacturer's specification.

Maximum towing weight

The maximum towing weight shows how heavy a caravan or trailer may be. The braked weight, indicating how much can be towed if the trailer is equipped with a braking installation, is always stated.

Luggage storage capacity

This is stated in litres. It always gives the volume of the boot or, in the case of hatchbacks, the luggage space up to window level. For models with a fold-down rear seat or even removable seats, two figures are given. Some saloons also have fold-down rear seats.

Combined fuel consumption

Fuel consumption is measured according to the ECE standard. This is the combined fuel consumption: a combination of town driving and driving on the open road. Fuel consumption is given in miles per gallon (mpg). However, the ECE standard is a laboratory test that says little about the daily driving conditions. In practice, it is almost impossible to achieve the stated consumption.

EuroNCAP

A large number of European consumer organisations and governments are working together on the European New Car Assessment Programme (EuroNCAP). This involves more than just collision tests although these have grown into the standard car safety test. Every manufacturer wants 'five stars' for their new model – and pays attention to that in the development phase.

Latest facelift

Sometimes a facelift is little more than a different grille or a different colour, but usually it also involves an improved engine and more extensive standard fittings. There is also a difference in model policy: European cars go on for a long time – often ten years or more – and are then replaced by something totally new. Sometimes there is a need for a facelift, even in the case of an evergreen like the Renault Twingo. The appearance of Japanese cars changes more often, but developments under the bonnet are more gradual.

Guarantee

In the UK most manufacturers give a two-year general warranty on new cars, to which is added another year at dealership level. Some Asian manufacturers even offer a five-year warranty.

Author's notes

The dynamism in the car world is unprecedented. Tastes are constantly changing and the stream of ideas about styling never lets up. In order to cater to the changing tastes of the consumer, the manufacturer must always look a few years ahead. After all, developing a new model is a time-consuming process.

As a result of market pressures, these processes have become increasingly short over recent decades. This has its downside, because quality has suffered. Not all systems could be optimally tested and not all materials comprehensively checked. This gave rise to practical problems. So manufacturers are retracing their steps and are now allowing more time for a test phase. This, however, does not affect the volume of new cars. In 2006 many models were replaced and new ones created. Every big car show had more than its fair share of innovations.

All the better for the creators of this car yearbook: we have plenty to do. We regard it as a challenge to provide our readers with as much insight as possible into the diversity of the car market.

Naturally, the price list can never be complete and is just a snapshot in time, but we think it important to give you a fair indication. We have to make choices in every respect and it is impossible to cover everything.

We have also tried to use as wide a variety of photographs as possible. After all, as well as a work of reference, this is also a picture book. And pictures say a lot more than words!

Henri Stolwijk

ALFA ROMEO 147 1.6 / 2.0

engine type	: petrol, inline-4
displacement	: 1598 / 1970 cc
max. power	: 88 kW (120 bhp) /
	110 kW (150 bhp)
@	: 6200 / 6300 rpm
max. torque	: 108 / 133 lb ft
@	: 4200 / 3800 rpm
gears	: 5
AT	: n.a.
drive	: FWD
brakes f/r	: vent. discs / discs
body type	: 3-, 5-dr. hatchback
l x w x h	: 4223 x 1729 x 1442 mm
wheelbase	: 2546 mm
turning circle	: 11.5 m

kerb weight	: 1175 / 1225 kg
towing weight	: 1300 kg
boot space	: 280 l – 1030 l
fuel capacity	: 60 l
consumption	: 34.4 / 31.7 mpg
acc. 0-62 mph	: 10.6 / 9.3 s
top speed	: 121 / 129 mph
EuroNCAP	: 3 stars
introduction	: October 2000
last revised in	: January 2005
warranty	: 2 years
miscellaneous	: Trendy Italian car, full of character. Rewarding driver because of excellent steering and responsive chassis. Basic version with 105 bhp 1.6 engine.

147 1.9 JTD 8V / 1.9 JTD 16V

engine type	: diesel, inline-4
displacement	: 1910 cc
max. power	: 88 kW (120 bhp) / 110 kW (150 bhp)
@	: 4000 rpm
max. torque	: 206 / 225 lb ft
@	: 2000 rpm
gears	: 5 / 6
kerb weight	: 1245 / 1265 kg
towing weight	: 1300 kg
consumption	: 48.7 mpg
acc. 0-60 mph	: 9.6 / 8.8 s
top speed	: 120 / 129 mph
miscellaneous	: 150 bhp Multijet diesel engine with lots of torque matches well with the 147. Excellent choice for hurried business people.

ALFA ROMEO 159 1.8 mpi / 1.9 JTS

engine type	: petrol, inline-4
displacement	: 1796 / 1859 cc
max. power	: 103 kW (140 bhp) / 118 kW (160 bhp)
@	: 6300 / 6500 rpm
max. torque	: 129 / 140 lb ft
@	: 3800 / 4500 rpm
gears	: 5 / 6
AT	: n.a.
drive	: FWD
brakes f/r	: vent. discs / discs
body type	: 4-dr. saloon
l x w x h	: 4660 x 1828 x 1417 mm
wheelbase	: 2700 mm
turning circle	: 11.1 m

kerb weight	: 1405 / 1455 kg
towing weight	: 1400 / 1500 kg
boot space	: 405 l
fuel capacity	: 70 l
consumption	: n.a. / 32.5 mpg
acc. 0-62 mph	: 10.2 / 9.7 s
top speed	: 128 / 132 mph
EuroNCAP	: 5 stars
introduction	: October 2005
last revised in	: n.a.
warranty	: 3 years
miscellaneous	: 1.8 mpi is the new entry level engine for the 159 range. All engines of saloon also available for Sportwagon.

159 2.2 JTS / 3.2 V6

engine type	: petrol, inline-4 / V6
displacement	: 2198 / 3195 cc
max. power	: 136 kW (185 bhp) / 191kW (260 bhp)
@	: 6500 / 6200 rpm
max. torque	: 170 / 238 lb ft
@	: 4500 rpm
gears	: 6
kerb weight	: 1490 / 1740 kg
towing weight	: 1500 kg
consumption	: 30.1 / 24.6 mpg
acc. 0-60 mph	: 8.8 / 7.0 s
top speed	: 138 / 149 mph
miscellaneous	: 3.2 V6 engine in 159 comes standard with 4WD, which makes it a rather heavy car.

ALFA ROMEO 159 SPORTWAGON 1.9 JTDM 8V / 1.9 JTDM 16V

engine type	: diesel, inline-4
displacement	: 1910 cc
max. power	: 88 kW (120 bhp) / 110 kW (150 bhp)
@	: 4000 rpm
max. torque	: 206 / 236 lb ft
@	: 2000 rpm
gears	: 6
AT	: n.a.
drive	: FWD
brakes f/r	: vent. discs / discs
body type	: 5-dr. stationwagon
l x w x h	: 4660 x 1828 x 1417 mm
wheelbase	: 2700 mm
turning circle	: 11.1 m

kerb weight	: 1550 / 1560 kg
towing weight	: 1500 kg
boot space	: 445 l
fuel capacity	: 70 l
consumption	: 46.3 mpg
acc. 0-62 mph	: 11.2 / 9.6 s
top speed	: 118 / 129 mph
EuroNCAP	: 5 stars
introduction	: March 2006
last revised in	: n.a.
warranty	: 2 years
miscellaneous	: The 120 bhp 8V JTdm engine is best suited for those who are not in a hurry. But if you want to exploit its chassis to the full, the 150 bhp 16V 4-cylinder is the engine of choice.

159 SPORTWAGON 2.4 JTDm

engine type	: diesel, inline-5
displacement	: 2387 cc
max. power	: 147 kW (200 bhp)
@	: 4000 rpm
max. torque	: 295 lb ft
@	: 2000 rpm
gears	: 6
kerb weight	: 1655 kg
towing weight	: 1500 kg
consumption	: 41.6 mpg
acc. 0-60 mph	: 8.6 s
top speed	: 140 mph
miscellaneous	: In addition to the 1.9 JTDm diesel engine, a 2.4 JTDm unit is also available in the 159.

ALFA ROMEO 166 2.0

engine type	: petrol, inline-4		kerb weight	: 1395 kg
displacement	: 1970 cc		towing weight	: 1500 kg
max. power	: 110 kW (150 bhp)		boot space	: 490 l
@	: 6300 rpm		fuel capacity	: 69 l
max. torque	: 133 lb ft		consumption	: 28.9 mpg
@	: 3800 rpm		acc. 0-62 mph	: 9.8 s
gears	: 6		top speed	: 131 mph
AT	: n.a.		EuroNCAP	: n.a.
drive	: FWD		introduction	: September 1998
brakes f/r	: vent. discs / discs		last revised in	: October 2003
body type	: 4-dr. sedan		warranty	: 2 years
l x w x h	: 4720 x 1800 x 1416 mm		miscellaneous	: Stylish flagship of Italian
wheelbase	: 2700 mm			manufacturer. Somewhat lacking in
turning circle	: 11.6 m			the ergonomics and build quality
				department, but facelift a success.

166 3.0 V6 / 3.2 V6

engine type	: petrol, V6
displacement	: 2959 / 3.179 cc
max. power	: 162 kW (220 bhp) /
	177 kW (240 bhp)
@	: 6200 / 6300 rpm
max. torque	: 195 / 213 lb ft
@	: 5000 / 4800 rpm
gears	: 4-speed automatic / 6
kerb weight	: 1525 / 1515 kg
towing weight	: 1500 kg
consumption	: 21.8 / 22.7 mpg
acc. 0-60 mph	: 8.6 / 7.4 s
top speed	: 147 /152 mph
miscellaneous	: Two V6 engines available, a 3.0 with automatic transmission and a 3.2 with a 6-speed manual gearbox. The bigger engine is sportier and quicker.

166 2.4 JTD 10V

engine type	: diesel, inline-5
displacement	: 2387 cc
max. power	: 110 kW (150 bhp)
@	: 4000 rpm
max. torque	: 225 lb ft
@	: 1800 rpm
gears	: 6 / optional 5-speed automatic
kerb weight	: 1465 kg
towing weight	: 1300 kg
consumption	: 39.4 mpg
acc. 0-60 mph	: 9.9 s
top speed	: 132 mph
miscellaneous	: Diesel-engined 166 is a good alternative for business drivers who want a car that is a bit different. Also available with 175 bhp strong 2.4 20V Multijet engine.

ALFA ROMEO GT COUPE 1.8 / 2.0

engine type	: petrol, inline-4	kerb weight	: 1265 / 1295 kg
displacement	: 1747 / 1970 cc	towing weight	: 1300 kg
max. power	: 103 kW (140 bhp) /	boot space	: 320 l – 905 l
	122 kW (165 bhp)	fuel capacity	: 63 l
@	: 6500 / 6400 rpm	consumption	: 33.4 / 32.6 mpg
max. torque	: 120 / 152 lb ft	acc. 0-62 mph	: 9.9 / 8.7 s
@	: 3900 / 3250 rpm	top speed	: 124 / 134 mph
gears	: 5	EuroNCAP	: n.a.
AT	: n.a.	introduction	: September 2003
drive	: FWD	last revised in	: -
brakes f/r	: vent. discs / discs	warranty	: 2 years
body type	: 2-dr. coupe	miscellaneous	: Stunning coupe, designed by
l x w x h	: 4489 x 1763 x 1362 mm		Bertone. 150 bhp 1.9 JTD is
wheelbase	: 2596 mm		available for those high mileage
turning circle	: 11.5 m		drivers, but petrolheads go for
			the 240 bhp 3.2 V6.

ALFA ROMEO BRERA / SPIDER 2.2 JTS / 3.2 V6

engine type	: petrol, inline-4 / V6
displacement	: 2198 / 3195 cc
max. power	: 136 kW (185 bhp) / 191 kW (260 bhp)
@	: 6500 / 6200 rpm
max. torque	: 170 / 238 lb ft
@	: 4500 rpm
gears	: 6
AT	: n.a.
drive	: FWD / 4WD
brakes f/r	: vent. discs / discs
body type	: 2-dr. coupe
l x w x h	: 4413 x 1830 x 1372 mm
wheelbase	: 2525 mm
turning circle	: 10.7 m

kerb weight	: 1445 / 1605 kg
towing weight	: 1450 / 1500 kg
boot space	: 300 l
fuel capacity	: 70 l
consumption	: 30.2 / 24.7 mpg
acc. 0-62 mph	: 8.6 / 6.8 s
top speed	: 138 / 149 mph
EuroNCAP	: n.a.
introduction	: November 2005
last revised in	: -
warranty	: 2 years
miscellaneous	: What will it be: the quick but heavy 3.2 V6 or the 2.2 JTS which is not as heavy and not as fast? A tough choice.

BRERA 2.4 JTDm

engine type	: diesel, inline-5
displacement	: 2387 cc
max. power	: 147 kW (200bhp)
@	: 4000 rpm
max. torque	: 295 lb ft
@	: 2000 rpm
gears	: 6
kerb weight	: 1600 kg
towing weight	: 1500 kg
consumption	: 41.7 mpg
acc. 0-60 mph	: 8.1 s
top speed	: 142 mph
miscellaneous	: Diesel engine sounds lovely and offers more torque than V6 petrol engine. A sporty yet economical version of the Brera.

ASTON MARTIN V8 VANTAGE

engine type	: petrol, V8		kerb weight	: 1570 kg
displacement	: 4280 cc		towing weight	: n.a.
max. power	: 283 kW (385 bhp)		boot space	: 300 l
@	: 7000 rpm		fuel capacity	: 77 l
max. torque	: 302 lb ft		consumption	: 20.3 mpg
@	: 5000 rpm		acc. 0-62 mph	: 5.0 s
gears	: 6		top speed	: 174 mph
AT	: optional 6-speed		EuroNCAP	: n.a.
drive	: RWD		introduction	: September 2005
brakes f/r	: vent. discs		last revised in	: -
body type	: 2-dr. coupe		warranty	: 2 years
l x w x h	: 4383 x 1866 x 1255 mm		miscellaneous	: The Vantage is the latest addition to
wheelbase	: 2600 mm			the Aston Martin range. The car
turning circle	: 11.1 m			is intended to compete with the
				Porsche 911 and Ferrari F430. A
				Volante version is in the making.

ASTON MARTIN DB9

engine type	: petrol, V12	kerb weight	: 1710 kg
displacement	: 5935 cc	towing weight	: n.a.
max. power	: 331 kW (450 bhp)	boot space	: 175 l
@	: 6000 rpm	fuel capacity	: 85 l
max. torque	: 420 lb ft	consumption	: 20.3 mpg
@	: 5000 rpm	acc. 0-62 mph	: 4.9 s
gears	: 6	top speed	: 186 mph
AT	: optional 6-speed	EuroNCAP	: n.a.
drive	: RWD	introduction	: July 2004
brakes f/r	: vent. discs	last revised in	: -
body type	: 2-dr. coupe	warranty	: 2 years
l x w x h	: 4710 x 1875 x 1318 mm	miscellaneous	: With its gorgeous lines, this car is
wheelbase	: 2740 mm		a serious contender for the title of
turning circle	: 11.5 m		Most Beautiful Car in this book.
			Performance fabulous too. Also
			available as Volante.

ASTON MARTIN V12 VANQUISH S

engine type	: petrol, V12		kerb weight	: 1820 kg
displacement	: 5935 cc		towing weight	: -
max. power	: 388 kW (520 bhp)		boot space	: 240 l
@	: 7000 rpm		fuel capacity	: 80 l
max. torque	: 426 lb ft		consumption	: 17 mpg
@	: 5800 rpm		acc. 0-62 mph	: 4.8 s
gears	: 6, seq.		top speed	: > 200 mph
AT	: -		EuroNCAP	: n.a.
drive	: RWD		introduction	: July 2001
brakes f/r	: vent. discs		last revised in	: -
body type	: 2-dr. coupe		warranty	: 2 years
l x w x h	: 4665 x 1923 x 1318 mm		miscellaneous	: The ultimate GT from Newport
wheelbase	: 2690 mm			Pagnell. Positioned above the DB9
turning circle	: 12.8 m			but only marginally faster. Demand
				for the 'ordinary' 460 bhp Vanquish
				has plummeted since the arrival of
				the more powerful Vanquish S.

AUDI A3 1.6 / 1.6 FSI

engine type	: petrol, inline-4	kerb weight	: 1205 / 1275 kg
displacement	: 1595 / 1598 cc	towing weight	: 1200 kg
max. power	: 75 kW (102 bhp) / 85 kW (115 bhp)	boot space	: 350 l – 1080 l
@	: 5600 / 6000 rpm	fuel capacity	: 55 l
max. torque	: 109/ 114 lb ft	consumption	: 40.5 / 43.8 mpg
@	: 3800 / 4000 rpm	acc. 0-62 mph	: 11.9 / 10.9 s
gears	: 5 / 6	top speed	: 115 / 122 mph
AT	: -	EuroNCAP	: 4 stars
drive	: FWD	introduction	: June 2003
brakes f/r	: vent. discs / discs	last revised in	: July 2005
body type	: 3-dr. hatchback	warranty	: 2 years
l x w x h	: 4203 x 1765 x 1421 mm	miscellaneous	: New entry level Audi after the
wheelbase	: 2578 mm		demise of the A2. Fairly sporty
turning circle	: 10.7 m		chassis. All petrol engines also
			available in A3 Sportback.

A3 1.8 TFSI / 2.0 TFSI

engine type	: petrol, inline-4
displacement	: 1781 / 1984 cc
max. power	: 118 kW (160 bhp) / 147 kW (200 bhp)
@	: n.a. / 5100 rpm
max. torque	: 184 / 206 lb ft
@	: n.a. / 1800 rpm
gears	: 6, optional 6-speed automatic
kerb weight	: n.a. / 1245 kg
towing weight	: n.a. / 1800 kg
consumption	: n.a. / 37.3 mpg
acc. 0-60 mph	: 8.2 / 6.9 s
top speed	: 137 / 147 mph
miscellaneous	: With the 2.0 TFSI engine under the bonnet, the A3 offers the performance of a VW Golf GTI, but in a rather less ostentatious suit.

A3 3.2 V6 / S3

engine type	: petrol, V6 / inline-4
displacement	: 3189 / 1984 cc
max. power	: 184 kW (250 bhp) / 195 kW (265 bhp)
@	: 6300 / 6000 rpm
max. torque	: 236 / 258 lb ft
@	: 2500 rpm
gears	: 6, optional 6-speed automatic
kerb weight	: 1495 kg / n.a.
towing weight	: 1600 kg / n.a.
consumption	: 26.8 / 31.0 mpg
acc. 0-60 mph	: 6.5 / 5.7 s
top speed	: 155 mph
miscellaneous	: The über-Audi A3. Rare beast because of high price.

AUDI A3 SPORTBACK 1.9 TDI

engine type	: diesel, inline-4		**kerb weight**	: 1335 kg
displacement	: 1896		**towing weight**	: 1700 kg
max. power	: 77 kW (105 bhp)		**boot space**	: 370 l – 1120 l
@	: 4000 rpm		**fuel capacity**	: 55 l
max. torque	: 184 lb ft		**consumption**	: 55.6 mpg
@	: 1900 rpm		**acc. 0-62 mph**	: 11.7 s
gears	: 5		**top speed**	: 116 mph
AT	: -		**EuroNCAP**	: n.a.
drive	: FWD		**introduction**	: September 2004
brakes f/r	: vent. discs / discs		**last revised in**	: -
body type	: 5-dr. hatchback		**warranty**	: 2 years
l x w x h	: 4286 x 1765 x 1423 mm		**miscellaneous**	: Sportback not just a 5-door A3
wheelbase	: 2578 mm			hatchback, but more of a
turning circle	: 10.7 m			stationwagon in appearance. All
				diesel engines also
				available in 3-door A3.

A3 SPORTBACK 2.0 TDI

engine type	: diesel, inline-4
displacement	: 1968 cc
max. power	: 103 kW (140 bhp)
@	: 4000 rpm
max. torque	: 236 lb ft
@	: 1750 rpm
gears	: 6, optional S-tronic
kerb weight	: 1380 kg
towing weight	: 1700 kg
consumption	: 51.6 mpg
acc. 0-60 mph	: 9.7 s
top speed	: 129 mph
miscellaneous	: Both 2.0 TDI versions also available with quattro 4WD.

AUDI A4 1.6 / 1.8 T

engine type	: petrol, inline-4
displacement	: 1595 / 1781 cc
max. power	: 75 kW (102 bhp) /
	120 kW (163 bhp)
@	: 5600 / 5700 rpm
max. torque	: 109 /166 lb ft
@	: 3800 / 1950 rpm
gears	: 5
AT	: - / optional CVT
drive	: FWD
brakes f/r	: vent. discs / discs
body type	: 4-dr. sedan
l x w x h	: 4586 x 1772 x 1427 mm
wheelbase	: 2648 mm
turning circle	: 11.1 m

kerb weight	: 1300 / 1390 kg
towing weight	: 1200 / 1400 kg
boot space	: 460 l – 720 l
fuel capacity	: 70 l
consumption	: 36.8 / 34.6 mpg
acc. 0-62 mph	: 12.6 / 8.6 s
top speed	: 118 / 142 mph
EuroNCAP	: 4 stars
introduction	: January 2001
last revised in	: November 2004
warranty	: 2 years
miscellaneous	: Most recent facelift saw the introduction of the big Audi grille, which looks good on the car. Steering very direct, build quality excellent. Serious competition for BMW 3 Series and Mercedes-Benz C-class.

A4 2.0 / 2.0 T FSI

engine type	: petrol, inline-4
displacement	: 1984 cc
max. power	: 96 kW (130 bhp) /
	147 kW (200 bhp)
@	: 5700 / 5100 rpm
max. torque	: 144 / 206 lb ft
@	: 3500 / 1800 rpm
gears	: - / optional CVT
kerb weight	: 1340 / 1427 kg
towing weight	: 1300 / 1400 kg
consumption	: 35.4 / 36.8 mpg
acc. 0-60 mph	: 9.8 / 7.3 s
top speed	: 132 / 150 mph
miscellaneous	: 2.0 TFSI engine lauded 'Engine of the Year'. A fine, smooth engine indeed.

AUDI A4 AVANT 1.9 TDI / 2.0 TDI

engine type	: diesel, inline-4
displacement	: 1896 / 1968 cc
max. power	: 77 kW (105 bhp) / 103 kW (140 bhp)
@	: 4000 rpm
max. torque	: 184 / 236 lb ft
@	: 1900 / 1750 rpm
gears	: 5 / 6
AT	: n.a.
drive	: FWD
brakes f/r	: vent. discs / discs
body type	: 5-dr. stationwagon
l x w x h	: 4586 x 1772 x 1427 mm
wheelbase	: 2648 mm
turning circle	: 11.1 m

kerb weight	: 1450 / 1490 kg
towing weight	: 1500 / 1600 kg
boot space	: 442 l – 1184 l
fuel capacity	: 70 l
consumption	: 49.8 / 48.9 mpg
acc. 0-62 mph	: 11.5 / 9.9 s
top speed	: 122 / 129 mph
EuroNCAP	: n.a.
introduction	: July 2001
last revised in	: November 2004
warranty	: 2 years
miscellaneous	: Avant is prettier than its saloon sibling, but load capacity is restricted. Also available with 170 bhp 2.0 TDI.

A4 Avant 2.7 TDI / 3.0 TDI

engine type	: diesel, V6
displacement	: 2698 / 2967 cc
max. power	: 132 kW (180 bhp) / 150 kW (204 bhp)
@	: 3300 / 3500 rpm
max. torque	: 280 / 332 lb ft
@	: 1400 rpm
gears	: 6, optional CVT / 6, optional 6 speed automatic
kerb weight	: 1600 / 1660 kg
towing weight	: 1800 / 1800 kg
consumption	: 41.7 / 37.8mpg
acc. 0-60 mph	: 8.6 / 7.4 s
top speed	: 139 / 144 mph
miscellaneous	: With an engine range that includes two 6-cylinder diesels, the A4 is popular in the car lease market. 2.7 TDI is latest diesel addition. All diesel engines also available in saloon.

AUDI A4 CABRIOLET 1.8 T / 2.0 T FSI

engine type	: petrol, inline-4	kerb weight	: 1540 / 1600 kg
displacement	: 1781 / 1984 cc	towing weight	: 1600 kg
max. power	: 120 kW (163 pk) /	boot space	: 315 l
	147 kW (200 bhp)	fuel capacity	: 70 l
@	: 5700 / 5100 rpm	consumption	: 32.8 / 33.6 mpg
max. torque	: 166 / 206 lb ft	acc. 0-62 mph	: 9.4 / 8.2 s
@	: 1950 / 1800 rpm	top speed	: 135 /144 mph
gears	: 5 / 6	EuroNCAP	: n.a.
AT	: optional CVT	introduction	: June 2006
drive	: FWD	last revised in	: -
brakes f/r	: vent. discs / discs	warranty	: 2 years
body type	: 2-dr. convertible	miscellaneous	: Still a pretty convertible. Facelift
l x w x h	: 4573 x 1777 x 1391 mm		includes upgraded engine range.
wheelbase	: 2650 mm		
turning circle	: 11.1 m		

A4 CABRIOLET 3.2 FSI / S4

engine type	: petrol, V6 / V8
displacement	: 3123 / 4163 cc
max. power	: 188 kW (255 bhp) /
	253 kW (344 pk)
@	: 6500 / 7000 rpm
max. torque	: 244 / 302 lb ft
@	: 3250 / 3500 rpm
gears	: 6, optional CVT / 6
kerb weight	: 1695 / 1855 kg
towing weight	: 1800 kg / n.a.
consumption	: 25.7 / 20.6 mpg
acc. 0-60 mph	: 6.8 / 5.9 s
top speed	: 155 mph
miscellaneous	: For speed-hungry drivers who think even the S4 is not quick enough, the RS4 Cabriolet is the one to choose. We think the 3.2 FSI will do.

A4 CABRIOLET 2.0 TDI / 2.7 TDI

engine type	: diesel, inline-4 / V6
displacement	: 1968 / 2698 cc
max. power	: 103 kW (140 bhp) /
	132 kW (180 pk)
@	: 4000 / 3300 rpm
max. torque	: 236 / 280 lb ft
@	: 1750 / 1400 rpm
gears	: 6
kerb weight	: 1600 / 1745 kg
towing weight	: 1800 kg
consumption	: 43.5 / mpg
acc. 0-60 mph	: 9.7 / 9.0 s
top speed	: 132 / 138 mph
miscellaneous	: The A4 Cabriolet is available with a wide selection of diesel engines, including a 233 bhp 3.0 TDI. Particle filter standard equipment.

AUDI RS4

engine type	: petrol, V8
displacement	: 4163 cc
max. power	: 309 kW (420 bhp)
@	: 7800 rpm
max. torque	: 317 lb ft
@	: 5500 rpm
gears	: 6
AT	: n.a.
drive	: 4WD
brakes f/r	: vent. discs
body type	: 4-dr. sedan
l x w x h	: 4589 x 1816 x 1415 mm
wheelbase	: 2648 mm
turning circle	: 11.5 m

kerb weight	: 1650 kg
towing weight	: n.a.
boot space	: 460 l
fuel capacity	: 66 l
consumption	: 21.2 mpg
acc. 0-62 mph	: 4.8 s
top speed	: 155 mph
EuroNCAP	: 4 stars
introduction	: October 2005
last revised in	: -
warranty	: 2 years
miscellaneous	: The hottest A4 around, for those who find the S4 somewhat lacking in performance... Avant version of RS4 also available. First production V8 with direct fuel injection.

S4

engine type	: petrol, V8
displacement	: 4163 cc
max. power	: 253 kW (344 bhp)
@	: 7000 rpm
max. torque	: 302 lb ft
@	: 3500 rpm
gears	: 6
kerb weight	: 1635 kg
towing weight	: n.a.
consumption	: 21.3 mpg
acc. 0-60 mph	: 5.6 s
top speed	: 155 mph
miscellaneous	: Car not as fast as RS4, but nevertheless very potent. Avant and convertible versions available too.

AUDI A6 2.4 / 3.2 FSI

engine type	: petrol, inline-4 / V6	kerb weight	: 1525 / 1540 kg
displacement	: 2393 / 3123 cc	towing weight	: 1700 / 2000 kg
max. power	: 130 kW (177 bhp) /	boot space	: 546 l
	188 kW (256 bhp)	fuel capacity	: 70 l
@	: 6000 / 6500 rpm	consumption	: 29.2 / 29.1 mpg
max. torque	: 170 / 243 lb ft	acc. 0-62 mph	: 8.9 / 6.9 s
@	: 3000 / 3250 rpm	top speed	: 144 / 155 mph
gears	: 6	EuroNCAP	: 5 stars
AT	: - / optional 6-speed tiptronic	introduction	: April 2004
drive	: FWD	last revised in	: -
brakes f/r	: vent. discs / discs	warranty	: 2 years
body type	: 4-dr. saloon	miscellaneous	: Good-looking car, balanced design
l x w x h	: 4915 x 1855 x 1460 mm		in spite of prominent grille. Also
wheelbase	: 2845 mm		available as Avant.
turning circle	: 11.9 m		

A6 4.2 FSI / S6

engine type	: petrol, V8 / V10
displacement	: 4163 / 5204 cc
max. power	: 257 kW (350 bhp) /
	320 kW (435 bhp)
@	: 6800 rpm
max. torque	: 325 / 398 lb ft
@	: 3500 / 4000 rpm
gears	: 6 speed tiptronic
kerb weight	: 1770 / 1910 kg
towing weight	: 2100 kg / n.a.
consumption	: 26.3 / 21.2 mpg
acc. 0-60 mph	: 5.9 / 5.2 s
top speed	: 155 mph
miscellaneous	: V10 engine in S6 borrowed from
	subsidiary Lamborghini. Even more
	powerful RS6 version is on its way.

AUDI A6 AVANT 3.0 TDI QUATTRO

engine type	: diesel, V6
displacement	: 2967 cc
max. power	: 165 kW (224 bhp)
@	: 4000 rpm
max. torque	: 332 lb ft
@	: 1400 rpm
gears	: 6
AT	: optional 6-speed tiptronic
drive	: 4WD
brakes f/r	: vent. discs / discs
body type	: 5-dr. stationwagon
l x w x h	: 4933 x 1855 x 1463 mm
wheelbase	: 2845 mm
turning circle	: 11.9 m

kerb weight	: 1805 kg
towing weight	: 1660 kg
boot space	: 565 l
fuel capacity	: 80 l
consumption	: 35.0 mpg
acc. 0-62 mph	: 7.3 s
top speed	: 149 mph
EuroNCAP	: 5 stars
introduction	: April 2004
last revised in	: -
warranty	: 2 years
miscellaneous	: Very potent diesel engine with 332 lb ft of torque. Thankfully, 4WD is standard fitment on cars with this engine. Engine also available in saloon.

A6 AVANT 2.0 TDI / 2.7 TDI

engine type	: diesel, inline-4 / V6
displacement	: 1968 / 2698 cc
max. power	: 103 kW (140 bhp) / 132 kW (180 bhp)
@	: 4000 / 3300 rpm
max. torque	: 236 / 280 lb ft
@	: 1750 / 1400 rpm
gears	: 6
kerb weight	: 1610 / 1695 kg
towing weight	: 1800 / 1900 kg
consumption	: 46.5 / 40.5 mpg
acc. 0-60 mph	: 10.5 / 8.3 s
top speed	: 127 / 140 mph
miscellaneous	: 2.0 TDI is entry level diesel, 2.7 TDI the better choice however since it is almost as fast as the 3-litre but much cheaper. Engines also available in saloon.

AUDI A6 ALLROAD QUATTRO 3.2 FSI / 4.2 FSI

engine type	: petrol, V6 / V8	kerb weight	: 1760 / 1880 kg
displacement	: 3123 / 4163 cc	towing weight	: 2100 kg
max. power	: 188 kW (255 bhp) /	boot space	: 565 l
	257 kW (350 bhp)	fuel capacity	: 80 l
@	: 6500 / 6800 rpm	consumption	: 25.8 / 25.3 mpg
max. torque	: 243 / 325 lb ft	acc. 0-62 mph	: 7.2 / 6.3 s
@	: 3250 / 3500 rpm	top speed	: 150 mph
gears	: 6 / 6-speed tiptronic	EuroNCAP	: n.a.
AT	: optional 6-speed tiptronic / -	introduction	: March 2006
drive	: 4WD	last revised in	: -
brakes f/r	: vent. discs / discs	warranty	: 2 years
body type	: 5-dr. stationwagon	miscellaneous	: Offroad vehicle derived from A6
l x w x h	: 4934 x 1832 x 1519 mm		Avant. Good alternative for
wheelbase	: 2833 mm		traditional SUV.
turning circle	: 11.9 m		

ALLROAD QUATTRO 2.7 TDI / 3.0 TDI

engine type	: diesel, V6
displacement	: 2698 / 2967 cc
max. power	: 132 kW (180 bhp) /
	171 kW (233 bhp)
@	: 3300 / 4000 rpm
max. torque	: 280 / 332 lb ft
@	: 1400 rpm
gears	: 6-speed tiptronic
kerb weight	: 1875 / 1880 kg
towing weight	: 2100 kg
consumption	: 32.6 / 32.2 mpg
acc. 0-60 mph	: 9.3 / 7.8 s
top speed	: 134 / 143 mph
miscellaneous	: As it should be: both diesel engines
	feature a particle filter as standard.

AUDI A8 3.2 FSI / 4.2 FSI QUATTRO

engine type	: petrol, V6 / V8
displacement	: 3123 / 4163 cc
max. power	: 191 kW (260 bhp) /
	257 kW (350 bhp)
@	: 6500 / 6800 rpm
max. torque	: 243 / 324 lb ft
@	: 3250 / 3500 rpm
gears	: 6 / n.a.
AT	: optional, CVT / 6-speed tiptronic
drive	: FWD / 4WD
brakes f/r	: vent. discs
body type	: 4-dr. saloon
l x w x h	: 5051 x 1894 x 1444 mm
wheelbase	: 2944 mm
turning circle	: 6.1 m

kerb weight	: 1690 / 1800 kg
towing weight	: 2100 / 2300 kg
boot space	: 500 l
fuel capacity	: 90 l
consumption	: 28.5 / 26 mpg
acc. 0-62 mph	: 7.7 / 6.1 s
top speed	: 155 mph
EuroNCAP	: n.a.
introduction	: November 2002
last revised in	: July 2005
warranty	: 3 years
miscellaneous	: 3.2 FSI frankly does not leave much to be desired. Direct fuel injection now on 4.2 V8 too. Wheelbase of A8 'Lang' version 130 mm longer.

A8 6.0 W12 / S8

engine type	: petrol, W12 / V10
displacement	: 5998 / 5204 cc
max. power	: 331 kW (450 bhp)
@	: 6200 / 7000 rpm
max. torque	: 427 / lb ft
@	: 4000 / 3500 rpm
gears	: 6-speed tiptronic
kerb weight	: 1960 / 1940 kg
towing weight	: 2300 kg
consumption	: 20 / 21.2 mpg
acc. 0-60 mph	: 5.1 s
top speed	: 155 mph
miscellaneous	: Stylish or sporty? Performance-wise you cannot go wrong with either of these, since they are equally fast.

A8 3.0 TDI / 4.2 TDI QUATTRO

engine type	: diesel, V6 / V8
displacement	: 2967 / 4134 cc
max. power	: 171 kW (233 bhp) /
	240 kW (326 bhp)
@	: 4000 / 3750 rpm
max. torque	: 332 / 479 lb ft
@	: 1400 / 1600 rpm
gears	: 6-speed tiptronic
kerb weight	: 1830 / 1940 kg
towing weight	: 2300 kg
consumption	: 32.8 / 29.4 mpg
acc. 0-60 mph	: 7.8 / 5.9 s
top speed	: 151 / 155 mph
miscellaneous	: Fat diesel engines offer more torque than petrol versions. Diesel power hardly noticeable due to excellent noise insulation.

AUDI TT 2.0 T FSI

engine type	: petrol, inline-4
displacement	: 1984 cc
max. power	: 147 kW (200 bhp)
@	: 5100 rpm
max. torque	: 206 lb ft
@	: 1800 rpm
gears	: 6
AT	: optional 6-speed S-Tronic
drive	: FWD
brakes f/r	: vent. discs / discs
body type	: 2-dr. coupe
l x w x h	: 4178 x 1842 x 1352 mm
wheelbase	: 2468 mm
turning circle	: 11.0 m

kerb weight	: 1260 kg
towing weight	: -
boot space	: 290 l
fuel capacity	: 55 l
consumption	: 36.8 mpg
acc. 0-62 mph	: 6.6 s
top speed	: 149 mph
EuroNCAP	: n.a.
introduction	: June 2006
last revised in	: -
warranty	: 2 years
miscellaneous	: Aluminium body reduces weight of new TT. Handsome and capable coupe. Diesel versions and Roadster soon to follow.

TT 3.2 FSI QUATTRO

engine type	: petrol, V6
displacement	: 3189 cc
max. power	: 184 kW (250 bhp)
@	: 6300 rpm
max. torque	: 236 lb ft
@	: 2500 rpm
gears	: 6
kerb weight	: 1410 kg
towing weight	: n.a.
consumption	: 27.5 mpg
acc. 0-60 mph	: 5.9 s
top speed	: 155 mph
miscellaneous	: 4WD comes standard on the fastest TT, at the penalty of extra weight.

AUDI Q7 3.0 TDI

engine type	: diesel, V6		**kerb weight**	: 2295 kg
displacement	: 2967 cc		**towing weight**	: 3500 kg
max. power	: 171 kW (233 bhp)		**boot space**	: 330 - 2035
@	: 4000 rpm		**fuel capacity**	: n.a.
max. torque	: 368 lb ft		**consumption**	: 26.9 mpg
@	: 1750 - 2750 rpm		**acc. 0-62 mph**	: 9.1 s
gears	: n.a.		**top speed**	: 134 mph
AT	: 6-speed tiptronic		**EuroNCAP**	: n.a.
drive	: 4WD		**introduction**	: September 2005
brakes f/r	: vent. discs		**last revised in**	: -
body type	: 5-dr. SUV		**warranty**	: 2 years
l x w x h	: 5086 x 1983 x 1737 mm		**miscellaneous**	: Long-awaited, good-looking SUV.
wheelbase	: 3002 mm			Diesel version probably more
turning circle	: 11.9 m			popular in Europe, V8 petrol engine
				across the pond.

Q7 4.2 V8

engine type	: petrol, V8
displacement	: 4163
max. power	: 257 kW (350 bhp)
@	: 6800 rpm
max. torque	: 325 lb ft
@	: 3500 rpm
gears	: 6 speed tiptronic
kerb weight	: 2275 kg
towing weight	: 3500 kg
consumption	: 20.8 mpg
acc. 0-60 mph	: 7.4 s
top speed	: 154 mph
miscellaneous	: Shares components with Volkswagen Touareg, but is superior in every respect, including price.

BENTLEY CONTINENTAL GT

engine type	: petrol, W12	kerb weight	: 2385 kg
displacement	: 5998 cc	towing weight	: -
max. power	: 411 kW (552 bhp)	boot space	: 370 l
@	: 6100 rpm	fuel capacity	: 90 l
max. torque	: 479 lb ft	consumption	: 16.5 mpg
@	: 1600 rpm	acc. 0-62 mph	: 4.8 s
gears	: n.a.	top speed	: 198 mph
AT	: 6-speed tiptronic	EuroNCAP	: n.a.
drive	: 4WD	introduction	: September 2002
brakes f/r	: vent. discs	last revised in	: -
body type	: 2-dr. coupe	warranty	: 3 years
l x w x h	: 4807 x 1918 x 1390 mm	miscellaneous	: Extremely fast, relatively affordable
wheelbase	: 2745 mm		'supercar' with drivetrain from
turning circle	: 11.4 m		Volkswagen. Now also available as
			an open-topped car, dubbed GTC.

BENTLEY CONTINENTAL FLYING SPUR

engine type	: petrol, W12		kerb weight	: 2500 kg
displacement	: 5998 cc		towing weight	: -
max. power	: 411 kW (552 bhp)		boot space	: 475 l
@	: 6100 rpm		fuel capacity	: 90 l
max. torque	: 479 lb ft		consumption	: 16 mpg
@	: 1600 rpm		acc. 0-62 mph	: 5.2 s
gears	: n.a.		top speed	: 195 mph
AT	: 6-speed tiptronic		EuroNCAP	: n.a.
drive	: 4WD		introduction	: February 2005
brakes f/r	: vent. discs		last revised in	: -
body type	: 4-dr. saloon		warranty	: 3 years
l x w x h	: 5307 x 2118 x 1479 mm		miscellaneous	: The fastest 4-door saloon in the
wheelbase	: 3065 mm			world, don't let its introvert
turning circle	: 11.8 m			appearance fool you.

BENTLEY ARNAGE R / T

engine type	: petrol, V8	kerb weight	: 2585 kg
displacement	: 6750 cc	towing weight	: -
max. power	: 298 kW (405 bhp) /	boot space	: 375 l
	336 kW (457 bhp)	fuel capacity	: 100 l
@	: 4000 / 4100 rpm	consumption	: 14.5 mpg
max. torque	: 645 / 738 lb ft	acc. 0-62 mph	: 6.3 / 5.8 s
@	: 3250 rpm	top speed	: 168 / 179 mph
gears	: n.a.	EuroNCAP	: n.a.
AT	: 4-speed automatic	introduction	: May 1998
drive	: RWD	last revised in	: June 2004
brakes f/r	: vent. discs	warranty	: 3 years
body type	: 4-dr. saloon	miscellaneous	: The ultimate Bentley. Very potent
l x w x h	: 5405 x 1930 x 1515 mm		car in angular disguise, ideally
wheelbase	: 3115 mm		suited for those who think Jaguars
turning circle	: 12.4 m		are ordinary.

BENTLEY AZURE

engine type	: petrol, V8	kerb weight	: 2695 kg
displacement	: 6750 cc	towing weight	: -
max. power	: 336 kW / 457 bhp	boot space	: 310 l
@	: 4100 rpm	fuel capacity	: 96 l
max. torque	: 738 lb ft	consumption	: n.a.
@	: 3250 rpm	acc. 0-62 mph	: 6.0 s
gears	: n.a.	top speed	: 179 mph
AT	: 4-speed automatic	EuroNCAP	: n.a.
drive	: RWD	introduction	: April 2006
brakes f/r	: vent. discs	last revised in	: -
body type	: 2-dr. convertible	warranty	: 3 years
l x w x h	: 5410 x 190 x 1485 mm	miscellaneous	: The finest convertible on today's
wheelbase	: 3115 mm		market. Unrivalled luxury and
turning circle	: n.a.		exclusivity, but very, very expensive.

BMW 116i / 118i

engine type	: petrol, inline-4	kerb weight	: 1180 / 1205 kg
displacement	: 1596 / 1995 cc	towing weight	: 1200 kg
max. power	: 85 kW (115 bhp) / 95 kW (129 bhp)	boot space	: 330 l – 1150 l
@	: 6000 / 5750 rpm	fuel capacity	: 50 l
max. torque	: 110/ 133 lb ft	consumption	: 37.7 / 38.7 mpg
@	: 4300 / 3250 rpm	acc. 0-62 mph	: 10.8 / 9.4 s
gears	: 5	top speed	: 124 / 129 mph
AT	: - / optional 6-speed	EuroNCAP	: 5 stars
drive	: RWD	introduction	: May 2004
brakes f/r	: vent. discs / discs	last revised in	: -
body type	: 5-dr. hatchback	warranty	: 2 years
l x w x h	: 4227 x 1751 x 1430 mm	miscellaneous	: Rear-wheel drive is unique in this segment but makes for a cramped interior cabin.
wheelbase	: 2660 mm		
turning circle	: 10.7 m		

120i / 130i

engine type	: petrol, inline-4 / inline-6
displacement	: 1995 / 2996 cc
max. power	: 110 kW (150 bhp) / 195 kW (265 bhp)
@	: 6200 / 6600 rpm
max. torque	: 148 / 232 lb ft
@	: 3600 / 2500 rpm
gears	: 6, optional 6-speed / n.a.
kerb weight	: 1235 / 1450 kg
towing weight	: 1200 kg / n.a.
consumption	: 37.7 / 30.7 mpg
acc. 0-60 mph	: 8.7 / 6.1 s
top speed	: 135 / 155 mph
miscellaneous	: Energetic cars. Lots of power, relatively low weight. Ideally suited for powerdrifters and performance-wise superior to many fast cars.

118d / 120d

engine type	: diesel, inline-4
displacement	: 1995 cc
max. power	: 90 kW (122 bhp) / 120 kW (163 pk)
@	: 4000 rpm
max. torque	: 206 / 250 lb ft
@	: 2000 rpm
gears	: 6 / 6, optional 6-speed
kerb weight	: 1285 / 1315 kg
towing weight	: 1200 kg
consumption	: 50.4 / 49.6 mpg
acc. 0-60 mph	: 10 / 7.9 s
top speed	: 125 / 137 mph
miscellaneous	: Powerful diesel engines go well with the BMW 1 Series. It comes as no surprise that these models are very popular as lease cars.

BMW 318i / 320i SEDAN

engine type	: petrol, inline-4
displacement	: 1995 cc
max. power	: 95 kW (129 bhp) /
	110 kW (150 bhp)
@	: 5750 / 6200 rpm
max. torque	: 133 / 148 lb ft
@	: 3250 / 3600 rpm
gears	: 6
AT	: optional 6-speed
drive	: RWD
brakes f/r	: vent. discs / discs
body type	: 4-dr. saloon
l x w x h	: 4520 x 1817 x 1421 mm
wheelbase	: 2760 mm
turning circle	: 11.0 m

kerb weight	: 1335 / 1320 kg
towing weight	: n.a. / 1400 kg
boot space	: 460 l
fuel capacity	: 60 l
consumption	: 38.7 / 38.2 mpg
acc. 0-62 mph	: 10.0 / 9.0 s
top speed	: 129 / 137 mph
EuroNCAP	: 5 stars
introduction	: October 2004
last revised in	: -
warranty	: 2 years
miscellaneous	: New 3 Series endowed with more common looks than other current BMWs, which accounts for its wide appeal. As is usual with BMW, the range of available engines is enormous.

325i / 330i SEDAN

engine type	: petrol, inline-6
displacement	: 2497 / 2996 cc
max. power	: 160 kW (218 bhp) /
	190 kW (258 bhp)
@	: 6500 / 6600 rpm
max. torque	: 184 / 221 lb ft
@	: 2750 / 2500 rpm
gears	: 6, optional 6-speed
kerb weight	: 1390 / 1425 kg
towing weight	: 1600 / 1700 kg
consumption	: 33.6 / 32.5 mpg
acc. 0-60 mph	: 7.0 / 6.3 s
top speed	: 152 / 155 mph
miscellaneous	: BMWs are almost synonymous with 6-cylinder in-line engines. Unfortunately, a much higher pricetag comes with the extra horsepower.

BMW 318d / 320d TOURING

engine type	: diesel, inline-4	kerb weight	: 1480 kg
displacement	: 1995 cc	towing weight	: 1600 kg
max. power	: 90 kW (122 bhp) /	boot space	: 460 - 1385 l
	120 kW (163 bhp)	fuel capacity	: 61 l
@	: 4000 rpm	consumption	: 48.7 / 47.9 mpg
max. torque	: 206 / 250 lb ft	acc. 0-62 mph	: 10.9 / 8.6 s
@	: 1750 / 2000 rpm	top speed	: 127 / 139 mph
gears	: 5 / 6	EuroNCAP	: 5 stars
AT	: optional 6-speed	introduction	: June 2005
drive	: RWD	last revised in	: -
brakes f/r	: vent. discs / discs	warranty	: 2 years
body type	: 5-dr. stationwagon	miscellaneous	: The 3 Series Touring does not offer
l x w x h	: 4520 x 1817 x 1418 mm		more space than its saloon sibling,
wheelbase	: 2760 mm		but its outward appearance is more
turning circle	: 11.0 m		balanced.

330d TOURING

engine type	: diesel, inline-6
displacement	: 2996 cc
max. power	: 170 kW (231 bhp)
@	: 4000 rpm
max. torque	: 368 lb ft
@	: 1750 rpm
gears	: 6, optional 6-speed
kerb weight	: 1675 kg
towing weight	: 1800 kg
consumption	: 42.2 mpg
acc. 0-60 mph	: 6.8 s
top speed	: 154 mph
miscellaneous	: The diesel engines are also available in the saloon.

BMW 325i / 330i COUPE

engine type	: petrol, inline-6	kerb weight	: 1495 / 1545 kg
displacement	: 2497 / 2996 cc	towing weight	: 1600 / 1700 kg
max. power	: 160 kW (218 bhp) / 200 kW (272 bhp)	boot space	: 440 l
@	: 6500 / 6650 rpm	fuel capacity	: 63 l
max. torque	: 184 / 221 lb ft	consumption	: 33.8 / 32.2 mpg
@	: 2750 rpm	acc. 0-62 mph	: 6.9 / 6.1 s
gears	: 6	top speed	: 153 / 155 mph
AT	: optional 6-speed	EuroNCAP	: n.a.
drive	: RWD	introduction	: September 2006
brakes f/r	: vent. discs	last revised in	: -
body type	: 2-dr. coupe	warranty	: 2 years
l x w x h	: 4580 x 1782 x 1395 mm	miscellaneous	: The coupe version shares no body
wheelbase	: 2760 mm		panels with the saloon. Elegant
turning circle	: 11.0 m		looking car. Also available as 330d.

335i COUPE

engine type	: petrol, inline-6
displacement	: 2996 cc
max. power	: 225 kW (306 bhp)
@	: 5800 rpm
max. torque	: 295 lb ft
@	: 1300 rpm
gears	: 6, optional 6-speed
kerb weight	: 1600 kg
towing weight	: 2005 kg
consumption	: 29.9 mpg
acc. 0-60 mph	: 5.5 s
top speed	: 155 mph
miscellaneous	: Almost as fast as the old M3. Performance is excellent thanks to two turbos, fuel consumption remains acceptable.

BMW 318i / 320i CONVERTIBLE

engine type	: petrol, inline-4 / inline-6
displacement	: 1995 / 2171 cc
max. power	: 105 kW (143 bhp) / 125 kW (170 bhp)
@	: 6000 / 6100 rpm
max. torque	: 148 / 155 lb ft
@	: 3750 / 3500 rpm
gears	: 5
AT	: optional 5-speed
drive	: RWD
brakes f/r	: vent. discs
body type	: 2-dr. convertible
l x w x h	: 4488 x 1757 x 1372 mm
wheelbase	: 2725 mm
turning circle	: 10.5 m

kerb weight	: 1440 / 1495 kg
towing weight	: 1400 / 1600 kg
boot space	: 300 l
fuel capacity	: 63 l
consumption	: 36.2 / 30.1 mpg
acc. 0-62 mph	: 10.4 / 9.1 s
top speed	: 129 / 138 mph
EuroNCAP	: 4 stars
introduction	: 2000
last revised in	: 2003
warranty	: 2 years
miscellaneous	: Beautiful convertible of timeless design. Engine power more than adequate for cruising along boulevards at 30 mph. Four-seater car.

325Ci / 330Ci CONVERTIBLE

engine type	: petrol, inline-6
displacement	: 2494 / 2979 cc
max. power	: 141 kW (192 bhp) / 170 kW (231 bhp)
@	: 6000 / 5900 rpm
max. torque	: 180 / 221 lb ft
@	: 3500 rpm
gears	: 5, optional 5-speed or SMG/ 6, optional 5-speed or SMG
kerb weight	: 1515 / 1560 kg
towing weight	: 1600 kg
consumption	: 29.4 / 29.4 mpg
acc. 0-60 mph	: 8.0 / 6.9 s
top speed	: 145 / 153 mph
miscellaneous	: 325Ci best balanced. 330Ci a trifle racy for a relaxing drive with the top down, the M3 convertible even more so.

320Cd / 330Cd CONVERTIBLE

engine type	: diesel, inline-4 / inline-6
displacement	: 1995 / 2996 cc
max. power	: 110 kW (150 bhp) / 150 kW (204 bhp)
@	: 4000 rpm
max. torque	: 243 / 302 lb ft
@	: 2000 / 3250 rpm
gears	: 6, optional 5-speed
kerb weight	: 1580 / 1675 kg
towing weight	: 1600 kg
consumption	: 44.8 / 40.4 mpg
acc. 0-60 mph	: 9.7 / 7.8 s
top speed	: 131 / 145 mph
miscellaneous	: When both Audi and Mercedes-Benz started offering diesel power in their convertibles, BMW felt it had to follow suit, with these road-burning convertibles as a result.

BMW 523i / 525i

engine type	: petrol, inline-6
displacement	: 2497 cc
max. power	: 130 kW (177 bhp) /
	160 kW (218 bhp)
@	: 5800 / 6500 rpm
max. torque	: 170 / 184 lb ft
@	: 3500 / 2750 rpm
gears	: 6
AT	: optional 6-speed
drive	: RWD
brakes f/r	: vent. discs
body type	: 4-dr. sedan
l x w x h	: 4840 x 1845 x 1470 mm
wheelbase	: 2890 mm
turning circle	: 11.4 m

kerb weight	: 1445 / 1450 kg
towing weight	: 1600 kg
boot space	: 520 l
fuel capacity	: 70 l
consumption	: 33.2 / 32.5 mpg
acc. 0-62 mph	: 8.5 / 7.5 s
top speed	: 146 / 152 mph
EuroNCAP	: 4 stars
introduction	: July 2003
last revised in	: -
warranty	: 2 years
miscellaneous	: Dubbed a controversial design at first, but now widely accepted. 4WD is an option on the 525i. Also available as 530i.

540i / 550i

engine type	: petrol, V8
displacement	: 4000 / 4799cc
max. power	: 225 kW (306 bhp) /
	270 kW / 367 bhp
@	: 6300 rpm
max. torque	: 288 / 362 lb ft
@	: 3500 / 3400 rpm
gears	: 6, optional 6-speed or SMG
kerb weight	: 1725 / 1735 kg
towing weight	: 2000 kg
consumption	: 25.7 / 25.4 mpg
acc. 0-60 mph	: 6.2 / 5.5 s
top speed	: 155 mph
miscellaneous	: Porsche-like performance in a 4-door saloon. The M5 version hits the rev limiter even quicker.

BMW 520d / 525d TOURING

engine type	: diesel, inline-4 / inline-6	kerb weight	: 1675 / 1750 kg
displacement	: 1995 / 2497 cc	towing weight	: 1800 / 2000 kg
max. power	: 120 kW (163 bhp) /	boot space	: 500 - 1650 l
	130 kW (177 bhp)	fuel capacity	: 70 l
@	: 4000 rpm	consumption	: 47.9 / 42.2 mpg
max. torque	: 250 / 295 lb ft	acc. 0-62 mph	: 8.9 / 8.3 s
@	: 2000 rpm	top speed	: 139 / 143 mph
gears	: 6	EuroNCAP	: 4 stars
AT	: optional 6-speed	introduction	: March 2004
drive	: RWD	last revised in	: -
brakes f/r	: vent. discs	warranty	: 2 years
body type	: 5-dr. stationwagon	miscellaneous	: Powerful diesel engine and chassis
l x w x h	: 4840 x 1845 x 1470 mm		make a wonderful combination. Car
wheelbase	: 2890 mm		eats up the miles.
turning circle	: 11.4 m		

530d / 535d TOURING

engine type	: diesel, inline-6
displacement	: 2993 cc
max. power	: 170 kW (231 bhp) /
	225 kW (272 bhp)
@	: 4000 rpm
max. torque	: 368 / 413 lb ft
@	: 1750 / 2000 rpm
gears	: 6, optional 6-speed
kerb weight	: 1660 / 1730 kg
towing weight	: 2000 kg
consumption	: 42.2 / 34.6 mpg
acc. 0-60 mph	: 7.2 / 6.6 s
top speed	: 155 mph
miscellaneous	: All diesel engines available in
	saloon. Diesel power is engine of
	choice in 5 Series. With the
	introduction of a particle filter, end
	pipes of exhaust system are now
	cut off straight.

BMW 630i / 650i COUPE

engine type	: petrol, inline-6 / V8	kerb weight	: 1465 / 1590 kg
displacement	: 2996 / 4800 cc	towing weight	: -
max. power	: 190 kW (258 bhp) /	boot space	: 450 l
	270 kW (367 bhp)	fuel capacity	: 70 l
@	: 6600 / 6100 rpm	consumption	: 31.4 / 23.7 mpg
max. torque	: 221 / 362 lb ft	acc. 0-62 mph	: 6.5 / 5.4 s
@	: 2500 / 3600 rpm	top speed	: 155 mph
gears	: 6	EuroNCAP	: n.a.
AT	: optional 6-speed	introduction	: September 2003
drive	: RWD	last revised in	: -
brakes f/r	: vent. discs	warranty	: 2 years
body type	: 2-dr. coupe	miscellaneous	: Of bold design, this splendid coupe
l x w x h	: 4820 x 1855 x 1373 mm		is a real head turner. Both engines
wheelbase	: 2780 mm		also available in beautiful
turning circle	: 11.4 m		convertible.

BMW M5

engine type	: petrol, V10	kerb weight	: 1685 kg
displacement	: 4999 cc	towing weight	: -
max. power	: 373 kW (507 bhp)	boot space	: 520 l
@	: 7750 rpm	fuel capacity	: 70 l
max. torque	: 384 lb ft	consumption	: 19.1 mpg
@	: 6100 rpm	acc. 0-62 mph	: 4.7 s
gears	: 7-speed SMG	top speed	: 155 mph
AT	: -	EuroNCAP	: 4 stars
drive	: RWD	introduction	: August 2004
brakes f/r	: vent. discs	last revised in	: -
body type	: 4-dr. saloon	warranty	: 2 years
l x w x h	: 4855 x 1846 x 1469 mm	miscellaneous	: The M5 is a Formula I car for the
wheelbase	: 2889 mm		road, it even has a launch control
turning circle	: 11.4 m		system. State-of-the-art technology.

M6

engine type	: petrol, V10
displacement	: 4999cc
max. power	: 373 kW (507 bhp)
@	: 7750 rpm
max. torque	: 384 lb ft
@	: 6100 rpm
gears	: 7-speed SMG
kerb weight	: 1685 kg
towing weight	: n.a.
consumption	: 19.1 mpg
acc. 0-60 mph	: 4.6 s
top speed	: 155 mph
miscellaneous	: The M6 has one of the most expensive car roofs in the world, made of carbonfibre for reduced weight and lower centre of gravity. Marginally faster than M5.

BMW 730i / 740i

engine type	: petrol, inline-6 / V8
displacement	: 2996 / 4000 cc
max. power	: 190 kW (258 bhp) / 225 kW (306 bhp)
@	: 6600 / 6300 rpm
max. torque	: 222 / 288 lb ft
@	: 2500 / 3500 rpm
gears	: 6-speed automatic
AT	: n.a.
drive	: RWD
brakes f/r	: vent. discs
body type	: 4-dr. saloon
l x w x h	: 5039 x 1902 x 1491 mm
wheelbase	: 2990 mm
turning circle	: 12.1 m

kerb weight	: 1780 / 1870 kg
towing weight	: 2000 / 2100 kg
boot space	: 500 l
fuel capacity	: 88 l
consumption	: 28 / 25.2 mpg
acc. 0-62 mph	: 7.8 / 6.6 s
top speed	: 152 / 155 mph
EuroNCAP	: n.a.
introduction	: November 2001
last revised in	: March 2005
warranty	: 2 years
miscellaneous	: It took a facelift for this model to become distinctive again. I-Drive system still difficult to master. All engine variants also available in long-wheelbase version, as is the 730d.

750i / 760i

engine type	: petrol, V8 / V12
displacement	: 4798 / 5972 cc
max. power	: 270 kW (367 bhp) / 327 kW (445 bhp)
@	: 6300 / 6000 rpm
max. torque	: 362 / 442 lb ft
@	: 3400 / 3950 rpm
gears	: 6-speed automatic
kerb weight	: 1885 / 2080 kg
towing weight	: 2100 kg
consumption	: 24 / 21.2 mpg
acc. 0-60 mph	: 5.9 / 5.5 s
top speed	: 155 mph
miscellaneous	: Limousine that makes life difficult for A6 W12, Phaeton and S600. For well-heeled and sporty people who are not worried by its fuel consumption.

BMW 730d / 745d

engine type	: diesel, inline-6 / V8
displacement	: 2993 / 4423 cc
max. power	: 170 kW (231 bhp) / 242 kW (330 bhp)
@	: 4000 rpm
max. torque	: 383 / 553 lb ft
@	: 2000 / 1750 rpm
gears	: 6-speed automatic
kerb weight	: 1875 / 2015 kg
towing weight	: 2100 kg
consumption	: 34.4 mpg / n.a.
acc. 0-60 mph	: 7.8 / 6.6 s
top speed	: 148 / 155 mph
miscellaneous	: Two diesel-engined models that make petrol versions redundant. 745d offers more power and torque than rivals from Audi and Mercedes-Benz. Astonishingly powerful, yet relatively frugal.

BMW X3 2.0i / 2.5si

engine type	: petrol, inline-4 / inline-6	kerb weight	: 1730 / 1805 kg
displacement	: 1995 / 2494 cc	towing weight	: 1600 / 1800 kg
max. power	: 110 kW (150 bhp) / 160 kW (218 bhp)	boot space	: 480 - 1560 l
@	: 6200 / 6500 rpm	fuel capacity	: 67 l
max. torque	: 148 / 218 lb ft	consumption	: 30.4 / 28.5 mpg
@	: 3750 / 2750 rpm	acc. 0-62 mph	: 11.5 / 8.5 s
gears	: 6	top speed	: 123 / 130 mph
AT	: optional 6-speed	EuroNCAP	: n.a.
drive	: 4WD	introduction	: September 2003
brakes f/r	: vent. discs	last revised in	: September 2006
body type	: 5-dr. SUV	warranty	: 2 years
l x w x h	: 4565 x 1853 x 1674 mm	miscellaneous	: New X3 benefits from facelift.
wheelbase	: 2795 mm		Although still not very capable
turning circle	: 11.7 m		offroad, it is one of the best driving
			SUVs onroad.

X3 3.0si

engine type	: petrol, inline-6
displacement	: 2996 cc
max. power	: 200 kW (272 bhp)
@	: 6650 rpm
max. torque	: 232 lb ft
@	: 2750 rpm
gears	: 6-speed automatic
kerb weight	: 1840 kg
towing weight	: 2000 kg
consumption	: 27.4 mpg
acc. 0-60 mph	: 7.5 s
top speed	: 130 mph
miscellaneous	: Substantial power increase for 3.0 6-cylinder engine makes X3 3.0si a very quick car, but biggest diesel version is still the best.

X3 2.0d / 3.0d

engine type	: diesel, inline-4 / inline-6
displacement	: 1995 cc
max. power	: 110 kW (150 bhp) / 160 kW (218 pk)
@	: 4000 rpm
max. torque	: 243 / 368 lb ft
@	: 2000 / 1750 rpm
gears	: 6, optional 6-speed automatic
kerb weight	: 1820 / 1880 kg
towing weight	: 1700 / 2000 kg
consumption	: 39.2 / 35.8 mpg
acc. 0-60 mph	: 10.2 / 7.4 s
top speed	: 123 / 130 mph
miscellaneous	: Latest addition is the 3.0sd which packs a 286 bhp twin turbo diesel engine under the bonnet. But the smaller 2.0d is the more economical choice.

BMW X5 3.0si / 4.8i

engine type	: petrol, inline-6 / V8		**kerb weight**	: n.a.
displacement	: 2996 / 4799 cc		**towing weight**	: n.a.
max. power	: 200 kW (272 bhp) /		**boot space**	: 620 - 1750 l
	261 kW (355 bhp)		**fuel capacity**	: n.a.
@	: n.a.		**consumption**	: 26 / 22.7 mpg
max. torque	: 232 / 350 lb ft		**acc. 0-62 mph**	: 8.1 / 6.5 s
@	: 2750 / 3400 rpm		**top speed**	: 140 / 149 mph
gears	: -		**EuroNCAP**	: n.a.
AT	: 6-speed automatic		**introduction**	: September 2006
drive	: 4WD		**last revised in**	: -
brakes f/r	: vent. discs		**warranty**	: 2 years
body type	: 5-dr. SUV		**miscellaneous**	: BMW decided to enlarge the X5
l x w x h	: 4854 x 1933 x 1715 mm			model to widen the gap with the X3.
wheelbase	: 2920 mm			Available as 7-seater. Engines more
turning circle	: n.a.			powerful and economical.

X5 3.0d

engine type	: diesel, inline-6
displacement	: 2993 cc
max. power	: 170 kW (231 bhp)
@	: n.a.
max. torque	: 383 lb ft
@	: 2000 rpm
gears	: 6-speed automatic
kerb weight	: n.a.
towing weight	: n.a.
consumption	: 32.6 mpg
acc. 0-60 mph	: 8.3 s
top speed	: 134 mph
miscellaneous	: The sensible choice in the X5 range. With the 3-litre diesel engine, the car is just as good as its 3.0 petrol-engined sibling.

BMW Z4 2.0i / 2.5i

engine type	: petrol, inline-4 / inline-6	**kerb weight**	: 1195 / 1225 kg
displacement	: 1995 / 2497 cc	**towing weight**	: -
max. power	: 110 kW (150 bhp) / 130 kW (177 bhp)	**boot space**	: 260 l
@	: 6200 / 5800 rpm	**fuel capacity**	: 55 l
max. torque	: 148 / 170 lb ft	**consumption**	: 37.7 / 34.4 mpg
@	: 3600 / 3500 rpm	**acc. 0-62 mph**	: 8.2 / 7.7 s
gears	: 6	**top speed**	: 137 / 142 mph
AT	: optional 6-speed	**EuroNCAP**	: 4 stars
drive	: RWD	**introduction**	: March 2003
brakes f/r	: vent. discs	**last revised in**	: October 2005
body type	: 2-dr. convertible	**warranty**	: 2 years
l x w x h	: 4091 x 1781 x 1299 mm	**miscellaneous**	: Roadster was given a technical
wheelbase	: 2495 mm		and optical makeover. Also available
turning circle	: 9.8 m		as 2.5si with 218 bhp.

Z4 3.0si / M

engine type	: inline-6
displacement	: 2996 / 3246 cc
max. power	: 195 kW (265 bhp) /
	252 kW (343 bhp)
@	: 6600 / 7900 rpm
max. torque	: 232 / 269 lb ft
@	: 2750 / 4900 rpm
gears	: 6, optional 6-speed automatic
kerb weight	: 1285 / 1385 kg
towing weight	: -
consumption	: 32.8 / 23.3 mpg
acc. 0-60 mph	: 5.7 / 5.0 s
top speed	: 155 mph
miscellaneous	: M-badge and coupe body are latest additions to the Z4 range. Handsome coupe only available with these two petrol engines.

BUGATTI VEYRON 16.4

engine type	: petrol, W16		kerb weight	: 1888 kg
displacement	: 7993 cc		towing weight	: -
max. power	: 736 kW (1,001 bhp)		boot space	: n.a.
@	: 6000 rpm		fuel capacity	: 100 l
max. torque	: 922 lb ft		consumption	: 11.8 mpg
@	: 2200 rpm		acc. 0-62 mph	: 2.5 s
gears	: -		top speed	: 253 mph
AT	: 7-speed seq.		EuroNCAP	: n.a.
drive	: 4WD		introduction	: August 2005
brakes f/r	: vent. discs		last revised in	: -
body type	: 2-dr. coupe		warranty	: 2 years
l x w x h	: 4462 x 1998 x 1204 mm		miscellaneous	: After years of postponement due to
wheelbase	: 2710 mm			development problems, the first
turning circle	: 11.6 m			batch of Veyrons has finally taken to
				the road. Remarkable car in every
				respect, but unattainable for nearly
				everyone on earth.

CADILLAC BLS 2.0t / 2.8 T V6

engine type	: petrol, inline-4 / V6	kerb weight	: 1450 / 1560 kg
displacement	: 1988 / 2792 cc	towing weight	: n.a.
max. power	: 131 kW (175 bhp) /	boot space	: 425 l
	186 kW (255 bhp)	fuel capacity	: 58 l
@	: 5500 rpm	consumption	: 37.2 / 27.7 mpg
max. torque	: 195 / 258 lb ft	acc. 0-62 mph	: 8.7 / 6.9 s
@	: 2500 / 2000 rpm	top speed	: 137 / 155 mph
gears	: 5 / 6	EuroNCAP	: n.a.
AT	: optional 5-speed automatic /	introduction	: September 2005
	optional 6-speed automatic	last revised in	: -
drive	: FWD	warranty	: 3 years
brakes f/r	: vent. discs / discs	miscellaneous	: Cadillac BLS is built alongside
body type	: 4-dr. saloon		technically identical Saab 9-3.
l x w x h	: 4679 x 1762 x 1449 mm		Striking appearance is strongpoint,
wheelbase	: 2675 mm		but small dealer network is not.
turning circle	: 10.9 m		Also available as 2.0 T with
			210 bhp.

BLS 1.9 D

engine type	: diesel, inline-4
displacement	: 1910 cc
max. power	: 110 kW (150 bhp)
@	: 4000 rpm
max. torque	: 236 lb ft
@	: 2000 rpm
gears	: 6, optional 6-speed automatic
kerb weight	: 1510 kg
towing weight	: n.a.
consumption	: 46.3 mpg
acc. 0-60 mph	: 9.8 s
top speed	: 131 mph
miscellaneous	: First diesel-engined car from Cadillac, apart from the disastrous V8 in the Seventies. Diesel engine already familiar from Saab and Vauxhall however.

CADILLAC CTS 2.8 / 3.6

engine type	: petrol, V6	kerb weight	: 1680 / 1706 kg
displacement	: 2792 / 3564 cc	towing weight	: 1815 kg
max. power	: 158 kW (215 bhp) /	boot space	: 420 l
	189 kW (257 bhp)	fuel capacity	: 64 l
@	: 7000 / 6200 rpm	consumption	: 24.2 / 24.4 mpg
max. torque	: 194 / 251 lb ft	acc. 0-62 mph	: 8.2 / 7.0 s
@	: 3000 / 3200 rpm	top speed	: 140 / 145 mph
gears	: 6	EuroNCAP	: n.a.
AT	: optional 5-speed automatic	introduction	: April 2003
drive	: RWD	last revised in	: -
brakes f/r	: vent. discs	warranty	: 3 years
body type	: 4-dr. saloon	miscellaneous	: Bold design and excellent driving
l x w x h	: 4828 x 1795 x 1441 mm		characteristics are its forte in
wheelbase	: 2880 mm		the battle with the European top
turning circle	: 10.8 m		marques. Rarely seen on our roads,
			undeservedly so.

CTS-V

engine type	: petrol, V8
displacement	: 5665 cc
max. power	: 298 kW (405 bhp)
@	: 6000 rpm
max. torque	: 393 lb ft
@	: 4800 rpm
gears	: 6
kerb weight	: 1746 kg
towing weight	: n.a.
consumption	: n.a.
acc. 0-60 mph	: 4.6 s
top speed	: 163 mph
miscellaneous	: A 4-door Corvette: exciting, wild and ultrafast. Perfectly suited for those who enjoy going sideways in a car. CTS-V faster on the Nürburgring than previous BMW M5 model.

CADILLAC STS 3.6 / 4.6

engine type	: petrol, V6 / V8	kerb weight	: 1782 / 1825 kg
displacement	: 3564 / 4565 cc	towing weight	: 1928 kg
max. power	: 189 kW (257 bhp) /	boot space	: 464 l
	239 kW (325 bhp)	fuel capacity	: 66 l
@	: 6500 / 6400 rpm	consumption	: 22.9 / 19.7 mpg
max. torque	: 252 / 315 lb ft	acc. 0-62 mph	: 7.4 / 6.2 s
@	: 3200 / 4400 rpm	top speed	: 142 / 155 mph
gears	: -	EuroNCAP	: n.a.
AT	: 5-speed automatic	introduction	: February 2005
drive	: RWD	last revised in	: -
brakes f/r	: vent. discs	warranty	: 3 years
body type	: 4-dr. saloon	miscellaneous	: Not your average billowing ship
l x w x h	: 4985 x 1845 x 1465 mm		from America this time. Much better
wheelbase	: 2957 mm		car than preceding model, for the
turning circle	: 11.5 m		discerning buyer. V8 version
			available with AWD.

STS-V

engine type	: petrol, V8
displacement	: 4371cc
max. power	: 328 kW (446 bhp)
@	: 6400 rpm
max. torque	: 430 lb ft
@	: 3600 rpm
gears	: 6-speed automatic
kerb weight	: 1950 kg
towing weight	: -
consumption	: n.a.
acc. 0-60 mph	: < 5 s
top speed	: > 155 mph
miscellaneous	: Heavyweight, but more nimble thanks to big supercharged V8. Fine tuning at the Nürburgring paid off. Nice alternative if you think the M5 and E55 AMG are ordinary.

CADILLAC XLR

engine type	: petrol, V8		kerb weight	: 1655 kg
displacement	: 4565 cc		towing weight	: -
max. power	: 239 kW (325 bhp)		boot space	: 125 - 330 l
@	: 6400 rpm		fuel capacity	: 68 l
max. torque	: 315 lb ft		consumption	: 13.2 mpg
@	: 4400 rpm		acc. 0-62 mph	: 5.9 s
gears	: -		top speed	: 155 mph
AT	: 5-speed automatic		EuroNCAP	: n.a.
drive	: RWD		introduction	: January 2003
brakes f/r	: vent. discs		last revised in	: -
body type	: 2-dr. convertible		warranty	: 3 years
l x w x h	: 4515 x 1835 x 1280 mm		miscellaneous	: Aggressively styled and luxuriously
wheelbase	: 2685 mm			appointed coupe-convertible. Sales
turning circle	: 11.9 m			disappointing however because of
				hefty price. Top-of-the-range model
				is the 446 bhp XLR-V.

CADILLAC SRX 3.6 V6 / 4.6 V8

engine type	: petrol, V6	kerb weight	: 1996 / 2051 kg
displacement	: 2792 / 3564 cc	towing weight	: 2268 kg
max. power	: 158 kW (215 bhp) /	boot space	: 240 / 1970 l
	189 kW (257 bhp)	fuel capacity	: 76 l
@	: 7000 / 6200 rpm	consumption	: 19.2 / 20.2 mpg
max. torque	: 194 / 251 lb ft	acc. 0-62 mph	: 8.1 / 7.4 s
@	: 3000 / 3200 rpm	top speed	: 125 / 140 mph
gears	: 6	EuroNCAP	: n.a.
AT	: optional 5-speed automatic	introduction	: October 2004
drive	: 4WD	last revised in	: -
brakes f/r	: vent. discs	warranty	: 3 years
body type	: 5-dr. SUV	miscellaneous	: For those who are torn between a
l x w x h	: 4950 x 1845 x 1721 mm		stationwagon and a SUV. Good
wheelbase	: 2880 mm		alternative for X5 and XC90. V8
turning circle	: 10.8 m		engine sounds great.

CADILLAC ESCALADE

engine type	: petrol, V8		**kerb weight**	: -
displacement	: 6199 cc		**towing weight**	: -
max. power	: 301 kW (409 bhp)		**boot space**	: 479 - 3084 l
@	: 5700 rpm		**fuel capacity**	: -
max. torque	: 417 lb ft		**consumption**	: -
@	: 4500 rpm		**acc. 0-62 mph**	: -
gears	: -		**top speed**	: -
AT	: 6-speed automatic		**EuroNCAP**	: -
drive	: 4WD		**introduction**	: May 2006
brakes f/r	: vent. discs		**last revised in**	: n.a.
body type	: 5-dr. SUV		**warranty**	: 3 years
l x w x h	: 5150 x 2007 x 1887 mm		**miscellaneous**	: Impressively large car, but much
wheelbase	: 2946 mm			too big for Europe. With seating for
turning circle	: 11.9 m			8 people though.

CHEVROLET MATIZ 0.8 / 1.0

engine type	: petrol, inline-3	kerb weight	: 770 kg
displacement	: 796 / 995 cc	towing weight	: -
max. power	: 38 kW (51 bhp) / 48 kW (65 bhp)	boot space	: 170 l
@	: 6000 / 5400 rpm	fuel capacity	: 35 l
max. torque	: 53 / 67 lb ft	consumption	: 54.3 / 50.4 mpg
@	: 4400 / 4200 rpm	acc. 0-62 mph	: 18.2 / 14.1 s
gears	: 5	top speed	: 90 / 97 mph
AT	: -	EuroNCAP	: 3 stars
drive	: FWD	introduction	: May 2005
brakes f/r	: discs / drum brakes	last revised in	: -
body type	: 3-dr. hatchback	warranty	: 3 years
l x w x h	: 3495 x 1495 x 1500 mm	miscellaneous	: Practical, cute little car. Chevrolet
wheelbase	: 2345 mm		name normally not associated with
turning circle	: 9.2 m		this type of car, but all Daewoo
			models are now badged as
			Chevrolets in Europe.

CHEVROLET KALOS 1.2 / 1.4

engine type	: petrol, inline-4		**kerb weight**	: 955 / 1030 kg
displacement	: 1148 / 1399 cc		**towing weight**	: 1000 kg
max. power	: 53 kW (72 bhp) / 69 kW (94 bhp)		**boot space**	: 175 - 735 l
@	: 5400 / 5600 rpm		**fuel capacity**	: 45 l
max. torque	: 77 / 66 lb ft		**consumption**	: 44.1 / 42.1 mpg
@	: 4400 / 3400 rpm		**acc. 0-62 mph**	: 13.7 / 11.1 s
gears	: 5		**top speed**	: 98 / 109 mph
AT	: - / optional 4-speed automatic		**EuroNCAP**	: 3 stars
drive	: FWD		**introduction**	: January 2005
brakes f/r	: vent. discs		**last revised in**	: -
body type	: 3-, 5-dr. hatchback		**warranty**	: 3 years
l x w x h	: 3880 x 1670 x 1495 mm		**miscellaneous**	: Popular model which sells beyond
wheelbase	: 2480 mm			expectations. Also available with a
turning circle	: 9.8 m			83 bhp 1.4 engine. Aveo 1.4
				(pictured below) replaces the Kalos
				saloon.

CHEVROLET LACETTI 1.4 / 1.6

engine type	: petrol, inline-4
displacement	: 1399 / 1598 cc
max. power	: 68 kW (92 bhp) / 80 kW (109 bhp)
@	: 6000 / 5800 rpm
max. torque	: 97 / 110 lb ft
@	: 3600 / 4000 rpm
gears	: 5
AT	: optional 4-speed automatic
drive	: FWD
brakes f/r	: vent. discs / discs
body type	: 5-dr. hatchback
l x w x h	: 4295 x 1725 x 1445 mm
wheelbase	: 2600 mm
turning circle	: 10.4 m

kerb weight	: 1145 kg
towing weight	: 1200 kg
boot space	: 275 - 1045 l
fuel capacity	: 60 l
consumption	: 39.2 / 39.7 mpg
acc. 0-62 mph	: 11.6 / 10.7 s
top speed	: 97 / 110 mph
EuroNCAP	: n.a.
introduction	: January 2005
last revised in	: -
warranty	: 3 years
miscellaneous	: Sporty, well-equipped car, competitively priced at that. Drives well, especially in 1.6 form.

LACETTI 1.8

engine type	: petrol, inline-4
displacement	: 1799 cc
max. power	: 90 kW (122 bhp)
@	: 5800 rpm
max. torque	: 122 lb ft
@	: 4000 rpm
gears	: 5, optional 4-speed automatic
kerb weight	: 1180 kg
towing weight	: 1200 kg
consumption	: 38.1 mpg
acc. 0-60 mph	: 9.5 s
top speed	: 121 mph
miscellaneous	: Not overtly better car than 1.6 model, just a bit quicker and better suited to tow a caravan. Unfortunately, not available with a diesel engine.

CHEVROLET LACETTI SALOON 1.6 / 1.8

engine type	: petrol, inline-4	**kerb weight**	: 1180 / 1210 kg
displacement	: 1598 / 1799cc	**towing weight**	: 1200 kg
max. power	: 80 kW (109 bhp) / 90 kW (122 bhp)	**boot space**	: 405 l
@	: 6000 rpm	**fuel capacity**	: 60 l
max. torque	: 110 / 119 lb ft	**consumption**	: 40 / 37.8 mpg
@	: 3400 / 4000 rpm	**acc. 0-62 mph**	: 12.4 / 11.0 s
gears	: 5	**top speed**	: 116 / 121 mph
AT	: - / optional 4-speed automatic	**EuroNCAP**	: n.a.
drive	: FWD	**introduction**	: January 2005
brakes f/r	: vent. discs / discs	**last revised in**	: -
body type	: 4-dr. saloon	**warranty**	: 3 years
l x w x h	: 4500 x 1725 x 1440 mm	**miscellaneous**	: Also available with 94 bhp
wheelbase	: 2600 mm		1.4 engine. Old acquaintance from
turning circle	: 10.4 m		Daewoo, with minor changes only.
			Proper family car, but stationwagon
			offers even more space.

CHEVROLET EPICA 2.0 / 2.5

engine type	: petrol, inline-6		**kerb weight**	: 1435 / 1475 kg
displacement	: 1993 / 2492 cc		**towing weight**	: 1700 kg
max. power	: 105 kW (144 bhp) /		**boot space**	: 480 l
	115 kW (156 bhp)		**fuel capacity**	: 65 l
@	: 6400 / 4000 rpm		**consumption**	: 34.6 / 30.5 mpg
max. torque	: 144 / 175 lb ft		**acc. 0-62 mph**	: 9.9 s
@	: 4600 / 4000 rpm		**top speed**	: 129 / 130 mph
gears	: 5		**EuroNCAP**	: n.a.
AT	: - / optional 5-speed automatic		**introduction**	: July 2006
drive	: FWD		**last revised in**	: -
brakes f/r	: vent. discs / discs		**warranty**	: 3 years
body type	: 4-dr. saloon		**miscellaneous**	: Quiet, refined business car with a
l x w x h	: 4805 x 1810 x 1450 mm			friendly pricetag. Diesel-engined
wheelbase	: 2700 mm			version to follow.
turning circle	: 10.8 m			

CHEVROLET TACUMA 1.6 / 2.0

engine type	: petrol, inline-4		**kerb weight**	: 1245 / 1270 kg
displacement	: 1598 / 1998 cc		**towing weight**	: 1200 kg
max. power	: 77 kW (105 bhp) / 89 kW (121 bhp)		**boot space**	: 465 - 1165 l
@	: 6000 / 5600 rpm		**fuel capacity**	: 60 l
max. torque	: 105 / 130 lb ft		**consumption**	: 35.3 / 32.8 mpg
@	: 3400 / 4000 rpm		**acc. 0-62 mph**	: 11.8 / 10.5 s
gears	: 5		**top speed**	: 104 / 111 mph
AT	: - / optional 4-speed automatic		**EuroNCAP**	: n.a.
drive	: FWD		**introduction**	: January 2005
brakes f/r	: vent. discs / discs		**last revised in**	: -
body type	: 5-dr. MPV		**warranty**	: 3 years
l x w x h	: 4350 x 1755 x 1580 mm		**miscellaneous**	: Midsized MPV, already familiar from
wheelbase	: 2600 mm			its Daewoo period. Car looks dated
turning circle	: 10.6 m			in a segment with so many new
				additions.

CHEVROLET CAPTIVA 2.4 / 3.2

engine type	: petrol, inline-4 / V6	kerb weight	: 1760 / 1780 kg
displacement	: 2405 / 3195 cc	towing weight	: 1500 / 1700 kg
max. power	: 100 kW (136 bhp) /	boot space	: 465 - 1165 l
	169 kW (230 bhp)	fuel capacity	: 60 l
@	: 5000 / 6600 rpm	consumption	: 31.2 / 24.7 mpg
max. torque	: 156 / 214 lb ft	acc. 0-62 mph	: 13.5 / 10.5 s
@	: 4000 / 3600 rpm	top speed	: 109 / 115 mph
gears	: 5	EuroNCAP	: n.a.
AT	: - / optional 5-speed automatic	introduction	: June 2005
drive	: FWD	last revised in	: -
brakes f/r	: vent. discs / discs	warranty	: 3 years
body type	: 5-dr. SUV	miscellaneous	: Nice SUV. Captiva platform used
l x w x h	: 4635 x 1850 x 1720 mm		for Opel Antara too. 2.4 version also
wheelbase	: 2705 mm		available with 4WD.
turning circle	: 11.4 m		

CAPTIVA 2.0D

engine type	: diesel, inline-4
displacement	: 1991 cc
max. power	: 110 kW (150 bhp)
@	: 4000 rpm
max. torque	: 229 lb ft
@	: 2000 rpm
gears	: 5, optional 5-speed automatic
kerb weight	: 1795 kg
towing weight	: 2000 kg
consumption	: 38.4 mpg
acc. 0-60 mph	: 12.5 s
top speed	: 109 mph
miscellaneous	: Powerful diesel-engined version probably bestseller of Captiva range. Rightly so, since it is quicker and more economical than its two petrol-engined siblings.

CHRYSLER PT CRUISER 1.6 / 2.4

engine type	: petrol, inline-4
displacement	: 1598 / 2429 cc
max. power	: 85 kW (116 bhp) /
	105 kW (143 bhp)
@	: 6300 / 5200 rpm
max. torque	: 116 / 158 lb ft
@	: 6300 / 5200 rpm
gears	: 5
AT	: - / optional 4-speed automatic
drive	: FWD
brakes f/r	: vent. discs / discs
body type	: 5-dr. MPV
l x w x h	: 4288 x 1704 x 1601 mm
wheelbase	: 2616 mm
turning circle	: 11.6 m

kerb weight	: 1341 / 1410 kg
towing weight	: 1000 kg
boot space	: 521 - 2150 l
fuel capacity	: 57 l
consumption	: 36.8 / 30.1 mpg
acc. 0-62 mph	: 13.5 / 12.2 s
top speed	: 109 / 121 mph
EuroNCAP	: n.a.
introduction	: Summer 2000
last revised in	: Autumn 2005
warranty	: 2 years
miscellaneous	: Still genuinely retro-looking car, despite recent facelift. Also available as convertible. Replacement soon to follow.

PT CRUISER 2.4 TURBO

engine type	: petrol, inline-4
displacement	: 2429 cc
max. power	: 164 kW (223 bhp)
@	: 5100 rpm
max. torque	: 245 lb ft
@	: 3950 rpm
gears	: 5
kerb weight	: 1480 kg
towing weight	: 1000 kg
consumption	: 28.9 mpg
acc. 0-60 mph	: 7.5 s
top speed	: 124 mph
miscellaneous	: Reasonably quick car, but chassis is not entirely up to the job. Turbo engine endows soft-topped version with fine cruising characteristics.

PT CRUISER 2.2 CRD

engine type	: diesel, inline-4
displacement	: 2148 cc
max. power	: 89 kW (121 bhp)
@	: 4200 rpm
max. torque	: 221 lb ft
@	: 1600 rpm
gears	: 5
kerb weight	: 1485 kg
towing weight	: 1000 kg
consumption	: 47.2 mpg
acc. 0-60 mph	: 12.1 s
top speed	: 133 mph
miscellaneous	: Models destined for Europe are built in Austria. Diesel engine supplied by Mercedes-Benz available only in Europe.

CHRYSLER SEBRING 2.4i 16V / 2.7i V6

engine type	: petrol, inline-4 / V6	kerb weight	: 1491 / 1522 kg
displacement	: 2360 / 2736 cc	towing weight	: n.a.
max. power	: 129 kW (172 bhp) / 142 kW (190 bhp)	boot space	: 390 l
		fuel capacity	: 64 l
@	: 6000 / 6400 rpm	consumption	: n.a.
max. torque	: 164 / 220 lb ft	acc. 0-62 mph	: n.a.
@	: 4400 / 4000 rpm	top speed	: n.a.
gears	: -	EuroNCAP	: n.a.
AT	: 4-speed	introduction	: September 2006
drive	: FWD	last revised in	: -
brakes f/r	: vent. discs / discs	warranty	: 2 years
body type	: 4-dr. saloon	miscellaneous	: New Sebring model brings new opportunities for Chrysler. A 4-seater convertible and 156 bhp strong 2.0-litre version with manual gearbox will be included in the range.
l x w x h	: 4842 x 1808 x 1498 mm		
wheelbase	: 2765 mm		
turning circle	: 11.1 m		

SEBRING 2.0 CRD

engine type	: diesel, inline-4
displacement	: 1968 cc
max. power	: 103 kW (140 bhp)
@	: 4000 rpm
max. torque	: 229 lb ft
@	: 2500 rpm
gears	: 6
kerb weight	: n.a.
towing weight	: n.a.
consumption	: n.a.
acc. 0-60 mph	: n.a.
top speed	: n.a.
miscellaneous	: Volkswagen's diesel engine should help to make the Chrysler Sebring successful as a company car.

CHRYSLER 300 C 2.7L V6 / C 3.5L V6

engine type	: petrol, V6	kerb weight	: 1810 / 1824 kg
displacement	: 2736 / 3518 cc	towing weight	: 1500 / 1725 kg
max. power	: 142 kW (193 bhp) /	boot space	: 442 l
	183 kW (249 bhp)	fuel capacity	: 68 l
@	: 6400 rpm	consumption	: 26.3 / 25.5 mpg
max. torque	: 192 / 250 lb ft	acc. 0-62 mph	: 11.1 / 9.2 s
@	: 4000 / 3800 rpm	top speed	: 129 / 136 mph
gears	: -	EuroNCAP	: n.a.
AT	: 4-speed automatic	introduction	: Summer 2004
drive	: RWD	last revised in	: -
brakes f/r	: vent. discs	warranty	: 2 years
body type	: 4-dr. saloon	miscellaneous	: For managers who dare to be
l x w x h	: 4999 x 1881 x 1483 mm		different, but car has a lot to offer.
wheelbase	: 3048 mm		Also available with 5.7-litre V8.
turning circle	: 11.9 m		

CHRYSLER CROSSFIRE 3.2 V6 / SRT-6 AUTO

engine type	: petrol, V6	kerb weight	: 1352 / 1455 kg
displacement	: 3199 cc	towing weight	: -
max. power	: 160 kW (218 bhp) /	boot space	: 215 l / roadster 190 l
	246 kW (330 bhp)	fuel capacity	: 60 l
@	: 5700 / 6100 rpm	consumption	: 27.2 / 25.7 mpg
max. torque	: 229 / 310 lb ft	acc. 0-62 mph	: 6.5 / 5.0 s
@	: 3000 / 3500 rpm	top speed	: 155 mph
gears	: -	EuroNCAP	: n.a.
AT	: 5-speed automatic	introduction	: Late 2003, roadster summer 2004
drive	: RWD	last revised in	: -
brakes f/r	: vent. discs / discs	warranty	: 2 years
body type	: 2-dr. coupe	miscellaneous	: Drivetrain borrowed from previous
l x w x h	: 4058 x 1766 x 1307 mm		Mercedes-Benz SLK, in a striking
wheelbase	: 2400 mm		body with a charisma all of its own.
turning circle	: 10.3 m		Crossfire model stands out in the
			crowd.

300 C 3.0 CRD

engine type	: diesel, V6
displacement	: 2987 cc
max. power	: 160 kW (218 bhp)
@	: 3800 rpm
max. torque	: 376 lb ft
@	: 1600 rpm
gears	: 5-speed automatic
kerb weight	: 1916 kg
towing weight	: n.a.
consumption	: 34.6 mpg
acc. 0-60 mph	: 7.6 s
top speed	: 143 mph
miscellaneous	: Diesel-engined version is serious business for Chrysler. Modern engine the same as in Mercedes-Benz E-class.

CHRYSLER VOYAGER 2.4I / 3.3I V6 AUTO

engine type	: petrol, inline-4 / V6	**kerb weight**	: 1805 / 1850 kg
displacement	: 2429 / 3301 cc	**towing weight**	: 1600 kg
max. power	: 105 kW (144 bhp) /	**boot space**	: 660 - 3460 l
	128 kW (174 bhp)	**fuel capacity**	: 75 l
@	: 5200 / 5100 rpm	**consumption**	: 28.5 / 22.1 mpg
max. torque	: 161 / 205 lb ft	**acc. 0-62 mph**	: 12.4 / 11.9 s
@	: 4000 rpm	**top speed**	: 114 / 111 mph
gears	: 5 / n.a.	**EuroNCAP**	: n.a.
AT	: n.a. / 4-speed automatic	**introduction**	: November 2001
drive	: FWD	**last revised in**	: Spring 2004
brakes f/r	: vent. discs / discs	**warranty**	: 2 years
body type	: 5-dr. MPV	**miscellaneous**	: Very successful model, this first
l x w x h	: 4808 x 1997 x 1803 mm		American people carrier. Very
wheelbase	: 2878 mm		big, with clever Stow&Go seating
turning circle	: 12.0 m		arrangement. Wheelbase of Grand
			Voyager another 288 millimetres
			longer.

VOYAGER 2.5 CRD / 2.8 CRD LX

engine type	: diesel, inline-4
displacement	: 2499 / 2776 cc
max. power	: 105 kW (143 bhp) /
	110 kW (150 bhp)
@	: 4000 / 3800 rpm
max. torque	: 251 / 265 lb ft
@	: 2000 / 1800 rpm
gears	: 5
kerb weight	: 1925 / 1915 kg
towing weight	: 1600 kg
consumption	: 35.5 / 33.7mpg
acc. 0-60 mph	: 12.9 /11.9 s
top speed	: 115 / 112 mph
miscellaneous	: Voyager and Grand Voyager share
	a somewhat European look, but
	build quality is not up to European
	standards.

CHRYSLER 300 C TOURING 5.7 HEMI

engine type	: petrol, V8	kerb weight	: 1947 kg
displacement	: 5654 cc	towing weight	: 1725 kg
max. power	: 254 kW (340 bhp)	boot space	: 630 – 1602 l
@	: 5000 rpm	fuel capacity	: 71 l
max. torque	: 387 lb ft	consumption	: 22.6 mpg
@	: 4000 rpm	acc. 0-62 mph	: 6.4 s
gears	: -	top speed	: 155 mph
AT	: 5-speed automatic	EuroNCAP	: n.a.
drive	: RWD	introduction	: Summer 2004
brakes f/r	: vent. discs	last revised in	: -
body type	: 5-dr. stationwagon	warranty	: 2 years
l x w x h	: 4999 x 1881 x 1481 mm	miscellaneous	: Other engines available, but this is
wheelbase	: 3048 mm		the real thing. The word 'Hemi' has
turning circle	: 11.9 m		an iconic ring to it in the States.
			Spectacular V8 sound.

300 C TOURING SRT-8

engine type	: petrol, V8
displacement	: 6059 cc
max. power	: 317 kW (431 bhp)
@	: 6000 rpm
max. torque	: 420 lb ft
@	: 4800 rpm
gears	: 5-speed automatic
kerb weight	: 1725 kg
towing weight	: -
consumption	: 20.3 mpg
acc. 0-60 mph	: 5.0 s
top speed	: 165 mph
miscellaneous	: SRT-8 model is flagship of 300 C range, with an even bigger Hemi engine under the bonnet.

CITROËN C1 1.0

engine type	: petrol, inline-3		**kerb weight**	: 765 kg
displacement	: 998 cc		**towing weight**	: -
max. power	: 50 kW (68 bhp)		**boot space**	: 139 - 712 l
@	: 6000 rpm		**fuel capacity**	: 35 l
max. torque	: 69 lb ft		**consumption**	: 61.4 mpg
@	: 3600 rpm		**acc. 0-62 mph**	: 13.7 s
gears	: 5		**top speed**	: 98 mph
AT	: n.a.		**EuroNCAP**	: n.a.
drive	: FWD		**introduction**	: May 2005
brakes f/r	: vent. discs / drum brakes		**last revised in**	: -
body type	: 3, 5-dr. hatchback		**warranty**	: 2 years
l x w x h	: 3435 x 1630 x 1465 mm		**miscellaneous**	: One of three models that are trip-
wheelbase	: 2350 mm			lets: Citroën C1, Peugeot 107 and
turning circle	: 9.5 m			Toyota Aygo. Also available with
				5-door body.

C1 1.4 HDI

engine type	: diesel, inline-4
displacement	: 1398 cc
max. power	: 40 kW (55 bhp)
@	: 4000 rpm
max. torque	: 96 lb ft
@	: 1750 rpm
gears	: 5
kerb weight	: 880 kg
towing weight	: -
consumption	: 68.9 mpg
acc. 0-60 mph	: 15.6 s
top speed	: 96 mph
miscellaneous	: With the 1.4 HDI engine, the C1 is an even more economical car to drive.

CITROËN C2 1.1 / 1.4

engine type	: petrol, inline-4	kerb weight	: 932 / 991 kg
displacement	: 1124 / 1361 cc	towing weight	: 525 / 537 kg
max. power	: 44 kW (61 bhp) / 54 kW (75 bhp)	boot space	: 193 - 879 l
@	: 5500 / 5400 rpm	fuel capacity	: 41 l
max. torque	: 69 / 87 lb ft	consumption	: 48.7 / 47 mpg
@	: 3200 / 3300 rpm	acc. 0-62 mph	: 14.4 / 12.2 s
gears	: 5	top speed	: 98 / 105 mph
AT	: n.a. / optional SensoDrive	EuroNCAP	: 4 stars
drive	: FWD	introduction	: August 2003
brakes f/r	: vent. discs / drum brakes	last revised in	: -
body type	: 3-dr. hatchback	warranty	: 2 years
l x w x h	: 3666 x 1461 x 1659 mm	miscellaneous	: Rakish city car. Popular too, with
wheelbase	: 2315 mm		sales stimulated by low price.
turning circle	: 9.6 m		Baggage space is limited.

C2 1.6 16V

engine type	: petrol, inline-4
displacement	: 1587 cc
max. power	: 80 kW (110 bhp)
@	: 5705 rpm
max. torque	: 108 lb ft
@	: 4000 rpm
gears	: 5
kerb weight	: 1055 kg
towing weight	: 565 kg
consumption	: 44.8 mpg
acc. 0-60 mph	: 10.9 s
top speed	: 121 mph
miscellaneous	: Quick little car, in VTS trim even more fun with 125 bhp engine and manual gearbox that is preferable to the Sensodrive system.

C2 1.4 HDI

engine type	: diesel, inline-4
displacement	: 1398 cc
max. power	: 40 kW (55 bhp)
@	: 4000 rpm
max. torque	: 96 lb ft
@	: 1750 rpm
gears	: 5
kerb weight	: 996 kg
towing weight	: 548 kg
consumption	: 65.7 mpg
acc. 0-60 mph	: 13.5 s
top speed	: 103 mph
miscellaneous	: Frugal type. Nice to drive however, thanks to torquey diesel engine, but driving noise a bit high.

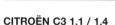

CITROËN C3 1.1 / 1.4

engine type	: petrol, inline-4	kerb weight	: 953 / 980 kg
displacement	: 1124 / 1361 cc	towing weight	: 926 / 1174 kg
max. power	: 44 kW (61 bhp) / 54 kW (75 bhp)	boot space	: 305 - 1310 l
@	: 5500 / 5400 rpm	fuel capacity	: 45 l
max. torque	: 69 / 87 lb ft	consumption	: 47.1 / 46.3 mpg
@	: 3200 / 3300 rpm	acc. 0-62 mph	: 16.6 / 13.6 s
gears	: 5	top speed	: 98 / 104 mph
AT	: - / optional SensoDrive	EuroNCAP	: 4 stars
drive	: FWD	introduction	: Spring 2002
brakes f/r	: vent. discs / drum brakes	last revised in	: Autumn 2005
body type	: 5-dr. hatchback	warranty	: 2 years
l x w x h	: 3850 x 1667 x 1519 mm	miscellaneous	: Still attractive. Reasonable interior
wheelbase	: 2460 mm		space and modern dashboard.
turning circle	: 10.1 m		

C3 1.6 16V

engine type	: petrol, inline-4
displacement	: 1587 cc
max. power	: 80 kW (110 bhp)
@	: 5705 rpm
max. torque	: 108 lb ft
@	: 4000 rpm
gears	: 5
kerb weight	: 1033 kg
towing weight	: 1176 kg
consumption	: 43.5 mpg
acc. 0-60 mph	: 10.6 s
top speed	: 118 mph
miscellaneous	: 16V 4-cylinder transforms C3 into a quick car. XT-R model features wilder bumpers and an engine with 90 or 110 bhp.

C3 1.4HDI

engine type	: diesel, inline-4
displacement	: 1398 cc
max. power	: 40 kW (55 bhp)
@	: 4000 rpm
max. torque	: 96 lb ft
@	: 1750 rpm
gears	: 5
kerb weight	: 997 kg
towing weight	: n.a.
consumption	: 64.2 mpg
acc. 0-60 mph	: 14.8 s
top speed	: 101 mph
miscellaneous	: Affordable, diesel-engined C3 a good alternative for a 206 HDi. Engine suits car well.

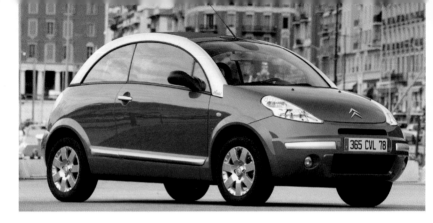

CITROËN C3 PLURIEL 1.4 / 1.6 16V

engine type	: petrol, inline-4
displacement	: 1361 / 1587 cc
max. power	: 54 kW (75 bhp) / 80 kW (110 bhp)
@	: 5400 / 5750 rpm
max. torque	: 87 / 108 lb ft
@	: 3300 / 4000 rpm
gears	: 5
AT	: - / optional SensoDrive
drive	: FWD
brakes f/r	: vent. discs / drum brakes
body type	: 2-dr. convertible
l x w x h	: 3934 x 1700 x 1559 mm
wheelbase	: 2460 mm
turning circle	: 10.1 m

kerb weight	: 1128 / 1175 kg
towing weight	: 850 kg
boot space	: 267 l
fuel capacity	: 47 l
consumption	: 41.5 / 42.2 mpg
acc. 0-62 mph	: 13.9 / 11.6 s
top speed	: 99 / 117 mph
EuroNCAP	: 4 stars
introduction	: Spring 2003
last revised in	: -
warranty	: 2 years
miscellaneous	: Nice roof construction, but Pluriel is not free from rattles. With the roof closed and a driving speed of over 75 mph, the wind noise is deafening. Therefore better suited for the city.

CITROËN C4 1.4 16V / 1.6 16V

engine type	: petrol, inline-4	kerb weight	: 1157 / 1175 kg
displacement	: 1361 / 1587cc	towing weight	: 1561 / 1511 kg
max. power	: 65 kW (90 bhp) / 80 kW (110 bhp)	boot space	: 320 - 1023 l
@	: 5250 / 5800 rpm	fuel capacity	: 60 l
max. torque	: 98 / 108 lb ft	consumption	: 44.1 / 39.8 mpg
@	: 3300 / 4000 rpm	acc. 0-62 mph	: 14.2 / 11.9 s
gears	: 5	top speed	: 113 / 121 mph
AT	: - / optional 4-speed	EuroNCAP	: 5 stars
drive	: FWD	introduction	: Autumn 2004
brakes f/r	: vent. discs / discs	last revised in	: -
body type	: 5-dr. hatchback	warranty	: 2 years
l x w x h	: 4260 x 1773 x 1471 mm	miscellaneous	: Good-looking car, pitched against
wheelbase	: 2608 mm		VW Golf. Citroën full of élan again.
turning circle	: 10.8 m		Non-revolving steering wheel centre
			and perfume device are very
			special.

C4 1.6HDI 90 / 2.0 HDiF 138

engine type	: diesel, inline-4
displacement	: 1560 / 1997 cc
max. power	: 66 kW (92 bhp) / 100 kW (138 bhp)
@	: 4000 rpm
max. torque	: 159 / 236 lb ft
@	: 1750 / 2000 rpm
gears	: 5 / 6
kerb weight	: 1232 / 1356 kg
towing weight	: 1636 / 1811 kg
consumption	: 60.1 / 51.4 mpg
acc. 0-60 mph	: 13.9 / 10.5 s
top speed	: 112 /125 mph
miscellaneous	: 1.6 HDI engine with 110 bhp also
	available. The larger diesel engine
	is equipped with a particle filter.

CITROËN C4 COUPE 2.0 16V 138 / 180 pk

engine type	: petrol, inline-4	kerb weight	: 1254 / 1312 kg
displacement	: 1997cc	towing weight	: 1611 / 1401 kg
max. power	: 100 kW (138 bhp) /	boot space	: 314 l
	130 kW (180 bhp)	fuel capacity	: 60 l
@	: 6000 / 7000 rpm	consumption	: 37.2 / 33.6 mpg
max. torque	: 148 / 149 lb ft	acc. 0-62 mph	: 10.1 / 8.9 s
@	: 4100 / 4750 rpm	top speed	: 129 / 141 mph
gears	: 5	EuroNCAP	: 5 stars
AT	: -	introduction	: Autumn 2004
drive	: FWD	last revised in	: -
brakes f/r	: vent. discs / discs	warranty	: 2 years
body type	: 3-dr. hatchback	miscellaneous	: Coupe with exciting looks. Same
l x w x h	: 4273 x 1769 x 1456 mm		engine range as saloon, except for
wheelbase	: 2608 mm		the 180 bhp VTS which is mounted
turning circle	: 10.8 m		exclusively in the Coupe.

CITROËN C5 1.8 16V / 2.0 16V

engine type	: petrol, inline-4		kerb weight	: 1290 / 1320 kg
displacement	: 1749 / 1997 cc		towing weight	: 1300 / 1500 kg
max. power	: 85 kW (117 bhp) / 104 kW (143 bhp)		boot space	: 455 - 1310 l
@	: 5500 / 6000 rpm		fuel capacity	: 66 l
max. torque	: 125 / 148 lb ft		consumption	: 37.2 / 35.3 mpg
@	: 4000 rpm		acc. 0-62 mph	: 12.1 / 10.1 s
gears	: 5		top speed	: 125 / 131 mph
AT	: - / optional 4-speed		EuroNCAP	: 4 stars
drive	: FWD		introduction	: March 2001
brakes f/r	: vent. discs / discs		last revised in	: Autumn 2004
body type	: 5-dr. hatchback		warranty	: 2 years
l x w x h	: 4618 x 1770 x 1476 mm		miscellaneous	: Front has gained most from recent
wheelbase	: 2750 mm			facelift, rear of car somewhat
turning circle	: 11.8 m			cluttered. Fortunately, the
				stationwagon is as beautiful as ever.

C5 3.0 V6

engine type	: petrol, V6
displacement	: 2946 cc
max. power	: 152 kW (210 bhp)
@	: 6000 rpm
max. torque	: 215 lb ft
@	: 3750 rpm
gears	: 5, optional 4-speed automatic
kerb weight	: 1480 kg
towing weight	: 1600 kg
consumption	: 28.2 mpg
acc. 0-60 mph	: 8.2 s
top speed	: 143 mph
miscellaneous	: Lovely grand tourer. In the C5, Paris is just around the corner. Suspension system defies convention, but is unmatched.

CITROËN C5 BREAK 1.6 HDiF 16V / 2.0 HDiF 16V

engine type	: petrol, inline-4	kerb weight	: 1585 kg
displacement	: 1596 / 1997 cc	towing weight	: 1600 kg
max. power	: 80 kW (110 bhp) / 104 kW (143 bhp)	boot space	: 563 - 1658 l
@	: 4000 rpm	fuel capacity	: 68 l
max. torque	: 125 / 148 lb ft	consumption	: 51.4 / 47.1 mpg
@	: 4000 rpm	acc. 0-62 mph	: 11.5 / 10.1 s
gears	: 5 / 6	top speed	: 116 / 125 mph
AT	: optional 4-speed automatic	EuroNCAP	: 4 stars
drive	: FWD	introduction	: Summer 2001
brakes f/r	: vent. discs / discs	last revised in	: Autumn 2004
body type	: 5-dr. stationwagon	warranty	: 2 years
l x w x h	: 4839 x 1780 x 1511 mm	miscellaneous	: Infinitely big baggage space.
wheelbase	: 2750 mm		Pleasant, modern diesel engines
turning circle	: 11.8 m		with particle filter, also available in
			saloon.

C5 BREAK 2.2 HDi 16V

engine type	: diesel, inline-4
displacement	: 2179 cc
max. power	: 125 kW (173 bhp)
@	: 4000 rpm
max. torque	: 273 lb ft
@	: 1500 rpm
gears	: 6
kerb weight	: 1585 kg
towing weight	: 1600 kg
consumption	: 45.8 mpg
acc. 0-60 mph	: 8.2 s
top speed	: 135 mph
miscellaneous	: With this model, Citroën joins the horsepower race in the diesel-engined business car segment.

CITROËN C6 3.0i V6

engine type	: petrol, V6		kerb weight	: 1791 kg
displacement	: 2946 cc		towing weight	: 1700 kg
max. power	: 155 kW (215 bhp)		boot space	: 421 l
@	: 6000 rpm		fuel capacity	: 72 l
max. torque	: 214 lb ft		consumption	: 25.2 / 32.5 mpg
@	: 3750 rpm		acc. 0-62 mph	: 9.4 s
gears	: -		top speed	: 143 mph
AT	: 6-speed		EuroNCAP	: 5 stars
drive	: FWD		introduction	: Autumn 2005
brakes f/r	: vent. discs		last revised in	: -
body type	: 4-dr. saloon		warranty	: 2 years
l x w x h	: 4908 x 1860 x 1464 mm		miscellaneous	: Unconventional design and
wheelbase	: 2900 mm			suspension system should win
turning circle	: 12.4 m			customers over, for the C6 is more
				expensive than similar offerings
				from Mercedes-Benz and BMW.

C6 2.7 HDiF V6

engine type	: diesel, V6
displacement	: 2720 cc
max. power	: 150 kW (204 bhp)
@	: 4000 rpm
max. torque	: 325 lb ft
@	: 1900 rpm
gears	: 6-speed automatic
kerb weight	: 1846 kg
towing weight	: 1700 kg
consumption	: 32.5 mpg
acc. 0-60 mph	: 8.9 s
top speed	: 143 mph
miscellaneous	: Best buy: refined diesel version of V6 engine is quicker and more economical than the petrol V6.

CITROËN BERLINGO 1.4 / 1.6 16V

engine type	: petrol, inline-4	kerb weight	: 1163 / 1226 kg
displacement	: 1361 / 1587cc	towing weight	: 900 / 1100 kg
max. power	: 55 kW (75 bhp) / 80 kW (110 bhp)	boot space	: 625 - 2800 l
@	: 5500 / 5800 rpm	fuel capacity	: 55 l
max. torque	: 89 / 108 lb ft	consumption	: 38.2 / 37.7 mpg
@	: 3300 / 4000 rpm	acc. 0-62 mph	: 17.5 / 13.1 s
gears	: 5	top speed	: 94 / 106 mph
AT	: -	EuroNCAP	: n.a.
drive	: FWD	introduction	: January 1997
brakes f/r	: vent. discs / drum brakes	last revised in	: September 2002
body type	: 5-dr. MPV	warranty	: -
l x w x h	: 4137 x 1724 x 1810 mm	miscellaneous	: 2 years
wheelbase	: 2696 mm		: The sensible choice. A lot of
turning circle	: 11.1 m		space for this kind of money.

BERLINGO 1.6 HDI 75 / 90

engine type	: diesel, inline-4
displacement	: 1560 cc
max. power	: 55 kW (75 bhp) / 66 kW (92 bhp)
@	: 4000 rpm
max. torque	: 125 / 168 lb ft
@	: 1750 / 1900 rpm
gears	: 5
kerb weight	: 1244 / 1215 kg
towing weight	: 1100 kg
consumption	: 52.3 mpg
acc. 0-60 mph	: 15.4 / 12.9 s
top speed	: 93 / 99 mph
miscellaneous	: More horsepower is tempting, but costs a great deal more. Not recommended really in a budget car like the Berlingo.

CITROËN XSARA PICASSO 1.6 16V / 2.0 16V

engine type	: petrol, inline-4	**kerb weight**	: 1240 / 1245 kg
displacement	: 1587 / 1997 cc	**towing weight**	: 900 / 1300 kg
max. power	: 80 kW (110 bhp) /	**boot space**	: 550 - 1970 l
	100 kW (137 bhp)	**fuel capacity**	: 55 l
@	: 6000 rpm	**consumption**	: 38.7 / 35.9 mpg
max. torque	: 108 / 141 lb ft	**acc. 0-62 mph**	: 15.0 / 12.2 s
@	: 4000 / 4100 rpm	**top speed**	: 112 / 118 mph
gears	: 5 / -	**EuroNCAP**	: 4 stars
AT	: - / optional 4-speed	**introduction**	: January 2000
drive	: FWD	**last revised in**	: March 2004
brakes f/r	: vent. discs / drum brakes	**warranty**	: 2 years
body type	: 5-dr. MPV	**miscellaneous**	: Those in search of a not too
l x w x h	: 4275 x 1751 x 1635 mm		expensive car with a lot of space,
wheelbase	: 2760 mm		need not look any further.
turning circle	: 11.5 m		

XSARA PICASSO 1.6 HDI / 1.6 HDiF

engine type	: diesel, inline-4
displacement	: 1560 cc
max. power	: 66 kW (90 bhp) / 80 kW (110 bhp)
@	: 4000 rpm
max. torque	: 159 / 192 lb ft
@	: 1750 rpm
gears	: 5
kerb weight	: 1265 / 1293 kg
towing weight	: 1300 kg
consumption	: 55.4 mpg
acc. 0-60 mph	: 12.1 / 10.8 s
top speed	: 109 / 114 mph
miscellaneous	: Particle filter standard equipment
	on HDiF version.

CITROËN C4 PICASSO 1.8 / 2.0

engine type	: petrol, inline-4	kerb weight	: 1510 / 1560 kg
displacement	: 1749 / 1997 cc	towing weight	: 1500 kg
max. power	: 92 kW (127 bhp) / 104 kW (143 bhp)	boot space	: 208 – 1951 l
@	: 6000 rpm	fuel capacity	: 60 l
max. torque	: 125 / 148 lb ft	consumption	: 35.3 mpg
@	: 3750 / 4000 rpm	acc. 0-62 mph	: 11.9 / 11.5 s
gears	: 5 / 6	top speed	: 115 / 121 mph
AT	: - / optional 4-speed	EuroNCAP	: n.a.
drive	: FWD	introduction	: September 2006
brakes f/r	: vent. discs / discs	last revised in	: -
body type	: 5-dr. MPV	warranty	: 2 years
l x w x h	: 4590 x 1830 x 1660 mm	miscellaneous	: The new C4 Picasso boasts seven
wheelbase	: 2728 mm		seats, but a 5-seater version will
turning circle	: 11.8 m		make its appearance later.

C4 PICASSO 1.6 HDIF / 2.0 HDIF

engine type	: diesel, inline-4
displacement	: 1560 / 1997 cc
max. power	: 80 kW (110 bhp) / 100 kW (138 bhp)
@	: 4000 rpm
max. torque	: 177 / 199 lb ft
@	: 1750 / 2000 rpm
gears	: 5 / 6
kerb weight	: 1530 / 1620 kg
towing weight	: 1180 / 1500 kg
consumption	: 47.9 / 46.3 mpg
acc. 0-60 mph	: 12.7 / 12.5 s
top speed	: 112 / 121 mph
miscellaneous	: Biggest diesel version sports a sequential gearbox. Extra interior space is an added advantage of this box, which is also mounted in the two-litre petrol version.

CITROËN C8 2.0 16V / 2.0 HDiF 16V

engine type	: petrol / diesel, inline-4	kerb weight	: 1606 / 1718 kg
displacement	: 1997 cc	towing weight	: 1700 / 1850 kg
max. power	: 104 kW (143 bhp) /	boot space	: 480 - 2948 l
	100 kW (138 bhp)	fuel capacity	: 80 l
@	: 6000 / 4000 rpm	consumption	: 31.4 / 40.9 mpg
max. torque	: 148 / 221 lb ft	acc. 0-62 mph	: 11.6 / 12.9 s
@	: 4100 / 2000 rpm	top speed	: 117 / 112 mph
gears	: 5 / 6	EuroNCAP	: n.a.
AT	: optional 4-speed / -	introduction	: May 2002
drive	: FWD	last revised in	: -
brakes f/r	: vent. discs / discs	warranty	: 2 years
body type	: 5-dr. MPV	miscellaneous	: Also available as HDiF with 110 bhp
l x w x h	: 4726 x 1854 x 1752 mm		and automatic transmission. It looks
wheelbase	: 2823 mm		like Citroën is gradually budging out
turning circle	: 10.9 m		of the segment of the large MPVs.

CORVETTE C6 / Z06

engine type	: petrol, V8	kerb weight	: 1492 kg
displacement	: 5967 cc	towing weight	: -
max. power	: 297 kW (404 bhp)	boot space	: 635 l
@	: 6000 rpm	fuel capacity	: 68 l
max. torque	: 416 lb ft	consumption	: 21.7 mpg
@	: 4400 rpm	acc. 0-62 mph	: 4.3 s
gears	: 6	top speed	: 186 mph
AT	: optional 4-speed	EuroNCAP	: n.a.
drive	: RWD	introduction	: January 2005
brakes f/r	: vent. discs	last revised in	: -
body type	: 2-dr. coupe	warranty	: 3 years
l x w x h	: 4435 x 1845 x 1245 mm	miscellaneous	: The Corvette is to the USA what
wheelbase	: 2685 mm		the Porsche 911 is to Germany.
turning circle	: 12.0 m		Capable and good alternative for
			European sportscars. Also available
			as Convertible.

Z06

engine type	: petrol, V8
displacement	: 7011 cc
max. power	: 377 kW (512 bhp)
@	: 6300 rpm
max. torque	: 470 lb ft
@	: 4800 rpm
gears	: 6
kerb weight	: 1393 kg
towing weight	: -
consumption	: 19.3 mpg
acc. 0-60 mph	: 7.6 s
top speed	: 143 mph
miscellaneous	: Fastest Corvette in history, born at the Nürburgring. But it is rumoured that an even more powerful version is already on its way.

DACIA LOGAN 1.4 / 1.6

engine type	: petrol, inline-4
displacement	: 1390 / 1598 cc
max. power	: 55 kW (75 bhp) / 66 kW (90 bhp)
@	: 5500 rpm
max. torque	: 83 / 64 lb ft
@	: 3000 rpm
gears	: 5
AT	: -
drive	: FWD
brakes f/r	: vent. discs / drum brakes
body type	: 4-dr. saloon
l x w x h	: 4250 x 1735 x 1525 mm
wheelbase	: 2630 mm
turning circle	: 10.5 m

kerb weight	: 975 / 980 kg
towing weight	: 1100 kg
boot space	: 510 l
fuel capacity	: 50 l
consumption	: n.a.
acc. 0-62 mph	: 13.0 / 11.5 s
top speed	: 101 / 109 mph
EuroNCAP	: n.a.
introduction	: November 2005
last revised in	: -
warranty	: 2 years
miscellaneous	: Dacia is a full subsidiary of Renault. A lot of car for the money. Stationwagon soon to follow.

LOGAN 1.5 dCi

engine type	: diesel, inline-4
displacement	: 1461 cc
max. power	: 50 kW (68 bhp)
@	: 4000 rpm
max. torque	: 118 lb ft
@	: 1700 rpm
gears	: 5
kerb weight	: 1040 kg
towing weight	: 1100 kg
consumption	: n.a.
acc. 0-60 mph	: 15.0 s
top speed	: 98 mph
miscellaneous	: Stationwagon soon to follow.

DAIHATSU CHARADE

engine type	: petrol, inline-3	kerb weight	: 695 kg
displacement	: 989 cc	towing weight	: 600 kg
max. power	: 43 kW (58 bhp)	boot space	: 157 - 826 l
@	: 6000 rpm	fuel capacity	: 36 l
max. torque	: 67 lb ft	consumption	: 58.9 mpg
@	: 4000 rpm	acc. 0-62 mph	: 12.8 s
gears	: 5	top speed	: 99 mph
AT	: optional 4-speed automatic	EuroNCAP	: n.a.
drive	: FWD	introduction	: April 2003
brakes f/r	: vent. discs / drum brakes	last revised in	: Autumn 2005
body type	: 3, 5-dr. hatchback	warranty	: 3 years
l x w x h	: 3410 x 1475 x 1500 mm	miscellaneous	: Cute car, but interior space
wheelbase	: 2345 mm		is inferior to that of other small cars.
turning circle	: 8.4 m		

DAIHATSU TREVIS

engine type	: petrol, inline-3
displacement	: 989 cc
max. power	: 43 kW (58 bhp)
@	: 6000 rpm
max. torque	: 67 lb ft
@	: 4000 rpm
gears	: 5
kerb weight	: 790 kg
towing weight	: n.a.
consumption	: 57.6 mpg
acc. 0-60 mph	: n.a.
top speed	: n.a.
miscellaneous	: Well-equipped but expensive variant of Cuore.

DAIHATSU SIRION 2 1.0 / 1.3

engine type	: petrol, inline-3 / inline-4	**kerb weight**	: 890 / 940 kg
displacement	: 989 / 1298 cc	**towing weight**	: 750 / 1000 kg
max. power	: 51 kW (71 bhp) / 64 kW (87 bhp)	**boot space**	: 225 l
@	: 6000 rpm	**fuel capacity**	: 40 l
max. torque	: 69 / 88 lb ft	**consumption**	: 56.5 / 48.7 mpg
@	: 3600 / 3200 rpm	**acc. 0-62 mph**	: 13.9 / 11.0 s
gears	: 5	**top speed**	: 99 / 106 mph
AT	: optional 4-speed automatic	**EuroNCAP**	: n.a.
drive	: FWD	**introduction**	: January 2005
brakes f/r	: vent. discs / drum brakes	**last revised in**	: -
body type	: 5-dr. hatchback	**warranty**	: 3 years
l x w x h	: 3600 x 1665 x 1550 mm	**miscellaneous**	: New design copied from Cuore
wheelbase	: 2430 mm		and YRV. Sirion 2 more tailored to
turning circle	: 8.6 m		European taste than previous model.

DAIHATSU TERIOS

engine type	: petrol, inline 4	kerb weight	: 1140 kg
displacement	: 1495 cc	towing weight	: 1350 kg
max. power	: 77 kW (105 bhp)	boot space	: 380 l
@	: 6000 rpm	fuel capacity	: 50 l
max. torque	: 103 lb ft	consumption	: 35.8 mpg
@	: 3600 / 3200 rpm	acc. 0-62 mph	: 12.4 s
gears	: 5	top speed	: 99 mph
AT	: -	EuroNCAP	: n.a.
drive	: FWD	introduction	: April 2006
brakes f/r	: vent. discs / drum brakes	last revised in	: -
body type	: 5-dr. SUV	warranty	: 3 years
l x w x h	: 4055 x 1695 x 1690 mm	miscellaneous	: 4WD is an option, but not really
wheelbase	: 2580 mm		necessary for normal road use.
turning circle	: 9.8 m		More mature car than predecessor.

DAIHATSU COPEN

engine type	: petrol, inline 4	kerb weight	: 825 kg
displacement	: 1298 cc	towing weight	: -
max. power	: 64 kW (87 bhp)	boot space	: 210 l
@	: 6000 rpm	fuel capacity	: 40 l
max. torque	: 74 lb ft	consumption	: 44.1 mpg
@	: 4400 rpm	acc. 0-62 mph	: n.a.
gears	: 5	top speed	: 106 mph
AT	: -	EuroNCAP	: n.a.
drive	: FWD	introduction	: Late 2004
brakes f/r	: vent. discs / drum brakes	last revised in	: Autumn 2005
body type	: 2-dr. convertible	warranty	: 3 years
l x w x h	: 3395 x 1475 x 1245 mm	miscellaneous	: Now available with a bigger petrol
wheelbase	: 2225 mm		engine. Not very practical, but still
turning circle	: n.a.		great fun.

DAIMLER SUPER EIGHT

engine type	: petrol, V8		**kerb weight**	: 1665 kg
displacement	: 4196 cc		**towing weight**	: 1900 kg
max. power	: 291 kW (400 bhp)		**boot space**	: 470 l
@	: 6100 rpm		**fuel capacity**	: 85 l
max. torque	: 399 lb ft		**consumption**	: n.a.
@	: 3500 rpm		**acc. 0-62 mph**	: 5.3 s
gears	: -		**top speed**	: 155 mph
AT	: 6-speed		**EuroNCAP**	: n.a.
drive	: RWD		**introduction**	: November 2005
brakes f/r	: vent. discs		**last revised in**	: -
body type	: 4-dr. saloon		**warranty**	: 3 years
l x w x h	: 5215 x 1860 x 1448 mm		**miscellaneous**	: If you think the LWB version of the
wheelbase	: 3159 mm			Jaguar XJ is too bourgeois, choose
turning circle	: 12.0 m			this super-de-luxe variant instead.
				Cabin full of wood and leather of
				the finest quality. For discerning
				buyers with money to spend.

DODGE CALIBER 1.8 / 2.0

engine type	: petrol, inline-4
displacement	: 1798 / 1998c
max. power	: 110 kW (150 bhp) / 115 kW (156 bhp)
@	: 6500 / 6300 rpm
max. torque	: 124 / 140 lb ft
@	: 5200 / 5100 rpm
gears	: 5 / -
AT	: - / optional CVT
drive	: FWD
brakes f/r	: vent. discs / discs
body type	: 5-dr. hatchback
l x w x h	: 4415 x 1800 x 1535 mm
wheelbase	: 2635 mm
turning circle	: 10.8 m

kerb weight	: 1295 / 1335 kg
towing weight	: 1200 kg
boot space	: 525 l
fuel capacity	: 51 l
consumption	: 38.9 / 35.0 mpg
acc. 0-62 mph	: 12.8 / 11.8 s
top speed	: 118 / 124 mph
EuroNCAP	: n.a.
introduction	: June 2006
last revised in	: -
warranty	: 3 years
miscellaneous	: The Caliber is the car that has to put Dodge back on the map in Europe.

CALIBER 2.0 CRD

engine type	: diesel, inline-4
displacement	: 1968 cc
max. power	: 103 kW (140 bhp)
@	: 4000 rpm
max. torque	: 236 lb ft
@	: 2500 rpm
gears	: 6
kerb weight	: 1400 kg
towing weight	: 1200 kg
consumption	: 47.1 mpg
acc. 0-60 mph	: 9.3 s
top speed	: 115 mph
miscellaneous	: With its original design and low price, its future looks promising.

DODGE NITRO 3.7 V6

engine type	: petrol, V6	kerb weight	: 1860 kg
displacement	: 1998 cc	towing weight	: n.a.
max. power	: 157 kW (210 bhp)	boot space	: 900 l
@	: 5200 rpm	fuel capacity	: 74 l
max. torque	: 235 lb ft	consumption	: n.a.
@	: 4000 rpm	acc. 0-62 mph	: 9.6 s
gears	: 6	top speed	: 107 mph
AT	: optional 4-speed	EuroNCAP	: n.a.
drive	: 4WD	introduction	: March 2007
brakes f/r	: vent. discs / discs	last revised in	: -
body type	: 5-dr. SUV	warranty	: 2 years
l x w x h	: 4544 x 1857 x 1756 mm	miscellaneous	: This Nitro is a lot of SUV for your
wheelbase	: 2763 mm		money, says Dodge. Diesel-engined
turning circle	: 11.1 m		version is on its way too.

DODGE VIPER SRT-10

engine type	: petrol, V10		kerb weight	: 1575 kg
displacement	: 8277 cc		towing weight	: -
max. power	: 372 kW (507 bhp)		boot space	: 238 l
@	: 5600 rpm		fuel capacity	: 70 l
max. torque	: 525 lb ft		consumption	: 13.3 mpg
@	: 4100 rpm		acc. 0-62 mph	: 4.0 s
gears	: 6		top speed	: 190 mph
AT	: -		EuroNCAP	: n.a.
drive	: RWD		introduction	: August 2005
brakes f/r	: vent. discs		last revised in	: -
body type	: 2-dr. convertible		warranty	: 3 years
l x w x h	: 4459 x 1944 x 1210 mm		miscellaneous	: Powerful beast, goes just as fast as
wheelbase	: 2510 mm			a Corvette Z06 but in a rather less
turning circle	: 12.4 m			subtle fashion.

DONKERVOORT D8 150 / 180

engine type	: petrol, inline-4	kerb weight	: 630 kg
displacement	: 1781 cc	towing weight	: -
max. power	: 110 kW (150 bhp) / 132 kW (180 bhp)	boot space	: 100 l
		fuel capacity	: 40 l
@	: 5700 / 5500 rpm	consumption	: 31.5 mpg
max. torque	: 155 /173 lb ft	acc. 0-62 mph	: 6.0 / 5.0 s
@	: 2000 / 1950 rpm	top speed	: 124 / 131 mph
gears	: 5	EuroNCAP	: n.a.
AT	: -	introduction	: January 2003
drive	: RWD	last revised in	: -
brakes f/r	: vent. discs / discs	warranty	: 2 years
body type	: 2-dr. convertible	miscellaneous	: A terrific car that offers bike-like
l x w x h	: 3410 x 1730 x 1100 mm		driving sensations. Far from cheap,
wheelbase	: 2300 mm		but depreciation is low. Also
turning circle	: 8.0 m		available with 210 bhp and 270 bhp
			engines.

FERRARI F430

engine type	: petrol, V8	**kerb weight**	: 1450 kg
displacement	: 4308 cc	**towing weight**	: -
max. power	: 360 kW (490 bhp)	**boot space**	: 250 l
@	: 8500 rpm	**fuel capacity**	: 95 l
max. torque	: 343 lb ft	**consumption**	: 15.4 mpg
@	: 5250 rpm	**acc. 0-62 mph**	: 4.0 s
gears	: 6	**top speed**	: 196 mph
AT	: -	**EuroNCAP**	: n.a
drive	: RWD	**introduction**	: October 2004
brakes f/r	: vent. discs	**last revised in**	: -
body type	: 2-dr. coupe	**warranty**	: 2 years
l x w x h	: 4512 x 1923 x 1214 mm	**miscellaneous**	: Unmistakably a Ferrari. Worthy
wheelbase	: 2600 mm		replacement for the 360 Modena.
turning circle	: 10.8 m		Also F1 version available with
			sequential gearshift.

FERRARI 599 GTB FIORANO

engine type	: petrol, V12	kerb weight	: 1690 kg
displacement	: 5999 cc	towing weight	: -
max. power	: 456 kW (620 bhp)	boot space	: 320 l
@	: 7600 rpm	fuel capacity	: 105 l
max. torque	: 448 lb ft	consumption	: 21.3 mpg
@	: 5600 rpm	acc. 0-62 mph	: 3.7 s
gears	: 6	top speed	: 205 mph
AT	: optional seq. gearbox	EuroNCAP	: n.a.
drive	: RWD	introduction	: January 2006
brakes f/r	: vent. discs	last revised in	: -
body type	: 2-dr. coupe	warranty	: 2 years
l x w x h	: 4665 x 1962 x 1336 mm	miscellaneous	: Successor to the 575 M Maranello, but a better car in every respect. Cluttered design takes some getting used to.
wheelbase	: 2750 mm		
turning circle	: n.a.		

FERRARI 612 SCAGLIETTI

engine type	: petrol, V12	kerb weight	: 1840 kg
displacement	: 5748 cc	towing weight	: -
max. power	: 397 kW (540 bhp)	boot space	: 240 l
@	: 7250 rpm	fuel capacity	: 108 l
max. torque	: 434 lb ft	consumption	: 13.6 mpg
@	: 5250 rpm	acc. 0-62 mph	: 4.2 s
gears	: 6	top speed	: 199 mph
AT	: optional seq. gearbox	EuroNCAP	: n.a.
drive	: RWD	introduction	: April 2004
brakes f/r	: vent. discs	last revised in	: -
body type	: 2-dr. coupe	warranty	: 2 years
l x w x h	: 4902 x 1957 x 1344 mm	miscellaneous	: Larger, lighter, more spacious and
wheelbase	: 2950 mm		more powerful than predecessor
turning circle	: 12.0 m		456 M GT. Not your average Ferrari,
			though, but different in many ways.

FIAT 600 1.1

engine type	: petrol, inline-4	**kerb weight**	: 710 kg
displacement	: 1108 cc	**towing weight**	: 400 kg
max. power	: 40 kW (54 bhp)	**boot space**	: 170- 810 l
@	: 5000 rpm	**fuel capacity**	: 38 l
max. torque	: 65 lb ft	**consumption**	: 47.3 mpg
@	: 2750 rpm	**acc. 0-62 mph**	: 14.5 s
gears	: 5	**top speed**	: 93 mph
AT	: -	**EuroNCAP**	: n.a.
drive	: FWD	**introduction**	: Spring 1998
brakes f/r	: discs / drum brakes	**last revised in**	: Autumn 2005
body type	: 3-dr. hatchback	**warranty**	: 2 years
l x w x h	: 3337 x 1508 x 1420 mm	**miscellaneous**	: Not as good as the Panda, but still
wheelbase	: 2200 mm		popular despite its age. Very low
turning circle	: 8.8 m		price is one of the reasons of its
			success.

FIAT PANDA 1.1 / 1.2

engine type	: petrol, inline-4	kerb weight	: 815 / 835 kg
displacement	: 1108 / 1242 cc	towing weight	: 800 kg
max. power	: 40 kW (54 bhp) / 44 kW (60 bhp)	boot space	: 206 – 775 l
@	: 5000 rpm	fuel capacity	: 35 l
max. torque	: 65 / 75 lb ft	consumption	: 49.6 / 50.4 mpg
@	: 2750 / 2500 rpm	acc. 0-62 mph	: 15.0 / 14.0 s
gears	: 5	top speed	: 93 / 96 mph
AT	: - / optional CVT	EuroNCAP	: 3 stars
drive	: FWD	introduction	: Autumn 2003
brakes f/r	: discs / drum brakes	last revised in	: -
body type	: 5-dr. hatchback	warranty	: 2 years
l x w x h	: 3538 x 1589 x 1540 mm	miscellaneous	: The Panda is proof of what Fiat
wheelbase	: 2299 mm		does best: building small cars.
turning circle	: 9.1 m		

PANDA 1.3 MULTIJET DYNAMIC

engine type	: diesel, inline-4
displacement	: 1248 cc
max. power	: 51 kW (bhp)
@	: 4000 rpm
max. torque	: 107 lb ft
@	: 1500 rpm
gears	: 5
kerb weight	: 910 kg
towing weight	: 900 kg
consumption	: 65.7 mpg
acc. 0-60 mph	: 13.0 s
top speed	: 99 mph
miscellaneous	: 1.3 diesel is the best engine in the Panda line-up: quiet, powerful and economical.

FIAT PANDA 4X4 CLIMBING

engine type	: petrol, inline-4		kerb weight	: 955 kg
displacement	: 1242 cc		towing weight	: 800 kg
max. power	: 44 kW (60 bhp)		boot space	: 206 l
@	: 5000 rpm		fuel capacity	: 30 l
max. torque	: 75 lb ft		consumption	: 43 mpg
@	: 2500 rpm		acc. 0-62 mph	: 20.0 s
gears	: 5		top speed	: 90 mph
AT	: -		EuroNCAP	: 3 stars
drive	: 4WD		introduction	: September 2004
brakes f/r	: vent. discs / discs		last revised in	: -
body type	: 5-dr. hatchback		warranty	: 2 years
l x w x h	: 3574 x 1605 x 1632 mm		miscellaneous	: Capable offroader, but less
wheelbase	: 2305 mm			suited as a city car. Sturdy looks.
turning circle	: 9.6 m			

PANDA 4X4 CROSS

engine type	: diesel, inline-4
displacement	: 1248 cc
max. power	: 51 kW (bhp)
@	: 4000 rpm
max. torque	: 107 lb ft
@	: 1500 rpm
gears	: 5
kerb weight	: 1065 kg
towing weight	: 900 kg
consumption	: 53.5 mpg
acc. 0-60 mph	: 18.0 s
top speed	: 93 mph
miscellaneous	: Not very quick either, but more powerful and better looking than the Climbing. More expensive too.

FIAT PUNTO 1.2

engine type	: petrol, inline-4		**kerb weight**	: 895 / 935 kg
displacement	: 1242 cc		**towing weight**	: 1000 kg
max. power	: 44 kW (60 bhp)		**boot space**	: 264 - 1080 l
@	: 5000 rpm		**fuel capacity**	: 47 l
max. torque	: 75 lb ft		**consumption**	: 50.4 mpg
@	: 2500 rpm		**acc. 0-62 mph**	: 14.3 s
gears	: 5		**top speed**	: 96 mph
AT	: -		**EuroNCAP**	: 4 stars
drive	: FWD		**introduction**	: September 1999
brakes f/r	: discs / drum brakes		**last revised in**	: Summer 2003
body type	: 3-, 5-dr. hatchback		**warranty**	: 2 years
l x w x h	: 3840 x 1660 x 1480 mm		**miscellaneous**	: The previous Punto is still in
wheelbase	: 2460 mm			production and serves as a cheaper
turning circle	: 10.5 m			alternative for the Grande Punto.

FIAT GRANDE PUNTO 1.2 / 1.4

engine type	: petrol, inline-4
displacement	: 1242 / 1368 cc
max. power	: 44 kW (65 bhp) / 57 kW (77 bhp)
@	: 5500 / 6000 rpm
max. torque	: 75 / 85 lb ft
@	: 3000 rpm
gears	: 5
AT	: -
drive	: FWD
brakes f/r	: discs / drum brakes
body type	: 3-, 5-dr. hatchback
l x w x h	: 4030 x 1687 x 1490 mm
wheelbase	: 2510 mm
turning circle	: 10.0 m

kerb weight	: 1015 / 105 kg
towing weight	: 900 / 1000 kg
boot space	: 275 l – n.a.
fuel capacity	: 45 l
consumption	: 47.9 / 47.9 mpg
acc. 0-62 mph	: 14.5 / 13.2 s
top speed	: 96 / 103 mph
EuroNCAP	: 5 stars
introduction	: September 2005
last revised in	: -
warranty	: 2 years
miscellaneous	: A lot bigger than its predecessor. Striking design. One of the most modern smaller cars on today's market. Also available with 95 bhp 1.4 engine.

GRANDE PUNTO 1.3 / 1.9 MULTIJET

engine type	: diesel, inline-4
displacement	: 1248 / 1910 cc
max. power	: 55 kW (75 bhp) / 88 kW (120 bhp)
@	: 4000 rpm
max. torque	: 140 / 206 lb ft
@	: 1750 / 2000 rpm
gears	: 5
kerb weight	: 1090 / 1205 kg
towing weight	: 1000 kg
consumption	: 62.8 / 48.7 mpg
acc. 0-60 mph	: 13.6 / 10.0 s
top speed	: 109 / 124 mph
miscellaneous	: Choosing can be difficult: also available are a 1.3 diesel with 90 bhp and a 1.9 diesel with 130 bhp. With the latter unit under the bonnet, the Grande Punto can top 125 mph.

FIAT STILO 1.4 / 1.6

engine type	: petrol, inline-4	**kerb weight**	: 1065 / 1225 kg
displacement	: 1368 / 1596 cc	**towing weight**	: 1000 / 1100 kg
max. power	: 70 kW (95 bhp) / 76 kW (103 bhp)	**boot space**	: 305 – 1002 l
@	: 5800 / 5750 rpm	**fuel capacity**	: 58 l
max. torque	: 107 / 114 lb ft	**consumption**	: 43.5 / 37.8 mpg
@	: 4500 rpm	**acc. 0-62 mph**	: 13.8 / 10.9 s
gears	: 5	**top speed**	: 112 / 116 mph
AT	: -	**EuroNCAP**	: 4 stars
drive	: FWD	**introduction**	: Autumn 2001
brakes f/r	: vent. discs / discs	**last revised in**	: Late 2004
body type	: 3-, 5-dr. hatchback	**warranty**	: 2 years
l x w x h	: 4182 x 1784 x 1475 mm	**miscellaneous**	: Stilo merits more success on the
wheelbase	: 2600 mm		basis of its virtues. Good alternative
turning circle	: 10.5 m		for a Golf or Astra. 3-door Stilo
			better looking than conservative
			5-door version.

STILO 1.8 / 2.4 ABARTH

engine type	: petrol, inline-4 / inline-5
displacement	: 1747 / 2446 cc
max. power	: 98 kW (133 bhp) / 125 kW (170 bhp)
@	: 6400 / 6000 rpm
max. torque	: 120 / 163 lb ft
@	: 3500 / 3500 rpm
gears	: 5
kerb weight	: 1270 / 1240 kg
towing weight	: 1200 / 1300 kg
consumption	: 35.9 / 29.6 mpg
acc. 0-60 mph	: 9.9 / 8.5 s
top speed	: 125 / 134 mph
miscellaneous	: Big 5-cylinder engine gives fastest Stilo a character of its own, but the 1.8 isn't exactly sluggish either.

FIAT STILO MULTIWAGON 1.6 / 1.8

engine type	: petrol, inline-4
displacement	: 1368 / 1596 cc
max. power	: 70 kW (95 bhp) / 76 kW (103 bhp)
@	: 5800 / 5750 rpm
max. torque	: 107 / 114 lb ft
@	: 4500 rpm
gears	: 5
AT	: -
drive	: FWD
brakes f/r	: vent. discs / discs
body type	: 5-dr. stationwagon
l x w x h	: 4516 x 1756 x 1570 mm
wheelbase	: 2600 mm
turning circle	: 10.5 m

kerb weight	: 1315 / 1360 kg
towing weight	: 1100 / 1200 kg
boot space	: 510 – 1480 l
fuel capacity	: 58 l
consumption	: 36.8 / 34.6 mpg
acc. 0-62 mph	: 11.4 / 10.8 s
top speed	: 114 / 124 mph
EuroNCAP	: 4 stars
introduction	: Late 2003
last revised in	: -
warranty	: 2 years
miscellaneous	: Taut lines, fine driving characteristics and long list of standard items make this an interesting proposition in a tough marketplace. Competitively priced. Also available with 95 bhp 1.4 petrol engine.

STILO WAGON 1.9 JTD 16V

engine type	: diesel, inline-4
displacement	: 1910 cc
max. power	: 85 kW (115 bhp) / 103 kW (140 bhp)
@	: 4000 rpm
max. torque	: 188 / 225 lb ft
@	: 2000 rpm
gears	: 6 / 6
kerb weight	: 1260 / 1260 kg
towing weight	: 1300 / 1300 kg
consumption	: 53.2 mpg
acc. 0-60 mph	: 12.0 / 9.7 s
top speed	: 118 / 126 mph
miscellaneous	: Also available with 100 bhp 1.9 JTD diesel engine.

FIAT CROMA 1.8 / 2.2

engine type	: petrol, inline-4
displacement	: 1796 / 2198 cc
max. power	: 103 kW (140 bhp) /
	108 kW (147 bhp)
@	: 6300 / 5800 rpm
max. torque	: 129 / 150 lb ft
@	: 3800 / 4000 rpm
gears	: 5
AT	: - / optional 5-speed automatic
drive	: FWD
brakes f/r	: vent. discs / discs
body type	: 5-dr. stationwagon
l x w x h	: 4756 x 1775 x 1597 mm
wheelbase	: 2700 mm
turning circle	: 10.9 m

kerb weight	: 1430 / 1485 kg
towing weight	: 1500 kg
boot space	: 500 – 1620 l
fuel capacity	: 62 l
consumption	: 38.2 / 32.8 mpg
acc. 0-62 mph	: 10.2 / 10.1 s
top speed	: 128 / 131 mph
EuroNCAP	: n.a.
introduction	: -
last revised in	: June 2005
warranty	: 2 years
miscellaneous	: Ambitious re-entry of Italian car manufacturer in medium-sized car segment. Unconventional design. Spacious interior and fine driving characteristics should bring more customers.

CROMA 1.9 / 2.4 JTD

engine type	: diesel, inline-4 / inline-5
displacement	: 1910 / 2387cc
max. power	: 110 kW (150 bhp) / 147 kW (200 bhp)
@	: 4000 rpm
max. torque	: 236 / 295 lb ft
@	: 2000 rpm
gears	: 6 / 6-speed automatic
kerb weight	: 1505 / 1625 kg
towing weight	: 1500 kg
consumption	: 46.3 / 35.3 mpg
acc. 0-60 mph	: 9.6 / 8.5 s
top speed	: 131 / 134 mph
miscellaneous	: Excellent diesel engines should promote sales of the Croma as a business car. Also available with 120 bhp 1.9 JTD diesel engine.

FIAT DOBLÒ 1.2 / 1.6 16V

engine type	: petrol, inline-4		kerb weight	: 1195 / 1250 kg
displacement	: 1242 / 1596 cc		towing weight	: 1100 kg
max. power	: 44 kW (65 bhp) / 74 kW (100 bhp)		boot space	: 750 - 3000 l
@	: 5500 / 4000 rpm		fuel capacity	: 60 l
max. torque	: 75 / 148 lb ft		consumption	: 38.3 / 44.9 mpg
@	: 3500 / 1500 rpm		acc. 0-62 mph	: 18.9 / 12.4 s
gears	: 5		top speed	: 88 / 104 mph
AT	: -		EuroNCAP	: 3 stars
drive	: FWD		introduction	: Late 2001
brakes f/r	: discs / drum brakes		last revised in	: -
body type	: 5-dr. MPV		warranty	: 2 years
l x w x h	: 4159 x 1714 x 1810 mm		miscellaneous	: More of a van than MPV, but an
wheelbase	: 2566 mm			excellent alternative for people who
turning circle	: 10.5 m			think twice when buying a car.

DOBLÒ 1.3 / 1.9 MULTIJET

engine type	: diesel, inline-4
displacement	: 1248 / 1910 cc
max. power	: 55 kW (75 bhp) / 77 kW (105 bhp)
@	: 4000 rpm
max. torque	: 148 / 155 lb ft
@	: 1750 / 2000 rpm
gears	: 5
kerb weight	: 1285 / 1295 kg
towing weight	: 1100 / 1100 kg
consumption	: 51.4 / 48.7 mpg
acc. 0-60 mph	: 16.1 / 12.4 s
top speed	: 97 / 102 mph
miscellaneous	: Angular design results in ample interior space. Hard-pressed drivers opt for the 105 bhp version.

FIAT SEDICI 1.2 / 1.6

engine type	: petrol, inline-4
displacement	: 1242 / 1596 cc
max. power	: 44 kW (65 bhp) / 74 kW (100 bhp)
@	: 5500 / 4000 rpm
max. torque	: 75 / 148 lb ft
@	: 3500 / 1500 rpm
gears	: 5
AT	: -
drive	: FWD
brakes f/r	: discs / drum brakes
body type	: 5-dr. MPV
l x w x h	: 4159 x 1714 x 1810 mm
wheelbase	: 2566 mm
turning circle	: 10.5 m
kerb weight	: 1195 / 1250 kg
towing weight	: 1100 kg
boot space	: 750 - 3000 l
fuel capacity	: 60 l
consumption	: 38.3 / 44.9 mpg
acc. 0-62 mph	: 18.9 / 12.4 s
top speed	: 88 / 104 mph
EuroNCAP	: 3 stars
introduction	: Late 2001
last revised in	: -
warranty	: 2 years
miscellaneous	: Fiat's Sedici was built in association with Suzuki. 4WD always comes as standard.

SEDICI 1.9 MULTIJET 8V

engine type	: diesel, inline-4
displacement	: 1248 / 1910 cc
max. power	: 55 kW (75 bhp) / 88 kW (120 bhp)
@	: 4000 rpm
max. torque	: 148 / 155 lb ft
@	: 1750 / 2000 rpm
gears	: 5
kerb weight	: 1285 / 1295 kg
towing weight	: 1100 / 1100 kg
consumption	: 51.4 / 48.7 mpg
acc. 0-60 mph	: 16.1 / 12.4 s
top speed	: 97 / 102 mph
miscellaneous	: Opt for the powerful diesel engine if you plan to use the Sedici in rough terrain.

FIAT IDEA 1.4 8V / 1.4 16V

engine type	: petrol, inline-4	**kerb weight**	: 1155 / 1155 kg
displacement	: 1368 / 1368 cc	**towing weight**	: 1000 kg
max. power	: 57 kW (77 bhp) / 70 kW (95 bhp)	**boot space**	: 320 - 1420 l
@	: 6000 / 5800 rpm	**fuel capacity**	: 47 l
max. torque	: 85 / 94 lb ft	**consumption**	: 46.3 / 43.5 mpg
@	: 3000 / 4500 rpm	**acc. 0-62 mph**	: 13.5 / 11.5 s
gears	: 5 / 6	**top speed**	: 101 / 109 mph
AT	: optional CVT	**EuroNCAP**	: n.a.
drive	: FWD	**introduction**	: Autumn 2003
brakes f/r	: discs / drum brakes	**last revised in**	: Autumn 2005
body type	: 5-dr. MPV	**warranty**	: 2 years
l x w x h	: 3930 x 1658 x 1660 mm	**miscellaneous**	: Hardly a big seller, despite its taut
wheelbase	: 2508 mm		design, pleasant driving behaviour,
turning circle	: 10.4 m		extensive equipment and
			competitive price.

IDEA 1.3 16V MULTI. / 1.9 JTD MULTIJET

engine type	: diesel, inline-4
displacement	: 1248 / 1910 cc
max. power	: 51 kW (70 bhp) / 74 kW (100 bhp)
@	: 4000 rpm
max. torque	: 148 / 155 lb ft
@	: 1750 rpm
gears	: 5
kerb weight	: 1200 / 1275 kg
towing weight	: 1000 / 1100 kg
consumption	: 56.3 / 52.2 mpg
acc. 0-60 mph	: 15.4 / 11.5 s
top speed	: 99 / 112 mph
miscellaneous	: Performance of smallest version far from disappointing, but 1.9 Multijet does everything just a tiny bit better.

FIAT MULTIPLA 1.6 / 1.9 JTD

engine type	: petrol / diesel, inline-4	kerb weight	: 1275 / 1345 kg
displacement	: 1596 / 1910 cc	towing weight	: 1200 / 1300 kg
max. power	: 76 kW (103 bhp) / 88 kW (120 bhp)	boot space	: 430 – 1850 l
@	: 5750 / 4000 rpm	fuel capacity	: 63 l
max. torque	: 107 / 155 lb ft	consumption	: 32.8 / 43.5 mpg
@	: 4000 / 1500 rpm	acc. 0-62 mph	: 12.6 / 12.2 s
gears	: 5	top speed	: 106 / 111 mph
AT	: -	EuroNCAP	: 3 stars
drive	: FWD	introduction	: Autumn 1998
brakes f/r	: vent. discs / drum brakes	last revised in	: Spring 2004
body type	: 5-dr. MPV	warranty	: 2 years
l x w x h	: 4089 x 1871 x 1695 mm	miscellaneous	: Spacious 6-seater, full of character
wheelbase	: 2666 mm		and practical solutions. 1.6 Multipla
turning circle	: 11.0 m		also available in a version that runs
			on natural gas.

FIAT ULYSSE 2.0 MULTIJET 120 / 136

engine type	: petrol, inline-4	kerb weight	: 1711 / 175 kg
displacement	: 1997 cc	towing weight	: 1800 / 1850 kg
max. power	: 88 kW (120 bhp) /	boot space	: 324 – 2948 l
	100 kW (136 bhp)	fuel capacity	: 80 l
@	: 4000 rpm	consumption	: 41.6 / 40.4 mpg
max. torque	: 221 / 251 lb ft	acc. 0-62 mph	: 12.9 / 11.4 s
@	: 2000 rpm	top speed	: 112 / 118 mph
gears	: 6	EuroNCAP	: 5 stars
AT	: -	introduction	: Autumn 2002
drive	: FWD	last revised in	: -
brakes f/r	: vent. discs / discs	warranty	: 2 years
body type	: 5-dr. MPV	miscellaneous	: Car is now available with diesel
l x w x h	: 4719 x 1863 x 1752 mm		engines only, including a 107 bhp
wheelbase	: 2823 mm		2.0 JTD combined with automatic
turning circle	: 10.9 m		transmission.

FORD KA 1.3

F

engine type	: petrol, inline-4	kerb weight	: 898 kg
displacement	: 1297 cc	towing weight	: -
max. power	: 51 kW (70 bhp)	boot space	: 186 – 724 l
@	: 5500 rpm	fuel capacity	: 40 l
max. torque	: 104 lb ft	consumption	: 37.2 mpg
@	: 3000 rpm	acc. 0-62 mph	: 13.7 s
gears	: 5	top speed	: 108 mph
AT	: -	EuroNCAP	: 3 stars
drive	: FWD	introduction	: Late 1997
brakes f/r	: vent. discs / drum brakes	last revised in	: -
body type	: 3-dr. hatchback	warranty	: 2 years
l x w x h	: 3620 x 1639 x 1385 mm	miscellaneous	: Only model left now from 'New Edge' period. Still a strong seller, with special editions that are offered at unbeatable prices.
wheelbase	: 2448 mm		
turning circle	: 9.9 m		

SPORTKA 1.6

engine type	: petrol, inline-4
displacement	: 1597 cc
max. power	: 70 kW (95 bhp)
@	: 5500 rpm
max. torque	: 100 lb ft
@	: 4250 rpm
gears	: 5
kerb weight	: 944 kg
towing weight	: -
consumption	: 37.8 mpg
acc. 0-60 mph	: 9.7 s
top speed	: 108 mph
miscellaneous	: Sportka benefits from tuned chassis and offers huge fun for a car in this price range.

FORD FIESTA 1.3 8V / 1.4 16V

engine type	: petrol, inline-4
displacement	: 1297 / 1388 cc
max. power	: 51 kW (70 bhp) / 59 kW (80 bhp)
@	: 5600 / 5700 rpm
max. torque	: 78 / 91 lb ft
@	: 2600 / 3500 rpm
gears	: 5
AT	: - / optional 5-speed automatic
drive	: FWD
brakes f/r	: vent. discs / drum brakes
body type	: 3-, 5-dr. hatchback
l x w x h	: 3916 x 1683 x 1430 mm
wheelbase	: 2486 mm
turning circle	: 9.8 m

kerb weight	: 1120 / 1105 kg
towing weight	: 800 / 900 kg
boot space	: 268 – 945 l
fuel capacity	: 45 l
consumption	: 45.8 / 44.3 mpg
acc. 0-62 mph	: 17.3 / 13.2 s
top speed	: 99 / 103 mph
EuroNCAP	: 4 stars
introduction	: Summer 2002
last revised in	: Late 2005
warranty	: 2 years
miscellaneous	: Model celebrated its 30th birthday in 2006. Looks fresh again after facelift. Also available with 100 bhp 1.6 petrol engine.

FIESTA ST

engine type	: petrol, inline-4
displacement	: 1999 cc
max. power	: 110 kW (150 bhp)
@	: 6000 rpm
max. torque	: 190 lb ft
@	: 4500 rpm
gears	: 5
kerb weight	: 1137 kg
towing weight	: -
consumption	: 38.3 mpg
acc. 0-60 mph	: 8.4 s
top speed	: 129 mph
miscellaneous	: Big engine for such a small car, but chassis is up to the job.

FORD FUSION 1.4 16V / 1.6 16V

engine type	: petrol, inline-4
displacement	: 1388 / 1596 cc
max. power	: 58 kW (80 bhp) / 74 kW (100 bhp)
@	: 5700 / 6000 rpm
max. torque	: 92 / 108 lb ft
@	: 3500 / 4000 rpm
gears	: 5
AT	: optional 4-speed automatic
drive	: FWD
brakes f/r	: vent. discs / drum brakes
body type	: 5-dr. hatchback
l x w x h	: 4020 x 1721 x 1498 mm
wheelbase	: 2486 mm
turning circle	: 9.8 m

kerb weight	: 1134 / 1171 kg
towing weight	: 900 kg
boot space	: 337 – 1175 l
fuel capacity	: 45 l
consumption	: 43 / 42.3 mpg
acc. 0-62 mph	: 14.0 / 11.1 s
top speed	: 98 / 109 mph
EuroNCAP	: n.a.
introduction	: Autumn 2002
last revised in	: Autumn 2005
warranty	: 2 years
miscellaneous	: Fusion is a crossover, according to Ford, but the car's interior has no added flexibility. It is simply a Fiesta with more interior space and higher seating position.

FUSION 1.4 TDCI / 1.6 16V TDCI

engine type	: diesel, inline-4
displacement	: 1399 / 1560 cc
max. power	: 50 kW (68 bhp) / 66 kW (90 bhp)
@	: 4000 rpm
max. torque	: 118 / 156 lb ft
@	: 2000 / 1750 rpm
gears	: 5
kerb weight	: 1192 / 1200 kg
towing weight	: 750 kg
consumption	: 62.8 / 62.8 mpg
acc. 0-60 mph	: 16.3 / 12.9 s
top speed	: 98 / 109 mph
miscellaneous	: Also available with 90 bhp 1.6 diesel engine.

FORD FOCUS 1.4 16V / 1.6 16V

engine type	: petrol, inline-4
displacement	: 1388 / 1596 cc
max. power	: 58 kW (80 bhp) / 74 kW (100 bhp)
@	: 5700 / 6000 rpm
max. torque	: 92 / 108 lb ft
@	: 3500 / 4000 rpm
gears	: 5
AT	: optional 4-speed automatic
drive	: FWD
brakes f/r	: vent. discs / drum brakes
body type	: 3-, 5-dr. hatchback
l x w x h	: 4342 x 1840 x 1501 mm
wheelbase	: 2640 mm
turning circle	: 10.4 m

kerb weight	: 1147 / 1127 kg
towing weight	: 700 / 1200 kg
boot space	: 385 – 1247 l
fuel capacity	: 55 l
consumption	: 42.8 / 42.2 mpg
acc. 0-62 mph	: 14.1 / 11.9 s
top speed	: 102 / 112 mph
EuroNCAP	: 5 stars
introduction	: -
last revised in	: -
warranty	: 2 years
miscellaneous	: The first Focus set new standards with its looks and handling. Second generation model longer and wider, and as a result also less agile. Also available with 115 bhp 1.6 petrol engine.

FOCUS ST

engine type	: petrol, inline-4
displacement	: 2522 cc
max. power	: 166 kW (225 bhp)
@	: 6100 rpm
max. torque	: 236 lb ft
@	: 1600 rpm
gears	: 6
kerb weight	: 1362 kg
towing weight	: n.a.
consumption	: 30.4 mpg
acc. 0-60 mph	: 6.8 s
top speed	: 152 mph
miscellaneous	: New top-of-the-range model borrows fat 5-cylinder from Volvo. Orange colour as seen on concept car available on production car.

FORD FOCUS ESTATE 1.6 TDCi / 1.8 TDCi

engine type	: diesel, inline-4
displacement	: 1560 / 1800 cc
max. power	: 81 kW (109 bhp) / 85 kW (115 bhp)
@	: 4000 / 3700 rpm
max. torque	: 177 / 206 lb ft
@	: 1750 / 1900 rpm
gears	: 5
AT	: CVT / -
drive	: FWD
brakes f/r	: vent. discs / discs
body type	: 5-dr. stationwagon
l x w x h	: 4475 x 1840 x 1501 mm
wheelbase	: 2640 mm
turning circle	: 10.4 m

kerb weight	: 1286 / 1426 kg
towing weight	: 1300 / 1500 kg
boot space	: 482 – 1525 l
fuel capacity	: 53 l
consumption	: 60.4 / 53.5 mpg
acc. 0-62 mph	: 11.2 / 10.9 s
top speed	: 117 / 119 mph
EuroNCAP	: 5 stars
introduction	: Spring 2005
last revised in	: -
warranty	: 2 years
miscellaneous	: Focus platform also used for estate and saloon variants (see below). Refer to Focus and Focus C-Max listings for specifications of available petrol engines. Also available with 90 bhp 1.6 TDCi diesel engine.

FOCUS ESTATE 2.0 TDCi

engine type	: diesel, inline-4
displacement	: 1999 cc
max. power	: 100 kW (136 bhp)
@	: 4000 rpm
max. torque	: 236 lb ft
@	: 2000 rpm
gears	: 5
kerb weight	: 1429 kg
towing weight	: 1300 kg
consumption	: 50.4 mpg
acc. 0-60 mph	: 9.5 s
top speed	: 126 mph
miscellaneous	: The Focus Estate is popular as a lease car, not in the least because of the strong diesel engines available.

FORD FOCUS C-MAX 1.8 16V / 2.0 16V

engine type	: petrol, inline-4	kerb weight	: 1409 / 1441 kg
displacement	: 1798 / 1999 cc	towing weight	: 1200 / 1400 kg
max. power	: 81 kW (110 bhp) / 107 kW (145 bhp)	boot space	: 460 – 1620 l
@	: 6000 / 6000 rpm	fuel capacity	: 55 l
max. torque	: 125 / 140 lb ft	consumption	: 39.8 / 38.7 mpg
@	: 4000 / 4000 rpm	acc. 0-62 mph	: 10.8 / 9.8 s
gears	: 5	top speed	: 120 / 127 mph
AT	: –	EuroNCAP	: 4 stars
drive	: FWD	introduction	: Autumn 2003
brakes f/r	: vent. discs / discs	last revised in	: –
body type	: 5-dr. MPV	warranty	: 2 years
l x w x h	: 4333 x 1825 x 1595 mm	miscellaneous	: Focus C-Max is not the most
wheelbase	: 2640 mm		spacious MPV, but it is definitely
turning circle	: 10.7 m		one of the best performing people
			carriers on today's market.

FORD FOCUS CC 1.6 / 2.0

engine type	: petrol, inline-4		kerb weight	: 1413 / 1465 kg
displacement	: 1596 / 1999 cc		towing weight	: 1000 / 1350 kg
max. power	: 74 kW (100 bhp) / 107 kW (145 bhp)		boot space	: 248 – 534 l
@	: 5500 / 6000 rpm		fuel capacity	: 55 l
max. torque	: 110 / 136 lb ft		consumption	: 39.8 / 37.7 mpg
@	: 4000 / 4500 rpm		acc. 0-62 mph	: 13.6 / 10.3 s
gears	: 5		top speed	: 114 / 130 mph
AT	: -		EuroNCAP	: n.a.
drive	: FWD		introduction	: Late 2006
brakes f/r	: vent. discs / discs		last revised in	: -
body type	: 2-dr. convertible		warranty	: 2 years
l x w x h	: 4509 x 1834 x 1456 mm		miscellaneous	: Fords rival to the VW Eos and
wheelbase	: 2640 mm			Vauxhall Astra Twin Top. Folding
turning circle	: 10.4 m			roof type construction makes it a
				rather long car.

FORD FOCUS CC 2.0 TDCi

engine type	: diesel, inline-4
displacement	: 1999 cc
max. power	: 100 kW (136 bhp)
@	: 4000 rpm
max. torque	: 236 lb ft
@	: 2000 rpm
gears	: 6
kerb weight	: 1548 kg
towing weight	: -
consumption	: 47.9 mpg
acc. 0-60 mph	: 10.3 s
top speed	: 128 mph
miscellaneous	: Convertibles are more and more being used for business. For this reason, the Focus CC is also available with diesel power.

FORD MONDEO 1.8 16V / 2.0 16V

engine type	: petrol, inline-4
displacement	: 1798 / 1999 cc
max. power	: 81 kW (110 bhp) / 107 kW (145 bhp)
@	: 5500 / 6000 rpm
max. torque	: 125 / 140 lb ft
@	: 3950 / 4000 rpm
gears	: 5
AT	: - / optional 4-speed automatic
drive	: FWD
brakes f/r	: vent. discs / discs
body type	: 4-dr. saloon / 5-dr. hatchback
l x w x h	: 4731 x 1812 x 1429 mm
wheelbase	: 2754 mm
turning circle	: 11.6 m

kerb weight	: 1360 / 1378 kg
towing weight	: 1500 / 1800 kg
boot space	: saloon: 500 – hatchback : 500 – 1370 l
fuel capacity	: 59 l
consumption	: 37.2 / 36.2 mpg
acc. 0-62 mph	: 11.6 / 9.8 s
top speed	: 127 / 134 mph
EuroNCAP	: 4 stars
introduction	: Autumn 2000
last revised in	: Autumn 2005
warranty	: 2 years
miscellaneous	: Mondeo was subjected to minor facelift. Spacious and well-built contender in the medium-sized car segment.

MONDEO 2.5 V6 24V / 3.0 V6 24V

engine type	: petrol, V6
displacement	: 2495 / 2967 cc
max. power	: 125 kW (170 bhp) / 150 kW (204 bhp)
@	: 6000 rpm
max. torque	: 162 / 194 lb ft
@	: 4250 / 4900 rpm
gears	: 6
kerb weight	: 1469 / 1503 kg
towing weight	: 1800 kg
consumption	: 27.7 / 27.4 mpg
acc. 0-60 mph	: 8.5 / 7.9 s
top speed	: 134 / 149 mph
miscellaneous	: Both V6 engines are strong performers, but high price hinders sales.

MONDEO ST220

engine type	: petrol, V6
displacement	: 2967 cc
max. power	: 166 kW (226 bhp)
@	: 6250 rpm
max. torque	: 210 lb ft
@	: 4900 rpm
gears	: 6
kerb weight	: 1495 kg
towing weight	: 1800 kg
consumption	: 27.2 mpg
acc. 0-60 mph	: 7.6 s
top speed	: 155 mph
miscellaneous	: A wolf in sheep's clothing. Introvert appearance, but with the heart of a lion underneath.

FORD MONDEO ESTATE 2.0 TDDi / 2.0 TDCI

engine type	: diesel, inline-4	kerb weight	: 1372 / 1569 kg
displacement	: 1998 cc	towing weight	: 1800 kg
max. power	: 66 kW (90 bhp) / 85 kW (115 bhp)	boot space	: 540 – 1700 l
@	: 4000 / 3950 rpm	fuel capacity	: 59 l
max. torque	: 210 / 210 lb ft	consumption	: 48.7 mpg
@	: 1900 rpm	acc. 0-62 mph	: 12.9 / 11.6 s
gears	: 5 / 6	top speed	: 112 / 121 mph
AT	: -	EuroNCAP	: 4 stars
drive	: FWD	introduction	: Autumn 2001
brakes f/r	: vent. discs / discs	last revised in	: Autumn 2005
body type	: 5-dr. stationwagon	warranty	: 2 years
l x w x h	: 4731 x 1812 x 1429 mm	miscellaneous	: Also available with 130 bhp
wheelbase	: 2754 mm		2.0 TDCI diesel engine.
turning circle	: 11.6 m		

MONDEO ESTATE 2.2 16V TDCI

engine type	: diesel, inline-4
displacement	: 2198 cc
max. power	: 114 kW (155 bhp)
@	: 3500 rpm
max. torque	: 266 lb ft
@	: 1800 rpm
gears	: 6
kerb weight	: 1574 kg
towing weight	: 1800 kg
consumption	: 46.3 mpg
acc. 0-60 mph	: 9.0 s
top speed	: 136 mph
miscellaneous	: 2.2-litre diesel engine is a good performer and is fitted with a particle filter. Car is also available in ST-trim.

FORD TOURNEO CONNECT 1.8

engine type	: petrol, inline-4		kerb weight	: 1420 kg
displacement	: 1796 cc		towing weight	: 1000 kg
max. power	: 85 kW (115 bhp)		boot space	: 1200 – 3200 l
@	: 5750 rpm		fuel capacity	: 60 l
max. torque	: 118 lb ft		consumption	: 34.2 mpg
@	: 4400 rpm		acc. 0-62 mph	: 12.7 s
gears	: 5		top speed	: 103 mph
AT	: -		EuroNCAP	: n.a.
drive	: FWD		introduction	: 2002
brakes f/r	: vent. discs / discs		last revised in	: -
body type	: 5-dr. MPV		warranty	: 2 years
l x w x h	: 4278 x 1795 x 1814 mm		miscellaneous	: Looks like a van with extra
wheelbase	: 2664 mm			sideglazing. Not very popular.
turning circle	: 11.0 m			

TOURNEO CONNECT 1.8 TDCI

engine type	: diesel, inline-4
displacement	: 1753 cc
max. power	: 66 kW (90 bhp)
@	: 4000 rpm
max. torque	: 162 lb ft
@	: 1750 rpm
gears	: 6
kerb weight	: 1485 kg
towing weight	: 1000 kg
consumption	: 43.6 mpg
acc. 0-60 mph	: 16.3 s
top speed	: 96 mph
miscellaneous	: Tourneo Connect faces tough opposition from Fiat Doblò and Renault Kangoo.

FORD GALAXY 2.0 16V

engine type	: petrol, inline-4		kerb weight	: 1697 kg
displacement	: 1999 cc		towing weight	: 1100 kg
max. power	: 107 kW (145 bhp)		boot space	: 308 – 2325 l
@	: 6000 rpm		fuel capacity	: 70 l
max. torque	: 140 lb ft		consumption	: 34.4 mpg
@	: 4500 rpm		acc. 0-62 mph	: 11.2 s
gears	: 5		top speed	: 121 mph
AT	: optional 4-speed		EuroNCAP	: n.a.
drive	: FWD		introduction	: May 2006
brakes f/r	: vent. discs / discs		last revised in	: -
body type	: 5-dr. MPV		warranty	: 2 years
l x w x h	: 4731 x 1812 x 1429 mm		miscellaneous	: New Galaxy was entirely developed
wheelbase	: 2754 mm			by Ford, without the help of VW.
turning circle	: 11.6 m			Biggest Ford model is a bit more
				practical than its stablemate, the
				S-Max.

GALAXY 2.0 TDCI

engine type	: diesel, inline-4
displacement	: 1999 cc
max. power	: 103 kW (140 bhp)
@	: 4000 rpm
max. torque	: 251 lb ft
@	: 1750 rpm
gears	: 6
kerb weight	: 1806 kg
towing weight	: 1700 kg
consumption	: 43.5 mpg
acc. 0-60 mph	: 10.5 s
top speed	: 120 mph
miscellaneous	: Less powerful diesel engines are also available.

FORD S-MAX 2.0 16V / 2.5

engine type	: petrol, inline-4 / inline-5		kerb weight	: 1605 / 1681 kg
displacement	: 1999 / 2522 cc		towing weight	: 1100 / 1700 kg
max. power	: 107 kW (145 bhp) /		boot space	: 285 – 2000 l
	162 kW (210 bhp)		fuel capacity	: 70 l
@	: 6000 / 5000 rpm		consumption	: 34.9 / 30.1 mpg
max. torque	: 140 / 239 lb ft		acc. 0-62 mph	: 10.9 / 7.9 s
@	: 4500 / 1500 rpm		top speed	: 143 mph
gears	: 5 / 6		EuroNCAP	: n.a.
AT	: -		introduction	: Spring 2006
drive	: FWD		last revised in	: -
brakes f/r	: vent. discs / discs		warranty	: 2 years
body type	: 5-dr. MPV		miscellaneous	: 2.5-litre engine stems from
l x w x h	: 4768 x 1884 x 1658 mm			Focus ST and transforms S-Max
wheelbase	: 2850 mm			into one of the fastest MPVs
turning circle	: 11.6 m			on the market.

S-MAX 2.0 TDCI

engine type	: diesel, inline-4
displacement	: 1999 cc
max. power	: 103 kW (140 bhp)
@	: 4000 rpm
max. torque	: 236 lb ft
@	: 1750 rpm
gears	: 6
kerb weight	: 1743 kg
towing weight	: 1700 kg
consumption	: 44.1 mpg
acc. 0-60 mph	: 10.2 s
top speed	: 122 mph
miscellaneous	: A particle filter is standard
	on this diesel engine.

HONDA JAZZ 1.2 / 1.4

engine type	: petrol, inline-4	kerb weight	: 815 / 835 kg
displacement	: 1246 / 1339 kg	towing weight	: 800 kg
max. power	: 57 kW (78 bhp) / 61 kW (83 bhp)	boot space	: 206 - 775
@	: 6000 / 5700 rpm	fuel capacity	: 35 l
max. torque	: 82 / 88 lb ft	consumption	: 51.6 / 48.9 mpg
@	: 2800 rpm	acc. 0-62 mph	: 13.7 / 12.0 s
gears	: 5	top speed	: 106 mph
AT	: optional CVT	EuroNCAP	: 4 stars
drive	: FWD	introduction	: Autumn 2001
brakes f/r	: vent. discs / discs	last revised in	: Autumn 2004
body type	: 5-dr. hatchback	warranty	: 2 years
l x w x h	: 3830 x 1675 x 1525 mm	miscellaneous	: Car of the Year in Japan.
wheelbase	: 2450 mm		Good-looking, spacious model,
turning circle	: 9.4 m		merits more recognition because of
			its fine qualities. Diesel power not
			available.

HONDA CIVIC 1.4 / 1.8

engine type	: petrol, inline-4
displacement	: 1339 / 1798 cc
max. power	: 61 kW (83 bhp) / 103 kW (140 bhp)
@	: 5700 / 6300 rpm
max. torque	: 88 / 128 lb ft
@	: 2800 / 4300 rpm
gears	: 6
AT	: optional 6-speed automatic
drive	: FWD
brakes f/r	: vent. discs / discs
body type	: 5-dr. hatchback
l x w x h	: 4250 x 1760 x 1460 mm
wheelbase	: 2635 mm
turning circle	: 11.0 m

kerb weight	: 1140 / 1165 kg
towing weight	: 1200 / 1400 kg
boot space	: 415 – 485 l
fuel capacity	: 50 l
consumption	: 47.9 / 44.1 mpg
acc. 0-62 mph	: 14.2 / 8.6 s
top speed	: 106 / 127 mph
EuroNCAP	: n.a.
introduction	: Autumn 2005
last revised in	: -
warranty	: 2 years
miscellaneous	: New Civic, hopefully more successful than previous model. Much more striking appearance. 1.8 petrol engine has low fuel consumption. 3-door Type-S also available. Range topper is Civic Type-R, with 200 bhp engine.

CIVIC 2.2 I-CTDI

engine type	: diesel, inline-4
displacement	: 2204 cc
max. power	: 103 kW (140 bhp)
@	: 4000 rpm
max. torque	: 251 lb ft
@	: 2000 rpm
gears	: 6
kerb weight	: 1310 kg
towing weight	: 1500 kg
consumption	: 62.8 / 62.8 mpg
acc. 0-60 mph	: 8.4 s
top speed	: 127 mph
miscellaneous	: More frugal type, but almost as quick as 1.8. Probably the best choice.

HONDA CIVIC HYBRID

engine type	: petrol, inline-4 + electrical engine		**kerb weight**	: 1297 kg
displacement	: 1339 cc		**towing weight**	: -
max. power	: 85 kW (115 bhp)		**boot space**	: 415 – 485 l
@	: 5700 / 6300 rpm		**fuel capacity**	: 50 l
max. torque	: 166 lb ft		**consumption**	: 61.4 mpg
@	: 1000 rpm		**acc. 0-62 mph**	: 12.1 s
gears	: 6		**top speed**	: 115 mph
AT	: -		**EuroNCAP**	: n.a.
drive	: FWD		**introduction**	: March 2006
brakes f/r	: vent. discs / discs		**last revised in**	: -
body type	: 4-dr. sedan		**warranty**	: 3 years
l x w x h	: 4545 x 1750 x 1430 mm		**miscellaneous**	: Latest hybrid technology not available (yet) in popular Civic hatchback, but only in this conservatively styled saloon. Interesting alternative for more expensive Toyota Prius.
wheelbase	: 2702 mm			
turning circle	: n.a.			

HONDA ACCORD 2.0I / 2.4I

engine type	: petrol, inline-4	**kerb weight**	: 1293 / 1356 kg
displacement	: 1998 / 2398 cc	**towing weight**	: 1500 kg
max. power	: 114 kW (155 bhp) /	**boot space**	: 459 l
	141 kW (190 bhp)	**fuel capacity**	: 65 l
@	: 6000 / 6800 rpm	**consumption**	: 38.2 / 31.4 mpg
max. torque	: 140 / 164 lb ft	**acc. 0-62 mph**	: 9.6 / 7.9 s
@	: 4500 rpm	**top speed**	: 137 / 141 mph
gears	: 5 / 6	**EuroNCAP**	: 4 stars
AT	: optional 5-speed automatic	**introduction**	: Autumn 2002
drive	: FWD	**last revised in**	: Autumn 2002
brakes f/r	: vent. discs / discs	**warranty**	: 2 years
body type	: 4-dr. saloon	**miscellaneous**	: Modern car with excellent build
l x w x h	: 4665 x 1760 x 1445 mm		quality. Rather limited model range
wheelbase	: 2680 mm		hinders sales. Stationcar has
turning circle	: 10.8 m		striking profile.

ACCORD 2.2 I-CTDI

engine type	: diesel, inline-4
displacement	: 2204 cc
max. power	: 103 kW (140 bhp)
@	: 4000 rpm
max. torque	: 251 lb ft
@	: 2000 rpm
gears	: 5
kerb weight	: 1545 kg
towing weight	: 1500 kg
consumption	: 51.4 mpg
acc. 0-60 mph	: 9.8 s
top speed	: 132 mph
miscellaneous	: It took some time for Honda to develop its own diesel engine, but it was worth the wait. One of the best diesel engines in its class.

HONDA LEGEND

engine type	: petrol, V6		**kerb weight**	: 1864 kg
displacement	: 3471 cc		**towing weight**	: 1600 kg
max. power	: 217 kW (295 bhp)		**boot space**	: 452 l
@	: 6200 rpm		**fuel capacity**	: 73 l
max. torque	: 259 lb ft		**consumption**	: 23.7 mpg
@	: 5000 rpm		**acc. 0-62 mph**	: 7.3 s
gears	: -		**top speed**	: 155 mph
AT	: 5-speed		**EuroNCAP**	: n.a.
drive	: 4WD		**introduction**	: July 2006
brakes f/r	: vent. discs / discs		**last revised in**	: -
body type	: 4-dr. saloon		**warranty**	: 3 years
l x w x h	: 4955 x 1845 x 1450 mm		**miscellaneous**	: Modern yet impersonal Japanese
wheelbase	: 2800 mm			business limousine. The price is
turning circle	: 11.6 m			rather high.

HONDA S2000

engine type	: petrol, inline-4	kerb weight	: 1220 kg
displacement	: 1997 cc	towing weight	: -
max. power	: 177 kW (240 bhp)	boot space	: 143 l
@	: 8300 rpm	fuel capacity	: 50 l
max. torque	: 153 lb ft	consumption	: 28.2 mpg
@	: 7500 rpm	acc. 0-62 mph	: 6.2 s
gears	: 6	top speed	: 150 mph
AT	: -	EuroNCAP	: n.a
drive	: RWD	introduction	: Spring 1999
brakes f/r	: vent. discs / discs	last revised in	: Spring 2004
body type	: 2-dr. convertible	warranty	: 3 years
l x w x h	: 4135 x 1750 x 1285 mm	miscellaneous	: Concept car SSM first shown in
wheelbase	: 2405 mm		1995, but resulting S2000 has a
turning circle	: 9.5 m		timeless design. Excellent driver's
			car with high-revving power unit.
			Now better than ever, following
			its second facelift.

HONDA FR-V 1.7 / 2.0

engine type	: petrol, inline-4	**kerb weight**	: 1366 / 1418 kg
displacement	: 1668 / 1998 cc	**towing weight**	: 1500 kg
max. power	: 92 kW (125 bhp) / 110 kW (150 bhp)	**boot space**	: 440 - 1600 l
@	: 6300 / 6500 rpm	**fuel capacity**	: 58 l
max. torque	: 114 / 142 lb ft	**consumption**	: 37.7 / 33.6 mpg
@	: 4800 / 4000 rpm	**acc. 0-62 mph**	: 12.3 / 10.5 s
gears	: 5 / 6	**top speed**	: 112 / 120 mph
AT	: -	**EuroNCAP**	: 4 stars
drive	: FWD	**introduction**	: Summer 2004
brakes f/r	: vent. discs / discs	**last revised in**	: -
body type	: 5-dr. MPV	**warranty**	: 2 years
l x w x h	: 4285 x 1810 x 1610 mm	**miscellaneous**	: Compact MPV but still wide enough to seat three people on the front row.
wheelbase	: 2685 mm		
turning circle	: 10.5 m		

FR-V 2.2 i-CDTi

engine type	: diesel, inline-4
displacement	: 2204 cc
max. power	: 103 kW (140 bhp)
@	: 4000 rpm
max. torque	: 251 lb ft
@	: 2000 rpm
gears	: 6
kerb weight	: 1645 kg
towing weight	: 1500 kg
consumption	: 44.8 mpg
acc. 0-60 mph	: 10.2 s
top speed	: 118 mph
miscellaneous	: Seating arrangement perfect for families with three children. One child can sit in the front.

HONDA CR-V 2.0

engine type	: petrol, inline-4		kerb weight	: n.a.
displacement	: 1998 cc		towing weight	: 1600 kg
max. power	: 110 kW (150 bhp)		boot space	: 527 – 1568 l
@	: 6200 rpm		fuel capacity	: 58 l
max. torque	: 140 lb ft		consumption	: 34.9 mpg
@	: 4200 rpm		acc. 0-62 mph	: 10.2 s
gears	: 6		top speed	: n.a.
AT	: n.a.		EuroNCAP	: n.a.
drive	: 4WD		introduction	: September 2006
brakes f/r	: vent. discs / discs		last revised in	: -
body type	: 5-dr. SUV		warranty	: 3 years
l x w x h	: 4635 x 1785 x 1710 mm		miscellaneous	: New CR-V is an SUV rather than an
wheelbase	: 2630 mm			offroader.
turning circle	: n.a.			

CR-V 2.2 i-CDTI

engine type	: diesel, inline-4
displacement	: 2204 cc
max. power	: 103 kW (140 bhp)
@	: 4000 rpm
max. torque	: 251 lb ft
@	: 2000 rpm
gears	: 6
kerb weight	: n.a.
towing weight	: 2000 kg
consumption	: 43.5 mpg
acc. 0-60 mph	: 12.2 s
top speed	: n.a.
miscellaneous	: CR-V is a much more interesting proposition thanks to Honda's own diesel engine.

HUMMER H3

engine type	: petrol, inline-5	**kerb weight**	: 2132 kg
displacement	: 3460 cc	**towing weight**	: 2041 kg
max. power	: 164 kW (220 bhp)	**boot space**	: 835 l
@	: 5600 rpm	**fuel capacity**	: 87 l
max. torque	: 225 lb ft	**consumption**	: n.a.
@	: 2800 rpm	**acc. 0-62 mph**	: < 10 s
gears	: 5	**top speed**	: > 105 mph
AT	: optional 4-speed automatic	**EuroNCAP**	: n.a.
drive	: 4WD	**introduction**	: Summer 2005
brakes f/r	: vent. discs / discs	**last revised in**	: -
body type	: 5-dr. SUV	**warranty**	: 3 years
l x w x h	: 4742 x 1897 x 1872 mm	**miscellaneous**	: Most credible model from Hummer, based on the Chevrolet Colorado pickup truck. Very capable offroad, but still too big for normal roads.
wheelbase	: 2842 mm		
turning circle	: 11.3 m		

HUMMER H2

engine type	: petrol, V8	**kerb weight**	: 2980 kg
displacement	: 5965 cc	**towing weight**	: 3182 kg
max. power	: 239 kW (325 bhp)	**boot space**	: 1132 – 2452 l
@	: 5200 rpm	**fuel capacity**	: 121 l
max. torque	: 365 lb ft	**consumption**	: n.a.
@	: 4000 rpm	**acc. 0-62 mph**	: < 10 s
gears	: -	**top speed**	: > 105 mph
AT	: 4-speed automatic	**EuroNCAP**	: n.a.
drive	: 4WD	**introduction**	: Summer 2004
brakes f/r	: vent. discs / discs	**last revised in**	: -
body type	: 5-dr. SUV	**warranty**	: 3 years
l x w x h	: 4821 x 2063 x 2080 mm	**miscellaneous**	: 'Smaller' H2 is in fact both higher
wheelbase	: 3119 mm		and longer than original Hummer
turning circle	: 13.5 m		and weighs about the same. Model
			variation with small, open load
			platform called H2 SUT.

HYUNDAI AMICA 1.1i

engine type	: petrol, inline-4		**kerb weight**	: 859 kg
displacement	: 1086 cc		**towing weight**	: 700 kg
max. power	: 47 kW (65 bhp)		**boot space**	: 220 - 889 l
@	: 5500 rpm		**fuel capacity**	: 35 l
max. torque	: 72 lb ft		**consumption**	: 52.3 mpg
@	: 3000 rpm		**acc. 0-62 mph**	: 15.8 s
gears	: 5		**top speed**	: 91 mph
AT	: optional 4-speed automatic		**EuroNCAP**	: 3 stars
drive	: FWD		**introduction**	: June 2003
brakes f/r	: discs / drum brakes		**last revised in**	: September 2005
body type	: 5-dr. hatchback		**warranty**	: 3 years
l x w x h	: 3565 x 1525 x 1570 mm		**miscellaneous**	: Much better-looking than original
wheelbase	: 2380 mm			Atos launched in 1997. One of the
turning circle	: 9.8 m			cheapest cars on today's market.

HYUNDAI GETZ 1.1 / 1.4

engine type	: petrol, inline-4	kerb weight	: 976 / 1025 kg
displacement	: 1086 / 1399 cc	towing weight	: 700 / 1000 kg
max. power	: 48 kW (65 bhp) / 70 kW (95 bhp)	boot space	: 254 - 977 l
@	: 5500 / 6000 rpm	fuel capacity	: 45 l
max. torque	: 73 / 92 lb ft	consumption	: 51.4 / 47.1 mpg
@	: 3200 / 3200 rpm	acc. 0-62 mph	: 15.6 / 11.2 s
gears	: 5	top speed	: 93 / 106 mph
AT	: - / optional 4-speed automatic	EuroNCAP	: n.a.
drive	: FWD	introduction	: July 2002
brakes f/r	: vent. discs / drum brakes	last revised in	: -
body type	: 3-, 5-dr. hatchback	warranty	: 2 years
l x w x h	: 3810 x 1665 x 1490 mm	miscellaneous	: Hyundai called in the help of Italian
wheelbase	: 2455 mm		designers. The outcome is very
turning circle	: 10.0 m		pleasing, with European looks.

GETZ 1.6

engine type	: petrol, inline-4
displacement	: 1599 cc
max. power	: 77 kW (105 bhp)
@	: 5800 rpm
max. torque	: 106 lb ft
@	: 3000 rpm
gears	: 5
kerb weight	: 1027 kg
towing weight	: 1100 kg
consumption	: 47.3 mpg
acc. 0-60 mph	: 9.6 s
top speed	: 112 mph
miscellaneous	: 1.6 engine endows Getz with performance characteristics of a small GTI. Direct steering response, fine chassis. All in all, a surprising package.

GETZ 1.5 CRDI

engine type	: diesel, inline-4
displacement	: 1493 cc
max. power	: 65 kW (88 bhp)
@	: 5800 rpm
max. torque	: 159 lb ft
@	: 1900 rpm
gears	: 5
kerb weight	: 1112 kg
towing weight	: 1100 kg
consumption	: 62.8 mpg
acc. 0-60 mph	: 12.1 s
top speed	: 106 mph
miscellaneous	: Diesel version is most economical Getz of all.

HYUNDAI ACCENT 1.4 / 1.6

engine type	: petrol, inline-4		**kerb weight**	: 1055 kg
displacement	: 1399 / 1599 cc		**towing weight**	: 1100 kg
max. power	: 70 kW (95 bhp) / 82 kW (112 bhp)		**boot space**	: n.a.
@	: 6000 rpm		**fuel capacity**	: 45 l
max. torque	: 92 / 108 lb ft		**consumption**	: 45.6 / 44.3 mpg
@	: 4700 / 4500 rpm		**acc. 0-62 mph**	: 12.3 / 10.2 s
gears	: 5		**top speed**	: 110 / 118 mph
AT	: -		**EuroNCAP**	: n.a.
drive	: FWD		**introduction**	: May 2006
brakes f/r	: vent. discs / drum brakes		**last revised in**	: -
body type	: 3-dr. hatchback/4-dr. saloon		**warranty**	: 3 years
l x w x h	: 4045 x 1695 x 1470 mm		**miscellaneous**	: 'Interim' model until the arrival of
wheelbase	: 2500 mm			the new Accent. Cheap and
turning circle	: 10.1 m			uncomplicated. Specifications apply
				to 3-dr. hatchback.

HYUNDAI MATRIX 1.6i / 1.8i

engine type	: petrol, inline-4
displacement	: 1599 / 1795 cc
max. power	: 76 kW (103 bhp) / 89 kW (121 bhp)
@	: 5800 / 6000 rpm
max. torque	: 104 / 119 lb ft
@	: 4500 / 4500 rpm
gears	: 5
AT	: optional 4-speed automatic
drive	: FWD
brakes f/r	: vent. discs / drum brakes
body type	: 5-dr. MPV
l x w x h	: 4025 x 1740 x 1635 mm
wheelbase	: 2600 mm
turning circle	: 10.4 m

kerb weight	: 1223 / 1270 kg
towing weight	: 1300 kg
boot space	: 354 – 1284 l
fuel capacity	: 55 l
consumption	: 39.8 / 34 mpg
acc. 0-62 mph	: 12.7 / 11.3 s
top speed	: 106 / 114 mph
EuroNCAP	: n.a.
introduction	: July 2001
last revised in	: August 2005
warranty	: 3 years
miscellaneous	: Originally styled mini-MPV by Pininfarina. With a longer lease of life again, thanks to minor facelift.

MATRIX 1.5 CRDI VGT

engine type	: diesel, inline-4
displacement	: 1493 cc
max. power	: 75 kW (102 bhp)
@	: 4000 rpm
max. torque	: 141 lb ft
@	: 2000 rpm
gears	: 5
kerb weight	: 1280 kg
towing weight	: 1300 kg
consumption	: 52.3 mpg
acc. 0-60 mph	: 14.3 s
top speed	: 99 mph
miscellaneous	: Matrix more interesting now with new 4-cylinder diesel engine.

HYUNDAI ELANTRA 1.6 / 2.0I

engine type	: petrol, inline-4
displacement	: 1599 / 1975 cc
max. power	: 76 kW (103 bhp) / 105 kW (143 bhp)
@	: 5800 / 6000 rpm
max. torque	: 104 / 119 lb ft
@	: 4500 / 4500 rpm
gears	: 5
AT	: optional 4-speed automatic
drive	: FWD
brakes f/r	: vent. discs / drum brakes
body type	: 4-dr. sedan
l x w x h	: 4495 x 1720 x 1425 mm
wheelbase	: 2610 mm
turning circle	: 10.1 m

kerb weight	: 1178 / 1223 kg
towing weight	: 1200 / 1400 kg
boot space	: 415 – 800 l
fuel capacity	: 55 l
consumption	: 38.3 / 34.5 mpg
acc. 0-62 mph	: 11.0 / 9.1 s
top speed	: 113 / 128 mph
EuroNCAP	: 3 stars
introduction	: September 2000
last revised in	: July 2003
warranty	: 3 years
miscellaneous	: Tidy medium-sized car with 4 or 5 doors, but rather dull-looking. Performance surprisingly good.

ELANTRA 2.0 CRDI

engine type	: diesel, inline-4
displacement	: 1991 cc
max. power	: 83 kW (112 bhp)
@	: 4000 rpm
max. torque	: 173 lb ft
@	: 1800 rpm
gears	: 5
kerb weight	: 1306 kg
towing weight	: 1400 kg
consumption	: 44.3 mpg
acc. 0-60 mph	: 11.7 s
top speed	: 118 mph
miscellaneous	: Diesel-powered Elantra better equipped than petrol versions, but not very successful on the lease market.

HYUNDAI COUPE 2.0 / 2.7 V6

engine type	: petrol, inline-4 / V6
displacement	: 1975 / 2656 cc
max. power	: 105 kW (143 bhp) / 123 kW (167 bhp)
@	: 4500 / 4000 rpm
max. torque	: 137 / 181 lb ft
@	: 4500 / 4000 rpm
gears	: 5 / 6
AT	: - / optional 4-speed automatic
drive	: FWD
brakes f/r	: vent. discs / discs
body type	: 3-dr. coupe
l x w x h	: 4395 x 1760 x 1330 mm
wheelbase	: 2530 mm
turning circle	: 10.9 m

kerb weight	: 1255 / 1308 kg
towing weight	: 1400 kg
boot space	: 418 l
fuel capacity	: 55 l
consumption	: 35.3 / 28.5 mpg
acc. 0-62 mph	: 9.1 / 8.2 s
top speed	: 129 / 137 mph
EuroNCAP	: n.a.
introduction	: September 2001
last revised in	: November 2004
warranty	: 3 years
miscellaneous	: Korean sportscars are thin on the ground, but here we have one. Rather stern face after facelift.

HYUNDAI SONATA 2.0i / 2.4i

engine type	: petrol, inline-4
displacement	: 1998 / 2359 cc
max. power	: 106 kW (145 bhp) / 119 kW (161 bhp)
@	: 6000 / 5800 rpm
max. torque	: 139 / 162 lb ft
@	: 4250 / 4250 rpm
gears	: 5
AT	: optional 4-speed automatic
drive	: FWD
brakes f/r	: vent. discs / discs
body type	: 4-dr. sedan
l x w x h	: 4800 x 1832 x 1475 mm
wheelbase	: 2730 mm
turning circle	: 10.9 m

kerb weight	: 1448 / 1438 kg
towing weight	: 1700 kg
boot space	: 523 l
fuel capacity	: 70 l
consumption	: 35.3 / 34.2 mpg
acc. 0-62 mph	: 10.5 / 8.9 s
top speed	: 127 / 132 mph
EuroNCAP	: n.a.
introduction	: September 2004
last revised in	: -
warranty	: 3 years
miscellaneous	: Good alternative for other, more customary business saloons. Well-built car with severe looks. Also available with 3.3-litre V6 engine.

SONATA 2.0 CRDI

engine type	: diesel, inline-4
displacement	: 1991 cc
max. power	: 103 kW (140 bhp)
@	: 4000 rpm
max. torque	: 224 lb ft
@	: 1800 rpm
gears	: 6
kerb weight	: 1566 kg
towing weight	: 1700 kg
consumption	: 46.3 mpg
acc. 0-60 mph	: 10.7 s
top speed	: 126 mph
miscellaneous	: Diesel engine should bring more customers.

HYUNDAI GRANDEUR 3.3 V6

engine type	: petrol, V6	kerb weight	: 1664 kg
displacement	: 3342 cc	towing weight	: 1800 kg
max. power	: 173 kW (235 bhp)	boot space	: 469 l
@	: 6000 rpm	fuel capacity	: 75 l
max. torque	: 224 lb ft	consumption	: 27.8 mpg
@	: 3500 rpm	acc. 0-62 mph	: 7.8 s
gears	: -	top speed	: 147 mph
AT	: 5-speed automatic	EuroNCAP	: n.a.
drive	: FWD	introduction	: Autumn 2005
brakes f/r	: vent. discs / discs	last revised in	: -
body type	: 4-dr. sedan	warranty	: 3 years
l x w x h	: 4895 x 1845 x 1490 mm	miscellaneous	: Successor to XG model. Car
wheelbase	: 2780 mm		deserves to be successful.
turning circle	: 11.4 m		

HYUNDAI TUCSON 2.0i CVVT / 2.7i V6

engine type	: petrol, inline-4 / V6	kerb weight	: 1600 kg
displacement	: 1975 / 2656 cc	towing weight	: 1400 - 4WD 1600 kg
max. power	: 105 kW (143 bhp) /	boot space	: 644 - 1856 l
	129 kW (175 bhp)	fuel capacity	: 65 l
@	: 6000 rpm	consumption	: 35.3 / 28.2 mpg
max. torque	: 136 / 178 lb ft	acc. 0-62 mph	: 10.4 / 10.5 s
@	: 4500 / 4000 rpm	top speed	: 108 / 112 mph
gears	: 5	EuroNCAP	: n.a.
AT	: optional 4-speed automatic	introduction	: March 2004
drive	: FWD	last revised in	: September 2005
brakes f/r	: vent. discs / discs	warranty	: 3 years
body type	: 5-dr. SUV	miscellaneous	: Highly successful model for
l x w x h	: 4325 x 1830 x 1730 mm		ambitious Korean car manufacturer.
wheelbase	: 2630 mm		
turning circle	: 10.8 m		

TUCSON 2.0 CRDI VGT

engine type	: diesel, inline-4
displacement	: 1991 cc
max. power	: 103 kW (140 bhp)
@	: 4000 rpm
max. torque	: 225 lb ft
@	: 1800 rpm
gears	: 6
kerb weight	: 1660 kg
towing weight	: 1600 kg
consumption	: 39.8 mpg
acc. 0-60 mph	: 12.0 s
top speed	: 110 mph
miscellaneous	: Diesel-powered Tucson available with 2WD and 4WD.

HYUNDAI SANTA FE 2.7 V6

engine type	: petrol, V6		kerb weight	: 1645 kg
displacement	: 2656 cc		towing weight	: 2000 kg
max. power	: 139 kW (189 bhp)		boot space	: 969 l
@	: 6000 rpm		fuel capacity	: 75 l
max. torque	: 183 lb ft		consumption	: 26.6 mpg
@	: 3500 rpm		acc. 0-62 mph	: 10.0 s
gears	: 5		top speed	: 111 mph
AT	: optional 4-speed automatic		EuroNCAP	: n.a.
drive	: FWD		introduction	: January 2006
brakes f/r	: vent. discs / discs		last revised in	: -
body type	: 5-dr. SUV		warranty	: 3 years
l x w x h	: 4675 x 1890 x 1725 mm		miscellaneous	: New Santa Fe positioned higher in the market to widen the gap with the Tucson. 2.7 also available with 4WD.
wheelbase	: 2700 mm			
turning circle	: 10.9 m			

SANTA FE 2.2 CRDI

engine type	: diesel, inline-4
displacement	: 2188 cc
max. power	: 110 kW (150 bhp)
@	: 4000 rpm
max. torque	: 247 lb ft
@	: 1800 rpm
gears	: 5
kerb weight	: 1718 kg
towing weight	: 2200 kg
consumption	: 38.7 mpg
acc. 0-60 mph	: 11.3 s
top speed	: 111 mph
miscellaneous	: Modern 2.2 diesel engine will soon find its way to other Hyundai models too.

HYUNDAI TERRACAN 3.5 V6

engine type	: petrol, V6	**kerb weight**	: 1958 kg
displacement	: 3497 cc	**towing weight**	: 2800 kg
max. power	: 143 kW (194 bhp)	**boot space**	: 1180 - 2000 l
@	: 5500 rpm	**fuel capacity**	: 75 l
max. torque	: 217 lb ft	**consumption**	: 18.7 mpg
@	: 3000 rpm	**acc. 0-62 mph**	: 10.7 s
gears	: -	**top speed**	: 111 mph
AT	: 4-speed automatic	**EuroNCAP**	: n.a.
drive	: 4WD	**introduction**	: July 2001
brakes f/r	: vent. discs / discs	**last revised in**	: August 2004
body type	: 5-dr. SUV	**warranty**	: 3 years
l x w x h	: 4710 x 1860 x 1790 mm	**miscellaneous**	: Biggest car in Hyundai model range, but of minor importance to the turnover figures of the Korean car manufacturer.
wheelbase	: 2750 mm		
turning circle	: 11.8 m		

TERRACAN 2.9 CRDI

engine type	: diesel, inline-4
displacement	: 2902 cc
max. power	: 120 kW (163 bhp)
@	: 3800 rpm
max. torque	: 253 lb ft
@	: 2000 rpm
gears	: 5, optional 4-speed automatic
kerb weight	: 2018 kg
towing weight	: 2800 kg
consumption	: 32.4 mpg
acc. 0-60 mph	: 13.7 s
top speed	: 104 mph
miscellaneous	: Classic offroader with potent engine, ideally suited to tow a boat or horse trailer.

HYUNDAI TRAJET 2.0 / 2.7 V6

engine type	: petrol, inline-4 / V6		kerb weight	: 1712 / 1752 kg
displacement	: 1997 / 2656 cc		towing weight	: 1800 / 1950 kg
max. power	: 103 kW (140 bhp) /		boot space	: 523 – 1801 l
	127 kW (173 bhp)		fuel capacity	: 65 / 75 l
@	: 5800 / 6000 rpm		consumption	: 33.5 / 24.9 mpg
max. torque	: 136 / 181 lb ft		acc. 0-62 mph	: 13.1 / 11.5 s
@	: 4600 / 4000 rpm		top speed	: 114 / 119 mph
gears	: 5 / -		EuroNCAP	: 3 stars
AT	: optional 4-speed automatic /		introduction	: February 2000
	4-speed automatic		last revised in	: April 2004
drive	: FWD		warranty	: 3 years
brakes f/r	: vent. discs / discs		miscellaneous	: Spacious and affordable, but on the
body type	: 5-dr. MPV			market for some time now. Exterior,
l x w x h	: 4695 x 1840 x 1760 mm			choice of materials and build quality
wheelbase	: 2830 mm			have improved since latest facelift.
turning circle	: 11.3 m			

INVICTA S1

engine type	: petrol, V8		**kerb weight**	: 1100 kg
displacement	: 4601 cc		**towing weight**	: -
max. power	: 239 kW (325 bhp)		**boot space**	: n.a.
@	: 5900 rpm		**fuel capacity**	: 100 l
max. torque	: 300 lb ft		**consumption**	: 25.1 mpg
@	: 4800 rpm		**acc. 0-62 mph**	: 5.0 s
gears	: 5		**top speed**	: 170 mph
AT	: -		**EuroNCAP**	: n.a.
drive	: RWD		**introduction**	: n.a.
brakes f/r	: vent. discs		**last revised in**	: -
body type	: 2-dr. coupe		**warranty**	: n.a.
l x w x h	: 4400 x 2000 x 1225 mm		**miscellaneous**	: Revival of illustrious British car
wheelbase	: 2500 mm			make dating back to the 1930s.
turning circle	: 11.5 m			Voluptuous carbonfibre body with
				big V8 from Ford Mustang
				underneath. Luxuriously appointed
				and very fast.

JAGUAR X-TYPE 2.5 V6 / 3.0 V6

engine type	: petrol, V6	kerb weight	: 1555 / 1575 kg
displacement	: 2495 / 2967 cc	towing weight	: 1500 / 1500 kg
max. power	: 144 kW (196 bhp) /	boot space	: 452 l
	166 kW (231 bhp)	fuel capacity	: 62 l
@	: 6800 / 6800 rpm	consumption	: 29.5 / 27.5 mpg
max. torque	: 180 / 209 lb ft	acc. 0-62 mph	: 8.3 / 7.0 s
@	: 3000 / 3000 rpm	top speed	: 140 / 146 mph
gears	: 5 / 5	EuroNCAP	: 4 stars
AT	: optional 5-speed automatic	introduction	: May 2001
drive	: 4WD	last revised in	: -
brakes f/r	: vent. discs	warranty	: 3 years
body type	: 4-dr. saloon	miscellaneous	: Jaguar's attempt to attract more
l x w x h	: 4672 x 1789 x 1392 mm		buyers. Not as successful as hoped
wheelbase	: 2710 mm		for. Car is based on Mondeo and
turning circle	: 10.8 m		drives very well. Also available in
			stylish Estate version.

X-TYPE 2.0D / 2.2D

engine type	: diesel, inline-4
displacement	: 1998 / 2198 cc
max. power	: 96 kW (130 bhp) /
	114 kW (152 bhp)
@	: 3800 / 3500 rpm
max. torque	: 244 / 270 lb ft
@	: 1800 / 1800 rpm
gears	: 5 / 6
kerb weight	: 1502 / 1525 kg
towing weight	: 1500 kg
consumption	: 49.1 / 47.1 mpg
acc. 0-60 mph	: 9.9 / 8.9 s
top speed	: 125 / 137 mph
miscellaneous	: First Jag with diesel power, identifiable by seemingly missing exhaust end pipes. After all, true aristocrats do not smoke in public.

JAGUAR S-TYPE 3.0 V6

engine type	: petrol, V6
displacement	: 2967 cc
max. power	: 175 kW (238 bhp)
@	: 6800 rpm
max. torque	: 221 lb ft
@	: 4100 rpm
gears	: 5
AT	: optional 6-speed automatic
drive	: RWD
brakes f/r	: vent. discs
body type	: 4-dr. saloon
l x w x h	: 4877 x 1818 x 1447 mm
wheelbase	: 2909 mm
turning circle	: 11.5 m

kerb weight	: 1720 kg
towing weight	: 1850 kg
boot space	: 400 - 810 l
fuel capacity	: 70 l
consumption	: 27.4 mpg
acc. 0-62 mph	: 7.5 s
top speed	: 146 mph
EuroNCAP	: n.a.
introduction	: October 1998
last revised in	: January 2004
warranty	: 3 years
miscellaneous	: New entry level version of S-type after demise of 2.5 engine. Full of character and now much more of a Jaguar after the facelift.

S-TYPE 4.2 V8 / R

engine type	: petrol, V8
displacement	: 4196 cc
max. power	: 219 kW (298 bhp) / 295 kW (395 bhp)
@	: 6000 / 6100 rpm
max. torque	: 310 / 408 lb ft
@	: 4100 / 3500 rpm
gears	: 6-speed automatic
kerb weight	: 1735 / 1800 kg
towing weight	: 1850 kg
consumption	: 24.5 / 22.7 mpg
acc. 0-60 mph	: 6.5 / 5.6 s
top speed	: 155 mph
miscellaneous	: R-version is a fast but modest car that does not flaunt its true potential. Thrilling supercharger whine. Jag for businessmen with deep enough pockets to pay the fuel bills.

S-TYPE 2.7D

engine type	: diesel, V6
displacement	: 2720 cc
max. power	: 152 kW (207 bhp)
@	: 4000 rpm
max. torque	: 320 lb ft
@	: 1500 rpm
gears	: 6, optional 6-speed automatic
kerb weight	: 1790 kg
towing weight	: 1850 kg
consumption	: 41.5 mpg
acc. 0-60 mph	: 8.5 s
top speed	: 143 mph
miscellaneous	: Refined twin turbo diesel engine matches S-type well. Power unit was developed with PSA.

JAGUAR XJ 3.0 V6 / 3.5 V6

engine type	: petrol, V6
displacement	: 2967 / 3555 cc
max. power	: 179 kW (240 bhp) / 196 kW (262 bhp)
@	: 6800 /3250 rpm
max. torque	: 221 / 247 lb ft
@	: 4100 / 4200 rpm
gears	: -
AT	: 6-speed automatic
drive	: RWD
brakes f/r	: vent. discs
body type	: 4-dr. saloon
l x w x h	: 5090 x 1860 x 1448 mm
wheelbase	: 3035 mm
turning circle	: 11.7 m

kerb weight	: 1545 / 1615 kg
towing weight	: 1900 kg
boot space	: 470 l
fuel capacity	: 85 l
consumption	: 27 / 26.8 mpg
acc. 0-62 mph	: 8.1 / 7.6 s
top speed	: 145 / 150 mph
EuroNCAP	: n.a.
introduction	: February 2003
last revised in	: -
warranty	: 3 years
miscellaneous	: Car exudes distinctive air, but styling is rather conservative. All-aluminium body reduces weight and enhances driving characteristics. Better performer than S-type. Also available in LWB-version, nearly 5 inches longer.

XJ 4.2 V8 / XJR

engine type	: petrol, V8
displacement	: 4196 cc
max. power	: 224 kW (300 bhp) / 298 kW (400 bhp)
@	: 6000 / 6100 rpm
max. torque	: 310 / 408 lb ft
@	: 4100 / 3500 rpm
gears	: 6-speed automatic
kerb weight	: 1615 / 1665 kg
towing weight	: 1900 kg
consumption	: 26 / 23 mpg
acc. 0-60 mph	: 6.6 / 5.3 s
top speed	: 155 mph
miscellaneous	: V8 is engine of choice for people who value comfort and speed in a car. XJR is even faster and boasts a truly sporty character.

XJ 2.7D

engine type	: diesel, V6
displacement	: 2720 cc
max. power	: 152 kW (207 bhp)
@	: 4000 rpm
max. torque	: 320 lb ft
@	: 1500 rpm
gears	: 6-speed automatic
kerb weight	: 1659 kg
towing weight	: 1900 kg
consumption	: 35 mpg
acc. 0-60 mph	: 8.2 s
top speed	: 141 mph
miscellaneous	: Diesel-powered version is aimed at higher business segment. Refined engine up to the job in the biggest Jaguar of all, but introduction of 3.6-litre V8 is at hand.

JAGUAR XK / XKR

engine type	: petrol, V8	kerb weight	: 1595 / 1732 kg
displacement	: 4196 cc	towing weight	: -
max. power	: 224 kW (300 bhp) /	boot space	: 327 l
	313 kW (420 bhp)	fuel capacity	: 75 l
@	: 6000 / 6250 rpm	consumption	: 25 / n.a. mpg
max. torque	: 310 / 413 lb ft	acc. 0-62 mph	: 5.9 / 4.9 s
@	: 4100 / 4000 rpm	top speed	: 155 mph
gears	: -	EuroNCAP	: n.a.
AT	: 6-speed automatic	introduction	: Spring 2006
drive	: RWD	last revised in	: -
brakes f/r	: vent. discs	warranty	: 3 years
body type	: 2-dr. coupe	miscellaneous	: Beautiful 2+2 seater replacement
l x w x h	: 4791 x 1832 x 1322 mm		for XK8. Aluminium body. Also
wheelbase	: 2752 mm		available as convertible.
turning circle	: 11.0 m		

JEEP COMPASS 2.4

engine type	: petrol, inline-4	**kerb weight**	: 1404 kg
displacement	: 2360 cc	**towing weight**	: n.a.
max. power	: 129 kW (172 bhp)	**boot space**	: 643 l
@	: 6000 rpm	**fuel capacity**	: 51 l
max. torque	: 164 lb ft	**consumption**	: n.a.
@	: 4400 rpm	**acc. 0-62 mph**	: n.a.
gears	: 5	**top speed**	: n.a.
AT	: optional CVT	**EuroNCAP**	: n.a.
drive	: FWD	**introduction**	: January 2007
brakes f/r	: vent. discs / discs	**last revised in**	: -
body type	: 5-dr. SUV	**warranty**	: 2 years
l x w x h	: 4405 x 1760 x 1632 mm	**miscellaneous**	: A bit of a turning point in the history of Jeep: the Compass is not an off-road vehicle but an SUV. It is, however, also available with 4WD.
wheelbase	: 2635 mm		
turning circle	: 10.8 m		

COMPASS 2.0 CRD

engine type	: diesel, inline-4
displacement	: 1968 cc
max. power	: 103 kW (140 bhp)
@	: 4000 rpm
max. torque	: 236 lb ft
@	: 2500 rpm
gears	: 6
kerb weight	: n.a.
towing weight	: n.a.
consumption	: n.a.
acc. 0-60 mph	: n.a.
top speed	: n.a.
miscellaneous	: Compass shares technology with Dodge Caliber. Both cars are available with diesel engine from Volkswagen.

JEEP PATRIOT 2.4

engine type	: petrol, inline-4	kerb weight	: n.a.
displacement	: 2360 cc	towing weight	: n.a.
max. power	: 129 kW (172 bhp)	boot space	: 652 l
@	: 6000 rpm	fuel capacity	: 51 l
max. torque	: 164 lb ft	consumption	: n.a.
@	: 4400 rpm	acc. 0-62 mph	: n.a.
gears	: 5	top speed	: n.a.
AT	: optional CVT	EuroNCAP	: n.a.
drive	: 4WD	introduction	: January 2007
brakes f/r	: vent. discs / discs	last revised in	: -
body type	: 5-dr. SUV	warranty	: 2 years
l x w x h	: 4411 x 1760 x 1637 mm	miscellaneous	: Patriot is more capable offroad than Compass. Also available with 2.0 CRD engine.
wheelbase	: 2635 mm		
turning circle	: 10.8 m		

JEEP WRANGLER

engine type	: petrol, v6		**kerb weight**	: 1706 kg
displacement	: 3778 cc		**towing weight**	: n.a.
max. power	: 153 kW (204 bhp)		**boot space**	: 490 l
@	: 5200 rpm		**fuel capacity**	: n.a.
max. torque	: 240 lb ft		**consumption**	: n.a.
@	: 4000 rpm		**acc. 0-62 mph**	: n.a.
gears	: 6		**top speed**	: n.a.
AT	: optional 4-speed automatic		**EuroNCAP**	: n.a.
drive	: 4WD		**introduction**	: January 2007
brakes f/r	: vent. discs / discs		**last revised in**	: -
body type	: 3-dr. SUV		**warranty**	: 2 years
l x w x h	: 3881 x 1872 x 1801 mm		**miscellaneous**	: New edition, now also available in
wheelbase	: 2423 mm			a 4-door version called Unlimited.
turning circle	: 10.6 m			Wranglers destined for Europe
				come either with a V6 petrol engine
				or 4-cylinder 2.8 CRD engine
				from the Chrysler Voyager.

JEEP CHEROKEE 2.4 / 3.7 V6

engine type	: petrol, inline-4 / V6		kerb weight	: 1717 / 1841 kg
displacement	: 2429 / 3701 cc		towing weight	: 2400 / 3360 kg
max. power	: 108 kW (147 bhp) /		boot space	: 820 - 1950 l
	150 kW (211 bhp)		fuel capacity	: 73 l
@	: 5200 rpm		consumption	: 25.8 / 23.2 mpg
max. torque	: 159 / 226 lb ft		acc. 0-62 mph	: 13.9 / 10.8 s
@	: 4000 rpm		top speed	: 102 / 112 mph
gears	: 5 / -		EuroNCAP	: 4 stars
AT	: - / optional 4-speed automatic		introduction	: September 2001
drive	: 4WD		last revised in	: January 2005
brakes f/r	: vent. discs / discs		warranty	: 2 years
body type	: 5-dr. SUV		miscellaneous	: Cherokee has less character than
l x w x h	: 4500 x 1820 x 1820 mm			its bigger brother, but is still quite
wheelbase	: 2650 mm			capable and fun to drive.
turning circle	: 11.5 m			

CHEROKEE 2.8 CRD

engine type	: diesel, inline-4
displacement	: 2776 cc
max. power	: 118 kW (160 bhp)
@	: 3800 rpm
max. torque	: 295 lb ft
@	: 1800 rpm
gears	: 5-speed automatic
kerb weight	: 1931 kg
towing weight	: 3360 kg
consumption	: 30.4 mpg
acc. 0-60 mph	: 12.6 s
top speed	: 108 mph
miscellaneous	: Diesel-powered Cherokee simply loves towing trailers.

JEEP GRAND CHEROKEE 4.7 V8 / 5.7 V8

engine type	: petrol, V8
displacement	: 4700 / 5654 cc
max. power	: 170 kW (231 bhp) / 240 kW (326 bhp)
@	: 4500 / 5000 rpm
max. torque	: 302 / 369 lb ft
@	: 3600 / 4000 rpm
gears	: -
AT	: 5-speed automatic
drive	: 4WD
brakes f/r	: vent. discs / discs
body type	: 5-dr. SUV
l x w x h	: 4750 x 2149 x 1740 mm
wheelbase	: 2780 mm
turning circle	: 11.2 m

kerb weight	: 2110 / 2150 kg
towing weight	: 3360 kg
boot space	: 978 - 1908 l
fuel capacity	: 79 l
consumption	: 19 / 18.3 mpg
acc. 0-62 mph	: 8.8 / 7.1 s
top speed	: 124 / 129 mph
EuroNCAP	: n.a.
introduction	: March 2005
last revised in	: -
warranty	: 2 years
miscellaneous	: With a big HEMI V8 engine under the bonnet, even this heavyweight turns into an agile performer. Not the best on-road behaviour though, but it really shines off road. Also available with a 218 bhp strong 3.0-litre diesel engine from Mercedes-Benz.

GRAND CHEROKEE SRT-8

engine type	: petrol, V8
displacement	: 6059 cc
max. power	: 313 kW (426 bhp)
@	: 6000 rpm
max. torque	: 420 lb ft
@	: 4600 rpm
gears	: 5-speed automatic
kerb weight	: 2220 kg
towing weight	: n.a.
consumption	: 17.2 mpg
acc. 0-60 mph	: 5.0 s
top speed	: 152 mph
miscellaneous	: Almost as capable as a Porsche Cayenne Turbo, but rather less costly.

JEEP COMMANDER 3.0 CRD

engine type	: diesel, V6	kerb weight	: 2315 kg
displacement	: 2987 cc	towing weight	: 3500 kg
max. power	: 160 kW (218 bhp)	boot space	: 212 - 1940 l
@	: 4000 rpm	fuel capacity	: 77 l
max. torque	: 376 lb ft	consumption	: 26.2 mpg
@	: 1600 rpm	acc. 0-62 mph	: 9.0 s
gears	: n.a.	top speed	: 118 mph
AT	: 5-speed automatic	EuroNCAP	: n.a.
drive	: 4WD	introduction	: Spring 2006
brakes f/r	: vent. discs / discs	last revised in	: -
body type	: 5-dr. SUV	warranty	: 2 years
l x w x h	: 4787 x 1900 x 1826 mm	miscellaneous	: Also available with 4.7 V8 and
wheelbase	: 2780 mm		5.7 V8 engines. Bigger and tougher
turning circle	: 11.8 m		than Grand Cherokee.

JMC LANDWIND 2.0 l / 2.4 l

engine type	: petrol, inline-4	kerb weight	: 1750 kg
displacement	: 1997 / 2351 cc	towing weight	: 2380 kg
max. power	: 84 kW (115 bhp) / 92 kW (125 bhp)	boot space	: n.a.
@	: 5500 / 5200 rpm	fuel capacity	: n.a.
max. torque	: 120 / 144 lb ft	consumption	: 33.4 / 31.5 mpg
@	: 3500 / 3000 rpm	acc. 0-62 mph	: n.a.
gears	: 5	top speed	: 99 / 109 mph
AT	: -	EuroNCAP	: -
drive	: 4WD	introduction	: Summer 2005
brakes f/r	: n.a.	last revised in	: -
body type	: 5-dr. SUV	warranty	: 2 years
l x w x h	: 4745 x 1800 x 1750 mm	miscellaneous	: Biggest petrol version also
wheelbase	: 2760 mm		available with 4WD. Sales of
turning circle	: 11.6 m		Landwind suffer from its alleged
			poor crashworthiness in
			German crash tests.

JMC LANDWIND 2.8 T

engine type	: diesel, inline-4
displacement	: 2771 cc
max. power	: 68 kW (92 bhp)
@	: 3600 rpm
max. torque	: 155 lb ft
@	: 2300 rpm
gears	: 5
kerb weight	: 1830 kg
towing weight	: 2265 kg
consumption	: 40.5 mpg
acc. 0-60 mph	: n.a.
top speed	: 90 mph
miscellaneous	: With an old and sluggish engine under the bonnet, the diesel-powered Landwind can hardly keep up with modern-day traffic.

KIA PICANTO 1.0

engine type	: petrol, inline-4	kerb weight	: 836 kg
displacement	: 999 cc	towing weight	: 700 kg
max. power	: 45 kW (61 bhp)	boot space	: 157 - 882 l
@	: 5600 rpm	fuel capacity	: 35 l
max. torque	: 64 lb ft	consumption	: 55.4 mpg
@	: 2800 rpm	acc. 0-62 mph	: 16.4 s
gears	: 5	top speed	: 93 mph
AT	: -	EuroNCAP	: n.a.
drive	: FWD	introduction	: February 2004
brakes f/r	: vent. discs / drum brakes	last revised in	: -
body type	: 5-dr. hatchback	warranty	: 3 years
l x w x h	: 3495 x 1595 x 1480 mm	miscellaneous	: Kind of a Korean Fiat Panda and
wheelbase	: 2370 mm		like its Italian rival very successful.
turning circle	: 9.2 m		Looks best in bright colours. Also
			available with 65 bhp 1.1 petrol
			engine and 4-speed automatic
			transmission.

PICANTO 1.1 CRDI VGT

engine type	: diesel, inline-3
displacement	: 1120 cc
max. power	: 55 kW (75 bhp)
@	: 4000 rpm
max. torque	: 113 lb ft
@	: 1900 rpm
gears	: 5
kerb weight	: 945 kg
towing weight	: 700 kg
consumption	: 64.5 mpg
acc. 0-60 mph	: n.a.
top speed	: 101 mph
miscellaneous	: Quick and economical car.

KIA RIO 1.4 / 1.6

engine type	: petrol, inline-4
displacement	: 1399 / 1599 cc
max. power	: 71 kW (97 bhp) / 82 kW (112 bhp)
@	: 6000 rpm
max. torque	: 92 / 108 lb ft
@	: 4700 / 4500 rpm
gears	: 5
AT	: - / optional 4-speed
drive	: FWD
brakes f/r	: vent. discs / discs
body type	: 5-dr. hatchback
l x w x h	: 3990 x 1695 x 1470 mm
wheelbase	: 2500 mm
turning circle	: 10.1 m

kerb weight	: 1154 / 1175 kg
towing weight	: 1100 kg
boot space	: 272 - 1107 l
fuel capacity	: 45 l
consumption	: 44.8 / 43.6 mpg
acc. 0-62 mph	: 12.3 / 10.2 s
top speed	: 110 / 117 mph
EuroNCAP	: n.a.
introduction	: Autumn 2005
last revised in	: -
warranty	: 3 years
miscellaneous	: New edition is totally different from previous Rio model. Well-built hatchback with European styling cues.

RIO 1.5 CRDi

engine type	: diesel, inline-4
displacement	: 1493 cc
max. power	: 81 kW (110 bhp)
@	: 4000 rpm
max. torque	: 173 lb ft
@	: 1900 rpm
gears	: 5
kerb weight	: 1221 kg
towing weight	: 1636 / 1811 kg
consumption	: 60.1 mpg
acc. 0-60 mph	: 11.5 s
top speed	: 110 mph
miscellaneous	: Fine diesel engine.

KIA CERATO 1.6 16V / 2.0 CVVT

engine type	: petrol, inline-4		**kerb weight**	: 1153 / 1220 kg
displacement	: 1599 / 1975 cc		**towing weight**	: 1200 / 1400 kg
max. power	: 77 kW (105 bhp) /		**boot space**	: 345 - 1494 l
	105 kW (143 bhp)		**fuel capacity**	: 55 l
@	: 5800 / 6000 rpm		**consumption**	: 40.4 / 37.7 mpg
max. torque	: 105 / 138 lb ft		**acc. 0-62 mph**	: 11 / 9 s
@	: 4500 rpm		**top speed**	: 115 / 129 mph
gears	: 5		**EuroNCAP**	: n.a.
AT	: - / optional 4-speed		**introduction**	: April 2004
drive	: FWD		**last revised in**	: -
brakes f/r	: vent. discs / discs		**warranty**	: 3 years
body type	: 5-dr. hatchback		**miscellaneous**	: Car with European looks and fine
l x w x h	: 4480 x 1735 x 1470 mm			driving characteristics. Deserves
wheelbase	: 2610 mm			more success. Also available as
turning circle	: 10.1 m			4-door saloon.

CERATO 1.6 CRDI VGT

engine type	: diesel, inline-4
displacement	: 1582 cc
max. power	: 85 kW (115 bhp)
@	: 4000 rpm
max. torque	: 174 lb ft
@	: 2000 rpm
gears	: 5
kerb weight	: 1254 kg
towing weight	: 1200 kg
consumption	: 57.6 mpg
acc. 0-60 mph	: n.a.
top speed	: 107 mph
miscellaneous	: New diesel engine makes its first appearance in the Cerato.

KIA CARENS 2.0

engine type	: petrol, inline-4
displacement	: 1997 cc
max. power	: 106 kW (144 bhp)
@	: 6000 rpm
max. torque	: 139 lb ft
@	: 4250 rpm
gears	: 5
AT	: optional 5-speed
drive	: FWD
brakes f/r	: vent. discs / discs
body type	: 5-dr. MPV
l x w x h	: 4545 x 1820 x 1650 mm
wheelbase	: 2700 mm
turning circle	: 10.8 m

kerb weight	: 1563 kg
towing weight	: n.a.
boot space	: 400 – 2106 l
fuel capacity	: 62 l
consumption	: 29.7 mpg
acc. 0-62 mph	: 10.8 s
top speed	: 118 mph
EuroNCAP	: n.a.
introduction	: August 2006
last revised in	: -
warranty	: 3 years
miscellaneous	: Carens now available as a 7-seater. Not a very innovative car, but it offers good value for money.

CARENS 2.0 CRDI

engine type	: diesel, inline-4
displacement	: 1991 cc
max. power	: 99 kW (135 bhp)
@	: 4000 rpm
max. torque	: 225 lb ft
@	: 1800 rpm
gears	: 6, optional 4-speed automatic
kerb weight	: 1619 kg
towing weight	: n.a.
consumption	: 42.8 mpg
acc. 0-60 mph	: 10.8 s
top speed	: 116 mph
miscellaneous	: Carens model range also includes a diesel-powered version, an engine we are already familiar with.

KIA SEDONA 2.7 V6

engine type	: petrol, V6
displacement	: 2656 cc
max. power	: 139 kW (189 bhp)
@	: 6000 rpm
max. torque	: 184 lb ft
@	: 4000 rpm
gears	: 5
AT	: optional 4-speed
drive	: FWD
brakes f/r	: vent. discs / drum brakes
body type	: 5-dr. MPV
l x w x h	: 4810 x 1985 x 1815 mm
wheelbase	: 2890 mm
turning circle	: 11.0 m

kerb weight	: 1924 kg
towing weight	: 2000 kg
boot space	: 364 l
fuel capacity	: 80 l
consumption	: 26.5 mpg
acc. 0-62 mph	: n.a.
top speed	: 117 mph
EuroNCAP	: n.a.
introduction	: May 2006
last revised in	: -
warranty	: 3 years
miscellaneous	: Updated Sedona positioned higher in the market now, in order to make room for the new Carens.

SEDONA 2.9 CRDI VGT

engine type	: diesel, inline-4
displacement	: 2902 cc
max. power	: 136 kW (185 bhp)
@	: 3800 rpm
max. torque	: 253 lb ft
@	: 2000 rpm
gears	: 5, optional 5-speed automatic
kerb weight	: 2068 kg
towing weight	: 2000 kg
consumption	: 36.4 mpg
acc. 0-60 mph	: n.a.
top speed	: 122 mph
miscellaneous	: Diesel-engined version still most economical choice, as with previous Sedona. But frankly, it is also the best of the range.

KIA MAGENTIS 2.0 / 2.7 V6

engine type	: petrol, inline-4 / V6	kerb weight	: 1383 / 1465 kg
displacement	: 1998 / 2656 cc	towing weight	: 1700 kg
max. power	: 106 kW (145 bhp) /	boot space	: 420 l
	138 kW (188 bhp)	fuel capacity	: 62 l
@	: 6000 rpm	consumption	: 36.7 / 30.7 mpg
max. torque	: 139 / 182 lb ft	acc. 0-62 mph	: 10.2 / 9.1 s
@	: 4250 / 4000 rpm	top speed	: 129 / 137 mph
gears	: 5 / -	EuroNCAP	: n.a.
AT	: - / optional 4-speed automatic	introduction	: February 2006
drive	: FWD	last revised in	: -
brakes f/r	: vent. discs / discs	warranty	: 3 years
body type	: 4-dr. saloon	miscellaneous	: New Magentis shares DNA with
l x w x h	: 4735 x 1805 x 1480 mm		Hyundai Sonata. Much better-
wheelbase	: 2720 mm		looking than predecessor.
turning circle	: 10.8 m		

MAGENTIS 2.0 CRDI

engine type	: diesel, inline-4
displacement	: 1991 cc
max. power	: 103 kW (140 bhp)
@	: 4000 rpm
max. torque	: 224 lb ft
@	: 1800 rpm
gears	: 6, optional 4-speed automatic
kerb weight	: 1500 kg
towing weight	: 1700 kg
consumption	: 47.1 mpg
acc. 0-60 mph	: n.a.
top speed	: 125 mph
miscellaneous	: Diesel engine already familiar from
	Hyundai, but upgraded recently
	with a turbo with variable geometry.

KIA OPIRUS

engine type	: petrol, V6	**kerb weight**	: 1675 kg
displacement	: 3778 cc	**towing weight**	: n.a.
max. power	: 166 kW (266 bhp)	**boot space**	: 450 l
@	: 6000 rpm	**fuel capacity**	: 70 l
max. torque	: 260 lb ft	**consumption**	: 26 mpg
@	: 4500 rpm	**acc. 0-62 mph**	: 7.5 s
gears	: -	**top speed**	: 143 mph
AT	: 5-speed automatic	**EuroNCAP**	: n.a.
drive	: FWD	**introduction**	: August 2003
brakes f/r	: vent. discs / discs	**last revised in**	: January 2007
body type	: 4-dr. saloon	**warranty**	: 3 years
l x w x h	: 4979 x 1850 x 1486 mm	**miscellaneous**	: Opirus benefits from new facelift
wheelbase	: 2800 mm		with more rounded lines. Much
turning circle	: 11.0 m		lighter, therefore faster and more
			economical.

KIA SPORTAGE 2.0 / 2.7 V6

engine type	: petrol, inline-4 / V6	kerb weight	: 1442 / 1570 kg
displacement	: 1998 / 2656 cc	towing weight	: 1400 / 1600 kg
max. power	: 104 kW (141 bhp) /	boot space	: 667 - 1886 l
	129 kW (179 bhp)	fuel capacity	: 58 / 65 l
@	: 6000 rpm	consumption	: 34.4 / 28.2 mpg
max. torque	: 136 / 178 lb ft	acc. 0-62 mph	: 10.4 / 10.5 s
@	: 4500 / 4000 rpm	top speed	: 112 / 104 mph
gears	: 5 / -	EuroNCAP	: n.a.
AT	: optional 4-speed automatic /	introduction	: September 2004
	4-speed automatic	last revised in	: -
drive	: FWD, optional 4WD	warranty	: 3 years
brakes f/r	: vent. discs / discs	miscellaneous	: Twin brother of Hyundai Tucson
body type	: 5-dr. SUV		and just as successful. Another Kia
l x w x h	: 4350 x 1800 x 1700 mm		hit after the Sorento.
wheelbase	: 2630 mm		
turning circle	: 10.8 m		

SPORTAGE 2.0 CRDI VGT

engine type	: diesel, inline-4
displacement	: 1991 cc
max. power	: 103 kW (140 bhp)
@	: 4000 rpm
max. torque	: 224 lb ft
@	: 1800 rpm
gears	: 6
kerb weight	: 1565 kg
towing weight	: 1400 kg
consumption	: 39.8 mpg
acc. 0-60 mph	: 12.0 s
top speed	: 104 mph
miscellaneous	: Diesel version now boasts
	more horsepower.

KIA SORENTO 3.3 V6

engine type	: petrol, V6	kerb weight	: n.a.
displacement	: 3342 cc	towing weight	: n.a.
max. power	: 177 kW (241 bhp)	boot space	: 486 - 1849 l
@	: 6000 rpm	fuel capacity	: 80 l
max. torque	: 216 lb ft	consumption	: n.a.
@	: 4500 rpm	acc. 0-62 mph	: 9.2 s
gears	: n.a.	top speed	: 118 mph
AT	: 5-speed automatic	EuroNCAP	: n.a.
drive	: 4WD	introduction	: May 2002
brakes f/r	: vent. discs / discs	last revised in	: January 2007
body type	: 5-dr. SUV	warranty	: 3 years
l x w x h	: 4567 x 1863 x 1724 mm	miscellaneous	: Still a very interesting proposition in a crowded segment, but overtaken by rivals in terms of looks and dynamic behaviour.
wheelbase	: 2710 mm		
turning circle	: 11.1 m		

SORENTO 2.5 CRDI VGT

engine type	: diesel, inline-4
displacement	: 2497 cc
max. power	: 125 kW (170 bhp)
@	: 3800 rpm
max. torque	: 289 lb ft
@	: 2000 rpm
gears	: 5, optional 5-speed automatic
kerb weight	: n.a.
towing weight	: n.a.
consumption	: 35.8 mpg
acc. 0-60 mph	: 12.0 s
top speed	: 104 mph
miscellaneous	: Bestseller of Sorento range, with delivery times of one year and more at the height of its success, but car begins to lose ground now.

KOENIGSEGG CCX

engine type	: petrol, V8	kerb weight	: 1180 kg
displacement	: 4700 cc	towing weight	: -
max. power	: 600 kW (816 bhp)	boot space	: 120 l
@	: 6900 rpm	fuel capacity	: 70 l
max. torque	: 678 lb ft	consumption	: 16.7 mpg
@	: 5700 rpm	acc. 0-62 mph	: 3.2 s
gears	: 6	top speed	: > 245 mph
AT	: -	EuroNCAP	: n.a.
drive	: RWD	introduction	: May 2004
brakes f/r	: vent. discs	last revised in	: March 2006
body type	: 2-dr. coupe	warranty	: n.a.
l x w x h	: 4293 x 1996 x 1120 mm	miscellaneous	: American legislation forced Koenigsegg to adapt its CCR model, resulting in CCX. Less expensive alternative to Bugatti Veyron.
wheelbase	: 2660 mm		
turning circle	: 11.0 m		

LADA 110 8V / 16V

engine type	: petrol, inline-4
displacement	: 1499 cc
max. power	: 59 kW (80 bhp) / 66 kW (90 bhp)
@	: 5200 / 5000 rpm
max. torque	: 89 / 97 lb ft
@	: 3000 / 3700 rpm
gears	: 5
AT	: -
drive	: FWD
brakes f/r	: vent. discs / drum brakes
body type	: 4-dr. saloon / 5-dr. stationwagon
l x w x h	: 4265 x 1680 x 1420 mm
wheelbase	: 2492 mm
turning circle	: 11.0 m

kerb weight	: 995 / 1015 kg
towing weight	: 1000 kg
boot space	: 415 - 1270 l
fuel capacity	: 43 l
consumption	: 38.9 / 38.3 mpg
acc. 0-62 mph	: 14 / 12 s
top speed	: 104 / 115 mph
EuroNCAP	: n.a.
introduction	: October 1999
last revised in	: -
warranty	: 2 years
miscellaneous	: Sales very disappointing. Car almost as rare as a Ferrari. Also available as a stationwagon, called 111.

112 16V

engine type	: petrol, inline-4
displacement	: 1499 cc
max. power	: 67 kW (90 bhp)
@	: 5600 rpm
max. torque	: 97 lb ft
@	: 3700 rpm
gears	: 5
kerb weight	: 1060 kg
towing weight	: 1000 kg
consumption	: 38.3 mpg
acc. 0-60 mph	: n.a.
top speed	: 115 mph
miscellaneous	: Hatchback version of Lada 110, also available with 80 bhp 8V engine. 16V versions have power steering.

LADA NIVA

engine type	: petrol, inline-4	**kerb weight**	: 1210 kg
displacement	: 1690 cc	**towing weight**	: 1500 kg
max. power	: 60 kW (82 bhp)	**boot space**	: 265 - 982 l
@	: 5000 rpm	**fuel capacity**	: 45 l
max. torque	: 95 lb ft	**consumption**	: 24.9 mpg
@	: 4000 rpm	**acc. 0-62 mph**	: 19.0 s
gears	: 5	**top speed**	: 85 mph
AT	: -	**EuroNCAP**	: n.a.
drive	: 4WD	**introduction**	: 1977
brakes f/r	: vent. discs / drum brakes	**last revised in**	: -
body type	: 3-dr. SUV	**warranty**	: 2 years
l x w x h	: 3720 x 1680 x 1640 mm	**miscellaneous**	: A prehistoric but durable and
wheelbase	: 2200 mm		charismatic car with offroad
turning circle	: 11.0 m		capability. Old bone-shaker
			that approaches cult car status.

LAMBORGHINI GALLARDO

engine type	: petrol, V10		**kerb weight**	: 1430 kg
displacement	: 5000 cc		**towing weight**	: -
max. power	: 383 kW (520 bhp)		**boot space**	: 110 l
@	: 7800 rpm		**fuel capacity**	: 90 l
max. torque	: 376 lb ft		**consumption**	: 14.5 mpg
@	: 4500 rpm		**acc. 0-62 mph**	: 3.9 s
gears	: 6		**top speed**	: 197 mph
AT	: optional 6-speed seq.		**EuroNCAP**	: n.a.
drive	: RWD		**introduction**	: January 2004
brakes f/r	: vent. discs		**last revised in**	: -
body type	: 2-dr. coupe - convertible		**warranty**	: 2 years
l x w x h	: 4300 x 1900 x 1165 mm		**miscellaneous**	: Also available as Special Edition
wheelbase	: 2560 mm			with a fixed roof in black. Roadster
turning circle	: 11.5 m			version offers similar performance
				with a foldable roof.

LAMBORGHINI MURCIÉLAGO / LP640

engine type	: petrol, V12	kerb weight	: 1650 kg
displacement	: 6192 / 6496 cc	towing weight	: -
max. power	: 426 kW (580 bhp) /	boot space	: 140 l
	471 kW (640 bhp)	fuel capacity	: 100 l
@	: 7500 / 8000 rpm	consumption	: 13.2 / 13.3 mpg
max. torque	: 479 / 486 lb ft	acc. 0-62 mph	: 3.8 / 3.4 s
@	: 5400 / 6000 rpm	top speed	: 205 / 211 mph
gears	: 6	EuroNCAP	: n.a.
AT	: optional 6-speed seq.	introduction	: January 2002
drive	: RWD	last revised in	: -
brakes f/r	: vent. discs	warranty	: 2 years
body type	: 2-dr. coupe - convertible	miscellaneous	: Latest addition is the wild LP640.
l x w x h	: 4580 x 2045 x 1140 mm		Murciélago also available as
wheelbase	: 2665 mm		Roadster, equally hot-tempered as
turning circle	: 12.5 m		the rest of the model range.

LANCIA YPSILON 1.2 / 1.2 16V

engine type	: petrol, inline-4
displacement	: 1242 cc
max. power	: 44 kW (60 bhp) / 59 kW (80 bhp)
@	: 5000 rpm
max. torque	: 75 / 84 lb ft
@	: 2500 / 4000 rpm
gears	: 5
AT	: -
drive	: FWD
brakes f/r	: discs / drum brakes
body type	: 3-dr. hatchback
l x w x h	: 3778 x 1704 x 1530 mm
wheelbase	: 2388 mm
turning circle	: 9.6 m

kerb weight	: 945 / 975 kg
towing weight	: 900 kg
boot space	: 215 – 910 l
fuel capacity	: 47 l
consumption	: 47.3 mpg
acc. 0-62 mph	: 16.8 / 11.2 s
top speed	: 95 / 108 mph
EuroNCAP	: n.a.
introduction	: October 2003
last revised in	: -
warranty	: 2 years
miscellaneous	: Best choice in this segment for those who value style and luxury. Drivetrain and equipment up-to-date. Also available as Bi-colore, with two-tone paintwork.

YPSILON 1.4 16V

engine type	: petrol, inline-4
displacement	: 1368 cc
max. power	: 70 kW (95 bhp)
@	: 5800 rpm
max. torque	: 95 lb ft
@	: 4500 rpm
gears	: 5
kerb weight	: 980 kg
towing weight	: 900 kg
consumption	: 43 mpg
acc. 0-60 mph	: 10.9 s
top speed	: 109 mph
miscellaneous	: Quick little car with responsive steering and strong performance. Echoes Lancia's past as a builder of sporty cars.

YPSILON 1.3 MULTIJET

engine type	: diesel, inline-4
displacement	: 1248 cc
max. power	: 51 kW (70 bhp)
@	: 4000 rpm
max. torque	: 140 lb ft
@	: 1750 rpm
gears	: 5
kerb weight	: 1045 kg
towing weight	: 900 kg
consumption	: 61.7 mpg
acc. 0-60 mph	: 15.1 s
top speed	: 103 mph
miscellaneous	: Lively diesel-powered version, very popular in mediterranean countries.

LANCIA MUSA 1.3 / 1.9 MULTIJET

engine type	: petrol, inline-4	kerb weight	: 1155 kg
displacement	: 1368 cc	towing weight	: 1100 kg
max. power	: 70 kW (95 bhp)	boot space	: 320 - 1420 l
@	: 5800 rpm	fuel capacity	: 47 l
max. torque	: 94 lb ft	consumption	: 43 mpg
@	: 4500 rpm	acc. 0-62 mph	: 11.5 s
gears	: 5	top speed	: 109 mph
AT	: -	EuroNCAP	: n.a.
drive	: FWD	introduction	: June 2004
brakes f/r	: discs / discs	last revised in	: -
body type	: 5-dr. MPV	warranty	: 2 years
l x w x h	: 3985 x 1698 x 1688 mm	miscellaneous	: More distinctive variation on Fiat
wheelbase	: 2508 mm		Idea, especially on the inside. Both
turning circle	: 10.4 m		diesel engines are economical and
			lively performers.

MUSA 1.4 16V

engine type	: diesel, inline-4
displacement	: 1248 / 1910 cc
max. power	: 51 kW (70 bhp) / 74 kW (100 bhp)
@	: 4000 rpm
max. torque	: 148 / 155 lb ft
@	: 1750 rpm
gears	: 5
kerb weight	: 1200 / 1275 kg
towing weight	: 1000 / 1100 kg
consumption	: 56.3 / 52.2 mpg
acc. 0-60 mph	: 15.4 / 11.5 s
top speed	: 99 / 112 mph
miscellaneous	: Petrol-engined version of Musa.
	8V petrol engine with 77 bhp also
	available.

LANCIA THESIS 2.4 / 3.0 V6

engine type	: petrol, inline-5 / V6		**kerb weight**	: 1685 / 1745 kg
displacement	: 2446 / 2959 cc		**towing weight**	: 1500 kg
max. power	: 125 kW (170 bhp) /		**boot space**	: 400 l
	158 kW (215 bhp)		**fuel capacity**	: 75 l
@	: 6000 / 6300 rpm		**consumption**	: 26.7 / 20.9 mpg
max. torque	: 167 / 194 lb ft		**acc. 0-62 mph**	: 9.5 / 9.2 s
@	: 3500 / 5000 rpm		**top speed**	: 135 / 145 mph
gears	: 6 / -		**EuroNCAP**	: n.a.
AT	: - / 5-speed automatic		**introduction**	: June 2002
drive	: FWD		**last revised in**	: -
brakes f/r	: vent. discs / discs		**warranty**	: 2 years
body type	: 4-dr. sedan		**miscellaneous**	: Too extreme for most executives,
l x w x h	: 4890 x 1830 x 1470 mm			therefore very exclusive. Good
wheelbase	: 2805 mm			looks, lots of charisma.
turning circle	: 12.2 m			Also available as 2.0 Turbo.

THESIS 3.2 V6

engine type	: petrol, V6
displacement	: 3.179 cc
max. power	: 169 kW (230 bhp)
@	: 6200 rpm
max. torque	: 289 lb ft
@	: 4800 rpm
gears	: 5-speed automatic
kerb weight	: 1820 kg
towing weight	: 1500 kg
consumption	: 19 mpg
acc. 0-60 mph	: 8.8 s
top speed	: 149 mph
miscellaneous	: Flagship of Thesis range performs marginally better than 3-litre model. Powerful, majestic and rare car.

THESIS 2.4 JTD 10V / 2.4 JTD 20V

engine type	: diesel, inline-5
displacement	: 2387 cc
max. power	: 110 kW (150 bhp) / 129 kW (175 bhp)
@	: 4000 rpm
max. torque	: 225 / 280 lb ft
@	: 1800 / 2000 rpm
gears	: 6 / optional 5-speed automatic
kerb weight	: 1715 / 1790 kg
towing weight	: 1500 kg
consumption	: 34.6 / 37.8 mpg
acc. 0-60 mph	: 10.1 / 9.8 s
top speed	: 128 / 140 mph
miscellaneous	: Spirited diesel engines with lots of horsepower and lots of torque. Expensive as a lease car because of high depreciation.

LANCIA PHEDRA 2.0 JTD 120 / 136

engine type	: petrol, inline-4	**kerb weight**	: 1660 / 1710 kg
displacement	: 1997 / 2179 cc	**towing weight**	: 1850 / 1850 kg
max. power	: 79 kW (108 bhp) / 94 kW (128 bhp)	**boot space**	: 324 – 2948 l
@	: 4000 rpm	**fuel capacity**	: 80 l
max. torque	: 199 / 232 lb ft	**consumption**	: 39.4 / 38.3 mpg
@	: 1750 / 2000 rpm	**acc. 0-62 mph**	: 13.4 / 12.6 s
gears	: 5	**top speed**	: 108 / 113 mph
AT	: -	**EuroNCAP**	: 5 stars
drive	: FWD	**introduction**	: June 2002
brakes f/r	: vent. discs / discs	**last revised in**	: -
body type	: 5-dr. MPV	**warranty**	: 2 years
l x w x h	: 4750 x 1863 x 1752 mm	**miscellaneous**	: MPV with style, grace and space.
wheelbase	: 2823 mm		Far more stylish than C8, 807 and
turning circle	: 10.9 m		Ulysse sister models.

LAND ROVER FREELANDER 3.2

engine type	: petrol, inline-6	kerb weight	: 1770 kg
displacement	: 3192 cc	towing weight	: 2000 kg
max. power	: 171 kW (233 bhp)	boot space	: 755 - 1670 l
@	: 6300 rpm	fuel capacity	: 59 l
max. torque	: 234 lb ft	consumption	: 24.5 mpg
@	: 3200 rpm	acc. 0-62 mph	: 8.9 s
gears	: -	top speed	: 124 mph
AT	: 6-speed	EuroNCAP	: n.a.
drive	: 4WD	introduction	: late 2006
brakes f/r	: vent. discs/ discs	last revised in	: -
body type	: 5-dr. SUV	warranty	: 3 years
l x w x h	: 4500 x 1910 x 1740 mm	miscellaneous	: New Freelander more of a sports utility than offroad vehicle. Better built now, but also rather more expensive than previous model.
wheelbase	: 2660 mm		
turning circle	: n.a.		

FREELANDER TD4

engine type	: diesel, inline-4
displacement	: 2179 cc
max. power	: 118 kW (160 bhp)
@	: 4000 rpm
max. torque	: 295 lb ft
@	: 2000 tpm
gears	: 6, optional 6-speed automatic
kerb weight	: 1770 kg
towing weight	: 2000 kg
consumption	: 37.8 mpg
acc. 0-60 mph	: 11.7 s
top speed	: 113 mph
miscellaneous	: With its diesel engine from Ford, TD4 model is destined to become the bestseller of the Freelander range.

LAND ROVER DEFENDER 90 / 110 TD5

engine type	: diesel, inline-5	kerb weight	: 1695 / 1870 kg
displacement	: 2495 cc	towing weight	: 3500 kg
max. power	: 90 kW (122 bhp)	boot space	: 1600 / 2300 l
@	: 4200 rpm	fuel capacity	: 60 / 75 l
max. torque	: 221 lb ft	consumption	: 28.2 mpg
@	: 1950 rpm	acc. 0-62 mph	: 16.8 / 18.8 s
gears	: 5	top speed	: 87 mph
AT	: -	EuroNCAP	: n.a.
drive	: 4WD	introduction	: January 1991
brakes f/r	: vent. discs/ drum brakes	last revised in	: November 2002
body type	: 3-, 5-dr. SUV	warranty	: 3 years
l x w x h	: 3883 / 4599 x 1790 x 1963 / 2035 mm	miscellaneous	: New diesel engine for updated Defender was borrowed from Ford Transit.
wheelbase	: 2360 / 2794 mm		
turning circle	: 12.3 / 12.8 m		

LAND ROVER DISCOVERY TDV6 / V8

engine type	: diesel, V6 / petrol, V8
displacement	: 2720 / 4394 cc
max. power	: 140 kW (190 bhp) /
	220 kW (300 bhp)
@	: 4000 / 5500 rpm
max. torque	: 324 / 314 lb ft
@	: 1900 / 4000 rpm
gears	: 6
AT	: optional 6-speed / 6-speed
drive	: 4WD
brakes f/r	: vent. discs/ discs
body type	: 5-dr. SUV
l x w x h	: 4835 x 2190 x 1887 mm
wheelbase	: 2885 mm
turning circle	: 11.5 m

kerb weight	: 2394 / 2436 kg
towing weight	: 3500 kg
boot space	: 280 - 2558 l
fuel capacity	: 82 / 86 l
consumption	: 30.1 / 18.8 mpg
acc. 0-62 mph	: 11.5 / 8.6 s
top speed	: 112 / 121 mph
EuroNCAP	: n.a.
introduction	: May 2004
last revised in	: -
warranty	: 3 years
miscellaneous	: Multi-talent. Unsurpassed offroad performance, but onroad driving characteristics fine too. Fresh, modern looks.

LAND ROVER RANGE ROVER SPORT V8 SUPERCHARGED

engine type	: petrol, V8		kerb weight	: 2550 / 2624 kg
displacement	: 4394 / 4196 cc		towing weight	: 3500 kg
max. power	: 225 kW (306 bhp) / 291 kW (396 bhp)		boot space	: 535 – 2091 l
			fuel capacity	: 100 l
@	: 5750 / 5750 rpm		consumption	: 27.7 / 17.8 mpg
max. torque	: 324 / 413 lb ft		acc. 0-62 mph	: 8.7 / 7.5 s
@	: 4000 / 4000 rpm		top speed	: 120 / 140 mph
gears	: -		EuroNCAP	: n.a.
AT	: 6-speed		introduction	: late 2002
drive	: 4WD		last revised in	: -
brakes f/r	: vent. discs/ vent. discs		warranty	: 3 years
body type	: 5-dr. SUV		miscellaneous	: Fabulous SUV, less blatant than flashy Cayenne and X5. German rivals are better performers though.
l x w x h	: 4950 x 2009 x 1863 mm			
wheelbase	: 2880 mm			
turning circle	: 11.6 m			

RANGE ROVER SPORT TDV6

engine type	: diesel, V8
displacement	: 3600 cc
max. power	: 200 kW (272 bhp)
@	: n.a.
max. torque	: 472 lb ft
@	: 2000 rpm
gears	: 6-speed
kerb weight	: n.a.
towing weight	: 3500 kg
consumption	: 24.5 mpg
acc. 0-60 mph	: 9.2 s
top speed	: 124 mph
miscellaneous	: At last, diesel power that is befitting for this model. Will find its way to other models too.

LAND ROVER RANGE ROVER 4.4 V8 / V8 SUPERCHARGED

engine type	: petrol, V8		**kerb weight**	: 2572 kg
displacement	: 4197 cc		**towing weight**	: 3500 kg
max. power	: 287 kW (390 bhp)		**boot space**	: 960 / 2013 l
@	: 5750 rpm		**fuel capacity**	: 88 l
max. torque	: 405 lb ft		**consumption**	: 17.8 mpg
@	: 3500 rpm		**acc. 0-62 mph**	: 7.2 s
gears	: -		**top speed**	: 140 mph
AT	: 6-speed		**EuroNCAP**	: -
drive	: 4WD		**introduction**	: March 2005
brakes f/r	: vent. discs / vent. discs		**last revised in**	: -
body type	: 5-dr. SUV		**warranty**	: 3 years
l x w x h	: 4788 x 1928 x 1817		**miscellaneous**	: Sporting version of Range Rover,
wheelbase	: 2745 mm			yet based on Discovery model.
turning circle	: 11.6 m			Also available without supercharger.

RANGE ROVER TDV8

engine type	: diesel, V6
displacement	: 2720 cc
max. power	: 140 kW (190 bhp)
@	: 4000 rpm
max. torque	: 324 lb ft
@	: 1900 rpm
gears	: 6-speed
kerb weight	: 2455 kg
towing weight	: 3500 kg
consumption	: 30.1 mpg
acc. 0-60 mph	: 12.7 s
top speed	: 112 mph
miscellaneous	: Performance of TDV6 engine not in keeping with Sport nomenclature. Thrifty alternative to thirsty V8 engines.

LEXUS IS 250

engine type	: petrol, V6
displacement	: 2500 cc
max. power	: 153 kW (208 bhp)
@	: 6400 rpm
max. torque	: 186 lb ft
@	: 4800 rpm
gears	: 6
AT	: optional 6-speed
drive	: RWD
brakes f/r	: vent. discs/ discs
body type	: 4-dr. saloon
l x w x h	: 4575 x 1800 x 1440 mm
wheelbase	: 2730 mm
turning circle	: 10.2 m

kerb weight	: 1570 kg
towing weight	: 1500 kg
boot space	: 378 l
fuel capacity	: 65 l
consumption	: 28.8 mpg
acc. 0-62 mph	: 8.1 s
top speed	: 144 mph
EuroNCAP	: n.a.
introduction	: December 2005
last revised in	: -
warranty	: 3 years
miscellaneous	: Lexus is obviously looking to introduce a family look for its models, for car resembles new GS model. Smallest Lexus to compete with 3-series, A4 and C-class. More engines on their way.

IS 220d

engine type	: diesel, inline-4
displacement	: 2231 cc
max. power	: 130 kW (177 bhp)
@	: 3600 rpm
max. torque	: 295 lb ft
@	: 2000 rpm
gears	: 6
kerb weight	: 1585 kg
towing weight	: 1500 kg
consumption	: 44.8 mpg
acc. 0-60 mph	: 8.9 s
top speed	: 134 mph
miscellaneous	: Serious competition for established European contenders. Lovely diesel engine, ecological too.

LEXUS GS 300 / GS 450H

engine type	: petrol, V6		**kerb weight**	: 1695 / 1865 kg
displacement	: 2995 / 3456 cc		**towing weight**	: 2000 kg
max. power	: 183 kW (249 bhp) /		**boot space**	: 430 l
	218 kW (296 bhp)		**fuel capacity**	: 71 / 65 l
@	: 6200 / 6400 rpm		**consumption**	: 28.8 / 35.8 mpg
max. torque	: 228 / 272 lb ft		**acc. 0-62 mph**	: 7.2 / 5.9 s
@	: 3500 / 4800 rpm		**top speed**	: 148 / 155 mph
gears	: -		**EuroNCAP**	: 5 stars
AT	: 6-speed		**introduction**	: February 2005
drive	: RWD		**last revised in**	: -
brakes f/r	: vent. discs		**warranty**	: 3 years
body type	: 4-dr. saloon		**miscellaneous**	: GS 430 was replaced by hybrid
l x w x h	: 4820 x 1820 x 1425 mm			GS 450h. V8 power available by
wheelbase	: 2850 mm			special order.
turning circle	: 10.4 m			

LEXUS LS 460

engine type	: petrol, V8		kerb weight	: 1945 kg
displacement	: 4608 / 5001 cc		towing weight	: 2000 kg
max. power	: 280 kW (380 bhp) /		boot space	: 510 l
	317 kW (430 bhp)		fuel capacity	: 84 l
@	: 6400 rpm		consumption	: 25.6 mpg
max. torque	: 364 lb ft		acc. 0-62 mph	: 5.7 s
@	: 4100 rpm		top speed	: 155 mph
gears	: -		EuroNCAP	: n.a.
AT	: 8-speed		introduction	: autumn 2006
drive	: RWD		last revised in	: -
brakes f/r	: vent. discs		warranty	: 3 years
body type	: 4-dr. saloon		miscellaneous	: Limousine of the highest order.
l x w x h	: 5030 x 1875 x 1465 mm			Hybrid LS 600h version a likewise
wheelbase	: 2970 mm			fine proposition in luxury saloon
turning circle	: 10.8 m			market.

LEXUS SC 430

engine type	: petrol, V8	kerb weight	: 1740 kg
displacement	: 4293 cc	towing weight	: -
max. power	: 210 kW (286 bhp)	boot space	: 135 - 450 l
@	: 5600 rpm	fuel capacity	: 75 l
max. torque	: 309 lb ft	consumption	: 23.6 mpg
@	: 3500 rpm	acc. 0-62 mph	: 6.4 s
gears	: -	top speed	: 155 mph
AT	: 5-speed	EuroNCAP	: n.a.
drive	: RWD	introduction	: June 2001
brakes f/r	: vent. discs	last revised in	: November 2005
body type	: 2-dr. coupe, cabriolet	warranty	: 3 years
l x w x h	: 4515 x 1830 x 1370 mm	miscellaneous	: Fast, elegant car, particularly
wheelbase	: 2620 mm		successful in the United States.
turning circle	: 10.8 m		Build quality and hardtop beyond
			reproach.

LEXUS RX 350

engine type	: petrol, V6	kerb weight	: 1810 kg
displacement	: 3456 cc	towing weight	: 2000 kg
max. power	: 203 kW (276 bhp)	boot space	: 490 - 2130 l
@	: 6200 rpm	fuel capacity	: 75 l
max. torque	: 252 lb ft	consumption	: 25.2 mpg
@	: 4700 rpm	acc. 0-62 mph	: 7.8 s
gears	: -	top speed	: 124 mph
AT	: 5-speed	EuroNCAP	: n.a.
drive	: 4WD	introduction	: October 2000
brakes f/r	: vent. discs / discs	last revised in	: February 2003
body type	: 5-dr. SUV	warranty	: 3 years
l x w x h	: 4740 x 1845 x 1660 mm	miscellaneous	: With a more powerful and more economical new engine under the bonnet, the RX 350 is still only slightly cheaper than the more modern RX 400h.
wheelbase	: 2715 mm		
turning circle	: 12.2 m		

RX 400H

engine type	: petrol, V6 + two electrical engines
displacement	: 3311 cc
max. power	: 155 kW (211 bhp)
@	: 5600 rpm
max. torque	: 212 lb ft
@	: 4400 rpm
gears	: CVT
kerb weight	: 2000 kg
towing weight	: 2000 kg
consumption	: 34.9 mpg
acc. 0-60 mph	: 7.6 s
top speed	: 124 mph
miscellaneous	: Combined peak power of petrol engine and twin electric motors is 272 bhp. Not bad. Environmentally friendly model, with fuel consumption of an average middle-class car.

LOTUS ELISE S / R

engine type	: petrol, inline-4
displacement	: 1796 cc
max. power	: 100 kW (136 bhp) / 141 kW (192 bhp)
@	: 6200 / 7800 rpm
max. torque	: 127 / 133 lb ft
@	: 4200 / 6800 rpm
gears	: 5
AT	: -
drive	: RWD
brakes f/r	: vent. discs
body type	: 2-dr. convertible
l x w x h	: 3785 x 1719 x 1143 mm
wheelbase	: 2301 mm
turning circle	: 10.5 m

kerb weight	: 860 kg
towing weight	: -
boot space	: 112 l
fuel capacity	: 38 l
consumption	: 34 / 32.1 mpg
acc. 0-62 mph	: 6.1 / 5.2 s
top speed	: 127 / 147 mph
EuroNCAP	: n.a.
introduction	: October 1997
last revised in	: July 2004
warranty	: 2 years
miscellaneous	: S model is new entry level Lotus. Just as quick as R model, but less hot-blooded and less expensive.

LOTUS EXIGE / EXIGE S

engine type	: petrol, inline-4	kerb weight	: 875 / 935 kg
displacement	: 1796 cc	towing weight	: -
max. power	: 141 kW (192 bhp) / 163 kW (221 bhp)	boot space	: 112 l
		fuel capacity	: 40 l
@	: 7800 rpm	consumption	: 32.1 / 31 mpg
max. torque	:133 /158 lb ft	acc. 0-62 mph	: 5.2 / 4.3 s
@	: 6800 / 5500 rpm	top speed	: 147 / 148 mph
gears	: 6	EuroNCAP	: n.a.
AT	: -	introduction	: February 2005
drive	: RWD	last revised in	: -
brakes f/r	: vent. discs	warranty	: 2 years
body type	: 2-dr. coupe	miscellaneous	: Make no mistake: 'S' denotes hottest Exige instead of entry level version. A real street racer.
l x w x h	: 3797 x 1727 x 1163 mm		
wheelbase	: 2301 mm		
turning circle	: 10.5 m		

LOTUS EUROPA S

engine type	: petrol, inline-4	**kerb weight**	: 995 kg
displacement	: 1998 cc	**towing weight**	: -
max. power	: 147 kW (200 bhp)	**boot space**	: 154 l
@	: 5400 rpm	**fuel capacity**	: 43.5 l
max. torque	: 194 lb ft	**consumption**	: 30.4 mpg
@	: 5000 rpm	**acc. 0-62 mph**	: 5.8 s
gears	: 6	**top speed**	: 140 mph
AT	: -	**EuroNCAP**	: n.a.
drive	: RWD	**introduction**	: July 2006
brakes f/r	: vent. discs	**last revised in**	: -
body type	: 2-dr. coupe	**warranty**	: 2 years
l x w x h	: 3900 x 1714 x 1120 mm	**miscellaneous**	: Softer Lotus, aimed at drivers
wheelbase	: 2330 mm		who value comfort over
turning circle	: n.a.		performance.

MASERATI COUPE / SPYDER

engine type	: petrol, V8	kerb weight	: 1670 / 1620 kg
displacement	: 4244 cc	towing weight	: -
max. power	: 287 kW (390 bhp)	boot space	: 315 / 300 l
@	: 7000 rpm	fuel capacity	: 88 l
max. torque	: 334 lb ft	consumption	: 15.2 mpg
@	: 4500 rpm	acc. 0-62 mph	: 4.9 / 5.0 s
gears	: 6	top speed	: 177 / 175 mph
AT	: optional seq. gearbox	EuroNCAP	: n.a.
drive	: RWD	introduction	: September 1998
brakes f/r	: vent. discs	last revised in	: March 2004
body type	: 2-dr. coupe / 2-dr. convertible	warranty	: 3 years
l x w x h	: 4523 x 1822 x 1305 mm	miscellaneous	: Exhilarating Coupe and Spyder have done wonders for Maserati sales in the past few years.
wheelbase	: 2660 / 2440 mm		
turning circle	: 12.0 m		

GRANSPORT

engine type	: petrol, V8
displacement	: 4244 cc
max. power	: 295 kW (400 bhp)
@	: 7000 rpm
max. torque	: 334 lb ft
@	: 4500 rpm
gears	: 6
kerb weight	: 1680 kg
towing weight	: -
consumption	: 16.1 mpg
acc. 0-60 mph	: 4.8 s
top speed	: 180 mph
miscellaneous	: Not all that much quicker than 'common' Coupe and Spyder models from Trident marque, but chassis in a higher state of tune.

MASERATI QUATTROPORTE

engine type	: petrol, V8		**kerb weight**	: 1930 kg
displacement	: 4244 cc		**towing weight**	: -
max. power	: 294 kW (400 bhp)		**boot space**	: 450 l
@	: 7000 rpm		**fuel capacity**	: 90 l
max. torque	: 333 lb ft		**consumption**	: 15 mpg
@	: 4500 rpm		**acc. 0-62 mph**	: 5.2 s
gears	: -		**top speed**	: 167 mph
AT	: seq. gearbox		**EuroNCAP**	: n.a.
drive	: RWD		**introduction**	: September 2003
brakes f/r	: vent. discs		**last revised in**	: -
body type	: 4-dr. saloon		**warranty**	: 3 years
l x w x h	: 5052 x 1895 x 1438 mm		**miscellaneous**	: Gorgeous looking car, and even
wheelbase	: 3064 mm			more fabulous to drive. Even
turning circle	: 12.3 m			though it has four doors, Italian flair
				doesn't come any better than this!

MAYBACH 57 / 62

engine type	: petrol, V12		**kerb weight**	: 2735 / 2855 kg
displacement	: 5513 cc		**towing weight**	: -
max. power	: 405 kW (550 bhp)		**boot space**	: 605 l
@	: 5250 rpm		**fuel capacity**	: 110 l
max. torque	: 664 lb ft		**consumption**	: 17.8 mpg
@	: 2300 rpm		**acc. 0-62 mph**	: 5.2 / 5.4 s
gears	: -		**top speed**	: 155 mph
AT	: 5-speed		**EuroNCAP**	: n.a.
drive	: RWD		**introduction**	: March 2002
brakes f/r	: vent. discs		**last revised in**	: -
body type	: 4-dr. saloon		**warranty**	: 4 years
l x w x h	: 5728 / 6165 x 1980 x 1572 mm		**miscellaneous**	: Ultra-luxurious barge with a
wheelbase	: 3390 / 3827 mm			pricetag that is way over our head
turning circle	: 13.4 / 14.8 m			and probably yours as well. Also
				available as 57 Special, with 612
				bhp strong 6.0 V12 engine and
				tweaked suspension.

MAZDA 2 1.2 / 1.4

engine type	: petrol, inline-4	**kerb weight**	: 1025 kg
displacement	: 1242 / 1388 cc	**towing weight**	: 600 / 900 kg
max. power	: 55 kW (75 bhp) / 57 kW (80 bhp)	**boot space**	: 335 l
@	: 6000 / 5600 rpm	**fuel capacity**	: 45 l
max. torque	: 81 / 92 lb ft	**consumption**	: 44.8 / 42.8 mpg
@	: 4000 / 3500 rpm	**acc. 0-62 mph**	: 15.1 / 13.9 s
gears	: 5	**top speed**	: 101 / 102 mph
AT	: - / optional 5-speed	**EuroNCAP**	: 4 stars
drive	: FWD	**introduction**	: February 2003
brakes f/r	: vent. discs / drum brakes	**last revised in**	: autumn 2005
body type	: 5-dr. hatchback	**warranty**	: 3 years
l x w x h	: 3925 x 1680 x 1530 mm	**miscellaneous**	: Small facelift should give
wheelbase	: 2490 mm		Mazda 2 a new lease of life.
turning circle	: 9.8 m		

2 1.6 / 1.4 CiTD

engine type	: petrol, inline-4 / diesel, inline-4
displacement	: 1596 / 1399 cc
max. power	: 74 KW (100 bhp) / 59 kW (68 bhp)
@	: 6000 / 4000 rpm
max. torque	: 108 / 118 lb ft
@	: 4000 / 2000 rpm
gears	: 5
kerb weight	: 1045 / 1055 kg
towing weight	: 900 / 800 kg
consumption	: 42.2 / 60.1 mpg
acc. 0-60 mph	: 11.4 / 15.0 s
top speed	: 112 / 99 mph
miscellaneous	: Diesel engine is a joy.

MAZDA 3 SPORT 1.6 / 2.0

engine type	: petrol, inline-4	kerb weight	: 1160 / 1210 kg
displacement	: 1598 / 1999 cc	towing weight	: 1200 / 1300 kg
max. power	: 77 kW (105 bhp) /	boot space	: 300 / 635 l
	110 kW (150 bhp)	fuel capacity	: 55 l
@	: 6000 rpm	consumption	: 40.9 / 35.8 mpg
max. torque	: 107 / 138 lb ft	acc. 0-62 mph	: 11.0 / 9.0 s
@	: 4000 / 4500 rpm	top speed	: 115 / 130 mph
gears	: 5	EuroNCAP	: n.a.
AT	: optional 4-speed / -	introduction	: September 2003
drive	: FWD	last revised in	: -
brakes f/r	: vent. discs / discs	warranty	: 3 years
body type	: 5-dr. hatchback	miscellaneous	: Compact model with refreshing
l x w x h	: 4420 x 1755 x 1465 mm		looks and pleasant road behaviour.
wheelbase	: 2640 mm		Also available with 84 bhp 1.4
turning circle	: 10.4 m		petrol engine. 4-door saloon
			available as well.

3 SPORT 1.6 CITD

engine type	: diesel, inline-4
displacement	: 1560 cc
max. power	: 81 kW (110 bhp)
@	: 4000 tpm
max. torque	: 177 lb ft
@	: 1750 rpm
gears	: 5
kerb weight	: 1250 kg
towing weight	: 1300 kg
consumption	: 58.9 mpg
acc. 0-60 mph	: 11.5 s
top speed	: 115 mph
miscellaneous	: Diesel engine performs adequately and is exceptionally fuel-efficient: 57 mpg is not unusual. Also available as saloon.

MAZDA 6 1.8 / 2.3 S-VT

engine type	: petrol, inline-4
displacement	: 1798 cc / 2261 cc
max. power	: 85 kW (115 bhp) /
	122 kW (166 bhp)
@	: 5300 / 6500 rpm
max. torque	: 122 / 152 lb ft
@	: 4000 / 4000 rpm
gears	: 5 / 6
AT	: - / optional 5-speed
drive	: FWD
brakes f/r	: vent. discs / discs
body type	: 4-dr. saloon
l x w x h	: 4505 x 1755 x 1665 mm
wheelbase	: 2750 mm
turning circle	: 11.8 m

kerb weight	: 1370 kg
towing weight	: 1300 / 1500 kg
boot space	: 500 l
fuel capacity	: 60 l
consumption	: 36.7 / 32.5 mpg
acc. 0-62 mph	: 11.4 / 8.9 s
top speed	: 122 / 131 mph
EuroNCAP	: n.a.
introduction	: June 2002
last revised in	: July 2005
warranty	: 3 years
miscellaneous	: Also available as 2.0 with 147 bhp. Model up-to-date again after latest facelift. Mazda 6 has an edge over most competitors because of fine driving characteristics.

6 2.0 CiTD

engine type	: diesel, inline-4
displacement	: 1998 cc
max. power	: 105 kW (143 bhp)
@	: 3500 rpm
max. torque	: 266 lb ft
@	: 2000 rpm
gears	: 6
kerb weight	: 1385 kg
towing weight	: 1600 kg
consumption	: 47.1 mpg
acc. 0-60 mph	: 10.8 s
top speed	: 127 mph
miscellaneous	: Well-mannered common-rail diesel engine with lots of torque. Popular lease model.

6 MPS

engine type	: petrol, inline-4
displacement	: 2261 cc
max. power	: 191 kW (260 bhp)
@	: 5500 rpm
max. torque	: 280 lb ft
@	: 3000 rpm
gears	: 6
kerb weight	: 1565 kg
towing weight	: n.b.
consumption	: 57.7 mpg
acc. 0-60 mph	: 6.6 s
top speed	: 149 mph
miscellaneous	: MPS stands for Mazda Performance Series and is used for top-of-the-range model, with a turbo engine and four-wheel drive. More comfortable than an Impreza or Lancer Evo.

MAZDA 5 1.8 / 2.0

engine type	: petrol, inline-4	kerb weight	: 1370 / 1375 kg
displacement	: 1798 / 1999 cc	towing weight	: 1300 / 1400 kg
max. power	: 85 kW (115 bhp) /	boot space	: 112 l
	107 kW (145 bhp)	fuel capacity	: 60 l
@	: 5300 / 6000 rpm	consumption	: 35.8 / 34.5 mpg
max. torque	: 122 / 136 lb ft	acc. 0-62 mph	: 11.4 / 10.8 s
@	: 4000 / 4500 rpm	top speed	: 113 / 122 mph
gears	: 5	EuroNCAP	: 5 stars
AT	: -	introduction	: February 2005
drive	: FWD	last revised in	: -
brakes f/r	: vent. discs / discs	warranty	: 3 years
body type	: 5-dr. MPV	miscellaneous	: Sharp, mid-sized people carrier
l x w x h	: 4505 x 1755 x 1665 mm		with stowable seats in the third row.
wheelbase	: 2750		Reasonably quick with 2.0 engine.
turning circle	: 11.2 m		

5 2.0 CiTD

engine type	: diesel, inline-4
displacement	: 1998 cc
max. power	: 81 kW (110 bhp) /
	105 kW (143 bhp)
@	: 3500 rpm
max. torque	: 228 / 266 lb ft
@	: 2000 rpm
gears	: 6
kerb weight	: 1510 kg
towing weight	: 1400 kg
consumption	: 44.9 / 44.9 mpg
acc. 0-60 mph	: 12.9 / 10.4 s
top speed	: 111 / 122 mph
miscellaneous	: Sales of Mazda 5 took off with
	introduction of diesel-powered
	version. Good match.

MAZDA MX-5 1.8 / 2.0

engine type	: petrol, inline-4	**kerb weight**	: 1055 / 1070 kg
displacement	: 1798 / 1999 cc	**towing weight**	: -
max. power	: 93 kW (126 bhp) /	**boot space**	: 150 l
	118 kW (160 bhp)	**fuel capacity**	: 50 l
@	: 6500 rpm	**consumption**	: 38.7 / 34.5 mpg
max. torque	:123 /138 lb ft	**acc. 0-62 mph**	: 9.4 / 7.9 s
@	: 4500 / 5000 rpm	**top speed**	: 122 / 131 mph
gears	: 5	**EuroNCAP**	: n.a.
AT	: -	**introduction**	: March 2006
drive	: RWD	**last revised in**	: -
brakes f/r	: vent. discs / discs	**warranty**	: 3 years
body type	: 2-dr. convertible	**miscellaneous**	: Third generation of very successful
l x w x h	: 3995 x 1720 x 1245 mm		convertible. Still a real driver's car,
wheelbase	: 2330 mm		now also available with a
turning circle	: 9.8 m		retractable hardtop roof. Manual
			6-speed gearbox is an option in
			biggest version.

MAZDA RX-8 RENESIS / RENESIS HP

engine type	: petrol, birotary engine	kerb weight	: 1394 / 1390 kg
displacement	: 2 x 645 cc	towing weight	: 1200 kg
max. power	: 141 kW (192 bhp) /	boot space	: 250 l
	179 kW (231 bhp)	fuel capacity	: 61 l
@	: 7000 / 8200 rpm	consumption	: 26.7 / 25.2 mpg
max. torque	: 162 /155 lb ft	acc. 0-62 mph	: 7.2 / 6.4 s
@	: 5000 / 5500 rpm	top speed	: 139 /146 mph
gears	: 6	EuroNCAP	: n.a.
AT	: optional seq. gearbox,	introduction	: February 2003
	seq. gearbox	last revised in	: -
drive	: RWD	warranty	: 3 years
brakes f/r	: vent. discs	miscellaneous	: Unique model because of rotary
body type	: 4-dr. coupe		engine and rear 'suicide' doors.
l x w x h	: 4330 x 1770 x 1340 mm		Lovely, high-revving machine.
wheelbase	: 2700 mm		
turning circle	: 10.6 m		

MAZDA CX-7

engine type	: petrol, inline-4	**kerb weight**	: 1683 kg
displacement	: 2260 cc	**towing weight**	: n.a.
max. power	: 182 kW (248 bhp)	**boot space**	: n.a.
@	: 5000 rpm	**fuel capacity**	: 69 l
max. torque	: 258 lb ft	**consumption**	: n.a.
@	: 2500 rpm	**acc. 0-62 mph**	: n.a.
gears	: -	**top speed**	: n.a.
AT	: 6-speed	**EuroNCAP**	: n.a.
drive	: FWD	**introduction**	: February 2007
brakes f/r	: vent. discs	**last revised in**	: -
body type	: 5-dr. SUV	**warranty**	: 3 years
l x w x h	: 4675 x 1872 x 1645 mm	**miscellaneous**	: Truly a sports utility vehicle, with matching performance. Diesel-powered version to follow in 2008.
wheelbase	: 2750 mm		
turning circle	: 11.4 m		

MERCEDES-BENZ A 150 / A 170

engine type	: petrol, inline-4
displacement	: 1498 / 1699 cc
max. power	: 70 kW (95 bhp) / 85 kW (116 bhp)
@	: 5200 / 5500 rpm
max. torque	: 104 / 114 lb ft
@	: 3500 rpm
gears	: 5
AT	: optional, CVT
drive	: FWD
brakes f/r	: vent. discs / discs
body type	: 3- , 5-dr. hatchback
l x w x h	: 3838 x1764 x 1593 mm
wheelbase	: 2568 mm
turning circle	: 10.9 m
kerb weight	: 1095 / 1110 kg
towing weight	: 1000 / 1300 kg
boot space	: 435 -1370 l
fuel capacity	: 54 l
consumption	: 45.6 / 42.8 mpg
acc. 0-62 mph	: 12.6 / 10.9 s
top speed	: 109 / 117 mph
EuroNCAP	: 5 stars
introduction	: July 2004
last revised in	: -
warranty	: 2 years
miscellaneous	: Smallest Merc, but with ample interior space due to its clever platform. Original, modern looks, especially in 3-door form.

A 200 / A 200 TURBO

engine type	: petrol, inline-4
displacement	: 2034 cc
max. power	: 100 kW (136 bhp) / 142 kW (192 bhp)
@	: 5750 / 5000 rpm
max. torque	: 124 / 141 mph
@	: 3500 / 1800 rpm
gears	: 5 / 6
kerb weight	: 1140 / 1175 kg
towing weight	: 1500 kg
consumption	: 39.2 / 34.9 mpg
acc. 0-60 mph	: 9.8 / 7.5 s
top speed	: 124 / 141 mph
miscellaneous	: All petrol engines also available in B-class.

MERCEDES-BENZ B 180 CDI / B 200 CDI

engine type	: diesel, inline-4
displacement	: 1991 cc
max. power	: 80 kW (109 bhp) / 103 kW (140 bhp)
@	: 4200 rpm
max. torque	: 184 /221 lb ft
@	: 1600 rpm
gears	: 6
AT	: optional, CVT
drive	: RWD
brakes f/r	: vent. discs / discs
body type	: 5-dr. hatchback
l x w x h	: 4270 x 1777 x 1603 mm
wheelbase	: 2778 mm
turning circle	: 12.0 m

kerb weight	: 1335 kg
towing weight	: 1500 kg
boot space	: 544 - 2245 l
fuel capacity	: 54 l
consumption	: 50.4 / 50.4 mpg
acc. 0-62 mph	: 11.3 / 9.6 s
top speed	: 114 / 124 mph
EuroNCAP	: -
introduction	: March 2005
last revised in	: -
warranty	: 2 years
miscellaneous	: 82 bhp 160 CDI engine from A-class not available in B-class, but B 150, B 170, B 200 and B 200 Turbo engines are.

MERCEDES-BENZ C 180 K / C 200 K SPORTS COUPE

engine type	: petrol, inline-4
displacement	: 1796 cc
max. power	: 105 kW (143 bhp) / 120 kW (163 bhp)
@	: 5200 / 5500 rpm
max. torque	: 162 / 177 lb ft
@	: 2500 / 3000 rpm
gears	: 6
AT	: optional, 5-speed
drive	: FWD
brakes f/r	: vent. discs / discs
body type	: 3-dr. hatchback
l x w x h	: 4343 x 1728 x 1406 mm
wheelbase	: 2715 mm
turning circle	: 10.7 m

kerb weight	: 1365 kg
towing weight	: 1500 kg
boot space	: 310 - 1100 l
fuel capacity	: 62 l
consumption	: 37.2 / 35.3 mpg
acc. 0-62 mph	: 9.7 / 9.1 s
top speed	: 139 / 145 mph
EuroNCAP	: 5 stars
introduction	: October 2000
last revised in	: February 2004
warranty	: 2 years
miscellaneous	: Smallest Benz with rear-wheel drive, competes with BMW 1-series and Audi A3. Twinpulse 1.8 also available as C 160 with 122 bhp.

C 230 / C 350 SPORTS COUPE

engine type	: petrol, V6
displacement	: 2496 / 3498 cc
max. power	: 150 kW (204 bhp) / 200 kW (272 bhp)
@	: 6100 / 6000 rpm
max. torque	:180 / 258 lb ft
@	: 2900 / 2400 rpm
gears	: 6
kerb weight	: 1415 / 1440 kg
towing weight	: 1500 kg
consumption	: 30.4 / 29.1 mpg
acc. 0-60 mph	: 8.4 / 6.4 s
top speed	: 150 / 155 mph
miscellaneous	: Two brand-new V6 engines that perform well, particularly in combination with the 7-speed auto box.

C 200 CDI / C 220 CDI SPORTS COUPE

engine type	: diesel, inline-4
displacement	: 2148 cc
max. power	: 90 kW (122 bhp) / 110 kW (150 bhp)
@	: 4200 rpm
max. torque	: 199 / 250 lb ft
@	: 1600 / 2000 rpm
gears	: 6
kerb weight	: 1390 / 1405 kg
towing weight	: 1500 / 1200 kg
consumption	: 43.5 / 42.8 mpg
acc. 0-60 mph	: 11.7 / 10.3 s
top speed	: 129 / 139 mph
miscellaneous	: 200 and 220 share the same engine, but they differ in horsepower. Their performance is more than adequate.

MERCEDES-BENZ C 180 KOMPRESSOR / C 200 KOMPRESSOR

engine type	: petrol, inline-4	kerb weight	: 1385 kg
displacement	: 1796 cc	towing weight	: 1500 kg
max. power	: 105 kW (143 bhp) / 120 kW (163 bhp)	boot space	: 455 l
@	: 4200 rpm	fuel capacity	: 62 l
max. torque	: 162 / 177 lb ft	consumption	: 37.2 / 35.3 mpg
@	: 1600 / 2000 rpm	acc. 0-62 mph	: 9.7 / 9.1 s
gears	: 6	top speed	: 139 / 145mph
AT	: optional, 5-speed	EuroNCAP	: 5 stars
drive	: RWD	introduction	: March 2000
brakes f/r	: vent. discs / discs	last revised in	: February 2004
body type	: 4 dr. saloon	warranty	: 2 years
l x w x h	: 4526 x 1728 x 1427 mm	miscellaneous	: Fine, representative car with rather
wheelbase	: 2715 mm		conservative styling. Wide choice of
turning circle	: 10.7 m		engines, ranging from 143 bhp
			strong 1.8 to 5.4 V8.

C 280

engine type	: petrol, V6
displacement	: 2996 cc
max. power	: 170 kW (231 bhp)
@	: 6000 rpm
max. torque	: 221 lb ft
@	: 2500 rpm
gears	: 6
kerb weight	: 1435 kg
towing weight	: 1500 kg
consumption	: 30.1 mpg
acc. 0-60 mph	: 7.3 s
top speed	: 155 mph
miscellaneous	: Also available as C 230 and C 350. Refer to Sports Coupe for specifications.

C 55 AMG

engine type	: petrol, V8
displacement	: 5439 cc
max. power	: 270 kW (367 bhp)
@	: 5750 rpm
max. torque	: 376 lb ft
@	: 4000 rpm
gears	: 5-speed automatic
kerb weight	: 1535 kg
towing weight	: 1500 kg
consumption	: 23.7 mpg
acc. 0-60 mph	: 5.2 s
top speed	: 155 mph
miscellaneous	: Colossal V8 turns C 55 into a monster. Also available as stationwagon.

MERCEDES-BENZ C 200 CDI ESTATE / C 220 CDI ESTATE

engine type	: diesel, inline-4	kerb weight	: 1465 kg
displacement	: 2148 cc	towing weight	: 1500 kg
max. power	: 90 kW (122 bhp) /	boot space	: 470 -1384 l
	110 kW (150 bhp)	fuel capacity	: 62 l
@	: 4200 rpm	consumption	: 41.5 / 40.9 mpg
max. torque	: 199 /250 lb ft	acc. 0-62 mph	: 11.2 / 10.5 s
@	: 1600 / 2000 rpm	top speed	: 126 / 135 mph
gears	: 6	EuroNCAP	: 5 stars
AT	: optional, 5-speed	introduction	: March 2000
drive	: RWD	last revised in	: February 2004
brakes f/r	: vent. discs / discs	warranty	: 2 years
body type	: 5-dr. stationwagon	miscellaneous	: Diesel-powered versions are
l x w x h	: 4541 x 1728 x 1466 mm		bestsellers among C-class
wheelbase	: 2715 mm		stationwagon models.
turning circle	: 10.7 m		

C 320 CDI ESTATE

engine type	: diesel, V6
displacement	: 2987 cc
max. power	: 165 kW (224 bhp)
@	: 3800 rpm
max. torque	: 376 lb ft
@	: 1600 rpm
gears	: 6
kerb weight	: 1580 kg
towing weight	: 1500 kg
consumption	: 35.8 mpg
acc. 0-60 mph	: 8.3 s
top speed	: 150 mph
miscellaneous	: Powerful V6 is only diesel
	alternative to 4-cylinder diesel
	engines in this model range.

MERCEDES-BENZ E 280 / E 350

engine type	: petrol, V6
displacement	: 2996 / 3498 cc
max. power	: 170 kW (231 bhp) / 200 kW (272 bhp)
@	: 6000 rpm
max. torque	: 222 / 258 lb ft
@	: 2500 / 2400 rpm
gears	: 6 / -
AT	: optional 7-speed / 7-speed
drive	: RWD
brakes f/r	: vent. discs
body type	: 4-dr. saloon
l x w x h	: 4856 x 1822 x 1483 mm
wheelbase	: 2854 mm
turning circle	: 11.4 m

kerb weight	: 1560 / 1590 kg
towing weight	: 1900 kg
boot space	: 540 l
fuel capacity	: 80 l
consumption	: 33.2 / 29.1 mpg
acc. 0-62 mph	: 7.3 / 6.9 s
top speed	: 154 / 155 mph
EuroNCAP	: 5 stars
introduction	: February 2002
last revised in	: April 2006
warranty	: 2 years
miscellaneous	: Facelifted E-class more reliable, now problems with electronics are over, says Mercedes. Also available as E 200 Kompressor.

E 200 CDI / E 220 CDI

engine type	: diesel, inline-4
displacement	: 2148 cc
max. power	: 100 kW (136 bhp) / 125 kW (170 bhp)
@	: 3800 rpm
max. torque	: 251 / 295 lb ft
@	: 2000 rpm
gears	: 6
kerb weight	: 1515 kg
towing weight	: 1900 kg
consumption	: 46.2 / 44.8 mpg
acc. 0-60 mph	: 9.9 / 8.4 s
top speed	: 133 / 141 mph
miscellaneous	: With facelift came more power for the 4-cylinder CDI-engines. E 200 NGT version runs on natural gas.

E 420 CDI

engine type	: diesel, V8
displacement	: 3996 cc
max. power	: 231 kW (314 bhp)
@	: 3600 rpm
max. torque	: 538 lb ft
@	: 2200 rpm
gears	: 7-speed automatic
kerb weight	: 1810 kg
towing weight	: n.a.
consumption	: 30.5 mpg
acc. 0-60 mph	: 6.1 s
top speed	: 155 mph
miscellaneous	: Strongest diesel engine fitted in saloon only.

MERCEDES-BENZ E 280 CDI ESTATE / E 320 CDI ESTATE

engine type	: diesel, V6
displacement	: 2987 cc
max. power	: 140 kW (190 bhp) / 165 kW (224 bhp)
@	: 4000 / 3800 rpm
max. torque	: 324 / 398 lb ft
@	: 1400 / 1600 rpm
gears	: 6 / -
AT	: optional / 7-speed
drive	: RWD
brakes f/r	: vent. discs / discs
body type	: 5-dr. stationwagon
l x w x h	: 4888 x 1822 x 1506 mm
wheelbase	: 2854 mm
turning circle	: 11.4 m

kerb weight	: 1745 / 1785 kg
towing weight	: 2100 kg
boot space	: 690 -1950 l
fuel capacity	: 70 / 80 l
consumption	: 37.2 / 37.2 mpg
acc. 0-62 mph	: 9.1 / 7.3 s
top speed	: 143 / 149 mph
EuroNCAP	: 5 stars
introduction	: February 2002
last revised in	: April 2006
warranty	: 2 years
miscellaneous	: Also available with 4MATIC, Mercedes' 4WD-system.

E 500 ESTATE / E 63 AMG ESTATE

engine type	: petrol, V8
displacement	: 5461 / 6208 cc
max. power	: 285 kW (388 bhp) / 378 kW (514 bhp)
@	: 6000 / 6800 rpm
max. torque	: 391 / 464 lb ft
@	: 2800 / 5200 rpm
gears	: 7-speed automatic
kerb weight	: 1795 / 1890 kg
towing weight	: 2100 kg / -
consumption	: 23.9 / 19.5 mpg
acc. 0-60 mph	: 5.4 / 4.6 s
top speed	: 155 mph
miscellaneous	: New addition to E-class range, much more powerful than E 55 AMG despite absence of supercharger.

MERCEDES-BENZ CLS 350 / CLS 500

engine type	: petrol, V6 / V8	kerb weight	: 1630 / 1710 kg
displacement	: 3498 / 5461 cc	towing weight	: n.a.
max. power	: 200 kW (272 bhp) /	boot space	: 505 l
	285 kW (388 bhp)	fuel capacity	: 80 l
@	: 6000 / 6000 rpm	consumption	: 31 / 24.4 mpg
max. torque	: 31 / 34.4 mpg	acc. 0-62 mph	: 7.0 / 6.1 s
@	: 2400 / 2800 - 4800 rpm	top speed	: 155 / 155 mph
gears	: -	EuroNCAP	: n.a.
AT	: 7-speed	introduction	: July 2004
drive	: RWD	last revised in	: -
brakes f/r	: vent. discs	warranty	: 2 years
body type	: 4-dr. saloon	miscellaneous	: One of the most striking cars to
l x w x h	: 4913 x 1873 x 1390 / 1403 mm		emerge in a decade, this 4-door
wheelbase	: 2854 mm		coupe from das Haus. Also
turning circle	: 11.2 m		available as 320 CDI and very
			potent 63 AMG version.

MERCEDES-BENZ S 350 / S 500

engine type	: petrol, V6 / V8
displacement	: 3498 / 5461 cc
max. power	: 200 kW (272 bhp) / 285 kW (388 bhp)
@	: 6000 rpm
max. torque	: 258 / 391 lb ft
@	: 2400 / 2800 rpm
gears	: -
AT	: 7-speed
drive	: RWD
brakes f/r	: vent. discs
body type	: 4-dr. saloon
l x w x h	: 5076 x 1871 x 1473 mm
wheelbase	: 3035 mm
turning circle	: 11.7 m

kerb weight	: 1780 kg
towing weight	: 2100 kg
boot space	: 560 l
fuel capacity	: 88 l
consumption	: 28 / 24.1 mph
acc. 0-62 mph	: 7.2 / 5.4 s
top speed	: 155 mph
EuroNCAP	: n.a.
introduction	: autumn 2005
last revised in	: -
warranty	: 2 years
miscellaneous	: Newest S-class model as usual a showcase of latest technology. Also available as S 450 with 340 bhp.

S 600 / S 65 AMG

engine type	: petrol, V12
displacement	: 5513 / 5981 cc
max. power	: 380 kW (517 bhp) / 450 (612 bhp)
@	: 5000 / 5950 rpm
max. torque	: 612 / 737 lb ft
@	: 1800 / 2000 rpm
gears	: 5-speed automatic
kerb weight	: 2080 / 2150 kg
towing weight	: 2100 kg / -
consumption	: 19.8 / 19.2 mpg
acc. 0-60 mph	: 4.6 / 4.4 s
top speed	: 155 mph
miscellaneous	: Both models available only on LWB-platform. 'Old' AMG-powerhouse still going strong in S-class.

S 320 CDI

engine type	: diesel, V6
displacement	: 2987 cc
max. power	: 173 kW (235 bhp)
@	: 3600 rpm
max. torque	: 398 lb ft
@	: 1600 rpm
gears	: 7-speed automatic
kerb weight	: 1855 kg
towing weight	: 2100 kg
consumption	: 33.6 mpg
acc. 0-60 mph	: 7.5 s
top speed	: 155 mph
miscellaneous	: For the time being the only diesel-powered unit available in the S-class range. Rivals have V8 diesel power to offer, so S 420 CDI model would be welcome addition.

MERCEDES-BENZ R 350 / R 500

engine type	: petrol, V6 / petrol, V8	kerb weight	: 2055 / 2090 kg
displacement	: 3498 / 4966 cc	towing weight	: 2100 kg
max. power	: 200 kW (272 bhp) /	boot space	: 314 – 2385 l
	225 kW (306 bhp)	fuel capacity	: 80 l
@	: 6000 / 5600 rpm	consumption	: 24.8 / 21.2 mpg
max. torque	: 258 / 339 lb ft	acc. 0-62 mph	: 8.3 / 6.9 s
@	: 2400 / 2700 rpm	top speed	: 143 / 149 mph
gears	: -	EuroNCAP	: n.a.
AT	: 7-speed automatic	introduction	: late 2005
drive	: 4WD	last revised in	: -
brakes f/r	: vent. discs / discs	warranty	: 2 years
body type	: 5-dr. MPV	miscellaneous	: 6-seater MPV, based on ML-class.
l x w x h	: 4780 x 1911 x 1779 mm		Big car, aimed at American market.
wheelbase	: 2915 mm		Longer version (wheelbase
turning circle	: 11.7 m		3215 mm) available. Range topped
			by 510 bhp R 63 AMG.

R 320 CDI

engine type	: diesel, V6
displacement	: 2987 cc
max. power	: 165 kW (224 bhp)
@	: 3800 rpm
max. torque	: 376 lb ft
@	: 1600 rpm
gears	: 6
kerb weight	: 1685 kg
towing weight	: 1500 kg
consumption	: 30.4 mpg
acc. 0-60 mph	: 8.6 s
top speed	: 134 mph
miscellaneous	: 'Economical' R-class model. Also available as R 280 CDI with 190 bhp.

MERCEDES-BENZ CLK 200 KOMPRESSOR / CLK 280

engine type	: petrol, inline-4 / V6
displacement	: 1796 cc / 2.996 cc
max. power	: 120 kW (163 bhp) /
	170 kW (231 bhp)
@	: 5500 / 6000 rpm
max. torque	: 177 / 222 lb ft
@	: 3000 / 2500 rpm
gears	: 6
AT	: optional, 5-speed / 7-speed
drive	: RWD
brakes f/r	: vent. discs
body type	: 2-dr. coupe
l x w x h	: 4652 x 1740 x 1413 mm
wheelbase	: 2715 mm
turning circle	: 10.8 m

kerb weight	: 1440 / 1480 kg
towing weight	: 1500 kg
boot space	: 435 l
fuel capacity	: 62 l
consumption	: 33.6 / 30.7 mpg
acc. 0-62 mph	: 9.3 / 7.4 s
top speed	: 142 / 155 mph
EuroNCAP	: n.a.
introduction	: March 2002
last revised in	: June 2005
warranty	: 2 years
miscellaneous	: C-class based coupe offers some additional exclusivity…

CLK 220 CDI / CLK 320 CDI

engine type	: diesel, inline-4
displacement	: 2148 / 2987 cc
max. power	: 110 kW (150 bhp) /
	165 kW (224 bhp)
@	: 4200 / 3800 rpm
max. torque	: 251 / 376 lb ft
@	: 2000 / 1400 rpm
gears	: 6
kerb weight	: 1475 / 1560 kg
towing weight	: 1500 kg
consumption	: 44.1 / 38.2 mpg
acc. 0-60 mph	: 10.2 / 8.2 s
top speed	: 135 / 155 mph
miscellaneous	: … without sacrificing interior space.

MERCEDES-BENZ CLK 350 / CLK 500 CABRIOLET

engine type	: petrol, V6 / V8		kerb weight	: 1635 / 1700 kg
displacement	: 3498 / 5462 cc		towing weight	: 1500 kg
max. power	: 200 kW (272 bhp) / 285 kW (388 bhp)		boot space	: 390 l
@	: 6000 rpm		fuel capacity	: 62 l
max. torque	: 258 / 391 lb ft		consumption	: 28 / 24.4 mpg
@	: 2400 / 2800 rpm		acc. 0-62 mph	: 6.4 / 5.3 s
gears	: -		top speed	: 155 / 155 mph
AT	: 7-speed		EuroNCAP	: n.a.
drive	: RWD		introduction	: March 2003
brakes f/r	: vent. discs		last revised in	: June 2005
body type	: 2-dr. convertible		warranty	: 2 years
l x w x h	: 4652 x 1740 x 1413 mm		miscellaneous	: Why buy the AMG-version if you
wheelbase	: 2715 mm			can have a CLK 500 with the
turning circle	: 10.8 m			new, powerful 5.5-litre V8 engine
				instead?

CLK 63 AMG

engine type	: petrol, V8
displacement	: 6208 cc
max. power	: 354 kW (481 bhp)
@	: 6800 rpm
max. torque	: 464 lb ft
@	: 5000 rpm
gears	: 7-speed automatic
kerb weight	: 1775 kg
towing weight	: -
consumption	: 19.6 mpg
acc. 0-60 mph	: 4.7 s
top speed	: 155 mph
miscellaneous	: Coupe version is current safety car
	in Formula 1. Also available as
	a convertible.

MERCEDES-BENZ CL 500 / CL 600

engine type	: petrol, V8 / V12	kerb weight	: 1895 / 2085 kg
displacement	: 5462 / 5514 cc	towing weight	: n.a.
max. power	: 285 kW (388 bhp) /	boot space	: 490 l
	380 kW (517 bhp)	fuel capacity	: 90 l
@	: 6000 / 5000 rpm	consumption	: 23.4 / 19.8 mpg
max. torque	: 391 / 612 lb ft	acc. 0-62 mph	: 5.5 / 4.6 s
@	: 2800 / 1900 rpm	top speed	: 155 / 155 mph
gears	: -	EuroNCAP	: n.a.
AT	: 7- / 5-speed automatic	introduction	: autumn 2006
drive	: RWD	last revised in	: -
brakes f/r	: vent. discs	warranty	: 2 years
body type	: 2-dr. coupe	miscellaneous	: Giant coupe finds favour with small
l x w x h	: 5065 x 1871 x 1418 mm		but loyal group of customers,
wheelbase	: 2955 mm		especially in Germany, the USA and
turning circle	: 11.6 m		the Middle East.

MERCEDES-BENZ SLR MCLAREN

engine type	: petrol, V8		kerb weight	: 1768 kg
displacement	: 5439 cc		towing weight	: -
max. power	: 460 kW (626 bhp)		boot space	: 272 l
@	: 6500 rpm		fuel capacity	: 98 l
max. torque	: 575 lb ft		consumption	: 14.8 mpg
@	: 3250 rpm		acc. 0-62 mph	: 3.8 s
gears	: -		top speed	: 208 mph
AT	: 5-speed		EuroNCAP	: n.a.
drive	: RWD		introduction	: autumn 2003
brakes f/r	: ceramic discs		last revised in	: -
body type	: 2-dr. coupe		warranty	: 2 years
l x w x h	: 4656 x 1908 x 1261 mm		miscellaneous	: Fastest and most expensive model
wheelbase	: 2700 mm			in current range from Stuttgart.
turning circle	: n.a.			Merc offers staggering performance
				but can still be used as a daily
				driver, which is more than can be
				said of a Porsche Carrera GT.

MERCEDES-BENZ SLK 200 KOMPRESSOR / SLK 350

engine type	: petrol, inline-4 / V6
displacement	: 1795 / 3498 cc
max. power	: 120 kW (163 bhp) / 200 kW (272 bhp)
@	: 5500 / 6000 rpm
max. torque	: 177 /258 lb ft
@	: 3000 / 3500 rpm
gears	: 6 u
AT	: optional, 5-speed
drive	: RWD
brakes f/r	: vent. discs / discs
body type	: 2-dr. convertible
l x w x h	: 4089 x 1777 x 1296 mm
wheelbase	: 2430 mm
turning circle	: 10.5 m

kerb weight	: 1290 / 1365 kg
towing weight	: -
boot space	: 210 - 300 l
fuel capacity	: 70 l
consumption	: 32.5 / 29.1 mpg
acc. 0-62 mph	: 7.9 / 5.6
top speed	: 143 / 155 mph
EuroNCAP	: n.a.
introduction	: January 2004
last revised in	: -
warranty	: 2 years
miscellaneous	: SLK of second generation is a proper sportscar now that competes with the BMW Z4 and Porsche Boxster. Also available as SLK 280 with 231 bhp.

SLK 55 AMG

engine type	: petrol, V8
displacement	: 5439 cc
max. power	: 265 kW (360 bhp)
@	: 5750 rpm
max. torque	: 376 lb ft
@	: 4000 rpm
gears	: 7-speed automatic
kerb weight	: 1440 kg
towing weight	: n.a.
consumption	: 23.5 mpg
acc. 0-60 mph	: 4.9 s
top speed	: 155 mph
miscellaneous	: A big engine indeed for such a small convertible. Spectacular performance level, lovely V8 sound from quadruple end pipes.

MERCEDES-BENZ SL 500 / SL 55 AMG

engine type	: petrol, V8	**kerb weight**	: 1810 / 1860 kg
displacement	: 5461 / 5439 cc	**towing weight**	: -
max. power	: 285 kW (388 bhp) /	**boot space**	: 317 l
	380 kW (517 bhp)	**fuel capacity**	: 80 l
@	: 6000 / 6100 rpm	**consumption**	: 23.2 / 20.9 mpg
max. torque	: 391 / 531 lb ft	**acc. 0-62 mph**	: 5.4 / 4.5 s
@	: 2800 / 2600 rpm	**top speed**	: 155 / 155 mph
gears	: -	**EuroNCAP**	: n.a.
AT	: 7-speed / 5-speed	**introduction**	: August 2001
drive	: RWD	**last revised in**	: February 2006
brakes f/r	: vent. discs	**warranty**	: 2 years
body type	: 2-dr. convertible	**miscellaneous**	: SL was given a minor facelift.
l x w x h	: 4535 x 1827 x 1298 mm		V6-engined SL 350 also available.
wheelbase	: 2560 mm		
turning circle	: 11.0 m		

SL 600 / SL 65 AMG

engine type	: petrol, V12
displacement	: 5513 / 5980 cc
max. power	: 380 kW (517 bhp) /
	450 kW (612 bhp)
@	: 6100 / 5950 rpm
max. torque	: 612 / 737 lb ft
@	: 1900 / 2000 rpm
gears	: 5-speed automatic
kerb weight	: 1945 / 2020 kg
towing weight	: -
consumption	: 19.8 / 18.7 mpg
acc. 0-60 mph	: 4.5 / 4.2 s
top speed	: 155 / 155 mph
miscellaneous	: Although the difference in price between the two is considerable, the AMG is only marginally quicker off the line.

MERCEDES-BENZ ML 280 CDI / ML 320 CDI

engine type	: diesel, V6	kerb weight	: 2085 kg
displacement	: 2987 cc	towing weight	: 3500 kg
max. power	: 140 kW (190 bhp) /	boot space	: 500 – 2050 l
	165 kW (224 bhp)	fuel capacity	: 95 l
@	: 4000 / 3800 rpm	consumption	: 9.8 / 8.6 s
max. torque	: 324 /376 lb ft	acc. 0-62 mph	: 127 / 136 mph
@	: 1400 / 1600 rpm	top speed	: n.a.
gears	: -	EuroNCAP	: October 2004
AT	: 7-speed	introduction	: -
drive	: 4WD	last revised in	: -
brakes f/r	: vent. discs	warranty	: 2 years
body type	: 5-dr. SUV	miscellaneous	: New ML better in every respect
l x w x h	: 4780 x 1911 x 1815 mm		than successful but less than
wheelbase	: 2915 mm		perfect predecessor.
turning circle	: 11.6 m		

ML 350 / ML 500

engine type	: petrol, V6 / V8
displacement	: 3498 / 4966 cc
max. power	: 200 kW (272 bhp) /
	225 kW (306 bhp)
@	: 6000 / 5600 rpm
max. torque	: 258 / 339 lb ft
@	: 2400 / 2700 rpm
gears	: 7-speed automatic
kerb weight	: 2035 / 2075 kg
towing weight	: 3500 kg
consumption	: 24.6 / 21.1 mpg
acc. 0-60 mph	: 8.4 / 6.9 s
top speed	: 133 / 140 mph
miscellaneous	: Top-of-the-range model
	is the ML 63 AMG.

MERCEDES-BENZ G 270 Lang

engine type	: diesel, inline-5	kerb weight	: 2310 kg
displacement	: 2685 cc	towing weight	: 3500 kg
max. power	: 115 kW (156 bhp)	boot space	: 480 - 2250 l
@	: 3800 rpm	fuel capacity	: 96 l
max. torque	: 295 lb ft	consumption	: 26 mpg
@	: 1800 rpm	acc. 0-62 mph	: 13.7 s
gears	: -	top speed	: 99 mph
AT	: 5-speed	EuroNCAP	: n.a.
drive	: 4WD	introduction	: 1979
brakes f/r	: vent. discs / discs	last revised in	: November 2000
body type	: 5-dr. SUV	warranty	: 2 years
l x w x h	: 4662 x 1760 x 1931 mm	miscellaneous	: Developed for the military in 1979.
wheelbase	: 2850 mm		Gradually evolved into a luxury
turning circle	: 13.3 m		workhorse. Also available as 5-door
			Wagon and Convertible.

G 500 lang / G 400 CDI lang

engine type	: petrol, V8 / diesel, V8
displacement	: 4966 / 3996 cc
max. power	: 218 kW (296 bhp) /
	184 kW (250 bhp)
@	: 5500 / 4000 rpm
max. torque	: 336 / 413 lb ft
@	: 2800 / 1700 rpm
gears	: 5
kerb weight	: 2300 / 2420 kg
towing weight	: 3500 kg
consumption	: 17 / 22.2 mpg
acc. 0-60 mph	: 10.2 / 10.3 s
top speed	: 118 / 113 mph
miscellaneous	: V8-engined Geländewagen doubles as the ultimate SUV for the well-heeled.

MERCEDES-BENZ GL 450 / GL 500

engine type	: petrol, V8
displacement	: 4663 / 5461 cc
max. power	: 250 kW (340 bhp) / 285 kW (388 bhp)
@	: 6000 rpm
max. torque	: 339 /391 lb ft
@	: 2700 / 2800 rpm
gears	: -
AT	: 7-speed
drive	: 4WD
brakes f/r	: vent. discs
body type	: 5-dr. SUV
l x w x h	: 5088 x 1920 x 1840 mm
wheelbase	: 3075 mm
turning circle	: 12.1 m

kerb weight	: 2330 / 2345 kg
towing weight	: 3500 kg
boot space	: 620 l
fuel capacity	: 100 l
consumption	: 21 / 20.4 mpg
acc. 0-62 mph	: 7.2 / 6.6 s
top speed	: 146 / 149 mph
EuroNCAP	: n.a.
introduction	: July 2006
last revised in	: -
warranty	: 2 years
miscellaneous	: Not a successor to the G-class models, but an enlarged version of the ML.

GL 320 CDI / GL 420 CDI

engine type	: diesel, V6 / V8
displacement	: 2987 / 3996 cc
max. power	: 165 kW (224 bhp) / 225 kW (306 bhp)
@	: 3800 / 3600 rpm
max. torque	: 376 / 516 lb ft
@	: 1600 / 2200 rpm
gears	: 7-speed automatic
kerb weight	: 2350 / 2450 kg
towing weight	: 3500 kg
consumption	: 28.9 / 24.6 mpg
acc. 0-60 mph	: 9.5 / 7.2 s
top speed	: 131 / 143 mph
miscellaneous	: V8 diesel engine also available in M-class.

MINI COOPER / COOPER S

engine type	: petrol, inline-4		**kerb weight**	: n.a.
displacement	: 1598 cc		**towing weight**	: -
max. power	: 88 kW (120 bhp) /		**boot space**	: n.a.
	128 kW (175 bhp)		**fuel capacity**	: n.a.
@	: 6000 / 5500 rpm		**consumption**	: 48.9 / 41.1 mpg
max. torque	: 118 /146 lb ft		**acc. 0-62 mph**	: 9.1 / 7.1 s
@	: 4250 / 1600 rpm		**top speed**	: 126 / 140 mph
gears	: 6		**EuroNCAP**	: 4 stars
AT	: optional, 6-speed		**introduction**	: June 2001
drive	: FWD		**last revised in**	: late 2006
brakes f/r	: vent. discs		**warranty**	: 2 years
body type	: 3-dr. hatchback		**miscellaneous**	: After 5 years, Mini deemed a facelift
l x w x h	: 3700 x 1688 x 1415 mm			appropriate. Range will be
wheelbase	: 2467 mm			expanded with a 95 bhp Mini One
turning circle	: n.a.			1.4 in 2007.

MINI ONE CONVERTIBLE

engine type	: petrol, inline-4	kerb weight	: 1140 kg
displacement	: 1598 cc	towing weight	: 650 kg
max. power	: 66 kW (90 bhp)	boot space	: 165 l
@	: 5500 rpm	fuel capacity	: 50 l
max. torque	: 103 lb ft	consumption	: 39.2 mpg
@	: 3000 rpm	acc. 0-62 mph	: 11.8 s
gears	: 5	top speed	: 109 mph
AT	: optional, CVT	EuroNCAP	: 4 stars
drive	: FWD	introduction	: April 2004
brakes f/r	: vent. discs / discs	last revised in	: -
body type	: 2-dr. convertible	warranty	: 2 years
l x w x h	: 3635 x 1688 x 1415 mm	miscellaneous	: Also available as Cooper and
wheelbase	: 2467 mm		Cooper S. New convertible not
turning circle	: 10.7 m		likely to make its appearance soon.

MITSUBISHI COLT 1.1 / 1.3

engine type	: petrol, inline-3 / inline-3
displacement	: 1124 / 1332 cc
max. power	: 55 kW (75 bhp) / 70 kW (95 bhp)
@	: 6000 rpm
max. torque	: 74 / 92 lb ft
@	: 3500 / 4000 rpm
gears	: 5
AT	: - / 6-speed seq.
drive	: FWD
brakes f/r	: vent. discs / discs
body type	: 5-dr. hatchback
l x w x h	: 3870 x 1695 x 1550 mm
wheelbase	: 2500 mm
turning circle	: 10.8 m

kerb weight	: 940 / 945 kg
towing weight	: 1000 kg
boot space	: 220 – 645 l
fuel capacity	: 47 l
consumption	: 51.4 / 47.1 mpg
acc. 0-62 mph	: 13.4 / 11.1 s
top speed	: 103 / 112 mph
EuroNCAP	: 4 stars
introduction	: April 2004
last revised in	: -
warranty	: 3 years
miscellaneous	: Pretty car that could help to make Mitsubishi profitable again. Also available with 1.5 engine.

COLT 1.5 DI-D

engine type	: diesel, inline-3
displacement	: 1493 cc
max. power	: 70 kW (95 bhp)
@	: 4000 rpm
max. torque	: 155 lb ft
@	: 1800 rpm
gears	: 5
kerb weight	: 1060 kg
towing weight	: 1000 kg
consumption	: 58.9 mpg
acc. 0-60 mph	: 9.9 s
top speed	: 112 mph
miscellaneous	: 68 bhp version of 3-cylinder diesel engine also available.

MITSUBISHI COLT CZ3 1.5 INSTYLE / CZT 1.5 TURBO

engine type	: petrol, inline-4	kerb weight	: 1045 / 935 kg
displacement	: 1499 cc	towing weight	: 1000 kg
max. power	: 80 kW (109 bhp) / 110 kW (150 bhp)	boot space	: 220 – 645 l
@	: 6000 rpm	fuel capacity	: 47 l
max. torque	: 107 / 155 lb ft	consumption	: 46.3 /41.5 mpg
@	: 4000 / 3500 rpm	acc. 0-62 mph	: 9.8 / 8 s
gears	: 5	top speed	: 118 / 131 mph
AT	: n.a.	EuroNCAP	: n.a.
drive	: FWD	introduction	: April 2004
brakes f/r	: vent. discs	last revised in	: -
body type	: 3-dr. hatchback	warranty	: 3 years
l x w x h	: 3810 x 1695 x 1520 mm	miscellaneous	: CZ3 also available with smaller
wheelbase	: 2500 mm		petrol engines. CZT is fastest of
turning circle	: 10.8 m		Colt range. Convertible is latest
			addition, with 1.5 and 1.5 turbo
			engines.

MITSUBISHI LANCER WAGON 1.6 / 2.0

engine type	: petrol, inline-4	**kerb weight**	: 1250 / 1295 kg
displacement	: 1584 / 1997 cc	**towing weight**	: 1200 kg
max. power	: 72 kW (98 bhp) / 99 kW (135 bhp)	**boot space**	: 344 - 1079 l
@	: 5000 / 6000 rpm	**fuel capacity**	: 50 / 50 l
max. torque	: 111 / 130 lb ft	**consumption**	: 41.5 / 33.6 mpg
@	: 4000 / 4500 rpm	**acc. 0-62 mph**	: 12.6 / 10.0 s
gears	: 5	**top speed**	: 114 / 127 mph
AT	: -	**EuroNCAP**	: n.a.
drive	: FWD	**introduction**	: summer 2003
brakes f/r	: vent. discs / discs	**last revised in**	: autumn 2005
body type	: 5-dr. stationwagon	**warranty**	: 3 years
l x w x h	: 4485 x 1695 x 1480 mm	**miscellaneous**	: 'Plain' Lancer model now also
wheelbase	: 2600 mm		available as saloon. New Lancer
turning circle	: 10.0 m		on its way.

MITSUBISHI LANCER EVOLUTION IX

engine type	: petrol, inline-4	kerb weight	: 1440 kg
displacement	: 1997 cc	towing weight	: 1200 kg
max. power	: 206 kW (280 bhp)	boot space	: 430 l
@	: 6500 rpm	fuel capacity	: 55 l
max. torque	: 285 lb ft	consumption	: 20.5 mpg
@	: 3500 rpm	acc. 0-62 mph	: 5.7 s
gears	: 6	top speed	: 157 mph
AT	: -	EuroNCAP	: n.a.
drive	: 4WD	introduction	: autumn 2005
brakes f/r	: vent. discs	last revised in	: -
body type	: 4-dr. saloon	warranty	: 3 years
l x w x h	: 4490 x 1770 x 1450 mm	miscellaneous	: Now available with even more
wheelbase	: 2625 mm		horsepower – up to 360 bhp!
turning circle	: 11.8 m		

MITSUBISHI GRANDIS 2.4

engine type	: petrol, inline-4	kerb weight	: 1620 kg
displacement	: 2378 cc	towing weight	: 1600 kg
max. power	: 121 kW (165 bhp)	boot space	: 320 - 1545 l
@	: 6000 rpm	fuel capacity	: 65 l
max. torque	: 160 lb ft	consumption	: 30.1 mpg
@	: 4000 rpm	acc. 0-62 mph	: 10.0 s
gears	5	top speed	: 124 mph
AT	: n.a.	EuroNCAP	: n.a.
drive	: FWD	introduction	: April 2004
brakes f/r	: vent. discs / discs	last revised in	: summer 2005
body type	: 5-dr. MPV	warranty	: 3 years
l x w x h	: 4765 x 1795 x 1655 mm	miscellaneous	: Attractive MPV with high-grade
wheelbase	: 2830 mm		interior and clever design features.
turning circle	: 11.1 m		

GRANDIS 2.0 DI-D

engine type	: diesel, inline-4
displacement	: 1968 cc
max. power	: 100 kW (136 bhp)
@	: 4000 rpm
max. torque	: 228 lb ft
@	: 1750 rpm
gears	: 6
kerb weight	: 1725 kg
towing weight	: 2000 kg
consumption	: 42.8 mpg
acc. 0-60 mph	: 10.8 s
top speed	: 121 mph
miscellaneous	: Diesel power courtesy of Volkswagen. Sensible choice.

MITSUBISHI OUTLANDER 2.0 / 2.4

engine type	: petrol, inline-4
displacement	: 1997 / 2378 cc
max. power	: 100 kW (136 bhp) /
	118 kW (160 bhp)
@	: 6000 / 5750 rpm
max. torque	: 130 / 159 lb ft
@	: 4500 / 4000 rpm
gears	: 5
AT	: - / optional 4-speed
drive	: FWD / 4WD
brakes f/r	: vent. discs / discs
body type	: 5-dr. SUV
l x w x h	: 4545 x 1750 x 1670 mm
wheelbase	: 2625 mm
turning circle	: 11.4 m

kerb weight	: 1540 / 1555 kg
towing weight	: 1500 kg
boot space	: 402 - 1049 l
fuel capacity	: 60 l
consumption	: 29.9 / 28.9 mpg
acc. 0-62 mph	: 11.4 / 9.9 s
top speed	: 119 / 124 mph
EuroNCAP	: n.a.
introduction	: late 2003
last revised in	: 2005
warranty	: 3 years
miscellaneous	: 2-litre version has front-wheel drive, 2.4 has 4WD. Production of this robust and versatile model ends next year.

OUTLANDER 2.0 4WD Turbo

engine type	: petrol, inline-4
displacement	: 1997 cc
max. power	: 148 kW (202 bhp)
@	: 5500 rpm
max. torque	: 224 lb ft
@	: 3500 rpm
gears	: 5
kerb weight	: 1505 kg
towing weight	: 1500 kg
consumption	: 28.1 mpg
acc. 0-60 mph	: 7.7 s
top speed	: 137 mph
miscellaneous	: Turbo-powered version is nice finale for popular crossover SUV.

MITSUBISHI OUTLANDER II DI-D

engine type	: diesel, inline-4	kerb weight	: n.a.
displacement	: 1968 cc	towing weight	: n.a.
max. power	: 103 kW (140 bhp)	boot space	: n.a.
@	: 4000 rpm	fuel capacity	: 60 l
max. torque	: 229 lb ft	consumption	: n.a.
@	: 1750 rpm	acc. 0-62 mph	: 10.5 s
gears	: 6	top speed	: 115 mph
AT	: -	EuroNCAP	: n.a.
drive	: 4WD	introduction	: early 2007
brakes f/r	: vent. discs / discs	last revised in	: -
body type	: 5-dr. SUV	warranty	: 3 years
l x w x h	: 4640 x 1800 x 1680 mm	miscellaneous	: Petrol engines soon to be
wheelbase	: 2670 mm		introduced in 7-seater SUV.
turning circle	: n.a.		Exit old Outlander.

MITSUBISHI SHOGUN SPORT 2.5 TD

engine type	: diesel, inline-4	kerb weight	: 1780 kg
displacement	: 2477 cc	towing weight	: 2800 kg
max. power	: 85 kW (115 bhp)	boot space	: 500 - 1720 l
@	: 4000 rpm	fuel capacity	: 74 l
max. torque	: 177 lb ft	consumption	: 27.2 mpg
@	: 2000 rpm	acc. 0-62 mph	: 18.5 s
gears	: 5	top speed	: 93 mph
AT	: -	EuroNCAP	: n.a.
drive	: 4WD	introduction	: September 2002
brakes f/r	: vent. discs	last revised in	: late 2005
body type	: 5-dr. SUV	warranty	: 3 years
l x w x h	: 4610 x 1695 x 1720 mm	miscellaneous	: Offroad vehicle based on pick-up
wheelbase	: 2725 mm		truck from Mitsubishi. Elegant, but
turning circle	: 11.8 m		no longer as refined as competitors.

PAJERO SPORT 3.0 V6 INTENSE AUTO

engine type	: petrol, V6
displacement	: 2972 cc
max. power	: 125 kW (170 bhp)
@	: 5000 rpm
max. torque	: 188 lb ft
@	: 4000 rpm
gears	: 4-speed automatic
kerb weight	: 1805 kg
towing weight	: 2800 kg
consumption	: 22.6 mpg
acc. 0-60 mph	: 13.2 s
top speed	: 109 mph
miscellaneous	: Rarely seen on our roads.

MITSUBISHI SHOGUN 3.2 DI-D

engine type	: diesel, inline-4	kerb weight	: n.a.
displacement	: 3200 cc	towing weight	: n.a.
max. power	: 118 kW (160 bhp)	boot space	: n.a.
@	: 3800 rpm	fuel capacity	: n.a.
max. torque	: 281 lb ft	consumption	: n.a.
@	: 2000 rpm	acc. 0-62 mph	: 11.5 s
gears	: 6	top speed	: 106 mph
AT	: -	EuroNCAP	: n.a.
drive	: 4WD	introduction	: 1999
brakes f/r	: vent. discs	last revised in	: September 2006
body type	: 3-dr. SUV	warranty	: 3 years
l x w x h	: 4295 x 1885 x 1845 mm	miscellaneous	: 3.2 DI-D version also available with
wheelbase	: 2545 mm		longer wheelbase of 2780 mm.
turning circle	: 10.6 m		

SHOGUN 3.8 V6

engine type	: petrol, V6
displacement	: 3800 cc
max. power	: 184 kW (250 bhp)
@	: n.a.
max. torque	: 243 lb ft
@	: n.a.
gears	: 5-speed automatic
kerb weight	: n.a.
towing weight	: n.a.
consumption	: n.a.
acc. 0-60 mph	: 10.7 s
top speed	: 121 mph
miscellaneous	: This long version measures 4810 mm. V6 engine used earlier in Mitsubishi models for the American market.

MORGAN 4/4 1.8 / MORGAN ROADSTER

engine type	: inline-4 / V6	kerb weight	: 868 / 940 kg
displacement	: 1798 / 2967 cc	towing weight	: n.a.
max. power	: 85 kW (115 bhp) / 166 kW (226 bhp)	boot space	: 102 l
@	: 5500 / 6000 rpm	fuel capacity	: 50 l
max. torque	: 118 / 206 lb ft	consumption	: 29.7 / 19.9 mpg
@	: 4400 / 4900 rpm	acc. 0-62 mph	: 8.9 / 4.9 s
gears	: 5	top speed	: 106 / 115 mph
AT	: -	EuroNCAP	: n.a.
drive	: RWD	introduction	: 1954
brakes f/r	: vent. discs / drum brakes	last revised in	: summer 2004
body type	: 2-dr. convertible	warranty	: 2 years
l x w x h	: 3890 x 1500 x 1290 mm /	miscellaneous	: Not your average contemporary
	4010 x 1720 x 1220 mm		model, but still on the shortlist of
wheelbase	: 2440 / 2500 mm		car buffs around the globe. Engines
turning circle	: 10.0 m		from Ford, including 2.0 with
			145 bhp. Plus 8 model replaced
			by Roadster.

MORGAN AERO 8

engine type	: petrol, V8	kerb weight	: 1145 kg
displacement	: 4398 cc	towing weight	: -
max. power	: 239 kW (325 bhp)	boot space	: n.a.
@	: 6100 rpm	fuel capacity	: 70 l
max. torque	: 331 lb ft	consumption	: 25.9 mpg
@	: 3600 rpm	acc. 0-62 mph	: 4.5 s
gears	: 6	top speed	: 170 mph
AT	: -	EuroNCAP	: n.a.
drive	: RWD	introduction	: late 2000
brakes f/r	: vent. discs	last revised in	: spring 2006
body type	: 2-dr. convertible	warranty	: 2 years
l x w x h	: 4120 x 1770 x 1200 mm	miscellaneous	: V8 from BMW and aluminium
wheelbase	: 2535 mm		chassis not in keeping with Morgan
turning circle	: 10.0 m		tradition, but ashwood bodyframe
			is. Fast, entertaining drive, but
			suspension is killing for your
			kidneys.

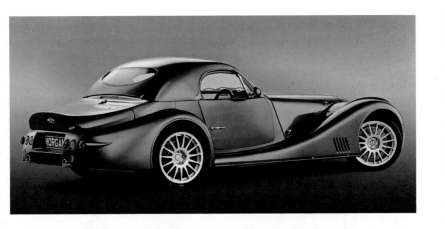

NISSAN MICRA 1.2 / 1.4

engine type	: petrol, inline-4
displacement	: 1240 / 1386 cc
max. power	: 48 kW (65 bhp) / 65 kW (88 bhp)
@	: 5200 rpm
max. torque	: 81 /94 lb ft
@	: 3600 / 3200 rpm
gears	: 5
AT	: - / optional, 4-speed
drive	: FWD
brakes f/r	: vent. discs / drum brakes
body type	: 3-, 5-dr. hatchback
l x w x h	: 3719 x 1660 x 1540 mm
wheelbase	: 2430 mm
turning circle	: 9.2 m

kerb weight	: 921 / 935 kg
towing weight	: 655 / 800 kg
boot space	: 251 – 982 l
fuel capacity	: 46 l
consumption	: 47.9 / 44.8 mpg
acc. 0-62 mph	: 16.3 / 11.9 s
top speed	: 104 / 107 mph
EuroNCAP	: 4 stars
introduction	: December 2002
last revised in	: summer 2005
warranty	: 3 years
miscellaneous	: Successful model. Attractive design and fine driving behaviour. Also available as 1.2 with 80 bhp.

MICRA 1.6

engine type	: petrol, inline-4
displacement	: 1598 cc
max. power	: 81 kW (110 bhp)
@	: 6000 rpm
max. torque	: 113 lb ft
@	: 4400 rpm
gears	: 5
kerb weight	: 992 kg
towing weight	: 800 kg
consumption	: 42.8 mpg
acc. 0-60 mph	: 9.8 s
top speed	: 114 mph
miscellaneous	: Horsepower not quite the 160 bhp its 160 SR badge suggests, but still a nice, lively car.

MICRA 1.5 DCI

engine type	: diesel, inline-4
displacement	: 1461 cc
max. power	: 60 kW (82 bhp)
@	: 4000 rpm
max. torque	: 147 lb ft
@	: 2000 rpm
gears	: 5
kerb weight	: 953 kg
towing weight	: 900 kg
consumption	: 60.1 mpg
acc. 0-60 mph	: 12.9 s
top speed	: 106 mph
miscellaneous	: Fine diesel engine from Renault, also available with 65 bhp.

NISSAN MICRA C+C 1.4 / 1.6

engine type	: petrol, inline-4	kerb weight	: 1135 / 1150 kg
displacement	: 1386 / 1598 cc	towing weight	: 750 kg
max. power	: 65 kW (88 bhp) / 81 kW (110 bhp)	boot space	: 255 / 457 l
@	: 5200 / 6000 rpm	fuel capacity	: 46 l
max. torque	: 94 / 113 lb ft	consumption	: 42.8 /42.2 mpg
@	: 3200 / 4400 rpm	acc. 0-62 mph	: 12.8 / 10.6 s
gears	: 5	top speed	: 109 / 119 mph
AT	: -	EuroNCAP	: n.a.
drive	: FWD	introduction	: early 2006
brakes f/r	: discs / drum brakes	last revised in	: -
body type	: 2-dr. convertible	warranty	: 3 years
l x w x h	: 3806 x 1668 x 1441 mm	miscellaneous	: Small convertibles abound in today's market, but Micra C+C stands out with panoramic glass roof and well-proportioned tail.
wheelbase	: 2432 mm		
turning circle	: n.a.		

NISSAN NOTE 1.4 / 1.6

engine type	: petrol, inline-4	kerb weight	: 967 / 1082 kg
displacement	: 1386 / 1598 cc	towing weight	: 945 / 1000 kg
max. power	: 65 kW (88 bhp) / 81 kW (110 bhp)	boot space	: 437 l
@	: 5200 / 6000 rpm	fuel capacity	: 46 l
max. torque	: 94 / 113 lb ft	consumption	: 44.8 / 42.8 mpg
@	: 3200 / 4400 rpm	acc. 0-62 mph	: 13.1 / 10.7 s
gears	: 5	top speed	: 103 / 114 mph
AT	: -	EuroNCAP	: 4 stars
drive	: FWD	introduction	: early 2006
brakes f/r	: discs / drum brakes	last revised in	: -
body type	: 5-dr. hatchback	warranty	: 3 years
l x w x h	: 4083 x 1690 x 1550 mm	miscellaneous	: New Note looks good and boasts
wheelbase	: 2600 mm		a clever interior. Built in Britain.
turning circle	: 11.0 m		

NOTE 1.5 DCI LP / 1.5 DCI HP

engine type	: diesel, inline-4
displacement	: 1461 cc
max. power	: 50 kW (68 bhp) / 63 kW (86 bhp)
@	: 4000 / 3750 rpm
max. torque	: 118 / 148 lb ft
@	: 2000 rpm
gears	: 5
kerb weight	: 1140 kg
towing weight	: 790 / 900 kg
consumption	: 55.8 / 55.4 mpg
acc. 0-60 mph	: 16.5 / 13.0 s
top speed	: 96 / 101 mph
miscellaneous	: Diesel power promotes career
	of Note as small business car.

NISSAN PRIMERA 1.8

engine type	: petrol, inline-4	kerb weight	: 1268 / 1315 kg
displacement	: 1769 cc	towing weight	: 1500 kg
max. power	: 85 kW (116 bhp)	boot space	: 450 l
@	: 5600 rpm	fuel capacity	: 62 l
max. torque	: 120 lb ft	consumption	: 38.2 mpg
@	: 4000 rpm	acc. 0-62 mph	: 11.9 / 9.6 s
gears	: 5	top speed	: 121 mph
AT	: optional, 4-speed automatic	EuroNCAP	: 4 stars
drive	: FWD	introduction	: February 2002
brakes f/r	: vent. discs	last revised in	: summer 2004
body type	: 4-dr. saloon	warranty	: 3 years
l x w x h	: 4567 x 1760 x 1482 mm	miscellaneous	: Middle-class contender from
wheelbase	: 2680 mm		Nissan not a big seller. Estate
turning circle	: 11.1 m		version also available.

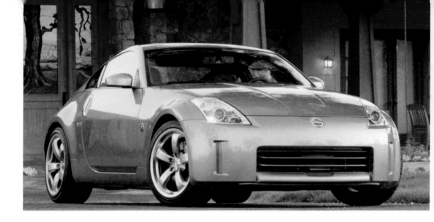

NISSAN 350Z

engine type	: petrol, V6	kerb weight	: 1549 kg
displacement	: 3498 cc	towing weight	: -
max. power	: 221 kW (300 bhp)	boot space	: 235 l
@	: 6400 rpm	fuel capacity	: 80 l
max. torque	: 260 lb ft	consumption	: 24.1 mpg
@	: 4800 rpm	acc. 0-62 mph	: 5.8 s
gears	: 6	top speed	: 155 mph
AT	: -	EuroNCAP	: n.a.
drive	: RWD	introduction	: March 2003
brakes f/r	: vent. discs	last revised in	: February 2006
body type	: 3-dr. coupe	warranty	: 3 years
l x w x h	: 4315 x 1815 x 1325 mm	miscellaneous	: 350Z benefits from recent facelift
wheelbase	: 2650 mm		and extra horsepower and is now
turning circle	: 11.3 m		even more difficult to beat for this
			kind of money. Roadster version
			also available.

NISSAN X-TRAIL 2.5

engine type	: petrol, inline-4		kerb weight	: 1470 kg
displacement	: 2488 cc		towing weight	: 2000 kg
max. power	: 121 kW (165 bhp)		boot space	: 350 - 1841 l
@	: 6000 rpm		fuel capacity	: 60 l
max. torque	: 170 lb ft		consumption	: 30.1 mpg
@	: 4000 rpm		acc. 0-62 mph	: 9.9 s
gears	: 5		top speed	: 118 mph
AT	: optional, 4-speed		EuroNCAP	: 4 stars
drive	: 4WD		introduction	: autumn 2001
brakes f/r	: vent. discs		last revised in	: October 2003
body type	: 5-dr. SUV		warranty	: 3 years
l x w x h	: 4510 x 1765 x 1750 mm		miscellaneous	: Successful crossover with sturdy looks and solid drivetrain. Outsells the Primera by a big margin.
wheelbase	: 2625 mm			
turning circle	: 10.6 m			

NISSAN QASHQAI 1.6 / 2.0

engine type	: petrol, inline-4	kerb weight	: n.a.
displacement	: 1598 / 1997 cc	towing weight	: n.a.
max. power	: 84 kW (115 bhp) / 103 kW	boot space	: n.a.
	(140 bhp)	fuel capacity	: n.a.
@	: 6000 rpm	consumption	: n.a.
max. torque	: 118 / 142 lb ft	acc. 0-62 mph	: n.a.
@	: 4400 / 4800 rpm	top speed	: n.a.
gears	: 5 / 6	EuroNCAP	: n.a.
AT	: - / optional CVT	introduction	: February 2007
drive	: FWD	last revised in	: -
brakes f/r	: vent. discs / discs	warranty	: 3 years
body type	: 5-dr. hatchback	miscellaneous	: Qashqai is a crossover to replace
l x w x h	: 4310 x 1780 x 1610 mm		the Almera.
wheelbase	: 2610 mm		
turning circle	: n.a.		

QASHQAI 1.5 DCI / 2.0 DCI

engine type	: diesel, inline-4
displacement	: 1461 / 1995 cc
max. power	: 78 kW (106 bhp) / 110 kW
	(150 bhp)
@	: 4000 / 3750 rpm
max. torque	: 177/ 236 lb ft
@	: 2000 rpm
gears	: 6
kerb weight	: n.a.
towing weight	: n.a.
consumption	: n.a.
acc. 0-60 mph	: n.a.
top speed	: n.a.
miscellaneous	: Latest model from Nissan promises
	to be a very competitive offer in this
	segment.

NISSAN MURANO 3.5 V6 SE

engine type	: petrol, V6	kerb weight	: 1500 kg
displacement	: 3498 cc	towing weight	: 438 - 1965 l
max. power	: 172 kW (234 bhp)	boot space	: 82 l
@	: 6000 rpm	fuel capacity	: 23 mpg
max. torque	: 235 lb ft	consumption	n.a.
@	: 3600 rpm	acc. 0-62 mph	: 8.9 s
gears	: -	top speed	: 124 mph
AT	: CVT	EuroNCAP	: n.a.
drive	: 4WD	introduction	: October 2004
brakes f/r	: vent. discs	last revised in	: -
body type	: 5-dr. SUV	warranty	: 3 years
l x w x h	: 4770 x 1880 x 1705 mm	miscellaneous	: No spare tyre on the rear door
wheelbase	: 2825 mm		of this modern SUV. Popular
turning circle	: 12.0 m		alternative to higher middle-class
			offerings. Available only with
			transversely mounted petrol engine
			and just one equipment level.

NISSAN PATROL 3.0 DI

engine type	: diesel, inline-4	**kerb weight**	: 2365 kg
displacement	: 2953 cc	**towing weight**	: 3500 kg
max. power	: 118 kW (160 bhp)	**boot space**	: 308 - 1652 l
@	: 3600 rpm	**fuel capacity**	: 95 l
max. torque	: 235 lb ft	**consumption**	: 26.2 mpg
@	: 2000 rpm	**acc. 0-62 mph**	: 14.8 s
gears	: 5	**top speed**	: 99 mph
AT	: optional, 4-speed	**EuroNCAP**	: n.a.
drive	: 4WD	**introduction**	: autumn 1997
brakes f/r	: vent. discs	**last revised in**	: autumn 2004
body type	: 5-dr. SUV	**warranty**	: 3 years
l x w x h	: 5045 x 1840 x 1855 mm	**miscellaneous**	: Classic offroader with externally
wheelbase	: 2970 mm		mounted spare tyre. Patrol often
turning circle	: 12.2 m		used professionally, more likely than
			not with a trailer on tow. Also
			available as 3-door with wheelbase
			of 2400 mm.

NISSAN PATHFINDER 2.5 DCI

engine type	: diesel, inline-4		kerb weight	: 2235 kg
displacement	: 2488 cc		towing weight	: 3000 kg
max. power	: 128 kW (174 bhp)		boot space	: 515 – 2091 l
@	: 4000 rpm		fuel capacity	: 80 l
max. torque	: 297 lb ft		consumption	: 31.4 mpg
@	: 2000 rpm		acc. 0-62 mph	: 11.5 s
gears	: 6		top speed	: 108 mph
AT	: optional, 5-speed automatic		EuroNCAP	: 4 stars
drive	: 4WD		introduction	: spring 2005
brakes f/r	: vent. discs		last revised in	: -
body type	: 5-dr. SUV		warranty	: 3 years
l x w x h	: 4740 x 1850 x 1760 mm		miscellaneous	: Impressively big SUV, yet
wheelbase	: 2850 mm			Americans refer to it as a
turning circle	: 11.9 m			'mid-sized' car. Capable
				offroader too.

PATHFINDER 4.0 V6

engine type	: petrol, V6
displacement	: 3954 cc
max. power	: 198 kW (269 bhp)
@	: 5600 rpm
max. torque	: 284 lb ft
@	: 4000 rpm
gears	: 5-speed automatic
kerb weight	: 2165 kg
towing weight	: 3000 kg
consumption	: 23.0 mpg
acc. 0-60 mph	: 8.9 s
top speed	: 118 mph
miscellaneous	: Manufacturer expects petrol version to be a slow seller, therefore only available with high level of equipment.

NOBLE M12 GTO-3R / M400

engine type	: petrol, V6	kerb weight	: 1080 / 1160 kg
displacement	: 2968 cc	towing weight	: -
max. power	: 239 kW (352 bhp) /	boot space	: -
	313 kW (425 bhp)	fuel capacity	: n.a.
@	: 6200 / 6500 rpm	consumption	: n.a.
max. torque	: 350 / 389 lb ft	acc. 0-62 mph	: 3.7 / 3.5 s
@	: 3500 / 5000 rpm	top speed	: 173 / 179 mph
gears	: 6	EuroNCAP	: n.a.
AT	: -	introduction	: 2004
drive	: RWD	last revised in	: -
brakes f/r	: vent. discs	warranty	: 2 years
body type	: 2-dr. coupé	miscellaneous	: Little gems from Englishman Lee
l x w x h	: 4089 x 1885 x 1143 mm		Noble, one of the best independent
wheelbase	: 2438 mm		sportscar manufacturers around.
turning circle	: n.a.		Fierce turbo engine and superb
			chassis.

NOBLE M15

engine type	: petrol, V6	kerb weight	: 1250 kg
displacement	: 2968 cc	towing weight	: -
max. power	: 339 kW (455 bhp)	boot space	: 185 l
@	: 6800 rpm	fuel capacity	: 70 l
max. torque	: 455 lb ft	consumption	: n.a.
@	: 4800 rpm	acc. 0-62 mph	: 3.5 s
gears	: 6	top speed	: 173 mph
AT	: -	EuroNCAP	: n.a.
drive	: RWD	introduction	: April 2006
brakes f/r	: vent. discs	last revised in	: -
body type	: 2-dr. coupe	warranty	: 2 years
l x w x h	: 4270 x 1905 x 1116 mm	miscellaneous	: M15 model intended to com-
wheelbase	: 2438 mm		bat with the likes of Ferrari and
turning circle	: n.a.		Porsche. Can be used as a
			shopping car as well, according to
			its maker.

OPEL (VAUXHALL) AGILA 1.0 / 1.2

engine type	: petrol, inline-3	kerb weight	: 940 / 955 kg
displacement	: 998 / 1229 cc	towing weight	: 650 kg
max. power	: 44 kW (60 bhp) / 59 kW (80 bhp)	boot space	: 240 -1250 l
@	: 5600 rpm	fuel capacity	: 41 l
max. torque	: 65 / 81 lb ft	consumption	: 48.7 / 47.1 mpg
@	: 3800 / 4000 rpm	acc. 0-62 mph	: 17.7 / 13.2 s
gears	: 5	top speed	: 90 / 100 mph
AT	: -	EuroNCAP	: n.a.
drive	: FWD	introduction	: summer 2000
brakes f/r	: vent. discs / drum brakes	last revised in	: late 2004
body type	: 5-dr. MPV	warranty	: 2 years
l x w x h	: 3535 x 1620 x 1660 mm	miscellaneous	: Smallest Vauxhall identical to
wheelbase	: 2360 mm		Suzuki Wagon R+. Popular with
turning circle	: 9.9 m		ladies and senior citizens alike.

OPEL (VAUXHALL) CORSA 1.2 / 1.4

engine type	: petrol, inline-4	kerb weight	: 1100 kg
displacement	: 1229 / 1364 cc	towing weight	: 1000 kg / n.a.
max. power	: 59 kW (80 bhp) / 66 kW (90 bhp)	boot space	: 285 – 1050 l
@	: 5600 rpm	fuel capacity	: n.a.
max. torque	: 81 / 92 lb ft	consumption	: 48.7 / 47.9 mpg
@	: 4000 rpm	acc. 0-62 mph	: 13.9 / 12.4 s
gears	: 5	top speed	: 109 / 111 mph
AT	: optional 5-speed / -	EuroNCAP	: n.a.
drive	: FWD	introduction	: September 2006
brakes f/r	: vent. discs / discs	last revised in	: -
body type	: 3-dr. hatchback	warranty	: 2 years
l x w x h	: 3999 x 1713 x 1488 mm	miscellaneous	: New Corsa has put on some
wheelbase	: 2511 mm		weight. Shares platform with Fiat
turning circle	: 10.2 m		Grande Punto. 5-door version and
			1.0 3-cylinder engine also available,
			but small engine too underpowered
			for heavy Corsa.

CORSA 1.3 CDTI

engine type	: diesel, inline-4
displacement	: 1248 cc
max. power	: 66 kW (90 bhp)
@	: 4000 rpm
max. torque	: 148 lb ft
@	: 1750 rpm
gears	: 6
kerb weight	: n.a.
towing weight	: 1200 kg
consumption	: 61.4 mpg
acc. 0-60 mph	: 12.7 s
top speed	: 107 mph
miscellaneous	: Corsa also available with 1.7 diesel engine with 125 bhp.

OPEL (VAUXHALL) TIGRA 1.4 / 1.8

engine type	: petrol, inline-4	kerb weight	: 1135 / 1165 kg
displacement	: 1364 / 1796 cc	towing weight	: -
max. power	: 66 kW (90 bhp) / 92 kW (125 bhp)	boot space	: 250 l
@	: 5600 / 6000 rpm	fuel capacity	: 45 l
max. torque	: 92 / 122 lb ft	consumption	: 46.3 / 36.7 mpg
@	: 4000 / 4600 rpm	acc. 0-62 mph	: 12.4 / 9.4 s
gears	: 5	top speed	: 112 / 127 mph
AT	: optional 5-speed / -	EuroNCAP	: n.a.
drive	: FWD	introduction	: late 2004
brakes f/r	: vent. discs / drum brakes	last revised in	: -
body type	: 2-dr. convertible	warranty	: 2 years
l x w x h	: 3921 x 1685 x 1364 mm	miscellaneous	: Charming convertible with
wheelbase	: 2491 mm		foldable steel hardtop, built by
turning circle	: 10.6 m		Karmann. More rare than a
			Peugeot 206 CC.

OPEL (VAUXHALL) TOUR 1.4

engine type	: petrol, inline-4		kerb weight	: 1135 kg
displacement	: 1364 cc		towing weight	: 1000 kg
max. power	: 66 kW (90 bhp)		boot space	: 510 -2695 l
@	: 5600 rpm		fuel capacity	: 52 l
max. torque	: 92 lb ft		consumption	: 44.8 mpg
@	: 4000 rpm		acc. 0-62 mph	: 14.0 s
gears	: 5		top speed	: 101 mph
AT	: -		EuroNCAP	: n.a.
drive	: FWD		introduction	: late 2002
brakes f/r	: vent. discs / drum brakes		last revised in	: autumn 2003
body type	: 5-dr. MPV		warranty	: 2 years
l x w x h	: 4332 x 1684 x 1801 mm		miscellaneous	: Corsa-based mini-MPV is not
wheelbase	: 2716 mm			nearly as successful as Meriva.
turning circle	: 10.8 m			

TOUR 1.3 CDTI / 1.7 CDTI

engine type	: diesel, inline-4
displacement	: 1248 / 1686 cc
max. power	: 55 kW (75 bhp) / 74 kW (100 bhp)
@	: 4000 / 4400 rpm
max. torque	: 125 / 148 lb ft
@	: 1750 / 2300 rpm
gears	: 5
kerb weight	: 1225 / 1265 kg
towing weight	: 1000 kg
consumption	: 55.4 / 54.3 mpg
acc. 0-60 mph	: 17.0 / 12.5 s
top speed	: 94 / 106 mph
miscellaneous	: No immediate successor planned on the basis of new Corsa.

OPEL (VAUXHALL) MERIVA 1.4 / 1.8

engine type	: petrol, inline-4	kerb weight	: 1230 / 1280 kg
displacement	: 1364 / 1796 cc	towing weight	: 1000 / 1200 kg
max. power	: 66 kW (90 bhp) / 92 kW (125 bhp)	boot space	: 415 l
@	: 5600 / 6000 rpm	fuel capacity	: 53 l
max. torque	: 92 / 122 lb ft	consumption	: 44.1 / 35.8 mpg
@	: 4000 / 4600 rpm	acc. 0-62 mph	: 13.8 / 11.3 s
gears	: 5	top speed	: 104 / 118 mph
AT	: optional 5-speed	EuroNCAP	: 4 stars
drive	: FWD	introduction	: spring 2003
brakes f/r	: vent. discs / discs	last revised in	: January 2006
body type	: 5-dr. MPV	warranty	: 2 years
l x w x h	: 4052 x 1694 x 1624 mm	miscellaneous	: Successful, class-leading crossover
wheelbase	: 2630 mm		between Corsa and Astra boasts a
turning circle	: 10.5 m		spacious, flexible interior. Also
			available with 1.6 engine.

MERIVA 1.3 CDTI / 1.7 CDTI

engine type	: diesel, inline-4
displacement	: 1248 / 1686 cc
max. power	: 55 kW (75 bhp) / 74 kW (100 bhp)
@	: 4400 rpm
max. torque	: 170 / 240 lb ft
@	: 1750 / 2300 rpm
gears	: 5
kerb weight	: 1293 / 1355 kg
towing weight	: 1200 / 1000 kg
consumption	: 56.5 / 54.3 mpg
acc. 0-60 mph	: 17.8 / 13.4 s
top speed	: 98 / 111 mph
miscellaneous	: Frugal Merivas, thanks to
	reliable diesel engines.

OPEL (VAUXHALL) ASTRA 1.4 / 1.6

engine type	: petrol, inline-4	kerb weight	: 1130 / 1165 kg
displacement	: 1364 / 1598 cc	towing weight	: 1000 / 1200 kg
max. power	: 66 kW (90 bhp) / 77 kW (105 bhp)	boot space	: 380 -1300 l
@	: 5600 / 6000 rpm	fuel capacity	: 52 l
max. torque	: 92 / 110 lb ft	consumption	: 44.8 / 42.8 mpg
@	: 4000 / 3900 rpm	acc. 0-62 mph	: 13.7 / 12.3 s
gears	: 5	top speed	: 111 / 115 mph
AT	: optional 5-speed	EuroNCAP	: 5 stars
drive	: FWD	introduction	: January 2004
brakes f/r	: vent. discs / drum brakes	last revised in	: -
body type	: 5-dr. hatchback	warranty	: 2 years
l x w x h	: 4249 x 1753 x 1460 mm	miscellaneous	: Undoubtedly a new bestseller in true Vauxhall tradition. Drives well, model range very wide. Refer to Astra Estate for diesel specifications.
wheelbase	: 2614 mm		
turning circle	: 10.8 m		

ASTRA 1.8 / 2.0 T

engine type	: petrol, inline-4
displacement	: 1796 / 1998 cc
max. power	: 103 kW (140 bhp) / 125 kW (170 bhp)
@	: 6300 / 5200 rpm
max. torque	: 129 / 184 lb ft
@	: 3800 / 1950 rpm
gears	: 5 / 6
kerb weight	: 1178 / 1285 kg
towing weight	: 1300 / 1500 kg
consumption	: 38.7 / 31.4 mpg
acc. 0-60 mph	: 10.2 / 8.7 s
top speed	: 123 / 135 mph
miscellaneous	: Two-litre turbo engine also available with 200 bhp. Fast and unobtrusive, with near-GTI performance.

OPEL (VAUXHALL) ASTRA ESTATE 1.3 CDTI / 1.9 CDTI

engine type	: diesel, inline-4	kerb weight	: n.a./ 1350 kg
displacement	: 1248 / 1910 cc	towing weight	: 1400 kg
max. power	: 66 kW (90 bhp) / 74 kW (100 bhp)	boot space	: 505 -1540 l
@	: 4000 / 3500 rpm	fuel capacity	: 52 l
max. torque	: 147 / 177 lb ft	consumption	: 58.9 / 56.5 mpg
@	: 1750 / 1700 rpm	acc. 0-62 mph	: 13.2 / 11.7 s
gears	: 6	top speed	: 107 / 112 mph
AT	: - / optional 6-speed	EuroNCAP	: 5 stars
drive	: FWD	introduction	: summer 2004
brakes f/r	: vent. discs / drum brakes	last revised in	: -
body type	: 5-dr. stationwagon	warranty	: 2 years
l x w x h	: 4515 x 1753 x 1500 mm	miscellaneous	: Spacious estate, also
wheelbase	: 2703 mm		available with petrol engines
turning circle	: 11.1 m		ranging from 90 up to 200 bhp.

ASTRA ESTATE 1.9 CDTI

engine type	: diesel, inline-4
displacement	: 1910 cc
max. power	: 88 kW (120 bhp) / 110 kW (150 bhp)
@	: 4000 rpm
max. torque	: 206 / 232 lb ft
@	: 2000 rpm
gears	: 6
kerb weight	: 1335 / 1350 kg
towing weight	: 1400 kg
consumption	: 47.9 mpg
acc. 0-60 mph	: 10.8 / 9.2 s
top speed	: 120 / 129 mph
miscellaneous	: Powerful diesel engines also available in 3-door and 5-door hatchback.

OPEL (VAUXHALL) ASTRA 2.0 T

engine type	: petrol, inline-4		kerb weight	: 1265 kg
displacement	: 1998 cc		towing weight	: 1500 kg
max. power	: 147 kW (200 bhp)		boot space	: 380 l
@	: 5400 rpm		fuel capacity	: 52 l
max. torque	: 193 lb ft		consumption	: 30.4 mpg
@	: 4200 rpm		acc. 0-62 mph	: 7.8 s
gears	: 6		top speed	: 145 mph
AT	: -		EuroNCAP	: 5 stars
drive	: FWD		introduction	: late 2005
brakes f/r	: vent. discs / discs		last revised in	: -
body type	: 3-dr. hatchback		warranty	: 2 years
l x w x h	: 4288 x 1753 x 1413 mm		miscellaneous	: 3-door hatchback visually very
wheelbase	: 2614 mm			different from 5-door version and
turning circle	: 10.8 m			more sporty. VXR fastest of Astra
				range with 240 bhp 2.0 turbo
				engine.

ASTRA VXR

engine type	: petrol, inline-4
displacement	: 1998 cc
max. power	: 177 kW (240 bhp)
@	: 5600 rpm
max. torque	: 236 lb ft
@	: 2400 rpm
gears	: 6
kerb weight	: 1293 kg
towing weight	: 1500 kg
consumption	: 30.7 mpg
acc. 0-60 mph	: 6.4 s
top speed	: 152 mph
miscellaneous	: Top-of-the-range model.
	Front-wheel drive is brave choice,
	considering the high output of
	the 2-litre turbo engine.

OPEL (VAUXHALL) ASTRA TWIN TOP 1.6 / 1.8

engine type	: petrol, inline-4	kerb weight	: 1415 / 1420 kg
displacement	: 1598 / 1796 cc	towing weight	: 1050 / 1200 kg
max. power	: 77 kW (105 bhp) /	boot space	: 205 - 440 l
	103 kW (140 bhp)	fuel capacity	: 52 l
@	: 6000 / 6300 rpm	consumption	: 40.4 / 36.7
max. torque	: 110 / 129 lb ft	acc. 0-62 mph	: 14.1 / 11.4 s
@	: 3900 / 3800 rpm	top speed	: 116 / 130 mph
gears	: 5	EuroNCAP	: n.a.
AT	: -	introduction	: April 2006
drive	: FWD	last revised in	: -
brakes f/r	: vent. discs / discs	warranty	: 2 years
body type	: 2-dr. convertible	miscellaneous	: Pretty 4-seater convertible with
l x w x h	: 4476 x 1831 x 1414 mm		clever roof top construction. Also
wheelbase	: 2614 mm		available as 2.0T with 170/200 bhp
turning circle	: 10.8 m		and 1.9 CDTi with 150 bhp.

OPEL (VAUXHALL) ZAFIRA 1.8 / 2.2

engine type	: petrol, inline-4
displacement	: 1796 / 2198 cc
max. power	: 103 kW (140 bhp) / 110 kW (150 bhp)
@	: 6300 / 5600 rpm
max. torque	: 129 / 159 lb ft
@	: 3800 / 4000 rpm
gears	: 5 / 6
AT	: - / optional 4-speed
drive	: FWD
brakes f/r	: vent. discs / discs
body type	: 5-dr. MPV
l x w x h	: 4467 x 1801 x 1635 mm
wheelbase	: 2703 mm
turning circle	: 10.9 m
kerb weight	: 1403 / 1470 kg
towing weight	: 1200 kg
boot space	: 140 - 1820 l
fuel capacity	: 58 l
consumption	: 36.2 / 34.4 mpg
acc. 0-62 mph	: 11.5 / 10.6 s
top speed	: 122 / 124 mph
EuroNCAP	: 5 stars
introduction	: summer 2005
last revised in	: -
warranty	: 2 years
miscellaneous	: Second generation of pioneering model, positioned somewhat higher in the market now to make room for Meriva. FLEX-7 seating concept retained. Also available as 1.6, 2.0 T and VXR.

ZAFIRA 1.9 CDTI

engine type	: diesel, inline-4
displacement	: 1910 cc
max. power	: 88 kW (120 bhp) / 110 kW (150 bhp)
@	: 3500 / 4000 rpm
max. torque	: 206 / 236 lb ft
@	: 1700 / 2000 rpm
gears	: 6
kerb weight	: 1513 / 1528 kg
towing weight	: 1200 / 1500 kg
consumption	: 46.3 / 45.6 lb ft
acc. 0-60 mph	: 12.0 / 10.4 s
top speed	: 116 / 126 lb ft
miscellaneous	: Particle filter comes as standard.

OPEL (VAUXHALL) VECTRA 1.8 16V / 2.2 16V

engine type	: petrol, inline-4
displacement	: 1796 / 2198 cc
max. power	: 103 kW (140 bhp) /
	114 kW (155 bhp)
@	: 6300 / 5600 rpm
max. torque	: 129 / 162 lb ft
@	: 3800 rpm
gears	: 5 / 6
AT	: - / optional 5-speed
drive	: FWD
brakes f/r	: vent. discs / discs
body type	: 4-dr. saloon
l x w x h	: 4596 x 1798 x 1460 mm
wheelbase	: 2700 mm
turning circle	: 11.0 m

kerb weight	: 1295 / 1335 kg
towing weight	: 1400 / 1500 kg
boot space	: 500 - 1050 l
fuel capacity	: 60 l
consumption	: 39.2 / 37.7 mpg
acc. 0-62 mph	: 10.7 / 9.6 s
top speed	: 131 / 135 mph
EuroNCAP	: 4 stars
introduction	: autumn 2001
last revised in	: autumn 2005
warranty	: 2 years
miscellaneous	: Successful middle-class lease car. Available as saloon and hatchback. New headlights introduced with facelift.

VECTRA 2.0 T

engine type	: petrol, inline-4
displacement	: 1998 cc
max. power	: 129 kW (175 bhp)
@	: 5500 rpm
max. torque	: 195 lb ft
@	: 2500 rpm
gears	: 6
kerb weight	: 1465 kg
towing weight	: 1700 kg
consumption	: 32.8 mpg
acc. 0-60 mph	: 9.4 s
top speed	: 143 mph
miscellaneous	: Good performance, high equipment level.

OPEL (VAUXHALL) VECTRA ESTATE 1.9 CDTI

engine type	: petrol, inline-4	kerb weight	: 1505 kg
displacement	: 1910 cc	towing weight	: 1500 kg
max. power	: 88 kW (120 bhp) /	boot space	: 530 - 1850 l
	110 kW (150 bhp)	fuel capacity	: 60 l
@	: 3500 / 4000 rpm	consumption	: 48.7 mpg
max. torque	: 206 / 232 lb ft	acc. 0-62 mph	: 12.0 / 10.5 s
@	: 2000 rpm	top speed	: 121 / 130 mph
gears	: 6	EuroNCAP	: 4 stars
AT	: - / optional 6-speed	introduction	: spring 2003
drive	: FWD	last revised in	: autumn 2005
brakes f/r	: vent. discs / discs	warranty	: 2 years
body type	: 5-dr. stationwagon	miscellaneous	: One of the biggest
l x w x h	: 4822 x 1798 x 1500 mm		stationwagons on the market, with
wheelbase	: 2830 mm		a giant flat loading platform. Also
turning circle	: 10.9 m		available with both 4- and
			6-cylinder petrol engines.

VECTRA ESTATE VXR

engine type	: petrol, inline-4
displacement	: 2792 cc
max. power	: 206 kW (280 bhp)
@	: 5500 rpm
max. torque	: 262 lb ft
@	: 1800 rpm
gears	: 6
kerb weight	: 1613 kg
towing weight	: 1800 kg
consumption	: 26.9 mpg
acc. 0-60 mph	: 6.5 s
top speed	: 155 mph
miscellaneous	: Recent power boost, but top speed limited to 155 mph. Previous VXR did 160 mph, enough to beat a BMW M5.

OPEL (VAUXHALL) SIGNUM 2.8 V6 TURBO / 3.0 V6 CDTI

engine type	: petrol, V6 / diesel, V6
displacement	: 2792 / 2958 cc
max. power	: 169 kW (230 bhp) /
	130 kW (184 bhp)
@	: 5500 / 4000 rpm
max. torque	: 243 / 295 lb ft
@	: 1800 / 1900 rpm
gears	: 6
AT	: optional 6-speed
drive	: FWD
brakes f/r	: vent. discs
body type	: 5-dr. hatchback
l x w x h	: 4636 x 1798 x 1466 mm
wheelbase	: 2830 mm
turning circle	: 11.4 m

kerb weight	: 1535 / 1610 kg
towing weight	: 1700 kg
boot space	: 365 - 1410 l
fuel capacity	: 60 l
consumption	: 26.6 / 40.4 mpg
acc. 0-62 mph	: 7.6 / 9.6 s
top speed	: 151 / 139 mph
EuroNCAP	: 4 stars
introduction	: March 2003
last revised in	: September 2005
warranty	: 2 years
miscellaneous	: Spacious hatchback on Vectra Estate platform, with two separate seats in the back.

OPEL (VAUXHALL) GT

engine type	: petrol, inline-4	kerb weight	: 1320 kg
displacement	: 1998 cc	towing weight	: -
max. power	: 191 kW (260 bhp)	boot space	: 153 l
@	: 5300 rpm	fuel capacity	: 52 l
max. torque	: 258 lb ft	consumption	: n.a.
@	: 2500 rpm	acc. 0-62 mph	: < 6.0 s
gears	: 5	top speed	: > 145 mph
AT	: -	EuroNCAP	: n.a.
drive	: RWD	introduction	: April 2007
brakes f/r	: vent. discs / discs	last revised in	: -
body type	: 2-dr. convertible	warranty	: 2 years
l x w x h	: 4091 x 1813 x 1274 mm	miscellaneous	: Famous GT badge revived,
wheelbase	: 2614 mm		this time on a roadster based
turning circle	: 10.6 m		on the Saturn Sky.

OPEL (VAUXHALL) ANTARA 2.4

engine type	: petrol, inline-4
displacement	: 2405 cc
max. power	: 103 kW (140 bhp)
@	: 5200 rpm
max. torque	: 162 lb ft
@	: 2400 rpm
gears	: 5
AT	: -
drive	: FWD
brakes f/r	: vent. discs / discs
body type	: 5-dr. SUV
l x w x h	: 4575 x 1850 x 1704 mm
wheelbase	: 2707 mm
turning circle	: 12.4 m

kerb weight	: 1805 / 1865 kg
towing weight	: 1500 / 2000 kg
boot space	: 405 l
fuel capacity	: 65 l
consumption	: 29.4 mpg
acc. 0-62 mph	: 11.9 s
top speed	: 109 mph
EuroNCAP	: n.a.
introduction	: September 2006
last revised in	: -
warranty	: 2 years
miscellaneous	: Based on the Chevrolet Captiva, but without the third row of seats. Antara faster and more economical than American.

ANTARA 2.0 CDTI

engine type	: diesel, inline-4
displacement	: 1991 cc
max. power	: 110 kW (150 bhp)
@	: 4000 rpm
max. torque	: 236 lb ft
@	: 2000 rpm
gears	: 5, optional 5-speed automatic
kerb weight	: n.a.
towing weight	: 2000 kg
consumption	: 37.7 mpg
acc. 0-60 mph	: 10.3 s
top speed	: 112 mph
miscellaneous	: Diesel-powered version likely to be bestseller of Antara range.

PAGANI ZONDA F

engine type	: petrol, V12		**kerb weight**	: approx. 1350 kg
displacement	: 7291 cc		**towing weight**	: -
max. power	: 443 kW (602 bhp)		**boot space**	: n.a.
@	: 6150 rpm		**fuel capacity**	: n.a.
max. torque	: 560 lb ft		**consumption**	: n.a.
@	: 4000 rpm		**acc. 0-62 mph**	: 3.6 s
gears	: 6		**top speed**	: > 215 mph
AT	: -		**EuroNCAP**	: n.a.
drive	: RWD		**introduction**	: April 2005
brakes f/r	: ceramic discs		**last revised in**	: n.v.t.
body type	: 2-dr. coupe		**warranty**	: n.a.
l x w x h	: 4435 x 2055 x 1141 mm		**miscellaneous**	: Unique sportscar from
wheelbase	: 2730 mm			Modena-based Horacio Pagani,
turning circle	: n.a.			with lots of carbonfibre and engines
				from Mercedes-Benz. More exotic
				than Ferrari Enzo. Also available
				as convertible.

PEUGEOT 107 1.0

engine type	: petrol, inline-3	kerb weight	: 865 kg
displacement	: 998 cc	towing weight	: -
max. power	: 50 kW (68 bhp)	boot space	: 139 - 751 l
@	: 6000 rpm	fuel capacity	: 35 l
max. torque	: 70 lb ft	consumption	: 61.4 mpg
@	: 3600 rpm	acc. 0-62 mph	: 13.7 s
gears	: 5	top speed	: 100 mph
AT	: optional 5-speed	EuroNCAP	: 4 stars
drive	: FWD	introduction	: December 2005
brakes f/r	: vent. discs / discs	last revised in	: -
body type	: 3- / 5-dr. hatchback	warranty	: 2 years
l x w x h	: 3430 x 1630 x 1470 mm	miscellaneous	: Front has typical Peugeot family
wheelbase	: 2340 mm		look. More versions of this budget
turning circle	: 9.5 m		car not planned.

PEUGEOT 1007 1.4 / 1.6 16V

engine type	: petrol, inline-4
displacement	: 1360 / 1587 cc
max. power	: 55 kW (75 bhp) / 80 kW (110 bhp)
@	: 5400 / 5800 rpm
max. torque	: 88 / 110 lb ft
@	: 3300 / 4000 rpm
gears	: 5
AT	: optional, 2Tronic
drive	: FWD
brakes f/r	: vent. discs, drum brakes / discs
body type	: 3-dr. hatchback
l x w x h	: 3731 x 1686 x 1620 mm
wheelbase	: 2315 mm
turning circle	: 10.1 m

kerb weight	: 1115 / 1178 kg
towing weight	: 987 / 1090 kg
boot space	: 326 - 977 l
fuel capacity	: 40 l
consumption	: 43.5 / 40.9 mpg
acc. 0-62 mph	: 15.6 / 11.1 s
top speed	: 103 / 118 mph
EuroNCAP	: 5 stars
introduction	: Summer 2005
last revised in	: -
warranty	: 2 years
miscellaneous	: Trendy city car with sliding doors for ease of entry in confined parking spaces. More expensive than comparable cars. Also 90 bhp 1.4 engine available.

1007 1.4 HDI

engine type	: diesel, inline-4
displacement	: 1398 cc
max. power	: 50 kW (70 bhp)
@	: 4000 rpm
max. torque	: 120 lb ft
@	: 2000 rpm
gears	: 5
kerb weight	: 1143 kg
towing weight	: 1137 kg
consumption	: 60.1 mpg
acc. 0-60 mph	: 16.7 s
top speed	: 99 mph
miscellaneous	: Diesel power makes small 1007 thrifty.

PEUGEOT PARTNER 1.4 / 1.6

engine type	: petrol, inline-4	kerb weight	: 1163 / 1226 kg
displacement	: 1360 / 1587 cc	towing weight	: 900 / 1100 kg
max. power	: 55 kW (75 bhp) / 80 kW (110 bhp)	boot space	: 624 - 2800 l
@	: 5500 / 5750 rpm	fuel capacity	: 55 l
max. torque	: 90 / 110 lb ft	consumption	: 39.8 / 37.5 mpg
@	: 3400 / 4000 rpm	acc. 0-62 mph	: 14.5 / 11.2 s
gears	: 5	top speed	: 93 / 107 mph
AT	: -	EuroNCAP	: n.a.
drive	: FWD	introduction	: 1996
brakes f/r	: vent. discs / drum brakes	last revised in	: September 2002
body type	: 4-dr. MPV	warranty	: 2 years
l x w x h	: 4137 x 1724 x 1801 mm	miscellaneous	: Already in its tenth year of
wheelbase	: 2693 mm		production. Good alternative to
turning circle	: 11.3 m		marginally higher positioned car
			when spaciousness is more
			important than chassis or looks.

PARTNER 1.6 HDI 90

engine type	: diesel, inline-4
displacement	: 1560 cc
max. power	: 66 kW (90 bhp)
@	: 4000 rpm
max. torque	: 161 lb ft
@	: 1900 rpm
gears	: 5
kerb weight	: 1244 / 1215 kg
towing weight	: 1100 kg
consumption	: 52.3 mpg
acc. 0-60 mph	: 12.9 s
top speed	: 99 mph
miscellaneous	: Diesel versions account for majority of commercial Partner sales. Version of 1.4 that runs on natural gas also available, for added tax benefits.

PEUGEOT 206 1.4 / 1.6 16V

engine type	: petrol, inline-4	
displacement	: 1360 / 1587 cc	
max. power	: 55 kW (75 bhp) / 80 kW (110 bhp)	
@	: 5500 / 5800 rpm	
max. torque	: 90 / 110 lb ft	
@	: 2800 / 4000 rpm	
gears	: 5 / -	
AT	: - / 4-speed	
drive	: FWD	
brakes f/r	: discs, drum brakes / vent. discs, discs	
body type	: 3-dr. hatchback	
l x w x h	: 3835 x 1652 x 1428 mm	
wheelbase	: 2442 mm	
turning circle	: 9.8 m	

kerb weight	: 925 / 988 kg
towing weight	: 1100 kg
boot space	: 245 - 1130 l
fuel capacity	: 50 l
consumption	: 44.1 / 38.1 mpg
acc. 0-62 mph	: 12.2 / 13.1 s
top speed	: 106 / 117 mph
EuroNCAP	: 4 stars
introduction	: July 1998
last revised in	: September 2002
warranty	: 2 years
miscellaneous	: Model retained in Peugeot range as cheaper alternative, like Renault Clio and Fiat Punto. Also available as stationwagon SW.

206 1.4 HDI

engine type	: diesel, inline-4
displacement	: 1398 cc
max. power	: 50 kW (68 bhp)
@	: 4000 rpm
max. torque	: 120 lb ft
@	: 1750 rpm
gears	: 5
kerb weight	: 949 kg
towing weight	: 1100 kg
consumption	: 64.2 mpg
acc. 0-60 mph	: 13.1 s
top speed	: 104 mph
miscellaneous	: SW version is available with 1.6 HDiF 16V diesel engine.

PEUGEOT 206 CC 1.6 16V / 2.0 16V

engine type	: petrol, inline-4	kerb weight	: 1115 / 1127 kg
displacement	: 1587 / 1997 cc	towing weight	: 1100 / 1100 kg
max. power	: 80 kW (110 bhp) /	boot space	: 175 l
	100 kW (138 bhp)	fuel capacity	: 50 l
@	: 5750 / 6000 rpm	consumption	: 40.3 / 32.8 mpg
max. torque	: 110 / 143 lb ft	acc. 0-62 mph	: 10.6 / 8.9 s
@	: 4000 / 4100 rpm	top speed	: 120 / 126 mph
gears	: 5	EuroNCAP	: n.a.
AT	: optional 4-speed / -	introduction	: September 2000
drive	: FWD	last revised in	: September 2002
brakes f/r	: vent. discs / discs	warranty	: 2 years
body type	: 2-dr. convertible	miscellaneous	: Big success. Charming looks,
l x w x h	: 3835 x 1673 x 1373 mm		popular as second car, which
wheelbase	: 2442 mm		promotes image of a ladies' car.
turning circle	: 10.5 m		Also available as 1.6 HDiF
			with 110 bhp.

PEUGEOT 207 1.4 16V / 1.6 16V

engine type	: petrol, inline-4
displacement	: 1360 / 1587 cc
max. power	: 65 kW (90 bhp) / 80 kW (110 bhp)
@	: 5250 / 5800 rpm
max. torque	: 100 / 110 lb ft
@	: 3250 / 4000 rpm
gears	: 5
AT	: -
drive	: FWD
brakes f/r	: vent. discs, drum brakes / discs
body type	: 3-dr. hatchback
l x w x h	: 4030 x 1750 x 1472 mm
wheelbase	: 2442 mm
turning circle	: 10.4 m

kerb weight	: 1114 / 1188 kg
towing weight	: 1150 kg
boot space	: 310 l
fuel capacity	: 50 l
consumption	: 44.1 / 40.3 mpg
acc. 0-62 mph	: 12.7 / 10.6 s
top speed	: 112 / 121 mph
EuroNCAP	: 5 stars
introduction	: March 2006
last revised in	: -
warranty	: 2 years
miscellaneous	: Bigger than predecessor and class-leading, but in a higher class now. More engines and bodytypes on their way.

207 1.4 HDI / 1.6 HDI

engine type	: diesel, inline-4
displacement	: 1398 / 1560 cc
max. power	: 50 kW (70 bhp) / 66 kW (90 bhp)
@	: 4000 rpm
max. torque	: 120 / 161 lb ft
@	: 1750 rpm
gears	: 5
kerb weight	: 1151 / 1172 kg
towing weight	: 1150 kg
consumption	: 62.7 mpg
acc. 0-60 mph	: 15.1 / 11.5 s
top speed	: 103 / 113 mph
miscellaneous	: Also available as 1.6 HDiF 16V with 110 bhp and particle filter.

PEUGEOT 307 1.4 16V / 1.6 16V

engine type	: petrol, inline-4	kerb weight	: 1133 / 1162 kg
displacement	: 1360 / 1587 cc	towing weight	: 1200 / 1200 kg
max. power	: 65 kW (90 bhp) / 80 kW (110 bhp)	boot space	: 420 - 1470 l
@	: 5250 / 5800 rpm	fuel capacity	: 60 l
max. torque	: 100 / 110 lb ft	consumption	: 43.5 / 38.2 mpg
@	: 3250 / 4000 rpm	acc. 0-62 mph	: 12.8 / 10.7 s
gears	: 5	top speed	: 107 / 118 mph
AT	: - / optional 5-speed	EuroNCAP	: 4 stars
drive	: FWD	introduction	: April 2001
brakes f/r	: vent. discs / discs	last revised in	: September 2005
body type	: 3-dr. hatchback	warranty	: 2 years
l x w x h	: 4212 x 1746 x 1510 mm	miscellaneous	: 307 has prominent grille, after 407.
wheelbase	: 2608 mm		A cornerstone of the French
turning circle	: 10.7 m		marque.

307 2.0 16V / 2.0 16V 177

engine type	: petrol, inline-4
displacement	: 1997 cc
max. power	: 103 kW (140 bhp) / 130 kW (180 bhp)
@	: 6000 / 7000 rpm
max. torque	: 150 / 152 Nm
@	: 4100 / 4750 rpm
gears	: 5, optional 5-speed
kerb weight	: 1218 / 1261 kg
towing weight	: 1500 / 1000 kg
consumption	: 36.7 / 33.6 mpg
acc. 0-60 mph	: 8.9 / 8.2 s
top speed	: 127 / 137 mph
miscellaneous	: Adequate performer, but no competition for faster hatchbacks around with over 200 bhp. Successor to 309 and 306 GTI models called for.

PEUGEOT 307 SW 1.6 HDI / 2.0 HDIF

engine type	: diesel, inline-4	kerb weight	: 1369 / 1475 kg
displacement	: 1560 / 1997 cc	towing weight	: 1300 / 1500 kg
max. power	: 66 kW (90 bhp) / 100 kW (136 bhp)	boot space	: 598 - 2082 l
@	: 4000 rpm	fuel capacity	: 60 / 60 l
max. torque	: 180 / 240 lb ft	consumption	: 55.3 / 50.4 mpg
@	: 1750 / 2000 rpm	acc. 0-62 mph	: 13.3 / 10.8 s
gears	: 5 / 6	top speed	: 114 / 122 mph
AT	: -	EuroNCAP	: n.a.
drive	: FWD	introduction	: April 2002
brakes f/r	: vent. discs / discs	last revised in	: September 2005
body type	: 5-dr. stationwagon	warranty	: 2 years
l x w x h	: 4432 x 1757 x 1544 mm	miscellaneous	: SW has glass roof section, Estate
wheelbase	: 2708 mm		has more sober equipment.
turning circle	: 11.0 m		Spacious and popular models.

PEUGEOT 307 CC 1.6 16V / CC 2.0 16V

engine type	: petrol, inline-4	kerb weight	: 1428 / 1443 kg
displacement	: 1587 / 1997 cc	towing weight	: 1200 / 1320 kg
max. power	: 80 kW (110 bhp) /	boot space	: 232 l
	103 kW (143 bhp)	fuel capacity	: 50 l
@	: 5800 / 6000 rpm	consumption	: 37.2 / 34.9 mpg
max. torque	: 110 / 150 lb ft	acc. 0-62 mph	: 12.7 / 10.1 s
@	: 4000 / 4000 rpm	top speed	: 119 / 129 mph
gears	: 5	EuroNCAP	: 4 stars
AT	: - / optional 4-speed	introduction	: April 2003
drive	: FWD	last revised in	: September 2005
brakes f/r	: vent. discs / discs	warranty	: 2 years
body type	: 2-dr. convertible	miscellaneous	: Former concept car now a big hit
l x w x h	: 4360 x 1759 x 1424 mm		in convertible market. Also available
wheelbase	: 2608 mm		with 2.0 diesel unit with particle
turning circle	: 11.0 m		filter and 136 bhp.

PEUGEOT 407 1.8 16V

engine type	: petrol, inline-4
displacement	: 1749 cc
max. power	: 92 kW (125 bhp)
@	: 6000 rpm
max. torque	: 127 lb ft
@	: 3750 rpm
gears	: 5
AT	: -
drive	: FWD
brakes f/r	: vent. discs / discs
body type	: 4-dr. saloon
l x w x h	: 4676 x 1811 x 1445 mm
wheelbase	: 2725 mm
turning circle	: 11.2 m

kerb weight	: 1375 kg
towing weight	: 1600 kg
boot space	: 407 l
fuel capacity	: 66 l
consumption	: 36.6 mpg
acc. 0-62 mph	: 10.3 s
top speed	: 126 mph
EuroNCAP	: 5 stars
introduction	: April 2004
last revised in	: -
warranty	: 2 years
miscellaneous	: Spacious, modern saloon with fine driving characteristics and bold design. Also available with four different diesel engines, refer to 407 SW for specifications.

407 2.0 16V / 2.2 16V

engine type	: petrol, inline-4
displacement	: 1997 / 2230 cc
max. power	: 103 kW (140 bhp) / 120 kW (163 bhp)
@	: 6000 / 5875 rpm
max. torque	: 150 / 165 lb ft
@	: 4000 / 4150 rpm
gears	: 5 / 6
kerb weight	: 1390 / 1491 kg
towing weight	: 1800 / 1800 kg
consumption	: 34.8 / 31.2 mpg
acc. 0-60 mph	: 9.1 / 9.0 s
top speed	: 132 / 137 mph
miscellaneous	: Strong petrol engines, but 3.0 V6 is best of them all. Refer to 407 Coupe for specifications of V6.

PEUGEOT 407 SW 1.6 HDIF 16V

engine type	: diesel, inline-4	kerb weight	: 1467 kg
displacement	: 1560 cc	towing weight	: 1000 kg
max. power	: 80 kW (110 bhp)	boot space	: 448 - 1365 l
@	: 4000 rpm	fuel capacity	: 66 l
max. torque	: 180 lb ft	consumption	: 50.4 mpg
@	: 1750 rpm	acc. 0-62 mph	: 12.1 s
gears	: 5	top speed	: 117 mph
AT	: -	EuroNCAP	: 5 stars
drive	: FWD	introduction	: September 2004
brakes f/r	: vent. discs / discs	last revised in	: -
body type	: 5-dr. stationwagon	warranty	: 2 years
l x w x h	: 4763 x 1811 x 1486 mm	miscellaneous	: Looks were more important than interior space, which is not unusual with more expensive middle-class stationwagons of this type.
wheelbase	: 2725 mm		
turning circle	: 11.2 m		

407 SW 2.0 HDIF 16V / 2.2 HDIF 16V

engine type	: diesel, inline-4
displacement	: 1997 / 2179 cc
max. power	: 100 kW (136 bhp) / 125 kW (170 bhp)
@	: 4000 rpm
max. torque	: 240 / 277 lb ft
@	: 2000 / 1500 rpm
gears	: 6
kerb weight	: 1523 / 1650 kg
towing weight	: 1600 / 1900 kg
consumption	: 47.1 / 45.5 mpg
acc. 0-60 mph	: 10.1 / 9.4 s
top speed	: 126 / 137 mph
miscellaneous	: Diesel engines in SW topped by 2.7 HDiF (refer to 407 Coupe), but 2.7 hardly faster than 2.2 and a lot more expensive.

PEUGEOT 407 COUPE 2.2 / 3.0 V6

P

engine type	: petrol, inline-4 / V6
displacement	: 2230 / 2946 cc
max. power	: 120 kW (163 bhp) /
	155 kW (211 bhp)
@	: 5875 / 6000 rpm
max. torque	: 165 / 218 lb ft
@	: 4150 / 3750 rpm
gears	: 6
AT	: - / optional 6-speed
drive	: FWD
brakes f/r	: vent. discs
body type	: 2-dr. coupe
l x w x h	: 4815 x 1868 x 1400 mm
wheelbase	: 2720 mm
turning circle	: 11.5 m

kerb weight	: 1525 / 1612 kg
towing weight	: n.a.
boot space	: 400 l
fuel capacity	: 66 l
consumption	: 30.7 / 27.6 mpg
acc. 0-62 mph	: 9.2 / 8.4 s
top speed	: 138 / 151 mph
EuroNCAP	: 5 stars
introduction	: January 2006
last revised in	: -
warranty	: 2 years
miscellaneous	: Stretched profile masks long front overhang. Designed in-house, whereas predecessors were styled by Pininfarina.

407 COUPE 2.7 HDIF

engine type	: diesel, V6
displacement	: 2720 cc
max. power	: 150 kW (205 bhp)
@	: 4000 rpm
max. torque	: 330 lb ft
@	: 1900 rpm
gears	: 6-speed automatic
kerb weight	: 1724 kg
towing weight	: n.a.
consumption	: 33.2 mpg
acc. 0-60 mph	: 8.5 s
top speed	: 143 mph
miscellaneous	: Top-of-the-range has diesel power under the bonnet, combined with a 6-speed automatic transmission.

PEUGEOT 607 2.2 16V / 3.0 V6 24V

engine type	: petrol, inline-4 / V6
displacement	: 2230 / 2946 cc
max. power	: 120 kW (163 bhp) / 155 kW (211 bhp)
@	: 5875 / 6000 rpm
max. torque	: 162 / 218 lb ft
@	: 4150 / 3750 rpm
gears	: 6 / -
AT	: - / 6-speed
drive	: FWD
brakes f/r	: vent. discs / discs
body type	: 4-dr. saloon
l x w x h	: 4902 x 1800 x 1442 mm
wheelbase	: 2800 mm
turning circle	: 11.4 m

kerb weight	: 1510 / 1619 kg
towing weight	: 1850 / 1800 kg
boot space	: 577 l
fuel capacity	: 80 l
consumption	: 30.7 / 27.7 mpg
acc. 0-62 mph	: 9.9 / 9.2 s
top speed	: 137 / 145 mph
EuroNCAP	: 4 stars
introduction	: September 1999
last revised in	: November 2005
warranty	: 2 years
miscellaneous	: It is traditionally difficult for outsiders to sell big cars in a segment that is dominated by expensive models from Germany. 607 is really a fine alternative but remains a rare car.

607 2.0 HDIF 16V / 2.2 HDIF 16V

engine type	: diesel, inline-4
displacement	: 1997 / 2179 cc
max. power	: 100 kW (136 bhp) / 125 kW (170 bhp)
@	: 4000 rpm
max. torque	: 240 / 277 lb ft
@	: 2000 / 1500 rpm
gears	: 6
kerb weight	: 1565 / 1595 kg
towing weight	: 1760 / 1800 kg
consumption	: 46.3 / 44.1 mpg
acc. 0-60 mph	: 10.8 / 9.3 s
top speed	: 128 / 139 mph
miscellaneous	: More horsepower now for 2.0 and 2.2 diesel engines.

607 2.7 HDIF V6

engine type	: diesel, V6
displacement	: 2720 cc
max. power	: 150 kW (204 bhp)
@	: 4000 rpm
max. torque	: 325 lb ft
@	: 1900 rpm
gears	: 6-speed automatic
kerb weight	: 1698 kg
towing weight	: 1700 kg
consumption	: 33.6 mpg
acc. 0-60 mph	: 8.7 s
top speed	: 143 mph
miscellaneous	: V6 engine developed by PSA and Ford but also used by Jaguar and Land Rover.

PEUGEOT 807 2.0 16V / 2.0 HDiF 16V

engine type	: petrol / diesel, inline-4		kerb weight	: 1606 / 1718 kg
displacement	: 1997 cc		towing weight	: 1700 / 1850 kg
max. power	: 103 kW (140 bhp) /		boot space	: 480 - 2948 l
	100 kW (136 bhp)		fuel capacity	: 80 l
@	: 6000 / 4000 rpm		consumption	: 31.4 / 39.8 mpg
max. torque	: 150 / 236 lb ft		acc. 0-62 mph	: 11.6 / 12.5 s
@	: 4000 / 2000 rpm		top speed	: 115 / 118 mph
gears	: 5 / 6		EuroNCAP	: 5 stars
AT	: optional 4-speed / -		introduction	: July 2002
drive	: FWD		last revised in	: -
brakes f/r	: vent. discs / discs		warranty	: 2 years
body type	: 5-dr. MPV		miscellaneous	: 807 model range much smaller
l x w x h	: 4727 x 1854 x 1752 mm			now, but 110 bhp HDiF version with
wheelbase	: 2825 mm			automatic transmission also
turning circle	: 10.8 m			available.

P

PORSCHE BOXSTER / BOXSTER S

engine type	: petrol, flat-6	kerb weight	: 1350 / 1395 kg
displacement	: 2687 / 3387 cc	towing weight	: n.a.
max. power	: 180 kW (245 bhp) /	boot space	: 280 l
	217 kW (295 bhp)	fuel capacity	: 64 l
@	: 6400 / 6250 rpm	consumption	: 30.4 / 26.6 mpg
max. torque	: 202 / 251 lb ft	acc. 0-62 mph	: 6.1 / 5.4 s
@	: 4600 / 4400 rpm	top speed	: 160 / 169 mph
gears	: 5 / 6	EuroNCAP	: n.a.
AT	: optional 5-speed	introduction	: July 2004
drive	: RWD	last revised in	: -
brakes f/r	: vent. discs	warranty	: 2 years
body type	: 2-dr. convertible	miscellaneous	: Boxster engine line-up now
l x w x h	: 4329 x 1801 x 1295 mm		identical to that of fixed-roof
wheelbase	: 2415 mm		Cayman.
turning circle	: 10.9 m		

PORSCHE CAYMAN S

engine type	: petrol, flat-6	kerb weight	: 1415 kg
displacement	: 3387 cc	towing weight	: -
max. power	: 217 kW (295 bhp)	boot space	: 410 l
@	: 6250 rpm	fuel capacity	: 64 l
max. torque	: 251 lb ft	consumption	: 26.6 mpg
@	: 4400 rpm	acc. 0-62 mph	: 5.4 s
gears	: 6	top speed	: 171 mph
AT	: optional 5-speed	EuroNCAP	: n.a.
drive	: RWD	introduction	: September 2005
brakes f/r	: vent. discs	last revised in	: -
body type	: 2-dr. coupe	warranty	: 2 years
l x w x h	: 4329 x 1801 x 1305 mm	miscellaneous	: Coupe based on Boxster. Also
wheelbase	: 2415 mm		available with 2.7 boxer engine
turning circle	: 10.9 m		with 245 bhp.

PORSCHE 911 CARRERA / CARRERA S

engine type	: petrol, flat-6
displacement	: 3596 / 3824 cc
max. power	: 239 kW (325 bhp) /
	261 kW (355 bhp)
@	: 6800 / 6600 rpm
max. torque	: 273 / 295 lb ft
@	: 4250 / 4600 rpm
gears	: 6
AT	: optional 5-speed
drive	: RWD
brakes f/r	: vent. discs
body type	: 2-dr. coupe
l x w x h	: 4427 x 1808 x 1310 mm
wheelbase	: 2350 mm
turning circle	: 12.1 m

kerb weight	: 1470 / 1495 kg
towing weight	: n.a.
boot space	: 135 l
fuel capacity	: 64 / 64 l
consumption	: 25.7 / 24.6 mpg
acc. 0-62 mph	: 5.0 / 4.8 s
top speed	: 177 / 182 mph
EuroNCAP	: n.a.
introduction	: July 2004
last revised in	: -
warranty	: 2 years
miscellaneous	: 997 model also available as Carrera 4 and 4S with 4WD and likewise with convertible body. All-round sportscar: spacious, very fast and great build quality. Expensive however.

PORSCHE 911 TURBO

engine type	: petrol, flat-6	kerb weight	: 1585 kg
displacement	: 3600 cc	towing weight	: -
max. power	: 353 kW (480 bhp)	boot space	: 105 l
@	: 6000 rpm	fuel capacity	: 67 l
max. torque	: 457 lb ft	consumption	: 22.1 mpg
@	: 1950 rpm	acc. 0-62 mph	: 3.9 s
gears	: 6	top speed	: 192 mph
AT	: optional 5-speed	EuroNCAP	: n.a.
drive	: 4WD	introduction	: July 2006
brakes f/r	: vent. discs	last revised in	: -
body type	: 2-dr. coupe	warranty	: 2 years
l x w x h	: 4450 x 1852 x 1300 mm	miscellaneous	: Porsche and turbo engines go well together. This newest version is not as mean as 930 Turbo from 1975, but it is incredibly quick.
wheelbase	: 2350 mm		
turning circle	: n.a.		

911 GT3

engine type	: petrol, flat-6
displacement	: 3600 cc
max. power	: 305 kW (415 bhp)
@	: 7600 rpm
max. torque	: 298 lb ft
@	: 5500 rpm
gears	: 6
kerb weight	: 1395 kg
towing weight	: -
consumption	: 21.7 mpg
acc. 0-60 mph	: 4.3 s
top speed	: 192 mph
miscellaneous	: Also available as GT3 RS, which weighs 20 kg less and is fractionally quicker. Only for purists.

PORSCHE CAYENNE / CAYENNE S

engine type	: petrol, V6 / V8
displacement	: 3189 / 4511 cc
max. power	: 184 kW (250 bhp) / 250 kW (340 bhp)
@	: 6000 / 6000 rpm
max. torque	: 228 / 310 lb ft
@	: 2500 / 2500 rpm
gears	: 6
AT	: optional 6-speed
drive	: 4WD
brakes f/r	: vent. discs
body type	: 5-dr. SUV
l x w x h	: 4782 x 1928 x 1699 mm
wheelbase	: 2855 mm
turning circle	: 11.4 m

kerb weight	: 2160 / 2225 kg
towing weight	: 3500 / 3500 kg
boot space	: 540 - 1770 l
fuel capacity	: 100 / 100 l
consumption	: 21.4 / 17.9 mpg
acc. 0-62 mph	: 9.1 / 6.8 s
top speed	: 132 / 150 mph
EuroNCAP	: n.a.
introduction	: April 2002
last revised in	: n.v.t.
warranty	: 2 years
miscellaneous	: Big hit from Porsche, one of the fastest SUVs on the market. V8 engine developed by Porsche, V6 borrowed from VW's Touareg.

TURBO / TURBO S

engine type	: petrol, V8
displacement	: 4511 cc
max. power	: 331 kW (450 bhp) / 383 kW (521 bhp)
@	: 6000 / 5500 rpm
max. torque	: 457 / 531 lb ft
@	: 2250 / 2750 rpm
gears	: 6-speed automatic
kerb weight	: 2355 kg
towing weight	: 3500 kg
consumption	: 18.0 mpg
acc. 0-60 mph	: 5.6 / 5.2 s
top speed	: 165 / 168 mph
miscellaneous	: Latest addition is Turbo S, a fuel-guzzler like the common Turbo but just a bit quicker.

RENAULT TWINGO 1.2 / 1.2 16V

engine type	: petrol, inline-4
displacement	: 1149 cc
max. power	: 43 kW (60 bhp) / 55 kW (75 bhp)
@	: 5250 / 5500 rpm
max. torque	: 69 / 77 lb ft
@	: 2500 / 4250 rpm
gears	: 5
AT	: optional 5-speed semi-automatic
drive	: FWD
brakes f/r	: vent. discs / drum brakes
body type	: 3-dr. hatchback
l x w x h	: 3433 x 1630 x 1423 mm
wheelbase	: 2347 mm
turning circle	: 9.6 m

kerb weight	: 795 / 805 kg
towing weight	: 600 kg
boot space	: 261 - 1096 l
fuel capacity	: 40 l
consumption	: 48.7 mpg
acc. 0-62 mph	: 13.7 / 11.7 s
top speed	: 94 / 104 mph
EuroNCAP	: 3 stars
introduction	: 1993
last revised in	: 2001
warranty	: 2 years
miscellaneous	: Still going strong, with its appealing design and favourable pricetag. A future classic perhaps, like the Citroën 2CV and Renault 4?

P
R

RENAULT KANGOO 1.2 16V / 1.6 16V

engine type	: petrol, inline-4	kerb weight	: 1010 / 1080 kg
displacement	: 1149 / 1598 cc	towing weight	: 1150 kg
max. power	: 55 kW (75 bhp) / 70 kW (95 bhp)	boot space	: 650 - 2600 l
@	: 5500 / 5000 rpm	fuel capacity	: 50 l
max. torque	: 78 / 109 lb ft	consumption	: 40.4 / 37.7 mpg
@	: 3500 / 3750 rpm	acc. 0-62 mph	: 14.2 / 10.7 s
gears	: 5	top speed	: 96 / 106 mph
AT	: - / optional 4-speed	EuroNCAP	: 4 stars
drive	: FWD	introduction	: December 1998
brakes f/r	: vent. discs / drum brakes	last revised in	: September 2005
body type	: 5-dr. MPV	warranty	: 2 years
l x w x h	: 4035 x 1672 x 1825 mm	miscellaneous	: Budget car, popular as delivery van.
wheelbase	: 2605 mm		Successor already spotted. 1.6
turning circle	: 10.4 m		version also available with 4WD.

KANGOO 1.5 DCI 70 / 1.5 DCI 85

engine type	: diesel, inline-4
displacement	: 1461 cc
max. power	: 50 kW (70 bhp) / 68 kW (85 bhp)
@	: 4000 / 3750 rpm
max. torque	: 118 / 148 lb ft
@	: 1500 / 1750 rpm
gears	: 5
kerb weight	: 1100 / 1110 kg
towing weight	: 1200 / 1150 kg
consumption	: 51.4 / 53.3 mpg
acc. 0-60 mph	: 16.0 / 11.3 s
top speed	: 92 / 98 mph
miscellaneous	: Low running costs, therefore popular as company car. Competition is stiff though. Also available as 1.5 dCi with 60 bhp.

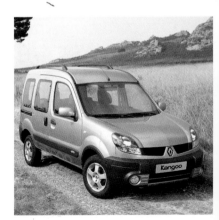

RENAULT CLIO CAMPUS 1.2 8V / 1.2 16V

engine type	: petrol, inline-4
displacement	: 1149 cc
max. power	: 43 kW (60 bhp) / 55 kW (75 bhp)
@	: 5250 / 5500 rpm
max. torque	: 68 / 78 lb ft
@	: 2500 / 4250 rpm
gears	: 5
AT	: -
drive	: FWD
brakes f/r	: vent. discs / drum brakes
body type	: 3- / 5-dr. hatchback
l x w x h	: 3812 x 1639 x 1417 mm
wheelbase	: 2472 mm
turning circle	: 10.3 m

kerb weight	: 890 / 920 kg
towing weight	: 1100 / 1150 kg
boot space	: 255 – 1035 l
fuel capacity	: 50 l
consumption	: 47.1 / 47.9 mpg
acc. 0-62 mph	: 15.0 / 13.0 s
top speed	: 98 / 106 mph
EuroNCAP	: 4 stars
introduction	: April 1998
last revised in	: July 2004
warranty	: 2 years
miscellaneous	: Entry level models of previous Clio still available, also with 1.4 16V and 1.5 dCi engines.

R

RENAULT CLIO 1.2 16V / 1.4 16V

engine type	: petrol, inline-4	kerb weight	: 1080 / 1135 kg
displacement	: 1149 / 1390 cc	towing weight	: 1200 kg
max. power	: 55 kW (75 bhp) / 72 kW (98 bhp)	boot space	: 288 – 1038 l
@	: 5500 / 5750 rpm	fuel capacity	: 55 l
max. torque	: 78 / 94 lb ft	consumption	: 47.9 / 42.8 mpg
@	: 4250 rpm	acc. 0-62 mph	: 13.4 / 11.3 s
gears	: 5	top speed	: 104 / 114 mph
AT	: optional 5-speed	EuroNCAP	: 5 stars
drive	: FWD	introduction	: September 2005
brakes f/r	: vent. discs / drum brakes	last revised in	: -
body type	: 3- / 5–dr. hatchback	warranty	: 2 years
l x w x h	: 3986 x 1707 x 1493 mm	miscellaneous	: Clio III is a lot bigger and safer
wheelbase	: 2575 mm		than predecessor. Voted
turning circle	: n.a.		'Car of the Year 2006'.

CLIO 1.6 16V / RS

engine type	: petrol, inline-4
displacement	: 1598 / 1998 cc
max. power	: 82 kW (112 bhp) / 145 kW (197 bhp)
@	: 6000 / 7250 rpm
max. torque	: 112 / 158 lb ft
@	: 4250 / 5550 rpm
gears	: 5 / 6
kerb weight	: 1115 / 1235 kg
towing weight	: 1200 kg / -
consumption	: 42.8 / 31.7 mpg
acc. 0-60 mph	: 10.2 / 6.9 s
top speed	: 118 / 134 mph
miscellaneous	: RS worthy replacement of old
	Clio Renault Sport and Clio
	Williams.

RENAULT MODUS 1.5 DCI 70 / 85

engine type	: diesel, inline-4		kerb weight	: 1155 / 1160 kg
displacement	: 1461 cc		towing weight	: 900 kg
max. power	: 50 kW (68 bhp) / 63 kW (86 bhp)		boot space	: 274 - 1283 l
@	: 4000 rpm		fuel capacity	: 49 l
max. torque	: 118 / 148 lb ft		consumption	: 60.1 / 62.8 mpg
@	: 1700 / 1900 rpm		acc. 0-62 mph	: 15.3 / 13.0 s
gears	: 5		top speed	: 97 / 106 mph
AT	: - / optional Quickshift		EuroNCAP	: 5 stars
drive	: FWD		introduction	: August 2004
brakes f/r	: vent. discs / drum brakes		last revised in	: -
body type	: 5-dr. MPV		warranty	: 2 years
l x w x h	: 3792 x 1695 x 1589 mm		miscellaneous	: Drivetrain shared with Clio. Refer to Clio for specifications of petrol engines.
wheelbase	: 2482 mm			
turning circle	: 9.9 m			

MODUS 1.5 DCI 105

engine type	: diesel, inline-4
displacement	: 1461 cc
max. power	: 78 kW (105 bhp)
@	: 4000 rpm
max. torque	: 177 lb ft
@	: 2000 rpm
gears	: 6
kerb weight	: 1175 kg
towing weight	: 900 kg
consumption	: 60.1 mpg
acc. 0-60 mph	: 11.2 s
top speed	: 116 mph
miscellaneous	: Excellent diesel engine, also fitted in Clio.

RENAULT MEGANE 1.4 16V / 1.6 16V

engine type	: petrol, inline-4	kerb weight	: 1140 / 1150 kg
displacement	: 1390 / 1598 cc	towing weight	: 1300 kg
max. power	: 72 kW (100 bhp) / 82 kW (110 bhp)	boot space	: 330 - 1190 l
@	: 6000 rpm	fuel capacity	: 60 l
max. torque	: 94 / 112 lb ft	consumption	: 40.9 mpg
@	: 3750 / 4250 rpm	acc. 0-62 mph	: 12.5 / 10.9 s
gears	: 5	top speed	: 114 / 119 mph
AT	: - / optional 4-speed	EuroNCAP	: 5 stars
drive	: FWD	introduction	: October 2002
brakes f/r	: vent. discs / discs	last revised in	: January 2006
body type	: 3- / 5-dr. hatchback	warranty	: 2 years
l x w x h	: 4209 x 1777 x 1457 mm	miscellaneous	: Already striking design
wheelbase	: 2625 mm		received minor facelift.
turning circle	: 10.5 m		

MEGANE 2.0 TURBO

engine type	: petrol, inline-4
displacement	: 1998 cc
max. power	: 165 kW (225 bhp)
@	: 5500 rpm
max. torque	: 221 lb ft
@	: 3000 rpm
gears	: 6
kerb weight	: 1330 kg
towing weight	: 1000 kg
consumption	: 32.1 mpg
acc. 0-60 mph	: 6.5 s
top speed	: 147 mph
miscellaneous	: Biggest engine available in Megane, but only in hatchback version with either 3 or 5 doors. Fast 'hot hatch' is built by Renault Sport in Dieppe.

RENAULT MEGANE SPORTS TOURER 1.5 DCI 85 / 105

engine type	: diesel, inline-4	kerb weight	: 1210 / 1235 kg
displacement	: 1461 cc	towing weight	: 1300 / 1250 kg
max. power	: 63 kW (85 bhp) / 78 kW (105 bhp)	boot space	: 520 - 1600 l
@	: 3750 / 4000 rpm	fuel capacity	: 60 l
max. torque	: 148 / 177 lb ft	consumption	: 60.1 mpg
@	: 1900 / 2000 rpm	acc. 0-62 mph	: 13.1 / 11.4 s
gears	: 5 / 6	top speed	: 108 / 115 mph
AT	: -	EuroNCAP	: 5 stars
drive	: FWD	introduction	: October 2002
brakes f/r	: vent. discs / discs	last revised in	: January 2006
body type	: 5-dr. stationwagon	warranty	: 2 years
l x w x h	: 4500 x 1777 x 1467 mm	miscellaneous	: Sports Tourer and Saloon share
wheelbase	: 2686 mm		same wheelbase, longer than
turning circle	: 10.7 m		hatchback. Engine range identical.

R

MEGANE SPORTS TOURER 1.9 DCI

engine type	: diesel, inline-4
displacement	: 1870 cc
max. power	: 96 kW (130 bhp)
@	: 4000 rpm
max. torque	: 222 lb ft
@	: 2000 rpm
gears	: 6
kerb weight	: 1285 kg
towing weight	: 1300 kg
consumption	: 51.4 mpg
acc. 0-60 mph	: 9.3 s
top speed	: 124 mph
miscellaneous	: 'FAP' addition to model name indicates standard fitment of particle filter.

RENAULT MEGANE COUPE-CABRIOLET 2.0 / 2.0 T

engine type	: petrol, inline-4	kerb weight	: 1365 / 1390 kg
displacement	: 1998 cc	towing weight	: 1200 kg
max. power	: 99 kW (135 bhp) / 120 kW (165 bhp)	boot space	: 490 l
@	: 5500 / 5000 rpm	fuel capacity	: 60 l
max. torque	: 141 / 199 lb ft	consumption	: 34.4 / 35.3 mpg
@	: 3750 / 3250 rpm	acc. 0-62 mph	: 9.9 / 8.7 s
gears	: 6	top speed	: 127 / 137 mph
AT	: optional 4-speed	EuroNCAP	: 5 stars
drive	: FWD	introduction	: September 2003
brakes f/r	: vent. discs / discs	last revised in	: January 2006
body type	: 2-dr. convertible	warranty	: 2 years
l x w x h	: 4355 x 1777 x 1404 mm	miscellaneous	: Comfortable 4-seater convertible which doubles as a coupe. Entry level model is 1.6 with 115 bhp. 165 bhp 2.0-litre turbo engine is faster and also available in hatchback.
wheelbase	: 2522 mm		
turning circle	: 10.1 m		

MEGANE COUPE-CABRIOLET 2.0 DCI

engine type	: diesel, inline-4
displacement	: 1995 cc
max. power	: 110 kW (150 bhp)
@	: 4000 rpm
max. torque	: 250 lb ft
@	: 2000 rpm
gears	: 6
kerb weight	: 1470 kg
towing weight	: 1200 kg
consumption	: 49.6 mpg
acc. 0-60 mph	: 9.6 s
top speed	: 132 mph
miscellaneous	: The number of diesel-powered convertibles continues to grow. Laid-back nature of diesel engine matches well with open-top motoring.

RENAULT SCENIC 1.4 16V / 1.6 16V

engine type	: petrol, inline-4
displacement	: 1390 / 1598 cc
max. power	: 72 kW (100 bhp) / 82 kW (110 bhp)
@	: 6000 rpm
max. torque	: 94 / 114 lb ft
@	: 3750 / 4250 rpm
gears	: 5 / 6
AT	: - / optional 4-speed
drive	: FWD
brakes f/r	: vent. discs / discs
body type	: 5-dr. MPV
l x w x h	: 4259 x 1805 x 1620 mm
wheelbase	: 2685 mm
turning circle	: 10.7 m

kerb weight	: 1290 / 1295 kg
towing weight	: 1300 kg
boot space	: 406 - 1840 l
fuel capacity	: 60 l
consumption	: 39.2 mpg
acc. 0-62 mph	: 14.3 / 11.8 s
top speed	: 108 / 115 mph
EuroNCAP	: 5 stars
introduction	: July 2003
last revised in	: September 2006
warranty	: 2 years
miscellaneous	: Received minor facelift like Megane sister. Refer to Grand Scenic with longer wheelbase for specifications of 2.0 and 2.0 T engines.

SCENIC 1.5 DCI 85 / 105

engine type	: diesel, inline-4
displacement	: 1461 cc
max. power	: 63 kW (85 bhp) / 78 kW (105 bhp)
@	: 4000 rpm
max. torque	: 148 / 177 lb ft
@	: 2000 rpm
gears	: 5 / 6
kerb weight	: 1315 / 1340 kg
towing weight	: 1300 kg
consumption	: 55.4 / 54.3 mpg
acc. 0-60 mph	: 14.6 / 12.4 s
top speed	: 104 / 111 mph
miscellaneous	: Two additional diesel engines available, more powerful still. Refer to Grand Scenic for specifications.

RENAULT GRAND SCENIC 2.0 16V / 2.0 T

engine type	: petrol, inline-4
displacement	: 1998 cc
max. power	: 99 kW (135 bhp) / 120 kW (165 bhp)
@	: 6000 / 5500 rpm
max. torque	: 141 / 199 lb ft
@	: 3750 / 3250 rpm
gears	: 6
AT	: optional, 4-speed / -
drive	: FWD
brakes f/r	: vent. discs / discs
body type	: 5-dr. MPV
l x w x h	: 4493 x 1810 x 1636 mm
wheelbase	: 2736 mm
turning circle	: 10.8 m

kerb weight	: 1455 / 1480 kg
towing weight	: 1300 kg
boot space	: 200 - 1920 l
fuel capacity	: 60 l
consumption	: 34.4 / 34.9 mpg
acc. 0-62 mph	: 10.9 / 9.6 s
top speed	: 121 / 128 mph
EuroNCAP	: 5 stars
introduction	: January 2004
last revised in	: September 2006
warranty	: 2 years
miscellaneous	: Grand Scenic can accommodate seven people, due to longer wheelbase and three rows of seats. Extra luggage possible as well of course.

GRAND SCENIC 1.9 DCI / 2.0 DCI

engine type	: diesel, inline-4
displacement	: 1870 / 1995 cc
max. power	: 96 kW (130 bhp) / 110 kW (150 bhp)
@	: 4000 rpm
max. torque	: 222 / 251 lb ft
@	: 2000 rpm
gears	: 6
kerb weight	: 1475 / 1505 kg
towing weight	: 1300 kg
consumption	: 47.1 / 48.7 mpg
acc. 0-60 mph	: 9.6 / 9.8 s
top speed	: 118 / 127 mph
miscellaneous	: Grand Scenic is now also available in 5-seater configuration.

RENAULT LAGUNA 1.6 16V / 2.0 16V

engine type	: petrol, inline-4
displacement	: 1598 / 1998 cc
max. power	: 82 kW (115 bhp) / 99 kW (135 bhp)
@	: 6000 / 5500 rpm
max. torque	: 111 / 141 lb ft
@	: 4250 / 3750 rpm
gears	: 5
AT	: - / optional 4-speed
drive	: FWD
brakes f/r	: vent. discs / discs
body type	: 5-dr. hatchback
l x w x h	: 4598 x 1774 x 1433 mm
wheelbase	: 2748 mm
turning circle	: 10.9 m

kerb weight	: 1245 / 1255 kg
towing weight	: 1300 kg
boot space	: 430 - 1340 l
fuel capacity	: 68 l
consumption	: 37.3 / 35.3 mpg
acc. 0-62 mph	: 11.5 / 9.8 s
top speed	: 122 / 129 mph
EuroNCAP	: 5 stars
introduction	: February 2005
last revised in	: February 2005
warranty	: 2 years
miscellaneous	: One of the first cars to score five stars in EuroNCAP crash tests. Successful model, spacious and pleasant to drive, but up against fierce competition.

LAGUNA 2.0 T 170 / 205

engine type	: petrol, inline-4
displacement	: 1998 cc
max. power	: 125 kW (170 bhp) / 150 kW (205 bhp)
@	: 5000 rpm
max. torque	: 199 / 221 lb ft
@	: 3250 / 3000 rpm
gears	: 6
kerb weight	: 1295 kg
towing weight	: 1350 kg
consumption	: 33.6 / 33.2 mpg
acc. 0-60 mph	: 8.4 / 7.2 s
top speed	: 138 / 146 mph
miscellaneous	: 2.0 turbo unit sporty engine choice for Laguna.

LAGUNA 3.0 V6 AUTO

engine type	: petrol, V6
displacement	: 2946 cc
max. power	: 152 kW (210 bhp)
@	: 6000 rpm
max. torque	: 206 lb ft
@	: 3750 rpm
gears	: 5-speed automatic
kerb weight	: 1405 kg
towing weight	: 1550 kg
consumption	: 28.5 mpg
acc. 0-60 mph	: 8.0 s
top speed	: 146 mph
miscellaneous	: Top-Laguna, but rarely seen on our roads.

RENAULT LAGUNA SPORTS TOURER 1.9 DCI 110 / 130

engine type	: diesel, inline-4	kerb weight	: 1325 / 1360 kg
displacement	: 1870 cc	towing weight	: 1500 kg
max. power	: 81 kW (110 bhp) / 96 kW (130 bhp)	boot space	: 475 - 1515 l
@	: 4000 rpm	fuel capacity	: 68 l
max. torque	: 192 / 221 lb ft	consumption	: 47.1 mpg
@	: 2000 rpm	acc. 0-62 mph	: 12.4 / 10.5 s
gears	: 6	top speed	: 119 / 125 mph
AT	: - / optional 4-speed	EuroNCAP	: 5 stars
drive	: FWD	introduction	: February 2001
brakes f/r	: vent. discs / discs	last revised in	: February 2005
body type	: 5-dr. stationwagon	warranty	: 2 years
l x w x h	: 4713 x 1774 x 1475 mm	miscellaneous	: Sports Tourer offers more space than saloon and sells in higher numbers. Available versions identical to saloon range.
wheelbase	: 2748 mm		
turning circle	: 10.9 m		

SPORTS TOURER 2.0 DCI 150 / 175

engine type	: diesel, inline-4
displacement	: 1995 cc
max. power	: 110 kW (150 bhp) / 127 kW (175 bhp)
@	: 4000 / 3750 rpm
max. torque	: 250 / 266 lb ft
@	: 2000 / 1750 rpm
gears	: 6
kerb weight	: 1430 / 1440 kg
towing weight	: 1500 kg
consumption	: 47.1 / 44.8 mpg
acc. 0-60 mph	: 9.8 / 8.6 s
top speed	: 132 / 138 mph
miscellaneous	: Lots of horsepower and torque. Automatic transmission available for 2.0 dCi 150.

RENAULT VEL SATIS 2.0 T / 3.5 V6

engine type	: petrol, inline-4 / V6
displacement	: 1998 / 3498 cc
max. power	: 125 kW (170 bhp) / 177 kW (245 bhp)
@	: 5000 / 6000 rpm
max. torque	: 199 / 243 lb ft
@	: 3250 / 3600 rpm
gears	: 6 / -
AT	: optional 5-speed / 5-speed
drive	: FWD
brakes f/r	: vent. discs / discs
body type	: 5-dr. hatchback
l x w x h	: 4860 x 1860 x 1577 mm
wheelbase	: 2840 mm
turning circle	: 11.3 m

kerb weight	: 1615 / 1695 kg
towing weight	: 1600 kg
boot space	: 460 - 1468 l
fuel capacity	: 80 l
consumption	: 30.1 / 24.6 mpg
acc. 0-62 mph	: 9.6 / 8.3 s
top speed	: 130 / 146 mph
EuroNCAP	: 5 stars
introduction	: April 2002
last revised in	: March 2005
warranty	: 2 years
miscellaneous	: Bold design for big middle-class Renault. Comfortable and spacious car, but not a success.

VEL SATIS 2.2 DCI / 3.0 DCI

engine type	: diesel, inline-4 / V6
displacement	: 2188 / 2958 cc
max. power	: 110 kW (150 bhp) / 130 kW (180 bhp)
@	: 4000 / 4400 rpm
max. torque	: 236 / 258 lb ft
@	: 1750 / 1800 rpm
gears	: 6 / 5
kerb weight	: 1635 / 1710 kg
towing weight	: 1600 / 1650 kg
consumption	: 39.8 / 32.5 mpg
acc. 0-60 mph	: 10.9 / 10.5 s
top speed	: 124 / 130 mph
miscellaneous	: Big, excellent diesel engines.

RENAULT ESPACE 2.0 16V / 2.0 T 16V

engine type	: petrol, inline-4	kerb weight	: 1640 / 1660 kg
displacement	: 1998 cc	towing weight	: 1800 / 2000 kg
max. power	: 100 kW (140 bhp) /	boot space	: 291 - 2860 l
	120 kW (165 bhp)	fuel capacity	: 83 l
@	: 5500 / 5000 rpm	consumption	: 30.1 / 29.1 mpg
max. torque	: 141 / 199 lb ft	acc. 0-62 mph	: 12.5 / 9.9 s
@	: 3750 / 2000 rpm	top speed	: 115 / 128 mph
gears	: 6	EuroNCAP	: 5 stars
AT	: - / optional 5-speed	introduction	: August 2002
drive	: FWD	last revised in	: February 2006
brakes f/r	: vent. discs / discs	warranty	: 2 years
body type	: 5-dr. MPV	miscellaneous	: The best of all the large MPVs.
l x w x h	: 4656 x 1860 x 1728 mm		Spacious, practical, original, safe.
wheelbase	: 2803 mm		Beats an aeroplane as means of
turning circle	: 11.0 m		transport on holidays.

ESPACE 3.5 V6 24V

engine type	: petrol, V6
displacement	: 3498 cc
max. power	: 177 kW (245 bhp)
@	: 6000 rpm
max. torque	: 243 lb ft
@	: 3600 rpm
gears	: 5-speed automatic
kerb weight	: 1745 kg
towing weight	: 2000 kg
consumption	: 23.5 mpg
acc. 0-60 mph	: 8.1 s
top speed	: 140 mph
miscellaneous	: V6 engine also available in
	Grand Espace version.

RENAULT GRAND ESPACE 1.9 DCI / 2.0 DCI

engine type	: diesel, inline-4	kerb weight	: 1730 / 1805 kg
displacement	: 1870 / 1998 cc	towing weight	: 2000 kg
max. power	: 88 kW (120 bhp) / 110 kW (150 bhp)	boot space	: 456 - 3050 l
@	: 4000 rpm	fuel capacity	: 83 l
max. torque	: 199 / 251 lb ft	consumption	: 40.9 / 37.6 mpg
@	: 2000 rpm	acc. 0-62 mph	: 13.2 / 10.6 s
gears	: 6	top speed	: 112 / 121 mph
AT	: -	EuroNCAP	: 5 stars
drive	: FWD	introduction	: August 2002
brakes f/r	: vent. discs / discs	last revised in	: February 2006
body type	: 5-dr. MPV	warranty	: 2 years
l x w x h	: 4856 x 1860 x 1746 mm	miscellaneous	: Also available as 2.0 dCi with
wheelbase	: 2868 mm		175 bhp, which makes 3.0 dCi
turning circle	: 11.4 m		virtually redundant. Automatic
			transmission only available in old
			2.2 dCi.

GRAND ESPACE 3.0 DCI V6 24V

engine type	: diesel, V6
displacement	: 2958 cc
max. power	: 130 kW (180 bhp)
@	: 4000 rpm
max. torque	: 295 lb ft
@	: 1800 rpm
gears	: 6-speed automatic
kerb weight	: 1865 kg
towing weight	: 2000 kg
consumption	: 29.7 mpg
acc. 0-60 mph	: 9.6 s
top speed	: 130 mph
miscellaneous	: Diesel power supplied by partner Nissan. 3.0 dCi version marginally faster thanks to new 6-speed automatic transmission.

ROLLS-ROYCE PHANTOM

engine type	: petrol, V12	kerb weight	: 2495 kg
displacement	: 6749 cc	towing weight	: n.a.
max. power	: 338 kW (453 bhp)	boot space	: 460 l
@	: 5350 rpm	fuel capacity	: 100 l
max. torque	: 531 lb ft	consumption	: 17.8 mpg
@	: 3500 rpm	acc. 0-62 mph	: 5.9 s
gears	: -	top speed	: 149 mph
AT	: 6-speed	EuroNCAP	: n.a.
drive	: RWD	introduction	: January 2003
brakes f/r	: vent. discs	last revised in	: -
body type	: 4-dr. saloon	warranty	: n.a.
l x w x h	: 5834 x 1990 x 1632	miscellaneous	: High-tech BMW drivetrain from
wheelbase	: 3570 mm		Germany, handcrafted interior
turning circle	: 13.8 m		from England. Monumental,
			colossal car. Also available in
			long wheelbase version with
			250 mm of extra legroom.

SAAB 9-3 1.8i / 1.8T

engine type	: petrol, inline-4	kerb weight	: 1350 / 1410 kg
displacement	: 1796 / 1998 cc	towing weight	: 1400 / 1600 kg
max. power	: 90 kW (122 bhp) /	boot space	: 425 l
	110 kW (150 bhp)	fuel capacity	: 58 l
@	: 6000 / 5500 rpm	consumption	: 35.8 / 34.9 mpg
max. torque	: 124 / 177 lb ft	acc. 0-62 mph	: 11.5 / 9.5 s
@	: 3800 / 2500 rpm	top speed	: 124 / 130 mph
gears	: 5	EuroNCAP	: 5 stars
AT	: optional 5-speed	introduction	: September 2002
drive	: FWD	last revised in	: -
brakes f/r	: vent. discs / discs	warranty	: 2 years
body type	: 4-dr. saloon	miscellaneous	: Saloon shares platform with
l x w x h	: 4635 x 1762 x 1466 mm		Vauxhall Vectra, but has character
wheelbase	: 2675 mm		of its own thanks to typical Saab
turning circle	: 10.8 m		interior and fine turbo engines.

R
S

9-3 2.0T 175 / 210 bhp

engine type	: petrol, inline-4
displacement	: 1998 cc
max. power	: 129 kW (175 bhp) /
	154 kW (210 bhp)
@	: 5500 / 5300 rpm
max. torque	: 196 / 221 lb ft
@	: 2500 / 2500 rpm
gears	: 5 / 5, optional 6-speed automatic
kerb weight	: 1425 / 1460 kg
towing weight	: 1600 kg
consumption	: 37.2 / 34.9 mpg
acc. 0-60 mph	: 8.5 / 8.0 s
top speed	: 140 / 146 mph
miscellaneous	: 210 bhp 2.0T version was flagship
	of 9-3 range, until the arrival of
	new Aero version.

SAAB 9-3 SPORTWAGON 1.9 TID

engine type	: diesel, inline-4	kerb weight	: 1595 / 1610 kg
displacement	: 1910 cc	towing weight	: 1500 / 1600 kg
max. power	: 88 kW (120 bhp) /	boot space	: 419 l
	110 kW (150 bhp)	fuel capacity	: 58 l
@	: 3500 / 4000 rpm	consumption	: 51.4 / 47.9 mpg
max. torque	: 206 / 236 lb ft	acc. 0-62 mph	: 12.0 / 10.2 s
@	: 2000 rpm	top speed	: 121 / 124 mph
gears	: 6	EuroNCAP	: 5 stars
AT	: - / optional 6-speed	introduction	: September 2002
drive	: FWD	last revised in	: -
brakes f/r	: vent. discs / discs	warranty	: 2 years
body type	: 5-dr. stationwagon	miscellaneous	: Long-awaited addition to 9-3 range,
l x w x h	: 4654 x 1762 x 1540 mm		with diesel power from Alfa Romeo.
wheelbase	: 2675 mm		
turning circle	: 11.0 m		

SAAB 9-3 CONVERTIBLE AERO

engine type	: petrol, V6		kerb weight	: 1750 kg
displacement	: 2792 cc		towing weight	: 1600 kg
max. power	: 184 kW (250 bhp)		boot space	: 352 l
@	: 5500 rpm		fuel capacity	: 58 l
max. torque	: 258 lb ft		consumption	: 26.6 mpg
@	: 2000 rpm		acc. 0-62 mph	: 7.2 s
gears	: 6		top speed	: 149 mph
AT	: optional 5-speed		EuroNCAP	: 5 stars
drive	: FWD		introduction	: September 2003
brakes f/r	: vent. discs		last revised in	: -
body type	: 2-dr. convertible		warranty	: 2 years
l x w x h	: 4635 x 1762 x 1460 mm		miscellaneous	: Conventional convertible with fabric
wheelbase	: 2675 mm			top, but fully winter-proof. After all,
turning circle	: 10.8 m			it is a Swedish car.

S

SAAB 9-5 2.0T / 2.3T

engine type	: petrol, inline-4	kerb weight	: 1470 kg
displacement	: 1985 / 2290 cc	towing weight	: 1800 kg
max. power	: 110 kW (150 bhp) /	boot space	: 500 l
	136 kW (185 bhp)	fuel capacity	: 75 l
@	: 5500 rpm	consumption	: 32.8 / 31.7 mpg
max. torque	: 177 / 206 lb ft	acc. 0-62 mph	: 9.8 / 8.3 s
@	: 1800 / 1800 rpm	top speed	: 134 / 143 mph
gears	: 5	EuroNCAP	: 5 stars
AT	: optional 5-speed	introduction	: July 1997
drive	: FWD	last revised in	: September 2005
brakes f/r	: vent. discs	warranty	: 2 years
body type	: 4-dr. saloon	miscellaneous	: 9-5 also available as
l x w x h	: 4827 x 1792 x 1449		environmentally friendly BioPower
wheelbase	: 2703 mm		version that runs on E85 (ethanol).
turning circle	: 10.8 m		2.3T with 220 bhp available too.

9-5 AERO

engine type	: petrol, inline-4
displacement	: 2290 cc
max. power	: 191 kW (260 bhp)
@	: 5300 rpm
max. torque	: 258 lb ft
@	: 5400 rpm
gears	: 5
kerb weight	: 1495 kg
towing weight	: 1800 kg
consumption	: 30.7 mpg
acc. 0-60 mph	: 6.9 s
top speed	: 155 mph
miscellaneous	: Fastest version, with 4-cylinder turbo engine in the best Saab tradition. V6 from Vauxhall no longer available.

SAAB 9-5 SPORT ESTATE 1.9 TiD

engine type	: diesel, inline-4	kerb weight	: 1555 kg
displacement	: 1910 cc	towing weight	: 1800 kg
max. power	: 110 kW (150 bhp)	boot space	: 416 – 1490 l
@	: 4000 rpm	fuel capacity	: 75 l
max. torque	: 236 lb ft	consumption	: 41.5 mpg
@	: 2000 rpm	acc. 0-62 mph	: 10.7 s
gears	: 5	top speed	: 127 mph
AT	: optional 5-speed	EuroNCAP	: 5 stars
drive	: FWD	introduction	: September 1998
brakes f/r	: vent. discs	last revised in	: September 2005
body type	: 5-dr. stationwagon	warranty	: 2 years
l x w x h	: 4828 x 1792 x 1459 mm	miscellaneous	: The only diesel unit available in
wheelbase	: 2703 mm		the 9-5, but a popular choice in
turning circle	: 10.8 m		business circles.

S

SAAB 9-7X 4.2 / 5.3 V8

engine type	: petrol, inline-6 / V8	kerb weight	: 2140 / 2180 kg
displacement	: 4195 / 5328 cc	towing weight	: 2540 / 2950 kg
max. power	: 213 kW (290 bhp) /	boot space	: 1127 – 2268 l
	220 kW (300 bhp)	fuel capacity	: 83 l
@	: 6000 / 5200 rpm	consumption	: 16.9 / 18.2 mpg
max. torque	: 275 / 330 lb ft	acc. 0-62 mph	: 8.9 / 7.8 s
@	: 3600 / 4000 rpm	top speed	: 118 mph
gears	: -	EuroNCAP	: n.a.
AT	: 4-speed	introduction	: October 2005
drive	: 4WD	last revised in	: -
brakes f/r	: vent. discs	warranty	: 2 years
body type	: 5-dr. SUV	miscellaneous	: Built in Ohio and based on
l x w x h	: 4930 x 1910 x 1790 mm		Chevrolet Trailblazer, but a better
wheelbase	: 2870 mm		car than its American sister model.
turning circle	: 11.5 m		But is it better than Volvo's XC90
			too?

SANTANA PS-10 PLUS

engine type	: diesel, inline-4		kerb weight	: 1960 kg
displacement	: 2798 cc		towing weight	: 3500 kg
max. power	: 92 kW (125 bhp)		boot space	: n.a.
@	: 3600 rpm		fuel capacity	: 100 l
max. torque	: 203 lb ft		consumption	: 27.7 mpg
@	: 1800 rpm		acc. 0-62 mph	: n.a.
gears	: 5		top speed	: 87 mph
AT	: -		EuroNCAP	: n.a.
drive	: 4WD		introduction	: January 2004
brakes f/r	: vent. discs / discs		last revised in	: -
body type	: 5-dr. SUV		warranty	: 2 years
l x w x h	: 4765 x 1840 x 2000 mm		miscellaneous	: Spanish version of Land Rover, built
wheelbase	: 2786 mm			under licence. Robust offroad
turning circle	: 13.0 m			vehicle, also available as 2-door
				pick-up and 2-door Shortline.

S

SEAT IBIZA 1.2 12V / 1.4 16V

engine type	: petrol, inline-3 / -4	kerb weight	: 995 / 1034 kg
displacement	: 1198 / 1390 cc	towing weight	: 800 kg
max. power	: 51 kW (70 bhp) / 63 kW (85 bhp)	boot space	: 267 - 960 l
@	: 5400 / 5000 rpm	fuel capacity	: 45 l
max. torque	: 83 / 96 lb ft	consumption	: 47.9 / 43.5 mpg
@	: 3000 / 3600 rpm	acc. 0-62 mph	: 14.2 / 11.9 s
gears	: 5	top speed	: 106 / 112 mph
AT	: -	EuroNCAP	: 4 stars
drive	: FWD	introduction	: April 2002
brakes f/r	: vent. discs / drum brakes	last revised in	: March 2006
body type	: 3-dr. hatchback	warranty	: 2 years
l x w x h	: 3953 x 1698 x 1441 mm	miscellaneous	: Dynamic, sporting alternative to
wheelbase	: 2460 mm		Volkswagen Polo and Skoda Fabia.
turning circle	: 10.6 m		1.4 16V also available with 100 bhp.

IBIZA 1.4 TDI / 1.9 TDI

engine type	: diesel, inline-3 / -4
displacement	: 1422/ 1896 cc
max. power	: 51 kW (70 bhp) / 74 kW (100 bhp)
@	: 4000 rpm
max. torque	: 114 / 177 lb ft
@	: 2200 / 1900 rpm
gears	: 5
kerb weight	: 1106 / 1165 kg
towing weight	: 1000 / 1200 kg
consumption	: 60.1 / 57.6 mpg
acc. 0-60 mph	: 14.8 / 10.8 s
top speed	: 103 / 118 mph
miscellaneous	: Engines also available in Cordoba.

SEAT IBIZA FR / CUPRA

engine type	: petrol, inline-4
displacement	: 1781 cc
max. power	: 110 kW (150 bhp) /
	132 kW (180 bhp)
@	: 5800 / 5500 rpm
max. torque	: 162 / 180 lb ft
@	: 1950 / 2000 rpm
gears	: 5
AT	: -
drive	: FWD
brakes f/r	: vent. discs / discs
body type	: 3-dr. hatchback
l x w x h	: 3953 x 1698 x 1441 mm
wheelbase	: 2460 mm
turning circle	: 10.6 m

kerb weight	: 1154 / 1177 kg
towing weight	: 1200 kg / -
boot space	: 267 - 960 l
fuel capacity	: 45 l
consumption	: 35.8 / 35.3 mpg
acc. 0-62 mph	: 8.4 / 7.3 s
top speed	: 134 / 143 mph
EuroNCAP	: 4 stars
introduction	: April 2002
last revised in	: March 2006
warranty	: 2 years
miscellaneous	: Compact, affordable and fiery models, but not that often found on buyers' shortlists.

S

IBIZA FR TDI / CUPRA TDI

engine type	: diesel, inline-4
displacement	: 1896 cc
max. power	: 96 kW (130 bhp) /
	118 kW (160 bhp)
@	: 4000 / 3750 rpm
max. torque	: 228 / 243 lb ft
@	: 1900 rpm
gears	: 6
kerb weight	: 1192 / 1215 kg
towing weight	: 1200 kg / -
consumption	: 53.3 / 51.4 mpg
acc. 0-60 mph	: 9.4 / 7.6 s
top speed	: 129 / 137 mph
miscellaneous	: 'FR' stands for Formula Racing. Engines also used in other cars of Volkswagen Group.

SEAT CORDOBA 1.4 16V

engine type	: petrol, inline-4	kerb weight	: 1082 / 1065 kg
displacement	: 1390 cc	towing weight	: 800 / 1000 kg
max. power	: 55 kW (75 bhp) / 74 kW (100 bhp)	boot space	: 485 - 1140 l
@	: 5000 / 6000 rpm	fuel capacity	: 45 l
max. torque	: 93 / 94 lb ft	consumption	: 37.7 / 42.8 mpg
@	: 3800 / 4400 rpm	acc. 0-62 mph	: 15.9 / 11.5 s
gears	: - / 5	top speed	: 107 / 120 mph
AT	: 4-speed / -	EuroNCAP	: 4 stars
drive	: FWD	introduction	: April 2002
brakes f/r	: vent. discs / drum brakes	last revised in	: March 2006
body type	: 4-dr. saloon	warranty	: 2 years
l x w x h	: 4280 x 1698 x 1441 mm	miscellaneous	: Current Cordoba not nearly as
wheelbase	: 2460 mm		successful as previous model.
turning circle	: 10.6 m		Also available with engines
			from Ibiza.

SEAT LEON FR / CUPRA

engine type	: petrol, inline-4		**kerb weight**	: 1334 kg / n.a.
displacement	: 1984 cc		**towing weight**	: 1400 kg / n.a.
max. power	: 147 kW (200 bhp) /		**boot space**	: 341 - 1166 l
	177 kW (240 bhp)		**fuel capacity**	: 55 l
@	: 5100 / 5700 rpm		**consumption**	: 35.8 / 32.8 mpg
max. torque	: 206 / 221 lb ft		**acc. 0-62 mph**	: 7.3 / 6.4 s
@	: 1800 / 2200 rpm		**top speed**	: 229 / 247 mph
gears	: 6		**EuroNCAP**	: 5 stars
AT	: -		**introduction**	: September 2005
drive	: FWD		**last revised in**	: -
brakes f/r	: vent. discs / discs		**warranty**	: 2 years
body type	: 5-dr. hatchback		**miscellaneous**	: Car with sporty looks and cleverly
l x w x h	: 4323 x 1768 x 1458 mm			disguised rear door handles. Also
wheelbase	: 2578 mm			available with less tweaked engines
turning circle	: 10.4 m			(refer to Altea and Toledo for
				specifications).

S

SEAT ALTEA 1.9 TDI

engine type	: diesel, inline-4		kerb weight	: 1380 kg
displacement	: 1896 cc		towing weight	: 1400 kg
max. power	: 77 kW (105 bhp)		boot space	: 409 l
@	: 4000 rpm		fuel capacity	: 55 l
max. torque	: 184 lb ft		consumption	: 51.4 mpg
@	: 1900 rpm		acc. 0-62 mph	: 12.3 s
gears	: 5		top speed	: 114 mph
AT	: -		EuroNCAP	: 5 stars
drive	: FWD		introduction	: November 2004
brakes f/r	: vent. discs / discs		last revised in	: -
body type	: 5-dr. hatchback		warranty	: 2 years
l x w x h	: 4280 x 1768 x 1568 mm		miscellaneous	: Engine range includes 102 bhp
wheelbase	: 2578 mm			strong 1.6 petrol engine and 2.0
turning circle	: 10.9 m			TFSI with 200 bhp.

ALTEA 2.0 TDI / 2.0 TDI FR

engine type	: diesel, inline-4
displacement	: 1968 cc
max. power	: 103 kW (140 bhp) / 125 kW (170 bhp)
@	
max. torque	: 4000 / 4200 rpm
@	: 236 / 258 lb ft
gears	: 1750 / 1800 rpm
kerb weight	: 6
towing weight	: 1405 / 1421 kg
consumption	: 1400 kg
acc. 0-60 mph	: 47.9 / 45.6 mpg
top speed	: 9.9 / 8.6 s
miscellaneous	: 125 / 130 mph
	: Also available with Volkswagen's DSG automatic transmission with double clutch, a fine alternative to a manual gearbox.

SEAT TOLEDO 1.6 / 2.0 FSI

engine type	: petrol, inline-4	**kerb weight**	: 1319 / 1350 kg
displacement	: 1595 / 1984 cc	**towing weight**	: 1200 / 1400 kg
max. power	: 75 kW (102 bhp) /	**boot space**	: 500 l
	110 kW (150 bhp)	**fuel capacity**	: 55 l
@	: 5600 / 6000 rpm	**consumption**	: 36.2 / 33.6 mpg
max. torque	: 109 / 147 lb ft	**acc. 0-62 mph**	: 12.9 / 9.7 s
@	: 3800 / 3500 rpm	**top speed**	: 181 / 206 mph
gears	: 5 / 6	**EuroNCAP**	: 5 stars
AT	: - / optional 6-speed	**introduction**	: November 2004
drive	: FWD	**last revised in**	: -
brakes f/r	: vent. discs / discs	**warranty**	: 2 years
body type	: 5-dr. hatchback	**miscellaneous**	: Also available with 1.9 TDI and
l x w x h	: 4457 x 1768 x 1568 mm		2.0 TDI.
wheelbase	: 2578 mm		
turning circle	: 10.9 m		

S

SEAT ALHAMBRA 2.0 / 1.8 T

engine type	: petrol, inline-4	kerb weight	: 1553 / 1574 kg
displacement	: 1984 / 1781 cc	towing weight	: 1800 / 1900 kg
max. power	: 85 kW (115 bhp) /	boot space	: 852 - 2610 l
	110 kW (150 bhp)	fuel capacity	: 70 l
@	: 5200 / 5800 rpm	consumption	: 30.1 mpg
max. torque	: 125 / 162 lb ft	acc. 0-62 mph	: 15.2 / 10.9 s
@	: 2600 / 1800 rpm	top speed	: 110 / 124 mph
gears	: 6 / 6	EuroNCAP	: 3 stars
AT	: - / optional 5-speed	introduction	: December 1997
drive	: FWD	last revised in	: April 2000
brakes f/r	: vent. discs / discs	warranty	: 2 years
body type	: 5-dr. MPV	miscellaneous	: Conventional MPV from Seat is
l x w x h	: 4634 x 1810 x 1759 mm		a relative of VW's Sharan.
wheelbase	: 2841 mm		Spacious interior.
turning circle	: 11.9 m		

ALHAMBRA 2.8 V6 AUTO

engine type	: petrol, V6
displacement	: 2792 cc
max. power	: 150 kW (204 bhp)
@	: 6200 rpm
max. torque	: 195 lb ft
@	: 3400 rpm
gears	: 5
kerb weight	: 1627 kg
towing weight	: 2000 kg
consumption	: 24.8 mpg
acc. 0-60 mph	: 10.4 s
top speed	: 132 mph
miscellaneous	: Powerful, refined V6 engine
	offers excellent performance.

ALHAMBRA 1.9 TDI / 2.0 TDI

engine type	: diesel, inline-4
displacement	: 1896 / 1968 cc
max. power	: 85 kW (115 bhp) /
	103 kW (140 bhp)
@	: 4000 rpm
max. torque	: 229 lb ft
@	: 1900 rpm
gears	: 6
kerb weight	: 1624 / 1640 kg
towing weight	: 2000 kg
consumption	: 43.3 / 42.2 mpg
acc. 0-60 mph	: 13.7 / 12.2 s
top speed	: 112 / 119 mph
miscellaneous	: Oldest model in Seat programme
	is still going strong.

SKODA FABIA 1.2 / 1.4 16V

engine type	: petrol, inline-3 / inline-4
displacement	: 1198 / 1390 cc
max. power	: 47 kW (64 bhp) / 55 kW (75 bhp)
@	: 5400 / 5000 rpm
max. torque	: 82 / 93 lb ft
@	: 3000 / 3800 rpm
gears	: 5
AT	: - / optional 4-speed
drive	: FWD
brakes f/r	: vent. discs / drum brakes
body type	: 5-dr. hatchback
l x w x h	: 3970 x 1646 x 1451 mm
wheelbase	: 2462 mm
turning circle	: 10.5 m

kerb weight	: 1035 kg
towing weight	: 800 kg
boot space	: 260 – 1016 l
fuel capacity	: 45 l
consumption	: 47.1 / 42.2 mpg
acc. 0-62 mph	: 15.9 / 13.8 s
top speed	: 99 / 103mph
EuroNCAP	: 4 stars
introduction	: September 1999
last revised in	: April 2004
warranty	: 2 years
miscellaneous	: Small hatchback of timeless design is a sensible choice of the thinking man. Also available with 55 bhp 1.2 engine.

S

FABIA 1.4 16V / 2.0

engine type	: petrol, inline-4
displacement	: 1390 / 1984 cc
max. power	: 74 kW (100 bhp) / 85 kW (115 bhp)
@	: 6000 / 5400 tpm
max. torque	: 93 / 125 lb ft
@	: 4400 / 2400 rpm
gears	: 5
kerb weight	: 1040 / 1085 kg
towing weight	: 850 / 1000 kg
consumption	: 42.2 / 36.7 mpg
acc. 0-60 mph	: 11.5 / 9.9 s
top speed	: 115 / 121 mph
miscellaneous	: With bigger engine, Fabia turns into a surprisingly comfortable tourer. All petrol engines available in estate version, with the exception of the smallest unit.

FABIA RS

engine type	: diesel, inline-4
displacement	: 1896 cc
max. power	: 96 kW (130 bhp)
@	: 4000 rpm
max. torque	: 228 lb ft
@	: 1900 rpm
gears	: 6
kerb weight	: 1220 kg
towing weight	: n.a.
consumption	: 53.3 mpg
acc. 0-60 mph	: 9.5 s
top speed	: 128 mph
miscellaneous	: Sporting flagship of Fabia range has diesel power under the bonnet. Excellent 6-speed gearbox and capable chassis. Only available as hatchback.

SKODA FABIA ESTATE 1.4 TDI

engine type	: diesel, inline-3	kerb weight	: 1130 / 1140 kg
displacement	: 1422 cc	towing weight	: 900 / 1000 kg
max. power	: 51 kW (70 bhp) / 59 kW (80 bhp)	boot space	: 426 - 1225 l
@	: 4000 rpm	fuel capacity	: 45 l
max. torque	: 114 / 144 lb ft	consumption	: 58.9 / 60.1 mpg
@	: 2200 rpm	acc. 0-62 mph	: 15.8 / 14.0 s
gears	: 5	top speed	: 104 / 105 mph
AT	: -	EuroNCAP	: 4 stars
drive	: FWD	introduction	: January 2001
brakes f/r	: vent. discs / drum brakes	last revised in	: August 2004
body type	: 5-dr. stationwagon	warranty	: 2 years
l x w x h	: 4232 x 1646 x 1452 mm	miscellaneous	: Popular family car. Same petrol engines available as in hatchback.
wheelbase	: 2462 mm		
turning circle	: 10.5 m		

FABIA ESTATE 1.9 TDI

engine type : diesel, inline-4
displacement : 1896 cc
max. power : 74 kW (100 bhp)
@ : 4000 rpm
max. torque : 177 lb ft
@ : 1800 rpm
gears : 5
kerb weight : 1155 kg
towing weight : 1000 kg
consumption : 56.5 mpg
acc. 0-60 mph : 11.6 s
top speed : 116 mph
miscellaneous : Proven 1.9 TDI strongest diesel engine available in estate version of Fabia. Older engine, but still adequate.

SKODA ROOMSTER 1.4 / 1.6

engine type	: petrol, inline-4	**kerb weight**	: 1155 / 1175 kg
displacement	: 1390 / 1598 cc	**towing weight**	: 900 / 1000 kg
max. power	: 63 kW (86 bhp) / 77 kW (105 bhp)	**boot space**	: 450 – 1780 l
@	: 5000 / 5600 rpm	**fuel capacity**	: 55 l
max. torque	: 97 / 113 lb ft	**consumption**	: 41.5 / 40.4 mpg
@	: 3800 rpm	**acc. 0-62 mph**	: 13.0 / 10.9 s
gears	: 5	**top speed**	: 106 / 114 mph
AT	: -	**EuroNCAP**	: n.a.
drive	: FWD	**introduction**	: September 2006
brakes f/r	: vent. discs / discs	**last revised in**	: -
body type	: 5-drs. MPV	**warranty**	: 2 years
l x w x h	: 4210 x 1684 x 1607 mm	**miscellaneous**	: Refreshing mini-MPV with
wheelbase	: 2620 mm		adjustable rear bench. Steep price
turning circle	: 10.5 m		not in the best Skoda tradition. Also
			available with 1.2 12V petrol engine
			and diesel power (refer to Fabia
			Estate for specifications).

S

SKODA OCTAVIA 1.4 / 1.6

engine type	: petrol, inline-4	kerb weight	: 1205 / 1230 kg
displacement	: 1390 / 1595 cc	towing weight	: 900 / 1200 kg
max. power	: 55 kW (75 bhp) / 75 kW (102 bhp)	boot space	: 560 - 1420 l
@	: 5000 / 5600 rpm	fuel capacity	: 55 l
max. torque	: 93 / 109 lb ft	consumption	: 40.4 / 39.8 mpg
@	: 3800 rpm	acc. 0-62 mph	: 15.5 / 12.4 s
gears	: 5	top speed	: 106 / 118 mph
AT	: optional 6-speed	EuroNCAP	: 4 stars
drive	: FWD	introduction	: June 2004
brakes f/r	: vent. discs / discs	last revised in	: -
body type	: 5-dr. hatchback	warranty	: 2 years
l x w x h	: 4572 x 1769 x 1462 mm	miscellaneous	: Octavia model resembles a saloon
wheelbase	: 2578 mm		but is in fact a hatchback. And
turning circle	: 10.9 m		successful at that.

OCTAVIA 1.6 FSI / 2.0 FSI

engine type	: petrol, inline-4
displacement	: 1598 / 1984 cc
max. power	: 85 kW (115 bhp) /
	110 kW (150 bhp)
@	: 6000 rpm
max. torque	: 114 / 148 lb ft
@	: 4000 / 3500 rpm
gears	: 5 / 6
kerb weight	: 1240 / 1285 kg
towing weight	: 1200 / 1300 kg
consumption	: 40.4 / 37.2 mpg
acc. 0-60 mph	: 11.4 / 9.3 s
top speed	: 123 / 132 mph
miscellaneous	: Modern engines run on leaner
	mixture in part of rev range,
	making them economical and
	powerful at the same time.

OCTAVIA RS

engine type	: petrol, inline-4
displacement	: 1984 cc
max. power	: 147 kW (200 bhp)
@	: 5100 rpm
max. torque	: 206 lb ft
@	: 1800 tpm
gears	: 6
kerb weight	: 1400 kg
towing weight	: 1300 kg
consumption	: 35.8 mpg
acc. 0-60 mph	: 7.3 s
top speed	: 149 mph
miscellaneous	: Fastest Skoda of them all, with
	200 bhp on tap. And rather more
	practical than a VW Golf GTI.

SKODA OCTAVIA ESTATE 1.9 TDI / 2.0 TDI

engine type	: diesel, inline-4	kerb weight	: 1300 / 1325 kg
displacement	: 1896 / 1968 cc	towing weight	: 1400 kg
max. power	: 77 kW (105 bhp) /	boot space	: 580 - 1620 l
	103 kW (140 bhp)	fuel capacity	: 55 l
@	: 4000 rpm	consumption	: 53.3 / 49.6 mpg
max. torque	: 184 / 236 lb ft	acc. 0-62 mph	: 11.9 / 9.7 s
@	: 1900 / 1750 rpm	top speed	: 119 / 129 mph
gears	: 5 / 6	EuroNCAP	: 4 stars
AT	: optional 6-speed	introduction	: June 2004
drive	: FWD	last revised in	: -
brakes f/r	: vent. discs / discs	warranty	: 2 years
body type	: 5-dr. stationwagon	miscellaneous	: Spacious stationwagon. Diesel
l x w x h	: 4572 x 1769 x 1468 mm		engines also available in hatchback,
wheelbase	: 2578 mm		petrol engines also in Estate. Now
turning circle	: 10.2 m		also available as wild Scout and
			170 bhp RS TDi.

S

SKODA SUPERB 2.0 / 1.8T

engine type	: petrol, inline-4
displacement	: 1984 / 1781 cc
max. power	: 85 kW (115 bhp) / 110 kW (150 bhp)
@	: 5400 / 5700 rpm
max. torque	: 127 / 155 lb ft
@	: 3500 / 1750 rpm
gears	: 5
AT	: optional 5-speed
drive	: FWD
brakes f/r	: vent. discs / discs
body type	: 4-dr. saloon
l x w x h	: 4803 x 1765 x 1469 mm
wheelbase	: 2803 mm
turning circle	: 11.8 m

kerb weight	: 1387 / 1413 kg
towing weight	: 1400 / 1300 kg
boot space	: 462 l
fuel capacity	: 62 l
consumption	: 32.8 / 34.0 mpg
acc. 0-62 mph	: 11.6 / 9.5 s
top speed	: 122 / 134 mph
EuroNCAP	: 4 stars
introduction	: July 2002
last revised in	: -
warranty	: 2 years
miscellaneous	: Biggest Skoda based on previous VW Passat. Lots of legroom in the back. A car fit for ministers of Central-European countries.

SUPERB V6 2.8 / V6 2.5 TDI

engine type	: petrol / diesel, V6
displacement	: 2771 / 2496 cc
max. power	: 142 kW (193 bhp) / 120 kW (163 bhp)
@	: 6000 / 4000 rpm
max. torque	: 206 / 258 lb ft
@	: 3200 / 1250 rpm
gears	: 5 / 6
kerb weight	: 1476 / 1545 kg
towing weight	: 1600 kg
consumption	: 29.1 / 35.8 mpg
acc. 0-60 mph	: 8.0 / 9.2 s
top speed	: 147 / 135 mph
miscellaneous	: Diesel power an obvious choice in this model.

SUPERB 1.9 TDI 74/96 KW

engine type	: diesel, inline-4
displacement	: 1896 cc
max. power	: 74 kW (101 bhp) / 96 kW (130 bhp)
@	: 4000 rpm
max. torque	: 184 / 236 lb ft
@	: 1900 / 1750 rpm
gears	: 5
kerb weight	: 1433 / 1440 kg
towing weight	: 1400 / 1600 kg
consumption	: 47.9 / 44.1 mpg
acc. 0-60 mph	: 13.2 / 10.4 s
top speed	: 119 / 133 mph
miscellaneous	: Popular as a taxi because of rear interior space and frugal but splendid diesel engines.

SMART FORTWO 50 bhp / 61 bhp

engine type	: petrol, inline-3
displacement	: 698 cc
max. power	: 37 kW (50 bhp) / 45 kW (61 bhp)
@	: 5250 rpm
max. torque	: 59 / 70 lb ft
@	: 1800 / 2000 rpm
gears	: 6
AT	: -
drive	: RWD
brakes f/r	: discs / drum brakes
body type	: 2-dr. hatchback
l x w x h	: 2500 x 1515 x 1549 mm
wheelbase	: 1812 mm
turning circle	: 8.7 m

kerb weight	: 730 kg
towing weight	: -
boot space	: 150 - 550 l
fuel capacity	: 33 l
consumption	: 60.1 mpg
acc. 0-62 mph	: 18.3 / 15.5 s
top speed	: 84 mph
EuroNCAP	: 3 stars
introduction	: September 1998
last revised in	: December 2003
warranty	: 2 years
miscellaneous	: Now sole Smart offering again, after demise of Forfour. Quick Brabus and convertible version also available.

S

SMART FORTWO CDI

engine type	: diesel, inline-3
displacement	: 799 cc
max. power	: 30 kW (41 bhp)
@	: 4200 rpm
max. torque	: 74 lb ft
@	: 1800 rpm
gears	: 6
kerb weight	: 730 kg
towing weight	: -
consumption	: 83.1 mpg
acc. 0-60 mph	: 19.8 s
top speed	: 84 mph
miscellaneous	: Both Coupé and Convertible available with diesel power. Open top motoring at a discount.

SPYKER C8

engine type	: petrol, V8	kerb weight	: approx. 1250 kg
displacement	: 4172 cc	towing weight	: -
max. power	: 298 kW (400 bhp)	boot space	: n.a.
@	: 7000 rpm	fuel capacity	: 75 l
max. torque	: 354 lb ft	consumption	: n.a.
@	: 3400 rpm	acc. 0-62 mph	: 4.5 s
gears	: 6	top speed	: 186 mph
AT	: -	EuroNCAP	: n.a.
drive	: RWD	introduction	: 2004
brakes f/r	: vent. discs	last revised in	: -
body type	: 2-dr. convertible	warranty	: 2 years
l x w x h	: 4185 x 1880 x 1080 mm	miscellaneous	: Small Dutch car manufacturer
wheelbase	: 2570 mm		builds on the foundations of
turning circle	: n.a.		forgotten pre-war luxury marque.
			Latest addition is C12 La Turbie
			model with 500 bhp Audi W12-
			engine.

SPYKER D12 PEKING-TO-PARIS

engine type	: petrol, W12		**kerb weight**	: 1850 kg
displacement	: 5998 cc		**towing weight**	: -
max. power	: 368 kW (500 bhp)		**boot space**	: n.a.
@	: n.a.		**fuel capacity**	: 100 l
max. torque	: 450 lb ft		**consumption**	: n.a.
@	: n.a.		**acc. 0-62 mph**	: 5.0 s
gears	: 6		**top speed**	: 186 mph
AT	: -		**EuroNCAP**	: n.a.
drive	: 4WD		**introduction**	: 2006
brakes f/r	: vent. discs		**last revised in**	: -
body type	: 4-dr. SUV		**warranty**	: 2 years
l x w x h	: 4950 x 2000 x 1680 mm		**miscellaneous**	: New SSUV, Spyker speak for Super Sports Utility Vehicle. Majority of customers to be found in Middle-East.
wheelbase	: 2855 mm			
turning circle	: n.a.			

S

SSANGYONG ACTYON 200 XDI

engine type	: diesel, inline-4	kerb weight	: n.a.
displacement	: 1998 cc	towing weight	: 2300 kg
max. power	: 104 kW (141 bhp)	boot space	: n.a.
@	: 4000 rpm	fuel capacity	: 75 l
max. torque	: 232 lb ft	consumption	: 36.2 mpg
@	: 1800 rpm	acc. 0-62 mph	: 14.4 s
gears	: 5	top speed	: 102 mph
AT	: optional 4-speed	EuroNCAP	: n.a.
drive	: 4WD	introduction	: September 2006
brakes f/r	: n.a.	last revised in	: -
body type	: 5-dr. SUV	warranty	: 3 years
l x w x h	: 4450 x 1880 x 1740 mm	miscellaneous	: Action inherits its bizarre styling
wheelbase	: 2740 mm		from the SsangYong Rodius.
turning circle	: n.a.		

SSANGYONG KYRON 200 XDI

engine type	: diesel, inline-4	kerb weight	: 1796 kg
displacement	: 1998 cc	towing weight	: 2100 kg
max. power	: 104 kW (141 bhp)	boot space	: 625 l
@	: 4000 rpm	fuel capacity	: 75 l
max. torque	: 229 lb ft	consumption	: 36.7 mpg
@	: 1800 rpm	acc. 0-62 mph	: 16.2 s
gears	: 5	top speed	: 104 mph
AT	: optional 4-speed	EuroNCAP	: n.a.
drive	: 2WD	introduction	: autumn 2005
brakes f/r	: vent. discs / discs	last revised in	: -
body type	: 3-dr. SUV	warranty	: 3 years
l x w x h	: 4660 x 1880 x 1755 mm	miscellaneous	: New model replaces Musso. Just
wheelbase	: 2740 mm		one engine available, but choice of
turning circle	: n.a.		2WD and 4WD. Better-looking than
			predecessor.

S

SSANGYONG REXTON 270

engine type	: diesel, inline-5	**kerb weight**	: 1961 kg
displacement	: 2696 cc	**towing weight**	: 3500 kg
max. power	: 121 kW (165 bhp)	**boot space**	: 935 – 1524 l
@	: 4000 rpm	**fuel capacity**	: 80 l
max. torque	: 250 lb ft	**consumption**	: 32.9 mpg
@	: 2400 rpm	**acc. 0-62 mph**	: 13.2 s
gears	: 5	**top speed**	: 111 mph
AT	: optional, 5-speed	**EuroNCAP**	: n.a.
drive	: 4WD	**introduction**	: December 2002
brakes f/r	: vent. discs / discs	**last revised in**	: July 2006
body type	: 5-dr. SUV	**warranty**	: 3 years
l x w x h	: 4720 x 1870 x 1830 mm	**miscellaneous**	: Cooperation with Mercedes-Benz
wheelbase	: 2820 mm		shows in front grille of new Rexton.
turning circle	: 11.2 m		Only available as yet as 270 Xdi.

SSANGYONG RODIUS 270

engine type	: diesel, inline-5		kerb weight	: 1982 kg
displacement	: 2696 cc		towing weight	: 2500 kg
max. power	: 121 kW (163 bhp)		boot space	: 893 - 3322 l
@	: 4000 rpm		fuel capacity	: 80 l
max. torque	: 165 lb ft		consumption	: 32.9 mpg
@	: 3000 rpm		acc. 0-62 mph	: 13.5 s
gears	: 5		top speed	: 105 mph
AT	: optional 5-speed		EuroNCAP	: n.a.
drive	: RWD		introduction	: July 2005
brakes f/r	: vent. discs		last revised in	: -
body type	: 5-dr. MPV		warranty	: 3 years
l x w x h	: 5125 x 1915 x 1845 mm		miscellaneous	: Very big car with lots of space and
wheelbase	: 3000 mm			8 seats. Old but capable diesel
turning circle	: 11.6 m			engine. Also available as SV 270X.

S

SUBARU G3X JUSTY

engine type	: petrol, inline-4	kerb weight	: 980 kg
displacement	: 1328 cc	towing weight	: 800 kg
max. power	: 69 kW (93 bhp)	boot space	: 236 l
@	: 6000 rpm	fuel capacity	: 41 l
max. torque	: 87 lb ft	consumption	: 40.9 mpg
@	: 4000 rpm	acc. 0-62 mph	: 11.7 s
gears	: 5	top speed	: 96 mph
AT	: -	EuroNCAP	: n.a.
drive	: 4WD	introduction	: December 2004
brakes f/r	: vent. discs / drum brakes	last revised in	: -
body type	: 5-dr. hatchback	warranty	: 3 years
l x w x h	: 3770 x 1605 x 1605 mm	miscellaneous	: Smallest Subaru is in fact a Suzuki
wheelbase	: 2360 mm		with different badging and 4-wheel
turning circle	: 10.0 m		drive. Bit of a maverick in Subaru
			programme.

SUBARU IMPREZA WRX / WRX STI

engine type	: petrol, flat-4	kerb weight	: 1380 / 1470 kg
displacement	: 2457 cc	towing weight	: 1200 kg
max. power	: 169 kW (230 bhp) /	boot space	: 401 / 395 l
	206 kW (280 bhp)	fuel capacity	: 60 l
@	: 5600 rpm	consumption	: 27.4 / 25.9 mpg
max. torque	: 236 / 289 lb ft	acc. 0-62 mph	: 5.9 / 5.4 s
@	: 3600 / 4000 rpm	top speed	: 143 / 158 mph
gears	: 5 / 6	EuroNCAP	: n.a.
AT	: -	introduction	: September 2000
drive	: 4WD	last revised in	: October 2005
brakes f/r	: vent. discs	warranty	: 3 years
body type	: 4-dr. saloon	miscellaneous	: Second nose job already for model
l x w x h	: 4465 x 1740 x 1440 mm		range that leans heavily on ultrafast
wheelbase	: 2525 mm		WRX and WRX STi versions.
turning circle	: 10.4 m		

S

IMPREZA 2.0R

engine type	: petrol, flat-4
displacement	: 1994 cc
max. power	: 118 kW (160 bhp)
@	: 6400 rpm
max. torque	: 137 lb ft
@	: 3200 rpm
gears	: 5
kerb weight	: 1285 kg
towing weight	: 1200 kg
consumption	: 31.4 mpg
acc. 0-60 mph	: 8.8 s
top speed	: 130 mph
miscellaneous	: Modest 2-litre version lives in the shadow of faster stablemates. Impreza also available as 5-door Plus.

SUBARU LEGACY 2.0R

engine type	: petrol, flat-4	**kerb weight**	: 1305 kg
displacement	: 1994 cc	**towing weight**	: 1300 kg
max. power	: 121 kW (165 bhp)	**boot space**	: 433 l
@	: 6800 rpm	**fuel capacity**	: 64 l
max. torque	: 138 lb ft	**consumption**	: 32.5 mpg
@	: 3200 rpm	**acc. 0-62 mph**	: 11.2 s
gears	: 5	**top speed**	: 133 mph
AT	: optional 4-speed	**EuroNCAP**	: n.a.
drive	: 4WD	**introduction**	: October 2003
brakes f/r	: vent. discs / discs	**last revised in**	: September 2006
body type	: 4-dr. saloon	**warranty**	: 3 years
l x w x h	: 4665 x 1730 x 1425 mm	**miscellaneous**	: Exclusively equipped Japanese
wheelbase	: 2670 mm		alternative for fast rivals from
turning circle	: 10.8 m		Germany. New 2.0 petrol engine
			replaces previous 2.0 as well as 2.5.
			Wagon version also available.

SUBARU OUTBACK 3.0R

engine type	: petrol, flat-6	kerb weight	: 1495 kg
displacement	: 3000 cc	towing weight	: 1800 kg
max. power	: 180 kW (245 bhp)	boot space	: 459 - 1649 l
@	: 6600 rpm	fuel capacity	: 64 l
max. torque	: 219 lb ft	consumption	: 28.5 mpg
@	: 4200 rpm	acc. 0-62 mph	: 8.5 s
gears	: -	top speed	: 139 mph
AT	: 5-speed	EuroNCAP	: 4 stars
drive	: 4WD	introduction	: October 2003
brakes f/r	: vent. discs / discs	last revised in	: September 2006
body type	: 5-dr. stationwagon	warranty	: 3 years
l x w x h	: 4730 x 1770 x 1545 mm	miscellaneous	: Outback is wilder version of Subaru
wheelbase	: 2670 mm		Legacy Wagon. 6-cylinder boxer
turning circle	: 10.8 m		engine refined and full of character.

S

SUBARU FORESTER 2.0 X / 2.5

engine type	: petrol, flat-4	kerb weight	: 1465 / 1560 kg
displacement	:1994 / 2457 cc	towing weight	: 1500 / 2000 kg
max. power	: 116 kW (158 bhp) /	boot space	: 387 – 1629 l
	169 kW (230 bhp)	fuel capacity	: 60 l
@	: 6400 / 5600 rpm	consumption	: 30.4 / 26.4 mpg
max. torque	: 137 / 236 lb ft	acc. 0-62 mph	: 9.7 / 6.0 s
@	: 3200 / 3600 rpm	top speed	: 122 / 134 mph
gears	: 5	EuroNCAP	: n.a.
AT	: optional 4-speed	introduction	: September1998
drive	: 4WD	last revised in	: September 2005
brakes f/r	: vent. discs / discs	warranty	: 3 years
body type	: 5-dr. stationwagon	miscellaneous	: Practical and spacious
l x w x h	: 4485 x 1735 x 1590 mm		Impreza-based stationwagon is
wheelbase	: 2525 mm		great tow car.
turning circle	: 10.6 m		

SUBARU B9 TRIBECA

engine type	: petrol, flat-6		**kerb weight**	: 1865 kg
displacement	: 3000 cc		**towing weight**	: 2000 kg
max. power	: 180 kW (245 bhp)		**boot space**	: n.a.
@	: 6600 rpm		**fuel capacity**	: 64 l
max. torque	: 219 lb ft		**consumption**	: 23.0 mpg
@	: 4200 rpm		**acc. 0-62 mph**	: n.a.
gears	: -		**top speed**	: 121 mph
AT	: 5-speed		**EuroNCAP**	: n.a.
drive	: 4WD		**introduction**	: November 2006
brakes f/r	: vent. discs		**last revised in**	: -
body type	: 5-dr. SUV		**warranty**	: 3 years
l x w x h	: 4855 x 1880 x 1675 mm		**miscellaneous**	: Stout crossover with spacious and
wheelbase	: 2750 mm			refined interior and fine driving
turning circle	: 11.4 m			characteristics.

S

SUZUKI ALTO 1.1

engine type	: petrol, inline-4	kerb weight	: 775 kg
displacement	: 1061 cc	towing weight	: 750 kg
max. power	: 46 kW (62 bhp)	boot space	: 177 - 725 l
@	: 6000 rpm	fuel capacity	: 35 l
max. torque	: 63 lb ft	consumption	: 57.6 mpg
@	: 3200 rpm	acc. 0-62 mph	: 14.8 s
gears	: 5	top speed	: 96 mph
AT	: optional 3-speed	EuroNCAP	: n.a.
drive	: FWD	introduction	: March 2002
brakes f/r	: vent. discs / drum brakes	last revised in	: -
body type	: 5-dr. hatchback	warranty	: 3 years
l x w x h	: 3495 x 1475 x 1455 mm	miscellaneous	: One of the smallest, most frugal
wheelbase	: 2360 mm		and affordable cars on the market.
turning circle	: 9.2 m		New model expected soon.

SUZUKI WAGON R⁺ 1.0 / 1.2

engine type	: petrol, inline-3 / inline-4	kerb weight	: 940 / 955 kg
displacement	: 998 / 1229 cc	towing weight	: 650 kg
max. power	: 44 kW (60 bhp) / 59 kW (80 bhp)	boot space	: 248 l
@	: 5600 rpm	fuel capacity	: 41 l
max. torque	: 65 / 81 lb ft	consumption	: 48.7 / 47.1 mpg
@	: 3800 / 4000 rpm	acc. 0-62 mph	: 17.7 / 13.2 s
gears	: 5	top speed	: 90 / 100 mph
AT	: -	EuroNCAP	: n.a.
drive	: FWD	introduction	: May 2000
brakes f/r	: vent. discs / drum brakes	last revised in	: -
body type	: 5-dr. MPV	warranty	: 3 years
l x w x h	: 3540 x 1600 x 1660 mm	miscellaneous	: Roomy and practical car with low
wheelbase	: 2360 mm		running costs. 94 bhp 1.3 also
turning circle	: 9.8 m		available, with either 5-speed
			manual or 4-speed automatic.

S

SUZUKI SWIFT 1.3 / 1.5

engine type	: petrol, inline-4		kerb weight	: 945 / 955 kg
displacement	: 1328 / 1490 cc		towing weight	: 1000 kg
max. power	: 68 kW (92 bhp) / 75 kW (102 bhp)		boot space	: 213 l
@	: 5800 / 5900 rpm		fuel capacity	: 45 l
max. torque	: 85 / 98 lb ft		consumption	: 46.3 / 45.6 mpg
@	: 4200 / 4100 rpm		acc. 0-62 mph	: 11.0 / 10.0 s
gears	: 5		top speed	: 109 / 115 mph
AT	: - / optional 4-speed		EuroNCAP	: 4 stars
drive	: FWD		introduction	: March 2005
brakes f/r	: vent. discs / drum brakes		last revised in	: -
body type	: 3- / 5-dr. hatchback		warranty	: 3 years
l x w x h	: 3695 x 1690 x 1500 mm		miscellaneous	: New Swift much better than
wheelbase	: 2380 mm			previous model. Modern looks, fine
turning circle	: 9.4 m			road behaviour. Also available as
				Sport with 125 bhp.

SWIFT 1.3 DIESEL

engine type	: diesel, inline-4
displacement	: 1248 cc
max. power	: 51 kW (69 bhp)
@	: 4000 rpm
max. torque	: 125 lb ft
@	: 2500 rpm
gears	: 5
kerb weight	: 1020 kg
towing weight	: 900 kg
consumption	: 61.4 mpg
acc. 0-60 mph	: 14.2 s
top speed	: 102 mph
miscellaneous	: Diesel-powered version is rather expensive and therefore only available by special order.

SUZUKI IGNIS 1.3 / 1.5

engine type	: petrol, inline-4	**kerb weight**	: 930 / 935 kg
displacement	: 1328 / 1490 cc	**towing weight**	: 800 kg
max. power	: 69 kW (94 bhp) / 73 kW (99 bhp)	**boot space**	: 236 l
@	: 6000 / 5900 rpm	**fuel capacity**	: 41 l
max. torque	: 87 / 99 lb ft	**consumption**	: 43.5 / 42.2 mpg
@	: 4100 rpm	**acc. 0-62 mph**	: 11.1 s / n.a.
gears	: 5	**top speed**	: 99 / 106 mph
AT	: -	**EuroNCAP**	: n.a.
drive	: FWD	**introduction**	: September 2003
brakes f/r	: vent. discs / drum brakes	**last revised in**	: -
body type	: 5-dr. hatchback	**warranty**	: 3 years
l x w x h	: 3770 x 1605 x 1605 mm	**miscellaneous**	: Model destined to step aside for
wheelbase	: 2360 mm		modern Swift and trendy SX4.
turning circle	: 10.0 m		

S

SUZUKI SX4 1.5 / 1.6 16V

engine type	: petrol, inline-4		kerb weight	: 1105 kg
displacement	: 1490 / 1586 cc		towing weight	: 1200 kg
max. power	: 73 kW (99 bhp) / 79 kW (107 bhp)		boot space	: 270 - 670 l
@	: 5600 rpm		fuel capacity	: 50 l
max. torque	: 98 / 107 lb ft		consumption	: 41.5 / 39.8 mpg
@	: 4100 / 4000 rpm		acc. 0-62 mph	: 11.0 / 10.7 s
gears	: 5		top speed	: 109 / 112 mph
AT	: - / optional 4-speed		EuroNCAP	: 4 stars
drive	: FWD		introduction	: April 2006
brakes f/r	: vent. discs / drum brakes		last revised in	: -
body type	: 5-dr. hatchback		warranty	: 3 years
l x w x h	: 4100 x 1730 x 1555 mm		miscellaneous	: Identical to Fiat Sedici, but cheaper since Italian sister car is offered with 4WD only. Wild SX4 4Grip model however also boasts 4 driven wheels.
wheelbase	: 2500 mm			
turning circle	: 10.6 m			

SX4 1.9 DDIS

engine type	: diesel, inline-4
displacement	: 1910 cc
max. power	: 88 kW (120 bhp)
@	: 4000 rpm
max. torque	: 206 lb ft
@	: 2000 rpm
gears	: 6
kerb weight	: 1240 kg
towing weight	: 1200 kg
consumption	: 44.8 mpg
acc. 0-60 mph	: 10.5 s
top speed	: 118 mph
miscellaneous	: Diesel version intended to promote SX4 as company car.

SUZUKI LIANA 1.6

engine type	: petrol, inline-4		**kerb weight**	: 1145 kg
displacement	: 1586 cc		**towing weight**	: 1200 kg
max. power	: 78 kW (106 bhp)		**boot space**	: 348 - 1062 l
@	: 5500 rpm		**fuel capacity**	: 50 l
max. torque	: 107 lb ft		**consumption**	: 40.9 mpg
@	: 4000 rpm		**acc. 0-62 mph**	: 11.7 s
gears	: 5		**top speed**	: 109 mph
AT	: optional 4-speed		**EuroNCAP**	: n.a.
drive	: FWD		**introduction**	: 2001
brakes f/r	: vent. discs / drum brakes		**last revised in**	: 2004
body type	: 5-dr. hatchback		**warranty**	: 3 years
l x w x h	: 4230 x 1690 x 1550 mm		**miscellaneous**	: 4-door saloon version lifted many a
wheelbase	: 2480 mm			rear wheel in famed British
turning circle	: 10.0 m			television car show. Car however
				not likely to be driven in anger on
				public roads.

S

SUZUKI JIMNY

engine type	: petrol, inline-4	kerb weight	: 1135 / 1220 kg
displacement	: 1328 cc	towing weight	: 1300 kg
max. power	: 63 kW (85 bhp)	boot space	: 113-816 l
@	: 6000 rpm	fuel capacity	: 40 l
max. torque	: 81 lb ft	consumption	: 38.7 mpg
@	: 4100 rpm	acc. 0-62 mph	: 14.1 s
gears	: 5	top speed	: 87 mph
AT	: -	EuroNCAP	: n.a.
drive	: 4WD	introduction	: September 1998
brakes f/r	: discs / drum brakes	last revised in	: December 2005
body type	: 2-dr. SUV	warranty	: 3 years
l x w x h	: 3625 x 1600 x 1670 mm	miscellaneous	: Suzuki built itself a reputation with
wheelbase	: 2250 mm		small offroad vehicles. Cute looks
turning circle	: 9.8 m		and determined behaviour. Also
			available as convertible.

SUZUKI GRAND VITARA 1.6 / 2.0

engine type	: petrol, inline-4	kerb weight	: 1370 / 1505 kg
displacement	: 1586 / 1995 cc	towing weight	: 1600 / 1850 kg
max. power	: 78 kW (106 bhp) /	boot space	: 184 – 964 / 398 – 1386 l
	103 kW (140 bhp)	fuel capacity	: 55 / 66 l
@	: 5900 / 6000 rpm	consumption	: 32.5 / 31.0 mpg
max. torque	: 107 / 135 lb ft	acc. 0-62 mph	: 14.4 / 12.5 s
@	: 4100 / 4000 rpm	top speed	: 99 / 109 mph
gears	: 5	EuroNCAP	: n.a.
AT	: - / optional 4-speed	introduction	: September 2005
drive	: 4WD	last revised in	: -
brakes f/r	: vent. discs / drum brakes	warranty	: 3 years
body type	: 3-dr. / 5-dr. SUV	miscellaneous	: Completely new model. 1.6 version
l x w x h	: 4005 /		only available with 3 doors, 2.0 only
	4470 (5-d) x 1810 x 1695 mm		with 5 doors. Fine companion with
wheelbase	: 2440 / 2640 (5-d) mm		adequate performance level.
turning circle	: 10.2 / 11.0 m		

GRAND VITARA 1.9 DDiS

engine type	: diesel, inline-4
displacement	: 1870 cc
max. power	: 95 kW (129 bhp)
@	: 3750 rpm
max. torque	: 221 lb ft
@	: 2000 rpm
gears	: 5
kerb weight	: 1495 kg
towing weight	: 1600 kg
consumption	: 36.7 mpg
acc. 0-60 mph	: 12.8 s
top speed	: 106 mph
miscellaneous	: Available with 3-door and
	5-door bodywork.

TOYOTA AYGO 1.0

engine type	: petrol, inline-3
displacement	: 998 cc
max. power	: 50 kW (68 bhp)
@	: 6000 rpm
max. torque	: 68 lb ft
@	: 3600 rpm
gears	: 5
AT	: optional 5-speed
drive	: FWD
brakes f/r	: vent. discs / drum brakes
body type	: 3- / 5-dr. hatchback
l x w x h	: 3410 x 1615 x 1465 mm
wheelbase	: 2340 mm
turning circle	: n.a.

kerb weight	: 765 kg
towing weight	: n.a.
boot space	: 130 - 782 l
fuel capacity	: 35 l
consumption	: 61.4 mpg
acc. 0-62 mph	: 14.2 s
top speed	: 98 mph
EuroNCAP	: 4 stars
introduction	: May 2005
last revised in	: -
warranty	: 3 years
miscellaneous	: Cute and original design, aimed at young clientele. Technically identical to Citroën C1 and Peugeot 107.

AYGO 1.4 DIESEL

engine type	: diesel, inline-4
displacement	: 1398 cc
max. power	: 40 kW (54 bhp)
@	: 4000 rpm
max. torque	: 96 lb ft
@	: 1750 rpm
gears	: 5
kerb weight	: 880 kg
towing weight	: n.a.
consumption	: 68.9 mpg
acc. 0-60 mph	: 16.8 s
top speed	: 96 mph
miscellaneous	: There are not that many cars around anymore of comparable size and weight.

TOYOTA YARIS 1.0 / 1.3

engine type	: petrol, inline-3 / inline-4	**kerb weight**	: 955 / 995 kg
displacement	: 998 / 1296 cc	**towing weight**	: 750 / 900 kg
max. power	: 51 kW (69 bhp) / 64 kW (87 bhp)	**boot space**	: 363 l
@	: 6000 rpm	**fuel capacity**	: 42 l
max. torque	: 68 / 90 lb ft	**consumption**	: 52.3 / 47.1 mpg
@	: 3600 / 4200 rpm	**acc. 0-62 mph**	: 15.7 / 11.5 s
gears	: 5	**top speed**	: 96 / 106 mph
AT	: optional 5-speed	**EuroNCAP**	: 5 stars
drive	: FWD	**introduction**	: January 2006
brakes f/r	: vent. discs	**last revised in**	: -
body type	: 3- / 5-dr. hatchback	**warranty**	: 3 years
l x w x h	: 3750 x 1695 x 1530 mm	**miscellaneous**	: New Yaris retains smart looks of previous model. Car is produced in Valenciennes in France.
wheelbase	: 2460 mm		
turning circle	: 9.4 m		

T

YARIS 1.4 D-4D

engine type	: diesel, inline-4
displacement	: 1364 cc
max. power	: 66 kW (90 bhp)
@	: 3800 rpm
max. torque	: 140 lb ft
@	: 1800 rpm
gears	: 5
kerb weight	: 1030 kg
towing weight	: 1050 kg
consumption	: 62.8 mpg
acc. 0-60 mph	: 10.7 s
top speed	: 109 mph
miscellaneous	: Consumption figures of car equipped with optional 5-speed gearbox with automatic clutch identical to manual version.

TOYOTA COROLLA 1.4 16V / 1.6 16V

engine type	: petrol, inline-4
displacement	: 1398 / 1598 cc
max. power	: 71 kW (97 bhp) / 81 kW (110 bhp)
@	: 6000 rpm
max. torque	: 96 / 110 lb ft
@	: 4600 / 4800 rpm
gears	: 5
AT	: - / optional 5-speed
drive	: FWD
brakes f/r	: vent. discs / discs
body type	: 3-dr. hatchback
l x w x h	: 4180 x 1710 x 1475 mm
wheelbase	: 2600 mm
turning circle	: 10.2 m

kerb weight	: 1105 / 1110 kg
towing weight	: 1000 / 1300 kg
boot space	: 289 - 1190 l
fuel capacity	: 55 l
consumption	: 42.2 / 40.4 mpg
acc. 0-62 mph	: 12.0 / 10.2 s
top speed	: 115 / 118 mph
EuroNCAP	: 4 stars
introduction	: 2001
last revised in	: June 2004
warranty	: 3 years
miscellaneous	: One of the most reliable cars on the market, also available with choice of two diesel engines. Successor expected soon, but possibly without the Corolla name tag.

COROLLA T-SPORT COMPRESSOR

engine type	: petrol, inline-4
displacement	: 1796 cc
max. power	: 165 kW (218 bhp)
@	: 8000 rpm
max. torque	: 158 lb ft
@	: 3600 rpm
gears	: 6
kerb weight	: 1305 kg
towing weight	: 1200 kg
consumption	: 30.7 mpg
acc. 0-60 mph	: 6.9 s
top speed	: 143 mph
miscellaneous	: Supercharger transforms engine character. No shortage of torque.

TOYOTA COROLLA WAGON 1.4 D4-D / 2.0 D4-D

engine type	: diesel, inline-4	**kerb weight**	: 1205 / 1305 kg
displacement	: 1364 / 1995 cc	**towing weight**	: 1300 kg
max. power	: 66 kW (90 bhp) / 85 kW (116 bhp)	**boot space**	: 402 - 1480 l
@	: 3800 / 3600 rpm	**fuel capacity**	: 55 l
max. torque	: 140 / 206 lb ft	**consumption**	: 58.8 / 50.4 mpg
@	: 1800 / 2000 rpm	**acc. 0-62 mph**	: 13.3 / 10.6 s
gears	: 5	**top speed**	: 112 / 115 mph
AT	: optional 5-speed / -	**EuroNCAP**	: 4 stars
drive	: FWD	**introduction**	: June 2004
brakes f/r	: vent. discs / discs	**last revised in**	: -
body type	: 5-dr. stationwagon	**warranty**	: 3 years
l x w x h	: 4410 x 1710 x 1520 mm	**miscellaneous**	: Corolla range includes both
wheelbase	: 2600 mm		stationwagon and saloon versions,
turning circle	: 10.2 m		also available with 1.4 and
			1.6 petrol engines.

T

TOYOTA VERSO 1.6 16V / 1.8 16V

engine type	: petrol, inline-4	kerb weight	: 1320 / 1340 kg
displacement	: 1598 / 1794 cc	towing weight	: 1200 / 1300 kg
max. power	: 81 kW (110 bhp) / 95 kW (129 bhp)	boot space	: 397 - 779 l
@	: 6000 rpm	fuel capacity	: 60 l
max. torque	: 111 / 126 lb ft	consumption	: 37.7 / 36.7 mpg
@	: 3800 / 4200 rpm	acc. 0-62 mph	: 12.7 / 10.8 s
gears	: 5	top speed	: 109 / 121 mph
AT	: - / optional 5-speed	EuroNCAP	: 5 stars
drive	: FWD	introduction	: February 2004
brakes f/r	: vent. discs / discs	last revised in	: -
body type	: 5-dr. MPV	warranty	: 3 years
l x w x h	: 4360 x 1770 x 1620 mm	miscellaneous	: Verso is a 7-seater with stowable
wheelbase	: 2750 mm		third row of seats. One of the best
turning circle	: 11.6 m		MPVs around.

VERSO 2.2 D-4D / T180

engine type	: diesel, inline-4
displacement	: 2231 cc
max. power	: 100 kW (136 bhp) / 130 kW (177 bhp)
@	: 3600 rpm
max. torque	: 228 / 295 lb ft
@	: 2000 rpm
gears	: 5
kerb weight	: 1450 kg
towing weight	: 1300 kg
consumption	: 44.8 / 41.5 mpg
acc. 0-60 mph	: 9.4 / 8.8 s
top speed	: 122 / 128 mph
miscellaneous	: Refined and powerful diesel option.

TOYOTA AVENSIS 1.6 16V / 1.8 16V

engine type	: petrol, inline-4	**kerb weight**	: 1255 kg
displacement	: 1598 / 1794 cc	**towing weight**	: 1300 kg
max. power	: 81 kW (110 bhp) / 95 kW (129 bhp)	**boot space**	: 520 l
@	: 6000 rpm	**fuel capacity**	: 60 l
max. torque	: 111 / 125 lb ft	**consumption**	: 39.2 mpg
@	: 3800 / 4200 rpm	**acc. 0-62 mph**	: 12.0 / 10.3 s
gears	: 5	**top speed**	: 121 / 124 mph
AT	: - / optional 4-speed	**EuroNCAP**	: 5 stars
drive	: FWD	**introduction**	: February 2003
brakes f/r	: vent. discs / discs	**last revised in**	: April 2006
body type	: 4-dr. saloon	**warranty**	: 3 years
l x w x h	: 4645 x 1760 x 1480 mm	**miscellaneous**	: Very successful car. Representative
wheelbase	: 2700 mm		looks, excellent build quality, fine
turning circle	: 10.8 m		engines, high safety level.

AVENSIS 2.0 D4 / 2.4 D4

engine type	: petrol, inline-4
displacement	: 1998 / 2362 cc
max. power	: 108 kW (147 bhp) / 120 kW (163 bhp)
@	: 5700 / 5800 rpm
max. torque	: 114 / 170 lb ft
@	: 4000 / 3800 rpm
gears	: 5 / 5-speed automatic
kerb weight	: 1305 kg
towing weight	: 1400 kg
consumption	: 34.9 / 29.7 mpg
acc. 0-60 mph	: 9.4 / 9.1 s
top speed	: 130 / 137 mph
miscellaneous	: D4 stands for direct fuel injection. Fine petrol engines.

TOYOTA AVENSIS TOURER T180

engine type	: diesel, inline-4	kerb weight	: 1460 kg
displacement	: 2231 cc	towing weight	: 1300 kg
max. power	: 130 kW (177 bhp)	boot space	: 520 - 1500 l
@	: 3600 rpm	fuel capacity	: 60 l
max. torque	: 295 lb ft	consumption	: 45.6 mpg
@	: 2000 rpm	acc. 0-62 mph	: 8.6 s
gears	: 6	top speed	: 137 mph
AT	: -	EuroNCAP	: 5 stars
drive	: FWD	introduction	: February 2003
brakes f/r	: vent. discs / discs	last revised in	: -
body type	: 5-dr. stationwagon	warranty	: 3 years
l x w x h	: 4700 x 1760 x 1525 mm	miscellaneous	: Catalytic convertor of diesel engine
wheelbase	: 2700 mm		very efficient against soot particles
turning circle	: 11.2 m		and nitrogen oxide. Toyota has a
			lead on rest of industry.

AVENSIS TOURER 2.0 D-4D / 2.2 D-4D

engine type	: diesel, inline-4
displacement	: 1995 / 2231 cc
max. power	: 93 kW (126 bhp) / 110 kW (150 bhp)
@	: 3600 rpm
max. torque	: 222 / 228 lb ft
@	: 2800 / 2000 rpm
gears	: 6
kerb weight	: 1440 / 1455 kg
towing weight	: 1300 kg
consumption	: 49.6 / 47.1 mpg
acc. 0-60 mph	: 10.6 / 9.3 s
top speed	: 124 / 130 mph
miscellaneous	: 2.0 D4-D engine upgraded
	together with facelift.

TOYOTA PRIUS HSD

engine type	: petrol, inline-4 + electrical engine	**kerb weight**	: 1104 kg
displacement	: 1497 cc	**towing weight**	: -
max. power	: 57 kW (77 bhp)	**boot space**	: 408 – 1210 l
@	: 5000 rpm	**fuel capacity**	: 50 l
max. torque	: 85 lb ft	**consumption**	: 65.7 mpg
@	: 4000 rpm	**acc. 0-62 mph**	: 10.9 s
gears	: -	**top speed**	: 106 mph
AT	: CVT	**EuroNCAP**	: 5 stars
drive	: FWD	**introduction**	: November 2003
brakes f/r	: vent. discs / discs	**last revised in**	: October 2005
body type	: 5-dr. hatchback	**warranty**	: 5 years
l x w x h	: 4450 x 1725 x 1490 mm	**miscellaneous**	: Complex hybrid drivetrain results
wheelbase	: 2700 mm		in low consumption and emission
turning circle	: 10.2 m		figures. Sales enhanced by unique
			looks and favourable tax conditions.

T

TOYOTA RAV4 2.0 16V

engine type	: petrol, inline-4	kerb weight	: 1440 kg
displacement	: 1998 cc	towing weight	: 2000 kg
max. power	: 112 kW (152 bhp)	boot space	: 513 l
@	: 6000 rpm	fuel capacity	: 60 l
max. torque	: 143 lb ft	consumption	: 32.8 mpg
@	: 4000 rpm	acc. 0-62 mph	: 10.6 s
gears	: 5	top speed	: 115 mph
AT	: optional 4-speed	EuroNCAP	: 4 stars
drive	: 4WD	introduction	: December 2005
brakes f/r	: vent. discs / discs	last revised in	: -
body type	: 5-dr. SUV	warranty	: 3 years
l x w x h	: 4395 x 1815 x 1720 mm	miscellaneous	: Third generation of successful SUV
wheelbase	: 2560 mm		much bigger than predecessors.
turning circle	: 10.2 m		Front-wheel drive and 3-door
			bodywork no longer available.

RAV4 2.2 D4-D

engine type	: diesel, inline-4
displacement	: 2231 cc
max. power	: 100 kW (136 bhp) /
	130 kW (177 bhp)
@	: 3600 rpm
max. torque	: 228 / 295 lb ft
@	: 2000 rpm
gears	: 6
kerb weight	: 1560 / 1570 kg
towing weight	: 2000 kg
consumption	: 42.8 / 40.4 mpg
acc. 0-60 mph	: 10.5 / 9.3 s
top speed	: 112 / 124 mph
miscellaneous	: Diesel-powered RAV4 shines with
	low consumption and emission
	figures. Not your average thirsty
	and polluting SUV therefore.

TOYOTA LAND CRUISER 3.0 D4-D / 4.0 V6

engine type	: diesel, inline-4 / petrol, V6
displacement	: 2982 / 3956 cc
max. power	: 127 kW (164 bhp) /
	183 kW (245 bhp)
@	: 3400 / 5200 rpm
max. torque	: 302 / 281 lb ft
@	: 1600 / 3800 rpm
gears	: 6 / -
AT	: optional 5-speed / 5-speed
drive	: 4WD
brakes f/r	: vent. discs
body type	: 5-dr. SUV
l x w x h	: 4810 x 1790 x 1890 mm
wheelbase	: 2790 mm
turning circle	: 11.4 m

kerb weight	: 1835 / 1845 kg
towing weight	: 2800 kg
boot space	: 620 l
fuel capacity	: 87 l
consumption	: 31.4 / 22.2 mpg
acc. 0-62 mph	: 11.5 / 9.1 s
top speed	: 109 / 112 mph
EuroNCAP	: n.a.
introduction	: December 2002
last revised in	: -
warranty	: 3 years
miscellaneous	: Although updated occasionally, looks of Land Cruiser remain unaltered. Robust offroader, comfortable too. 3.0 D4 version also available with 3-door body on shorter wheelbase.

T

TOYOTA LAND CRUISER AMAZON 4.2 TD

engine type	: diesel, inline-6	**kerb weight**	: 2420 kg
displacement	: 4164 cc	**towing weight**	: 3500 kg
max. power	: 150 kW (201 bhp)	**boot space**	: 1318 - 2212 l
@	: 3400 rpm	**fuel capacity**	: 96 l
max. torque	: 317 lb ft	**consumption**	: 25.4 mpg
@	: 1200 rpm	**acc. 0-62 mph**	: 13.6 s
gears	: 5	**top speed**	: 106 mph
AT	: optional 5-speed	**EuroNCAP**	: n.a.
drive	: 4WD	**introduction**	: 1998
brakes f/r	: vent. discs	**last revised in**	: December 2005
body type	: 5-dr. SUV	**warranty**	: 3 years
l x w x h	: 4890 x 1940 x 1890 mm	**miscellaneous**	: Bigger Land Cruiser Amazon also
wheelbase	: 2850 mm		available with V8 petrol engine.
turning circle	: 11.8 m		

TVR TUSCAN 2

engine type	: petrol, inline-6	kerb weight	: 1207 kg
displacement	: 3996 cc	towing weight	: -
max. power	: 287 kW (390 bhp)	boot space	: 275 l
@	: 7000 rpm	fuel capacity	: 57 l
max. torque	: 310 lb ft	consumption	: n.a.
@	: 5250 rpm	acc. 0-62 mph	: 3.8 s
gears	: 5	top speed	: 195 mph
AT	: -	EuroNCAP	: n.a.
drive	: RWD	introduction	: 2000
brakes f/r	: vent. discs	last revised in	: 2005
body type	: 2-dr. targa / convertible	warranty	: 2 years
l x w x h	: 4235 x 1810 x 1200 mm	miscellaneous	: The expression 'a hairy car' could
wheelbase	: 2361 mm		have been cued for TVRs in
turning circle	: n.a.		particular. Tuscan convertible
			available soon.

T

TVR SAGARIS

engine type	: petrol, inline-6	**kerb weight**	: 1078 kg
displacement	: 3996 cc	**towing weight**	: -
max. power	: 294 kW (400 bhp)	**boot space**	: n.a.
@	: 7000 rpm	**fuel capacity**	: 57 l
max. torque	: 350 lb ft	**consumption**	: n.a.
@	: 6000 rpm	**acc. 0-62 mph**	: 3.9 s
gears	: 5	**top speed**	: > 160 mph
AT	: -	**EuroNCAP**	: n.a.
drive	: RWD	**introduction**	: December 2005
brakes f/r	: vent. discs	**last revised in**	: -
body type	: 2-dr. coupe	**warranty**	: 2 years
l x w x h	: 4057 x 1850 x 1175 mm	**miscellaneous**	: Astonishing car with wild looks and wild engine. Phenomenal performance.
wheelbase	: 2361 mm		
turning circle	: n.a.		

VOLKSWAGEN FOX 1.2 / 1.4

engine type	: petrol, inline-3 / inline-4
displacement	: 1198 / 1390 cc
max. power	: 40 kW (55 bhp) / 55 kW (75 bhp)
@	: 4750 / 5000 rpm
max. torque	: 80 / 92 lb ft
@	: 3000 / 2750 rpm
gears	: 5
AT	: -
drive	: FWD
brakes f/r	: vent. discs / drum brakes
body type	: 3-dr. hatchback
l x w x h	: 3828 x 1660 x 1544 mm
wheelbase	: 2465 mm
turning circle	: 11.0 m

kerb weight	: 973 / 987 kg
towing weight	: -
boot space	: 260-1016 l
fuel capacity	: 45 l
consumption	: 46.3 / 41.5 mpg
acc. 0-62 mph	: 17.5 / 13.0 s
top speed	: 92 / 104 mph
EuroNCAP	: 4 stars
introduction	: September 2005
last revised in	: -
warranty	: 2 years
miscellaneous	: Cheapest VW in ages. Good alternative to Toyota Aygo and similar models. Spacious interior with adequate front and rear legroom.

VOLKSWAGEN FOX 1.4 TDI

engine type	: diesel, inline-3
displacement	: 1422 cc
max. power	: 51 kW (70 bhp)
@	: 4000 rpm
max. torque	: 114 lb ft
@	: 1600 rpm
gears	: 5
kerb weight	: 1060 kg
towing weight	: -
consumption	: 57.6 mpg
acc. 0-60 mph	: 14.7 s
top speed	: 100 mph
miscellaneous	: Smallest VW is built in Brazil. Only available in 3-door version, in order to make life easier for VW Polo.

VOLKSWAGEN POLO 1.2

engine type	: petrol, inline-3	kerb weight	: 989 / 991 kg
displacement	: 1198 cc	towing weight	: 700 / 800 kg
max. power	: 40 kW (55 bhp) / 47 kW (64 bhp)	boot space	: 270 -1030 l
@	: 4750 / 5400 rpm	fuel capacity	: 45 l
max. torque	: 80 / 83 lb ft	consumption	: 47.1 mpg
@	: 3000 rpm	acc. 0-62 mph	: 17.5 / 14.9 s
gears	: 5	top speed	: 95 / 101 mph
AT	: -	EuroNCAP	: 4 stars
drive	: FWD	introduction	: September 2001
brakes f/r	: vent. discs / drum brakes	last revised in	: September 2005
body type	: 3- / 5-dr. hatchback	warranty	: 2 years
l x w x h	: 3916 x 1650 x 1467 mm	miscellaneous	: Bestseller in B-segment. Also
wheelbase	: 2465 mm		available with 1.4 (75 or 80 bhp),
turning circle	: 10.6 m		1.6 (105 bhp) and four different TDi
			engines.

POLO GTI

engine type	: petrol, inline-4
displacement	: 1781 cc
max. power	: 110 kW (150 bhp)
@	: 5800 rpm
max. torque	: 162 lb ft
@	: 1950 rpm
gears	: 5
kerb weight	: 1139 kg
towing weight	: 800 kg
consumption	: 35.8 mpg
acc. 0-60 mph	: 8.2 s
top speed	: 134 mph
miscellaneous	: Engine from VW Golf IV GTI transforms Polo into a nice and quick 'hot hatch'.

VOLKSWAGEN POLO DUNE 1.4 16V / 1.6 16V

engine type	: petrol, inline-4	**kerb weight**	: 1062 / 1065 kg
displacement	: 1390 / 1598 cc	**towing weight**	: 800 / 1200 kg
max. power	: 59 kW (80 bhp) / 77 kW (105 bhp)	**boot space**	: 288 l
@	: 5000 / 5600 rpm	**fuel capacity**	: 45 l
max. torque	: 97 / 113 lb ft	**consumption**	: 42.2 / 40.9 mpg
@	: 3800 rpm	**acc. 0-62 mph**	: 13.5 / 12.1 s
gears	: 5	**top speed**	: 106 / 119 mph
AT	: optional 4-speed / optional 6-speed	**EuroNCAP**	: 4 stars
drive	: FWD	**introduction**	: March 2006
brakes f/r	: vent. discs / discs	**last revised in**	: -
body type	: 5-dr. hatchback	**warranty**	: 2 years
l x w x h	: 3908 x 1675 x 1527 mm	**miscellaneous**	: New Polo Dune is the first in a series of wild looking VWs.
wheelbase	: 2462 mm		
turning circle	: 10.6 m		

V

POLO DUNE 1.4 TDI / 1.9 TDI

engine type	: diesel, inline-3 / inline-4
displacement	: 1422 / 1896 cc
max. power	: 51 kW (70 bhp) / 74 kW (100 bhp)
@	: 4000 rpm
max. torque	: 114 / 177 lb ft
@	: 1600 / 1800 rpm
gears	: 5
kerb weight	: 1130 / 1165 kg
towing weight	: 900 / 1200 kg
consumption	: 56.5 / 55.4 mpg
acc. 0-60 mph	: 15.9 / 11.5 s
top speed	: 100 / 113 mph
miscellaneous	: Same 1.4 TDI engine also mounted in frugal Polo BlueMotion.

VOLKSWAGEN GOLF 1.4 16V / 1.4 TSI

engine type	: petrol, inline-4
displacement	: 1390 cc
max. power	: 59 kW (80 bhp) / 103 kW (140 bhp)
@	: 5000 / 5600 rpm
max. torque	: 97 / 162 lb ft
@	: 3800 / 1500 rpm
gears	: 5 / 6
AT	: -
drive	: FWD
brakes f/r	: vent. discs / discs
body type	: 3- / 5-dr. hatchback
l x w x h	: 4204 x 1759 x 1485 mm
wheelbase	: 2578 mm
turning circle	: 10.9 m

kerb weight	: 1129 / 1357 kg
towing weight	: 1000 / 1400 kg
boot space	: 350 – 1305 l
fuel capacity	: 55 l
consumption	: 39.8 / 39.2 mpg
acc. 0-62 mph	: 13.9 / 9.3 s
top speed	: 104 / 127 mph
EuroNCAP	: 5 stars
introduction	: September 2003
last revised in	: -
warranty	: 2 years
miscellaneous	: Golf 'V' sells in big numbers. Available with many different engines. Refer to Golf Plus, Touran and Jetta for specifications.

GOLF GT

engine type	: petrol, inline-4
displacement	: 1390 cc
max. power	: 125 kW (170 bhp)
@	: 6000 rpm
max. torque	: 177 lb ft
@	: 1750 rpm
gears	: 6
kerb weight	: 1277 kg
towing weight	: 1400 kg
consumption	: 38.2 mpg
acc. 0-60 mph	: 7.9 s
top speed	: 137 mph
miscellaneous	: High-tech engine economical yet powerful, thanks to combination of supercharger and turbo. Downsizing is the latest technical trend.

GOLF 2.0 SDI

engine type	: diesel, inline-4
displacement	: 1968 cc
max. power	: 55 kW (75 bhp)
@	: 4200 rpm
max. torque	: 103 lb ft
@	: 2200 rpm
gears	: 5
kerb weight	: 1227 kg
towing weight	: 1000 kg
consumption	: 52.3 mpg
acc. 0-60 mph	: 16.7 s
top speed	: 101 mph
miscellaneous	: Not a quick car, but still a good one. Spiritual successor to successful Golf II 1.6 D. Other diesel options: 1.9 TDI with 90/105 bhp and 2.0 TDI with 140/170 bhp.

VOLKSWAGEN GOLF GTI / R32

engine type	: petrol, inline-4 / V6		**kerb weight**	: 1303 / 1594 kg
displacement	: 1984 / 3189 cc		**towing weight**	: 1400 kg / n.a.
max. power	: 147 kW (200 bhp) /		**boot space**	: 350 – 1305 / 275 -1230 l
	184 kW (250 bhp)		**fuel capacity**	: 55 / 60 l
@	: 5100 / 6300 rpm		**consumption**	: 34.9 / 26.2 mpg
max. torque	: 207 / 236 lb ft		**acc. 0-62 mph**	: 7.2 / 6.5 s
@	: 1800 / 2500 rpm		**top speed**	: 146 / 155 mph
gears	: 6		**EuroNCAP**	: 5 stars
AT	: optional 6-speed DSG		**introduction**	: September 2004 / September 2005
drive	: FWD / 4WD		**last revised in**	: -
brakes f/r	: vent. discs, discs /		**warranty**	: 2 years
	vent. discs		**miscellaneous**	: Golf range features two top models.
body type	: 3- / 5-dr. hatchback			Legendary GTI makes a comeback,
l x w x h	: 4204 x 1759 x 1485 mm			6-cylinder R32 is even faster.
wheelbase	: 2578 mm			
turning circle	: 10.9 m			

V

VOLKSWAGEN GOLF PLUS 1.6 16V FSI / 2.0 16V FSI

engine type	: petrol, inline-4	kerb weight	: 1293 / 1348 kg
displacement	: 1598 / 1984 cc	towing weight	: 1200 / 1400 kg
max. power	: 85 kW (115 bhp) /	boot space	: 395 - 1450 l
	110 kW (150 bhp)	fuel capacity	: 55 l
@	: 6000 rpm	consumption	: 39.2 / 34.0 mpg
max. torque	: 114 / 148 lb ft	acc. 0-62 mph	: 11.8 / 9.2 s
@	: 4000 / 3500 rpm	top speed	: 117 / 127 mph
gears	: 6	EuroNCAP	: n.a.
AT	: optional 6-speed	introduction	: February 2005
drive	: FWD	last revised in	: -
brakes f/r	: vent. Discs / discs	warranty	: 2 years
body type	: 5-dr. hatchback	miscellaneous	: Also available as 1.4 with 80/
l x w x h	: 4206 x 1759 x 1580 mm		90 bhp and 1.6 with 102 bhp.
wheelbase	: 2578 mm		Original looks. Car 'competes' with
turning circle	: 10.8 m		smaller Golf and bigger Touran.
			Plus version almost 4 inches taller
			than normal Golf.

GOLF PLUS 1.9 TDI / 2.0 TDI

engine type	: diesel, inline-4
displacement	: 1896 / 1968 cc
max. power	: 77 kW (105 bhp) /
	103 kW (140 bhp)
@	: 4000 rpm
max. torque	: 184 / 236 lb ft
@	: 1900 / 1750 rpm
gears	: 5 / 6
kerb weight	: 1370 / 1401 kg
towing weight	: 1400 kg
consumption	: 50.4 / 47.9 mpg
acc. 0-60 mph	: 11.9 / 9.7 s
top speed	: 114 / 125 mph
miscellaneous	: Engines also available in Golf
	and a popular choice in
	company-owned cars.

VOLKSWAGEN CADDY KOMBI 1.4 16V / 1.6

engine type	: petrol, inline-4
displacement	: 1390 / 1598 cc
max. power	: 55 kW (75 bhp) / 75 kW (102 bhp)
@	: 5000 / 5600 rpm
max. torque	: 94 / 109 lb ft
@	: 3300 / 3800 rpm
gears	: 5
AT	: -
drive	: FWD
brakes f/r	: vent. discs
body type	: 5-dr. MPV
l x w x h	: 4405 x 1802 x 1833 mm
wheelbase	: 2682 mm
turning circle	: n.a.

kerb weight	: 1317 / 1336 kg
towing weight	: 1200 / 1300 kg
boot space	: 626 – 2300 l
fuel capacity	: 60 l
consumption	: 34.5 / 34.9 mpg
acc. 0-62 mph	: 17.9 / 13.7 s
top speed	: 92 / 102 mph
EuroNCAP	: n.a.
introduction	: April 2004
last revised in	: -
warranty	: 2 years
miscellaneous	: Sliding doors, sturdy grey-coloured bumpers and simple rear axle distinguish Caddy from equally spacious but more expensive Touran.

V

CADDY KOMBI 1.9 TDI

engine type	: diesel, inline-4
displacement	: 1895 / 1896 cc
max. power	: 55 kW (75 bhp) / 77 kW (105 bhp)
@	: 4000 rpm
max. torque	: 155 / 177 lb ft
@	: 1900 rpm
gears	: 5
kerb weight	: 1401 kg
towing weight	: 1400 / 1500 kg
consumption	: 45.6 / 47.1 mpg
acc. 0-60 mph	: 17.7 / 13.3 s
top speed	: 93 / 103 mph
miscellaneous	: 2.0 TDI engine reserved for other models.

VOLKSWAGEN TOURAN 1.6 16V FSI / 2.0 16V FSI

engine type	: petrol, inline-4	kerb weight	: 1398 / 1484 kg
displacement	: 1598 / 1984 cc	towing weight	: 1300 / 1500 kg
max. power	: 85 kW (115 bhp) /	boot space	: 695 – 1989 l
	110 kW (150 bhp)	fuel capacity	: 60 l
@	: 5800 / 6000 rpm	consumption	: 35.8 / 34.9 mpg
max. torque	: 114 / 148 lb ft	acc. 0-62 mph	: 11.9 / 10.4 s
@	: 4000 / 3500 rpm	top speed	: 116 / 125 mph
gears	: 6	EuroNCAP	: 5 stars
AT	: optional 6-speed	introduction	: February 2004
drive	: FWD	last revised in	: -
brakes f/r	: vent. Discs / discs	warranty	: 2 years
body type	: 5-dr. MPV	miscellaneous	: Exterior not exactly breathtaking,
l x w x h	: 4391 x 1794 x 1652 mm		but a popular choice nevertheless.
wheelbase	: 2678 mm		Long wheelbase and removable
turning circle	: 11.2 m		seats offer enough room to move
			large furniture.

TOURAN 2.0 TDI

engine type	: diesel, inline-4
displacement	: 1968 cc
max. power	: 125 kW (170 bhp)
@	: 4200 rpm
max. torque	: 258 lb ft
@	: 1750 rpm
gears	: 6
kerb weight	: 1551 kg
towing weight	: 1600 kg
consumption	: 42.8 mpg
acc. 0-60 mph	: 9.0 s
top speed	: 133 mph
miscellaneous	: Strongest 2-litre TDI now also available in Touran. DSG transmission optional.

VOLKSWAGEN JETTA 1.6 / 2.0 16V FSI

engine type	: petrol, inline-4	kerb weight	: 1243 / 1294 kg
displacement	: 1595 / 1984 cc	towing weight	: 1200 / 1400 kg
max. power	: 75 kW (102 bhp) / 110 kW (150 bhp)	boot space	: 527 l
@	: 5600 / 6000 rpm	fuel capacity	: 55 l
max. torque	: 109 / 148 lb ft	consumption	: 38.2 / 34.4 mpg
@	: 3800 / 3500 rpm	acc. 0-62 mph	: 12.2 / 9.2 s
gears	: 5 / 6	top speed	: 116 / 131 mph
AT	: - / optional 6-speed	EuroNCAP	: 5 stars
drive	: FWD	introduction	: September 2005
brakes f/r	: vent. discs / discs	last revised in	: -
body type	: 4-dr. saloon	warranty	: 2 years
l x w x h	: 4554 x 1781 x 1459 mm	miscellaneous	: Jetta no longer a Golf model with
wheelbase	: 2578 mm		a big bum. More of a small Passat
turning circle	: 10.9 m		with a big boot. Also available: 2.0
			TFSI, same engine as in Golf GTI.

JETTA 1.9 TDI / 2.0 TDI

engine type	: diesel, inline-4
displacement	: 1896 / 1968 cc
max. power	: 77 kW (105 bhp) /
	103 kW (140 bhp)
@	: 4000 rpm
max. torque	: 184 / 236 lb ft
@	: 1900 / 1750 rpm
gears	: 5 / 6
kerb weight	: 1320 / 1368 kg
towing weight	: 1400 kg
consumption	: 53.3 / 48.7 mpg
acc. 0-60 mph	: 11.9 / 9.7 s
top speed	: 117 / 129 mph
miscellaneous	: Jetta accounts for 40 per cent of
	Volkswagen sales in America. No
	chance of that in Europe.

VOLKSWAGEN NEW BEETLE 1.4 16V / 1.6

engine type	: petrol, inline-4
displacement	: 1390 / 1596 cc
max. power	: 55 kW (75 bhp) / 75 kW (102 bhp)
@	: 5000 / 5600 rpm
max. torque	: 93 / 109 lb ft
@	: 3300 / 3800 rpm
gears	: 5
AT	: -
drive	: FWD
brakes f/r	: vent. discs / discs
body type	: 3-dr. hatchback
l x w x h	: 4081 x 1724 x 1498 mm
wheelbase	: 2508 mm
turning circle	: 10.9 m

kerb weight	: 1157 / 1177 kg
towing weight	: 1000 kg
boot space	: 214 -769 l
fuel capacity	: 55 l
consumption	: 39.8 / 36.7 mpg
acc. 0-62 mph	: 14.6 / 11.6 s
top speed	: 100 / 111 mph
EuroNCAP	: 4 stars
introduction	: November 1998
last revised in	: September 2005
warranty	: 2 years
miscellaneous	: Long-term model received a minor facelift, in order to enhance sales. However, those who liked it, will already have bought one by now.

NEW BEETLE 1.9 TDI

engine type	: diesel, inline-4
displacement	: 1896 cc
max. power	: 77 kW (105 bhp)
@	: 4000 rpm
max. torque	: 177 lb ft
@	: 1800 rpm
gears	: 5
kerb weight	: 1266 kg
towing weight	: 1000 kg
consumption	: 51.4 mpg
acc. 0-60 mph	: 11.5 s
top speed	: 112 mph
miscellaneous	: Same engines used in hatchback and convertible.

VOLKSWAGEN NEW BEETLE CABRIOLET 2.0 / 1.8T

engine type	: petrol, inline-4	kerb weight	: 1304 / 1363 kg
displacement	: 1984 / 1781 cc	towing weight	: 1000 kg
max. power	: 85 kW (115 bhp) /	boot space	: 201 l
	110 kW (150 bhp)	fuel capacity	: 55 l
@	: 5200 / 5800 rpm	consumption	: 32.1 / 34.0 mpg
max. torque	: 127 / 162 lb ft	acc. 0-62 mph	: 11.7 / 9.3 s
@	: 3200 / 2000 rpm	top speed	: 114 / 125 mph
gears	: 5	EuroNCAP	: 4 stars
AT	: optional 4-speed / -	introduction	: April 2003
drive	: FWD	last revised in	: September 2005
brakes f/r	: vent. discs / discs	warranty	: 2 years
body type	: 2-dr. convertible	miscellaneous	: Romantic model in down-to-earth
l x w x h	: 4081 x 1724 x 1502 mm		Volkswagen programme.
wheelbase	: 2509 mm		
turning circle	: 10.9 m		

V

VOLKSWAGEN EOS 2.0 FSI / 2.0 TFSI

engine type	: petrol, inline-4	kerb weight	: 1481 / 1536 kg
displacement	: 1984 cc	towing weight	: 1500 kg
max. power	: 110 kW (150 bhp) /	boot space	: 400 l
	147 kW (200 bhp)	fuel capacity	: 55 l
@	: 6000 / 5100 rpm	consumption	: 34.0 / 33.6 mpg
max. torque	: 148 / 207 lb ft	acc. 0-62 mph	: 9.8 / 7.8 s
@	: 3500/ 1800 rpm	top speed	: 130 / 144 mph
gears	: 6	EuroNCAP	: n.a.
AT	: - / optional 6-speed DSG	introduction	: September 2005
drive	: FWD	last revised in	: -
brakes f/r	: vent. discs / discs	warranty	: 2 years
body type	: 2-dr. convertible	miscellaneous	: Beautiful 4-seater convertible with
l x w x h	: 4407 x 1791 x 1437 mm		detachable roof with three sections.
wheelbase	: 2578 mm		Late addition to segment, but worth
turning circle	: 10.9 m		the wait. Mixture of Golf and
			Passat, technically speaking.

VOLKSWAGEN PASSAT 1.6 / 1.6 16V FSI

engine type	: petrol, inline-4
displacement	: 1595 / 1598 cc
max. power	: 75 kW (102 bhp) / 85 kW (115 bhp)
@	: 5600 / 6000 rpm
max. torque	: 109 / 114 lb ft
@	: 3800 / 4000 rpm
gears	: 5 / 6
AT	: - / optional 6-speed
drive	: FWD
brakes f/r	: vent. discs / discs
body type	: 4-dr. saloon
l x w x h	: 4765 x 1820 x 1472 mm
wheelbase	: 2709 mm
turning circle	: 11.4 m

kerb weight	: 1318 / 1323 kg
towing weight	: 1300 kg
boot space	: 565 l
fuel capacity	: 70 l
consumption	: 36.7 / 36.2 mpg
acc. 0-62 mph	: 12.4 / 11.4 s
top speed	: 118 / 122 mph
EuroNCAP	: 5 stars
introduction	: November 2004
last revised in	: -
warranty	: 2 years
miscellaneous	: New Passat has striking front. Familiar, excellent build quality.

PASSAT 2.0 16V FSI / 2.0 TFSI

engine type	: petrol, inline-4
displacement	: 1984 cc
max. power	: 110 kW (150 bhp) / 147 kW (200 bhp)
@	: 6000 / 5100 rpm
max. torque	: 148 / 207 lb ft
@	: 3500 / 1800 rpm
gears	: 6
kerb weight	: 1364 / 1420 kg
towing weight	: 1500 / 1600 kg
consumption	: 33.2 / 34.4 mpg
acc. 0-60 mph	: 9.4 / 7.6 s
top speed	: 130 / 144 mph
miscellaneous	: FSI stands for Fuel Stratified Injection, Volkswagen speak for direct fuel injection. Lower consumption figures due to combustion of leaner mixture at constant engine speed.

PASSAT 3.2 V6 FSI

engine type	: petrol, V6
displacement	: 3189 cc
max. power	: 184 kW (250 bhp)
@	: 6400 rpm
max. torque	: 236 lb ft
@	: 3200 rpm
gears	: 6-speed DSG
kerb weight	: 1635 kg
towing weight	: 2200 kg
consumption	: 28.0 mpg
acc. 0-60 mph	: 7.2 s
top speed	: 151 mph
miscellaneous	: Previous Passat was related to Audi A4/A6, with longitudinal engines. New Passat has transverse engines, meaning V6 is in fact VR6. Now with fuel injection.

VOLKSWAGEN PASSAT ESTATE 2.0 TDI

engine type	: diesel, inline-4
displacement	: 1968 / 1968 cc
max. power	: 103 kW (140 bhp) / 125 kW (170 bhp)
@	: 4000 / 4200 rpm
max. torque	: 236 / 258 LB FT
@	: 1750 / 1800 rpm
gears	: 6
AT	: optional 6-speed DSG
drive	: FWD
brakes f/r	: vent. discs / discs
body type	: 5-dr. stationwagon
l x w x h	: 4774 x 1820 x 1517 mm
wheelbase	: 2709 mm
turning circle	: 11.4 m

kerb weight	: 1485 / 1432 kg
towing weight	: 1800 kg
boot space	: 603 -1731 l
fuel capacity	: 62 l
consumption	: 46.3 / 44.1 mpg
acc. 0-62 mph	: 10.1 / 8.6 s
top speed	: 128 / 137 mph
EuroNCAP	: 5 stars
introduction	: July 2005
last revised in	: -
warranty	: 2 years
miscellaneous	: Lots of space underneath flowing roofline. Available with same engines as saloon version, with the exception of the smallest 1.6 unit.

PASSAT ESTATE 1.9 TDI

engine type	: diesel, inline-4
displacement	: 1896 cc
max. power	: 77 kW (105 bhp)
@	: 4000 rpm
max. torque	: 184 lb ft
@	: 1900 rpm
gears	: 5
kerb weight	: 1452 kg
towing weight	: 1500 kg
consumption	: 47.9 mpg
acc. 0-60 mph	: 12.4 s
top speed	: 115 mph
miscellaneous	: No particle filter available on 1.9 TDI but an option on 140 bhp 2.0 TDI and standard fitment on the biggest 2.0 TDI.

VOLKSWAGEN PHAETON 3.2 V6 / 4.2 V8

engine type	: petrol, V6 / V8
displacement	: 3189 / 4172 cc
max. power	: 177 kW (241 bhp) / 246 kW (335 bhp)
@	: 6200 / 6500 rpm
max. torque	: 232 / 317 lb ft
@	: 2400 / 3500 rpm
gears	: -
AT	: 6-speed
drive	: 4WD
brakes f/r	: vent. discs
body type	: 4-dr. saloon
l x w x h	: 5055 x 1903 x 1450 mm
wheelbase	: 2881 mm
turning circle	: 12.0 m

kerb weight	: 2176 / 2232 kg
towing weight	: 2300 / 2400 kg
boot space	: 500 l
fuel capacity	: 90 l
consumption	: 23.2 / 21.6 mpg
acc. 0-62 mph	: 9.4 / 6.9 s
top speed	: 148 / 155 mph
EuroNCAP	: n.a.
introduction	: April 2002
last revised in	: -
warranty	: 2 years
miscellaneous	: Not to everyone's taste. Also available with longer wheelbase and with a choice of 2 separate seats or 3-seat bench in the rear.

V

PHAETON 6.0 W12

engine type	: petrol, W12
displacement	: 5998 cc
max. power	: 331 kW (450 bhp)
@	: 6050 rpm
max. torque	: 413 lb ft
@	: 2750 rpm
gears	: 5
kerb weight	: 2294 kg
towing weight	: 2400 kg
consumption	: 19.5 mpg
acc. 0-60 mph	: 6.1 s
top speed	: 155 mph
miscellaneous	: Compact 12-cylinder engine offers fabulous performance.

PHAETON 3.0 V6 TDI

engine type	: diesel, V6
displacement	: 2967 cc
max. power	: 165 kW (225 bhp)
@	: 4000 rpm
max. torque	: 332 lb ft
@	: 1400 rpm
gears	: 6
kerb weight	: 2227 kg
towing weight	: 2500 kg
consumption	: 29.4 mpg
acc. 0-60 mph	: 9.1 s
top speed	: 145 mph
miscellaneous	: Introduction of V6 diesel option has done wonders for popularity of big Phaeton.

VOLKSWAGEN TOUAREG 2.5 TDI / 3.0 V6 TDI

engine type	: diesel, inline-5 / V6	kerb weight	: 2179 / 2287 kg
displacement	: 2460 / 2967 cc	towing weight	: 3500 kg
max. power	: 128 kW (174 bhp) /	boot space	: 555 – 1570 l
	165 kW (225 bhp)	fuel capacity	: 100 l
@	: 3500 / 4000 rpm	consumption	: 28.8 / 25.9 mpg
max. torque	: 295 / 369 lb ft	acc. 0-62 mph	: 12.4 / 9.9 s
@	: 2000 / 1750 rpm	top speed	: 114 / 125 mph
gears	: 6 / -	EuroNCAP	: n.a.
AT	: optional / 6-speed	introduction	: September 2002
drive	: 4WD	last revised in	: -
brakes f/r	: vent. discs	warranty	: 2 years
body type	: 5-dr. SUV	miscellaneous	: Diesel power best choice for this
l x w x h	: 4754 x 1928 x 1726 mm		model. Successful VW SUV shares
wheelbase	: 2855 mm		technology with Porsche Cayenne.
turning circle	: 11.6 m		

TOUAREG 3.6 V6 / 4.2 V8

engine type	: petrol, V6 / V8
displacement	: 3597 / 4172 cc
max. power	: 206 kW (280 bhp) /
	228 kW (310 bhp)
@	: 6200 rpm
max. torque	: 266 / 302 lb ft
@	: 3000 rpm
gears	: 6
kerb weight	: 2204 / 2217 kg
towing weight	: 3500 kg
consumption	: 20.5 / 19.1 mpg
acc. 0-60 mph	: 8.7 / 8.1 s
top speed	: 134 / 135 mph
miscellaneous	: Strongest version is 450 bhp
	6.0 W12, available upon special
	request.

TOUAREG 5.0 V10 TDI

engine type	: diesel, V10
displacement	: 4921 cc
max. power	: 230 kW (313 bhp)
@	: 3750 rpm
max. torque	: 553 lb ft
@	: 2000 rpm
gears	: 6
kerb weight	: 2424 kg
towing weight	: 3500 kg
consumption	: 23.0 mpg
acc. 0-60 mph	: 7.8 s
top speed	: 140 mph
miscellaneous	: Fairly economical beast. Output of
	big diesel engine however already
	beaten by three other
	manufacturers from Germany.

VOLKSWAGEN SHARAN 2.0 / 1.8T

engine type	: petrol, inline-4
displacement	: 1984 / 1781 cc
max. power	: 85 kW (115 bhp) / 110 kW (150 bhp)
@	: 5200 / 5800 rpm
max. torque	: 125 / 162 lb ft
@	: 2600 / 1800 rpm
gears	: 6
AT	: optional 4- / 5-speed
drive	: FWD
brakes f/r	: vent. discs / discs
body type	: 5-dr. MPV
l x w x h	: 4634 x 1810 x 1759 mm
wheelbase	: 2841 mm
turning circle	: 11.0 m

kerb weight	: 1553 / 1574 kg
towing weight	: 1800 / 1900 kg
boot space	: 255 - 2610 l
fuel capacity	: 70 l
consumption	: 29.1 mpg
acc. 0-62 mph	: 15.2 / 10.9 s
top speed	: 110 / 124 mph
EuroNCAP	: 3 stars
introduction	: July 2000
last revised in	: -
warranty	: 2 years
miscellaneous	: Sharan model is past its prime. Also two diesel engines available, 1.9 TDI and 2.0 TDI. Refer to identical Seat Alhambra for specifications.

V

SHARAN 2.8 V6

engine type	: petrol, V6
displacement	: 2792 cc
max. power	: 150 kW (204 bhp)
@	: 6200 rpm
max. torque	: 195 lb ft
@	: 3400 rpm
gears	: 6, optional 5-speed automatic
kerb weight	: 1594 kg
towing weight	: 2000 kg
consumption	: 26.6 mpg
acc. 0-60 mph	: 9.9 s
top speed	: 135 mph
miscellaneous	: If you have money to spare, opt for the 2.8 V6 with 4Motion four-wheel drive. Ideally suited for winter sports holidays!

VOLVO C30 1.6

engine type	: petrol, inline-4	kerb weight	: n.a.
displacement	: 1596 cc	towing weight	: n.a.
max. power	: 74 kW (100 bhp)	boot space	: n.a.
@	: 6000 rpm	fuel capacity	: 55 l
max. torque	: 110 lb ft	consumption	: n.a.
@	: 4000 rpm	acc. 0-62 mph	: n.a.
gears	: 5	top speed	: n.a.
AT	: -	EuroNCAP	: n.a.
drive	: FWD	introduction	: April 2007
brakes f/r	: vent. discs	last revised in	: -
body type	: 3-dr. hatchback	warranty	: 2 years
l x w x h	: 4248 x 1780 x 1452 mm	miscellaneous	: Volvo's entry in Audi A3 and BMW
wheelbase	: 2640 mm		1-series class. Spiritual successor to
turning circle	: 10.6 m		Volvo 480, with styling cues of earlier
			P1800 ES.

VOLVO S40 1.8 / 2.0

engine type	: petrol, inline-4	kerb weight	: 1269 kg
displacement	: 1798 / 1999 cc	towing weight	: 1300 / 1350 kg
max. power	: 92 kW (125 bhp) / 107 kW (145 bhp)	boot space	: 404 l
@	: 6000 rpm	fuel capacity	: 55 l
max. torque	: 122 / 136 lb ft	consumption	: 39.2 / 38.2 mpg
@	: 4000 rpm	acc. 0-62 mph	: 10.9 / 9.5 s
gears	: 5	top speed	: 124 / 130 mph
AT	: -	EuroNCAP	: 5 stars
drive	: FWD	introduction	: September 2003
brakes f/r	: vent. discs	last revised in	: -
body type	: 4-dr. saloon	warranty	: 2 years
l x w x h	: 4468 x 1770 x 1452 mm	miscellaneous	: Youthful looking smaller Volvo
wheelbase	: 2640 mm		shares platform with Ford Focus and
turning circle	: 10.6 m		owes its fine driving behaviour to
			this. Also available with 100 bhp
			1.6 and 170 bhp 2.4 engines.

V

S40 T5

engine type	: petrol, inline-5
displacement	: 2521 cc
max. power	: 162 kW (220 bhp)
@	: 5000 rpm
max. torque	: 236 lb ft
@	: 1500 rpm
gears	: 6
kerb weight	: 1342 kg
towing weight	: 1500 kg
consumption	: 32.5 mpg
acc. 0-60 mph	: 7.5 s
top speed	: 140 mph
miscellaneous	: For people who like it fast but
	prefer plain looks: T5 version hardly
	distinguishable from common 1.8.
	Also available with AWD.

VOLVO V50 1.6D / 2.0D

engine type	: diesel, inline-4	kerb weight	: 1383 / 1472 kg
displacement	: 1560 / 1997 cc	towing weight	: 1500 kg
max. power	: 80 kW (109 bhp) /	boot space	: 417 – 1307 l
	100 kW (136 bhp)	fuel capacity	: 55 l
@	: 4000 rpm	consumption	: 56.5 / 48.7 mpg
max. torque	: 177 / 236 lb ft	acc. 0-62 mph	: 12.1 / 9.6 s
@	: 1750 / 2000 rpm	top speed	: 118 / 130 mph
gears	: 5	EuroNCAP	: 5 stars
AT	: -	introduction	: November 2004
drive	: FWD	last revised in	: -
brakes f/r	: vent. discs	warranty	: 2 years
body type	: 5-dr. stationwagon	miscellaneous	: Petrol engines same as in S40.
l x w x h	: 4514 x 1770 x 1452 mm		Popular, good-looking
wheelbase	: 2640 mm		stationwagon.
turning circle	: 10.6 m		

V50 D5

engine type	: diesel, inline-5
displacement	: 2401 cc
max. power	: 132 kW (180 bhp)
@	: 4000 rpm
max. torque	: 258 lb ft
@	: 1750 rpm
gears	: 5-speed automatic
kerb weight	: 1436 kg
towing weight	: 1500 kg
consumption	: 40.4 mpg
acc. 0-60 mph	: 8.5 s
top speed	: 140 mpg
miscellaneous	: Powerful diesel engine shared with S40. Available only in combination with 5-speed automatic transmission.

VOLVO S60 2.4 / 2.0T

engine type	: petrol, inline-5
displacement	: 2435 / 1984 cc
max. power	: 103 kW (140 bhp) / 132 kW (180 bhp)
@	: 4500 / 5300 rpm
max. torque	: 148 / 177 lb ft
@	: 3750 / 2200 rpm
gears	: 5
AT	: optional 6-speed
drive	: FWD
brakes f/r	: vent. discs
body type	: 4-dr. saloon
l x w x h	: 4603 x 1813 x 1428 mm
wheelbase	: 2715 mm
turning circle	: 10.8 m

kerb weight	: 1466 / 1388 kg
towing weight	: 1600 kg
boot space	: 424 – 1034 l
fuel capacity	: 70 l
consumption	: 31.7 mpg
acc. 0-62 mph	: 10.2 / 8.8 s
top speed	: 130 / 140 mph
EuroNCAP	: 4 stars
introduction	: July 2000
last revised in	: July 2004
warranty	: 2 years
miscellaneous	: S60 available with choice of ten different 5-cylinder engines, including three diesels. 2.4 also available with 170 bhp and in Bi-fuel version that runs both on petrol and natural gas.

V

S60 T5

engine type	: petrol, inline-5
displacement	: 2401 cc
max. power	: 191 kW (260 bhp)
@	: 5500 rpm
max. torque	: 258 lb ft
@	: 2100 rpm
gears	: 6
kerb weight	: 1477 kg
towing weight	: 1600 kg
consumption	: 30.4 mpg
acc. 0-60 mph	: 6.5 s
top speed	: 155 mph
miscellaneous	: Not the most spacious Volvo on offer, but often chosen for its sporty aura.

VOLVO V70 D / 2.4 D

engine type	: diesel, inline-5	kerb weight	: 1522 / 1535 kg
displacement	: 2401 cc	towing weight	: 1800 kg
max. power	: 92 kW (126 bhp) /	boot space	: 485 – 1641 l
	120 kW (163 bhp)	fuel capacity	: 70 l
@	: 4000 rpm	consumption	: 43.5 / 41.5 mpg
max. torque	: 221 / 250 lb ft	acc. 0-62 mph	: 12.3 / 9.5 s
@	: 1750 rpm	top speed	: 124 / 130 mph
gears	: 5 / 6	EuroNCAP	: 4 stars
AT	: - / optional 6-speed	introduction	: November 2000
drive	: FWD	last revised in	: July 2004
brakes f/r	: vent. discs	warranty	: 2 years
body type	: 5-dr. stationwagon	miscellaneous	: Highly successful model.
l x w x h	: 4710 x 1804 x 1465 mm		Businesslike, safe car with fine
wheelbase	: 2755 mm		driving characteristics and wide
turning circle	: 10.9 m		choice of engines and options.

V70 D5

engine type	: diesel, inline-5
displacement	: 2401 cc
max. power	: 136 kW (185 bhp)
@	: 4000 rpm
max. torque	: 295 lb ft
@	: 2000 rpm
gears	: 6
kerb weight	: 1536 kg
towing weight	: 1800 kg
consumption	: 41.5 mpg
acc. 0-60 mph	: 8.5 s
top speed	: 140 mph
miscellaneous	: One of the best diesel engines on the market. Also available in S60.

VOLVO XC70 D5 AWD / 2.5T AWD

engine type	: diesel / petrol, inline-5	**kerb weight**	: 1618 / 1642 kg
displacement	: 2401 / 2521 cc	**towing weight**	: 1800 kg
max. power	: 136 kW (185 bhp) /	**boot space**	: 485 - 1641 l
	154 kW (210 bhp)	**fuel capacity**	: 68 / 72 l
@	: 4000 / 5000 rpm	**consumption**	: 37.2 / 27.7 mpg
max. torque	: 295 / 236 lb ft	**acc. 0-62 mph**	: 9.5 / 8.1 s
@	: 2000 / 1500 rpm	**top speed**	: 130 mph
gears	: 5	**EuroNCAP**	: 4 stars
AT	: optional 5-speed	**introduction**	: July 2000
drive	: 4WD	**last revised in**	: July 2004
brakes f/r	: vent. discs	**warranty**	: 2 years
body type	: 5-dr. stationwagon	**miscellaneous**	: Only available with big engines
l x w x h	: 4733 x 1860 x 1562 mm		and four-wheel drive.
wheelbase	: 2763 mm		
turning circle	: 11.6 m		

VOLVO C70 2.4 / T5

engine type	: petrol, inline-5	**kerb weight**	: 1692 kg
displacement	: 2435 / 2521 cc	**towing weight**	: 1500 kg
max. power	: 103 kW (138 bhp) /	**boot space**	: 200 - 404 l
	162 kW (218 bhp)	**fuel capacity**	: 62 l
@	: 5000 rpm	**consumption**	: 31.7 / 31.0 mpg
max. torque	: 162 / 236 lb ft	**acc. 0-62 mph**	: 11.0 / 7.6 s
@	: 4000 / 1500 rpm	**top speed**	: 127 / 150 mph
gears	: 5 / 6	**EuroNCAP**	: n.a.
AT	: optional 5-speed	**introduction**	: November 2006
drive	: FWD	**last revised in**	: -
brakes f/r	: vent. discs	**warranty**	: 2 years
body type	: 2-dr. convertible	**miscellaneous**	: New model is the prettiest of Volvo
l x w x h	: 4580 x 1820 x 1400 mm		family. Beautiful convertible with
wheelbase	: 2640 mm		typical Volvo styling cues. Safer
turning circle	: 12.7 m		than many fixed-roof cars. Also
			available with 168 bhp 2.4i and D5
			diesel engine.

VOLVO S80 2.5T / 3.2

engine type	: petrol, inline-5 / inline-6	kerb weight	: 1415 / 1556 kg
displacement	: 2521 / 3192 cc	towing weight	: 1800 /kg
max. power	: 147 kW (200 bhp) /	boot space	: 480 l
	175 kW (238 bhp)	fuel capacity	: 70 l
@	: 4800 / 6200 rpm	consumption	: 30.7 / 28.5 mpg
max. torque	: 222 / 236 lb ft	acc. 0-62 mph	: 7.7 / 7.9 s
@	: 1500 / 3200 rpm	top speed	: 146 / 149 mph
gears	: 6 / -	EuroNCAP	: n.a.
AT	: optional, 6-speed / 6-speed	introduction	: April 2006
drive	: FWD	last revised in	: -
brakes f/r	: vent. discs	warranty	: 2 years
body type	: 4-dr. saloon	miscellaneous	: New S80 widens the gap with S60
l x w x h	: 4851 x 1861 x 1492 mm		and V70 models more so than
wheelbase	: 2835 mm		predecessor. Amiable car. Also
turning circle	: n.a.		available with V8 from XC90.

V

S80 2.4D / D5

engine type	: diesel, inline-5
displacement	: 2401 cc
max. power	: 120 kW (163 bhp) /
	136 kW (185 bhp)
@	: 4000 rpm
max. torque	: 251 / 295 lb ft
@	: 1750 / 2000 rpm
gears	: 6
kerb weight	: 1541 / 1545 kg
towing weight	: 1800 kg
consumption	: 44.8 / 44.1 mpg
acc. 0-60 mph	: 9.5 / 8.5 s
top speed	: 130 / 143 mph
miscellaneous	: D5 diesel option logical addition
	to engine range of flagship model.

VOLVO XC90 2.5T / 3.2

engine type	: petrol, inline-5 / inline-6
displacement	: 2521 / 3192 cc
max. power	: 154 kW (210 bhp) / 175 kW (231 bhp)
@	: 5000 / 6200 rpm
max. torque	: 236 lb ft
@	: 1500 / 3200 rpm
gears	: 6 / -
AT	: optional 5-speed / 6-speed
drive	: 4WD
brakes f/r	: vent. discs / discs
body type	: 5-dr. SUV
l x w x h	: 4807 x 1898 x 1784 mm
wheelbase	: 2857 mm
turning circle	: 12.5 m

kerb weight	: 1967 / 2025 kg
towing weight	: 2250 / 2250 kg
boot space	: 613 – 1837 l
fuel capacity	: 80 l
consumption	: 25.2 / 23.9 mpg
acc. 0-62 mph	: 9.5 s
top speed	: 130 mph
EuroNCAP	: 5 stars
introduction	: September 2002
last revised in	: April 2006
warranty	: 2 years
miscellaneous	: Big hit everywhere, in car parks of tennis clubs, shopping malls, you name it. Safe and fairly economical SUV with option of seven seats.

XC90 V8

engine type	: petrol, V8
displacement	: 4414 cc
max. power	: 232 kW (315 bhp)
@	: 5850 rpm
max. torque	: 324 lb ft
@	: 3900 rpm
gears	: 6-speed automatic
kerb weight	: 2077 kg
towing weight	: 2250 kg
consumption	: 20.9 mpg
acc. 0-60 mph	: 7.3 s
top speed	: 130 mph
miscellaneous	: V8 engine developed by Yamaha and aimed at American market.

XC90 D5

engine type	: diesel, inline-5
displacement	: 2401 cc
max. power	: 136 kW (185 bhp)
@	: 4000 rpm
max. torque	: 295 lb ft
@	: 2000 rpm
gears	: 6
kerb weight	: 2029 kg
towing weight	: 2250 kg
consumption	: 34.0 mpg
acc. 0-60 mph	: 10.9 s
top speed	: 121 mph
miscellaneous	: Perfect towing car for boat trailers and horse trailers.

Contacts

Marque	Postal address	Brochures	Web address
		0800 718 000	alfaromeo.co.uk
Alfa Romeo	240 Bath Road, Slough, Berkshire	0115 934 1414	sytner.co.uk
Alpina	Alpina GB, Sytner of Nottingham, Lenton Lane, Nottingham	01295 254 800	ascari.net
Ascari		01908 610 620	astonmartin.co.uk
Aston Martin	Banbury Road, Gaydon, Warwick	0845 699 777	audi.co.uk
Audi	Yeomans Drive, Blakelands, Milton Keynes MK14 5AN	01270 535 032	bentleymotors.co.uk
Bentley	Pyms Lane, Crewe, Cheshire CW1 3PL	0800 325 600	bmw.co.uk
BMW	Ellesfield Avenue, Bracknell, Berks RG12 8TA	01404 548 885	brookecars.co.uk
Brooke		0845 330 776	cadillaceurope.com
Cadillac	Trinity Court, Wokingham Road, Bracknell, Berks RG42 1PL	01883 333 700	caterham.co.uk
Caterham	Station Avenue, Caterham, Surrey, CR3 6LB	0800 666 222	chevrolet.co.uk
Chevrolet	Wyvern House, Kimpton Road, Luton LU2 0DW	0800 616 159	chryslerjeep.co.uk
Chrysler	Tongwell, Milton Keynes, Bucks MK15 8BA	0800 262 262	citroen.co.uk
Citroen	221 Bath Road, Slough, Berks SL1 4BA		stratstonecorvette.co.uk
Corvette	Wyvern House, Kimpton Road, Luton LU2 0DW	0800 618 618	daihatsu.co.uk
Daihatsu	Ryder Street, West Bromwich, West Midlands B70 0EJ	0800 616 159	dodge.co.uk
Dodge	Tongwell, Milton Keynes, Bucks MK15 8BA		ferrari.co.uk
Ferrari	272 Leigh Road, Slough, Berks SL1 4HF	0800 717 000	fiat.co.uk
Fiat	240 Bath Road, Slough, Berks SL1 4DX	08457 111 888	ford.co.uk
Ford	Eagle Way, Warley, Brentwood, Essex CM13 8BW	0845 200 8000	honda.co.uk
Honda	470 London Road, Slough, Berks SL3 8QY	0161 831 7447	hummer.co.uk
Hummer	325 Deansgate, Manchester, M3 4LQ	0800 981 981	hyundai.co.uk
Hyundai	St John's Court, Easton Street, High Wycombe, Bucks HP11 1JX	01249 651 000	invictacar.com
Invicta	9-12 Westpoint Business Park, Bumpers Farm, Chippenham, Wilts SN14 8RB		isuzu.co.uk
Isuzu	Ryder Street, West Bromwich, West Midlands B70 0EJ	0800 708 060	jaguar.com
Jaguar	Browns Lane, Allesley, Coventry, West Midlands CV5 9DR	0800 616 159	chryslerjeep.co.uk
Jeep	Tongwell, Milton Keynes, Bucks MK15 8BA	0800 775 777	kia.co.uk
Kia	2 The Heights, Brooklands, Weybridge, Surrey KT13 0NY	020 7589 1472	lamborghini.co.uk
Lamborghini	Melton Court, 25 Old Brompton Road, South Kensington, London SW7 3TD	0800 110 110	landrover.co.uk
Land Rover	Banbury Road, Gaydon, Warks CV35 0RR	0845 278 8888	lexus.co.uk
Lexus	Great Burgh, Burgh Heath, Epsom, Surrey KT18 5UX	0870 9000 565	lotuscars.co.uk
Lotus	Potash Lane, Hethel, Norfolk NR14 8EXZ	01373 301 376	marcos-eng.com
Marcos		0800 064 6468	maserati.co.uk
Maserati	272 Leigh Road, Slough, Berks SL1 4HF	08457 484 848	mazda.co.uk
Mazda	Riverbridge House, Anchor Boulevard, Dartford, Kent DA2 6QH	0800 181 361	mercedes.co.uk
Mercedes-Benz	Tongwell, Milton Keynes, Bucks MK15 8BA	08000 836 464	mini.co.uk
Mini	Ellesfield Avenue, Bracknell, Berks RG12 8TA	0845 070 2000	mitsubishi-cars.co.uk
Mitsubishi	Watermoor, Cirencester, Glos GL7 4LF	01684 573 104	morgan-motor.co.uk
Morgan	Pickersleigh Road, Malvern Link, Worcs WR14 2LL	08457 669 966	nissan.co.uk
Nissan	The Rivers Office Park, Denham Way, Maple Cross, Rickmansworth, Herts WD3 9YS	01455 844 052	noblecars.com
Noble	16 Moat Way Industrial Estate, Barwell, Leics LE9 8EY	01753 663 012	paganiautomobili.it
Pagani		01491 415 230	perodua-uk.com
Perodua	Craigmore House, Remenham Hill, Henley-on-Thames, Oxon RG9 3EP	08457 565 556	peugeot.co.uk
Peugeot	Aldermoor House, PO Box 227, Aldermoor Lane, Coventry CV3 1LT	08457 911 911	porsche.co.uk
Porsche	Bath Road, Calcot, Reading, Berks RG31 7SE	08000 521 521	proton.co.uk
Proton	Walton House, 56-58 Richmond Hill, Bournemouth BH2 6EX	0800 525 150	renault.co.uk
Renault	The Rivers Office Park, Denham Way, Maple Cross, Rickmansworth, Herts WD3 9YS	01243 384 000	rolls-royce.co.uk
Rolls-Royce	The Drive, Westhampnett, Chichester, West Sussex PO18 0SH	0800 626 556	saab.co.uk
Saab	150 Bath Road, Maidenhead, Berks FL6 4LB	0800 222 222	seat.co.uk
Seat	Yeomans Drive, Blakelands, Milton Keynes MK14 5AN	0845 774 745	skoda.co.uk
Skoda	Yeomans Drive, Blakelands, Milton Keynes MK14 5AN	08000 379 966	thesmart.co.uk
Smart	Tongwell, Milton Keynes, Bucks MK15 8BA	0118 976 6366	spyker-cars.co.uk
Spyker	Station Road, Pangbourne, Berkshire RG8 7AN	01252 775 428	syukcars.co.uk
SsangYong	1 St Andrew's Court, Wellington Street, Thame, Oxford OX9 3WT	08708 502 503	subaru.co.uk
Subaru	Ryder Street, West Bromwich, West Midlands B70 0EJ	01892 707 007	suzuki.co.uk
Suzuki	46-62 Gatwick Road, Crawley, West Sussex RH10 2XF	0845 275 5555	toyota.co.uk
Toyota	Great Burgh, Burgh Heath, Epsom, Surrey KT18 5UX	01253 509 055	tvr.co.uk
TVR	Bristol Avenue, Blackpool, Lancs FY2 0JF	08457 400 800	vauxhall.co.uk
Vauxhall	Griffin House, Osborne Road, Luton, Beds LU1 3YT	0800 333 666	volkswagen.co.uk
Volkswagen	Yeomans Drive, Blakelands, Milton Keynes MK14 5AN	0800 400 430	volvocars.co.uk
Volvo	Globe Park, Marlow, Bucks SL7 1YQ	01384 400 077	westfield-sportscars.co.uk
Westfield	Gibbons Industrial Park, Dudley Road, Kingswinford DY6 8XF		

New car prices in the UK

On the following pages are prices for every new car on sale in the United Kingdom, which were correct as of mid-October 2006. They're all on-the-road prices, which means all delivery and first registration charges have been taken into account. However, because they're list prices, they're not necessarily what you'll actually be charged if you come to buy a new car; some manuacturers are keener to haggle than others!

The list of models covered in the following pages is not exactly the same as the ones detailed already in this book. As this book went to press, we had technical details of some of the latest models, but not the costs. Examples of this include the Citroen C4 Picasso, Vauxhall Captiva and Alfa Romeo Spider – as well as replacement models such as the Audi S3 and Lexus LS460. Also, because of space constraints, it wasn't possible to include some of the very low-volume cars in the main section of the book, such as Ascari, Marcos and Westfield. However, because the prices are available, we've included them in the following pages.

Model	Derivative	BHP	UK price
ALFA ROMEO			
147	1.6 TS Turismo 3dr	120	13,850
147	1.6 TS Turismo 5dr	120	14,350
147	1.6 TS Lusso 5dr	120	15,350
147	2.0 TS Lusso 3dr	120	16,650
147	1.9 JTDm Turismo 8v 3dr	115	15,000
147	1.9 JTDm Turismo 8v 5dr	115	15,500
147	1.9 JTDm Lusso 16v 3dr	150	17,600
147	1.9 JTDm Lusso 16v 5dr	150	18,100
159	1.9 JTS Turismo	160	19,995
159	2.2 JTS Turismo	185	20,995
159	2.2 JTS Lusso	185	22,395
159	3.2 JTS Q4 Turismo	256	26,850
159	3.2 JTS Q4 Lusso	256	28,250
159	1.9 JTDm Turismo	150	20,495
159	1.9 JTDm Lusso	150	21,895
159	2.4 JTDm Turismo	200	24,395
159	2.4 JTDm Lusso	200	22,995
159	Sportwagon 1.9 JTS Turismo	160	21,095
159	Sportwagon 2.2 JTS Turismo	185	22,095
159	Sportwagon 2.2 JTS Lusso	185	23,495
159	Sportwagon 3.2 JTS Q4	256	29,350
159	Sportwagon 1.9 JTDm Turismo	150	21,595
159	Sportwagon 1.9 JTDm Lusso	150	22,995
159	Sportwagon 2.4 JTDm	200	25,495
GT	2.0 JTS	165	22,000
GT	3.2 V6	240	27,300
GT	1.9 JTDm	150	21,500
Brera	2.2 JTS	185	22,800
Brera	2.2 JTS SV	185	24,500
Brera	3.2 JTS Q4	256	28,750
Brera	3.2 JTS Q4 SV	256	29,850
Brera	2.4 JTDm	200	26,400
Brera	2.4 JTDm SV	200	27,500
ALPINA			
B3S	3.4	300	40,850
B3S	3.4 cabrio	300	43,850
D3	2.0d	197	26,995
B5	4.4 V8	500	63,850
B7	4.4 V8	500	79,850
Roadster S	3.4 S	300	37,850
Roadster S	3.4 S Lux	300	39,850
B6	Convertible	493	83,950
ASCARI			
KZ-1		500	235,000
ASTON MARTIN			
V8 Vantage	4.3 V8	380	82,800
DB9	5.9 coupé	450	109,750
DB9	5.9 Volante manual	450	118,750
Vanquish	S	520	177,100
AUDI			
A3	1.6 3dr	100	15,515
A3	1.6 SE 3dr	100	17,515

Model	Derivative	BHP	UK price
A3	1.6 Sport 3dr	100	17,515
A3	1.6 FSI 3dr	113	16,180
A3	1.6 FSI SE 3dr	113	18,180
A3	1.6 FSI S Line 3dr	113	19,730
A3	1.6 FSI Sport 3dr	113	18,180
A3	2.0 FSI 3dr	148	17,805
A3	2.0 FSI SE3dr	148	19,805
A3	2.0 FSI Sport 3dr	148	19,805
A3	2.0 FSI S Line 3dr	148	21,355
A3	2.0 T FSI Sport 3dr	197	22,455
A3	2.0 T FSI Sport DSG 3dr	197	21,095
A3	2.0 T FSI SE 3dr	197	21,095
A3	2.0 T FSI S Line 3dr	197	22,645
A3	2.0 T FSI S Line SE DSG 3dr	197	24,005
A3	2.0 T FSI quattro Sport 3dr	197	22,495
A3	2.0 T FSI quattro S Line 3dr	197	24,045
A3	2.0 T FSI quattro S Line SE 3dr	197	23,220
A3	3.2 quattro Sport 3dr	247	24,685
A3	3.2 quattro S Line 3dr	247	26,235
A3	1.9 TDI 3dr	103	16,725
A3	1.9 TDI SE 3dr	103	18,725
A3	1.9 TDI Sport 3dr	103	18,725
A3	2.0 TDI 3dr	138	18,080
A3	2.0 TDI SE 3dr	138	20,080
A3	2.0 TDI Sport 3dr	138	20,080
A3	2.0 TDI S Line 3dr	138	21,630
A3	2.0 TDI 170 SE 3dr	168	18,930
A3	2.0 TDI 170 Sport 3dr	168	20,930
A3	2.0 TDI 170 S Line 3dr	168	20,930
A3	2.0 TDI 170 quattro Sport 3dr	168	22,480
A3	2.0 TDI 170 quattro S Line 3dr	168	22,355
A3	1.6 Sportback	100	16,015
A3	1.6 SE Sportback	100	18,015
A3	1.6 Sport Sportback	100	18,030
A3	1.6 FSI Sportback	113	16,680
A3	1.6 FSI SE Sportback	113	18,680
A3	1.6 FSI Sport Sportback	113	18,680
A3	1.6 FSI S Line Sportback	113	20,230
A3	2.0 FSI Sportback	148	18,305
A3	2.0 FSI SE Sportback	148	20,305
A3	2.0 FSI Sport Sportback	148	20,305
A3	2.0 FSI S Line Sportback	148	21,855
A3	2.0 T FSI SE Sportback	197	19,745
A3	2.0 T FSI Sport Sportback	197	21,595
A3	2.0 T FSI S Line Sportback	197	21,595
A3	2.0 T FSI Sport DSG Sportback	197	23,145
A3	2.0 T FSI quattro Sport Sportback	197	22,955
A3	2.0 T FSI S Line SE Sportback	197	22,995
A3	2.0 T FSI quattro S Line Sportback	197	22,320
A3	2.0 T FSI S Line SE Sportback	197	24,545
A3	2.0 T FSI quattro S Line Sportback	197	23,680
A3	2.0 T FSI Sportback	197	23,720
A3	3.2 quattro Sport Sportback	247	25,185

Model	Derivative	BHP	UK price
A3	3.2 quattro S Line Sportback	247	26,735
A3	1.9 TDI Sportback	103	17,225
A3	1.9 TDI SE Sportback	103	19,225
A3	1.9 TDI Sport Sportback	103	19,225
A3	2.0 TDI Sportback	138	18,580
A3	2.0 TDI SE Sportback	138	20,580
A3	2.0 TDI Sport Sportback	138	20,580
A3	2.0 TDI S Line Sportback	138	22,130
A3	2.0 TDI 170 Sportback	168	19,430
A3	2.0 TDI 170 SE Sportback	168	21,430
A3	2.0 TDI 170 Sport Sportback	168	21,430
A3	2.0 TDI 170 S Line Sportback	168	22,980
A3	2.0 TDI 170 quattro Sport Sportback	168	22,855
A3	2.0 TDI 170 quattro S Line Sportback	168	24,405
A4	1.8 T	161	21,530
A4	1.8 T SE	161	21,530
A4	1.8 T S Line	161	22,280
A4	1.8 T quattro	161	22,930
A4	1.8 T quattro SE	161	22,930
A4	1.8 T quattro S Line	161	23,680
A4	2.0	129	19,900
A4	2.0 SE	129	19,900
A4	2.0 S Line	129	20,650
A4	2.0 T FSI	197	22,890
A4	2.0 T FSI SE	197	22,890
A4	2.0 T FSI S Line	197	23,640
A4	2.0 T FSI quattro	197	24,330
A4	2.0 T FSI quattro SE	197	24,330
A4	2.0 T FSI quattro S Line	197	25,080
A4	2.0 T FSI S Line SE	197	24,315
A4	2.0 T FSI quattro S Line SE	197	30,005
A4	3.2 FSI	252	27,760
A4	3.2 FSI SE	252	27,760
A4	3.2 FSI S Line	252	28,510
A4	3.2 FSI quattro	252	27,710
A4	3.2 FSI quattro SE	252	27,710
A4	3.2 FSI quattro S Line	252	28,460
S4	Saloon	339	37,160
RS4	Saloon	414	50,675
A4	1.9 TDI	114	21,075
A4	1.9 TDI SE	114	21,075
A4	1.9 TDI S Line	114	21,825
A4	2.0 TDI	138	22,370
A4	2.0 TDI SE	138	22,370
A4	2.0 TDI S Line	138	23,120
A4	2.0 TDI	170	23,305
A4	2.0 TDI S Line SE	170	25,605
A4	2.0 TDI quattro	170	24,730
A4	2.0 TDI quattro SE	170	24,730
A4	2.0 TDI quattro S Line	170	25,840
A4	2.0 TDI quattro S Line SE	170	27,030
A4	2.7 TDI	180	25,410
A4	2.7 TDI SE	180	25,410
A4	2.7 TDI S Line	180	26,160
A4	3.0 TDI quattro	201	27,800
A4	3.0 TDI quattro SE	201	27,800
A4	3.0 TDI quattro S Line	201	28,550
A4	Avant 2.0	129	21,025
A4	Avant 2.0 SE	129	21,025
A4	Avant 2.0 S Line	129	21,800
A4	Avant 1.8 T	161	22,065
A4	Avant 1.8 T SE	161	22,065
A4	Avant 1.8 T S Line	161	23,430
A4	Avant 1.8 T quattro	161	24,080
A4	Avant 1.8 T quattro SE	161	24,080
A4	Avant 1.8 T quattro S Line	161	24,830
A4	Avant 2.0 T FSI	197	24,080
A4	Avant 2.0 T FSI SE	197	24,080
A4	Avant 2.0 T FSI S Line	197	24,830
A4	Avant 2.0 T FSI quattro	197	25,480
A4	Avant 2.0 T FSI quattro SE	197	25,480
A4	Avant 2.0 T FSI quattro S Line	197	26,230
A4	Avant 2.0 T FSI S Line SE	197	25,465
A4	Avant 2.0 T FSI quattro S Line SE	197	26,865
A4	Avant 3.2 FSI	252	28,910
A4	Avant 3.2 FSI SE	252	28,910
A4	Avant 3.2 FSI S Line	252	29,660
A4	Avant 3.2 FSI quattro	252	28,860
A4	Avant 3.2 FSI quattro SE	252	28,860
S4	Avant quattro	339	38,310
RS4	Avant quattro	414	50,675
A4	Avant 1.9 TDI	114	22,225
A4	Avant 1.9 TDI SE	114	22,225
A4	Avant 1.9 TDI S Line	114	22,975
A4	Avant 2.0 TDI	140	23,520
A4	Avant 2.0 TDI SE	140	23,520
A4	Avant 2.0 TDI S Line	140	24,270
A4	Avant 2.0 TDI	170	24,455
A4	Avant 2.0 TDI SE	170	24,455
A4	Avant 2.0 TDI S Line	170	25,205
A4	Avant 2.0 TDI S Line SE	170	27,030
A4	Avant 2.0 TDI quattro	170	25,880
A4	Avant 2.0 TDI quattro SE	170	25,880
A4	Avant 2.0 TDI quattro S Line	170	26,630
A4	Avant 2.0 TDI quattro S Line SE	170	28,180
A4	Avant 2.7 TDI	180	26,560
A4	Avant 2.7 TDI SE	180	26,560
A4	Avant 2.7 TDI S Line	180	27,310
A4	Avant 3.0 TDI Quattro	201	28,950
A4	Avant 3.0 TDI Quattro SE	201	28,950
A4	Avant 3.0 TDI Quattro S Line	201	29,700
A4	Cabrio 1.8 T	161	25,955
A4	Cabrio 1.8 T Sport	161	26,705
A4	Cabrio 1.8 T S Line	161	28,355
A4	Cabrio 2.0 T FSI	197	27,605
A4	Cabrio 2.0 T FSI Sport	197	28,355
A4	Cabrio 2.0 T FSI S Line	197	30,055
A4	Cabrio 3.2 quattro	252	32,525
A4	Cabrio 3.2 quattro Sport	252	33,275
A4	Cabrio 3.2 quattro S Line	252	34,925
S4	Cabrio quattro	342	43,025
RS4	Cabrio quattro	414	59,625
A4	Cabrio 2.0 TDI	138	26,675
A4	Cabrio 2.0 TDI Sport	138	27,525
A4	Cabrio 2.0 TDI S Line	138	29,175
A4	Cabrio 3.0 TDI quattro	230	32,735
A4	Cabrio 3.0 TDI quattro Sport	230	33,710
A4	Cabrio 3.0 TDI quattro S Line	230	36,360
A6	2.0 T FSI SE	165	25,365
A6	2.0 T FSI S Line	165	28,405
A6	2.4 SE	177	25,425
A6	2.4 S Line	177	28,315
A6	2.4 quattro SE	177	27,025
A6	2.4 quattro S Line	177	29,915
A6	3.2 FSI SE	252	31,525
A6	3.2 FSI S Line	252	34,415
A6	3.2 FSI quattro SE	252	33,125
A6	3.2 FSI quattro S Line	252	36,015
A6	4.2 quattro SE	335	44,475
A6	4.2 quattro S Line	335	46,255
A6	4.2 FSI quattro	345	44,475
S6	Saloon	429	55,375
A6	2.0 TDI SE	138	25,250
A6	2.0 TDI S Line	138	28,290
A6	2.7 TDI SE	178	27,085
A6	2.7 TDI SE-Line	178	29,975
A6	3.0 TDI quattro SE	225	31,570
A6	3.0 TDI quattro S Line	225	34,460

Model	Derivative	BHP	UK price
A6	Avant 2.0 T FSI SE	165	26,935
A6	Avant 2.0 T FSI S Line	165	29,975
A6	Avant 2.4 SE	177	26,995
A6	Avant 2.4 S Line	177	29,885
A6	Avant 2.4 quattro SE	177	28,295
A6	Avant 2.4 quattro S Line	177	31,185
A6	Avant 3.2 FSI SE	252	33,095
A6	Avant 3.2 FSI S Line	252	35,985
A6	Avant 3.2 FSI quattro SE	252	34,395
A6	Avant 3.2 FSI quattro S Line	252	37,285
A6	Avant 4.2 quattro SE	335	45,745
A6	Avant 4.2 quattro S Line	335	47,525
A6	Avant 4.2 quattro	335	45,745
S6	Avant quattro	429	56,600
A6	Avant 2.0 TDI SE	138	26,820
A6	Avant 2.0 TDI S Line	138	29,860
A6	Avant 2.7 TDI SE	178	28,690
A6	Avant 2.7 TDI S Line	178	31,580
A6	Avant 3.0 TDI quattro SE	225	32,840
A6	Avant 3.0 TDI quattro S Line	225	35,730
A6	Allroad quattro 2.7 TDI	178	31,323
A6	Allroad quattro 3.0 TDI	201	34,980
A8	3.2 SE	256	50,225
A8	3.2 SE LWB	256	53,595
A8	3.2 Sport	256	52,725
A8	3.2 Sport LWB	256	56,095
A8	3.2 FSI quattro SE	256	52,125
A8	3.2 FSI quattro SE	256	54,625
A8	4.2 FSI quattro SE	325	59,815
A8	4.2 FSI quattro SE LWB	325	63,185
A8	4.2 FSI quattro Sport	325	61,715
A8	4.2 FSI quattro Sport LWB	325	65,085
A8	6.0 quattro	444	79,655
A8	3.0 TDI quattro SE	230	49,640
A8	3.0 TDI quattro SE LWB	230	53,030
A8	3.0 TDI quattro Sport	230	52,140
A8	3.0 TDI quattro Sport LWB	230	55,530
A8	4.2 TDI quattro SE	321	60,500
A8	4.2 TDI quattro SE LWB	321	63,870
A8	4.2 TDI quattro Sport	321	62,400
A8	4.2 TDI quattro Sport LWB	321	65,770
Q7	4.2 FSI quattro SE	345	47,725
Q7	4.2 FSI quattro S Line	345	48,625
Q7	3.0 TDI quattro	230	37,330
Q7	3.0 TDI quattro SE	230	39,830
Q7	3.0 TDI quattro S Line	230	40,730
TT	Coupé 2.0 T FSI	197	24,625
TT	Coupé 2.0 T FSI S-Tronic	197	26,025
TT	Coupé 3.2 quattro	247	29,285
TT	Coupé 3.2 quattro S-Tronic	247	30,685
TT	1.8 roadster	161	22,240
TT	1.8 T roadster	187	22,240
TT	3.2 V6 roadster	247	31,210

BENTLEY

Model	Derivative	BHP	UK price
Continental	GT	552	117,500
Continental	GTC	552	130,500
Continental	Flying Spur	552	117,500
Arnage	R	400	160,000
Arnage	T	450	170,000
Azure		450	222,500

BMW

Model	Derivative	BHP	UK price
116i		115	15,995
116i	ES	115	16,820
116i	SE	115	17,945
116i	Sport	115	17,945
116i	M Sport	115	19,690
118i		127	17,800
118i	ES	127	18,625
118i	SE	127	19,750
118i	Sport	127	19,750
118i	M Sport	127	21,495
120i		150	18,885
120i	ES	150	19,710
120i	SE	150	20,835
120i	Sport	150	20,735
120i	M Sport	150	22,510
130i	SE	261	24,770
130i	M Sport	261	26,540
118d		122	17,885
118d	ES	122	18,710
118d	SE	122	19,835
118d	Sport	122	19,835
118d	M Sport	122	21,580
120d		163	19,410
120d	ES	163	20,235
120d	SE	163	21,360
120d	Sport	163	21,260
120d	M Sport	163	23,035
318i		127	19,995
318i	ES	127	20,465
318i	SE	127	21,495
318i	M Sport	127	23,785
320i		150	21,625
320i	ES	150	22,095
320i	SE	150	23,125
320i	M Sport	150	25,415
320Si		170	25,000
320Si	SE	170	25,840
325i	SE	215	25,840
325i	M Sport	215	28,570
330i	SE	254	29,170
330i	M Sport	254	31,900
335i	SE	302	30,940
335i	M Sport	302	33,750
318d		122	22,340
318d	ES	122	22,810
318d	SE	122	23,840
318d	M Sport	122	26,130
320d		163	23,845
320d	ES	163	23,955
320d	SE	163	24,985
320d	M Sport	163	27,225
325d	SE	194	27,310
325d	M Sport	194	30,040
330d	SE	227	29,720
330d	M Sport	227	32,450
335d	SE	282	32,995
335d	M Sport	282	35,735
318i	ES Touring	127	21,645
318i	SE Touring	127	22,675
318i	M Sport Touring	127	24,965
320i	ES Touring	150	23,275
320i	SE Touring	150	24,305
320i	M Sport Touring	150	26,595
325i	SE Touring	215	27,020
325i	M Sport Touring	215	29,750
330i	SE Touring	254	30,340
330i	M Sport Touring	254	33,070
335i	SE Touring	302	32,110
335i	M Sport Touring	302	34,920
318d	ES Touring	121	24,015
318d	SE Touring	121	25,045
318d	M Sport Touring	121	27,335
320d	ES Touring	163	25,135
320d	SE Touring	163	26,165
320d	M Sport Touring	163	28,455
325d	SE Touring	194	28,490
325d	M Sport Touring	194	31,220

Model	Derivative	BHP	UK price
330d	SE Touring	231	30,890
330d	M Sport Touring	231	33,290
335d	SE Touring	282	34,165
335d	M Sport Touring	282	36,905
325i	SE coupé	218	28,090
335i	SE coupé	302	33,420
318Ci	SE cabrio	143	27,235
318Ci	M Sport cabrio	143	28,410
320Ci	SE cabrio	168	28,795
320Ci	M Sport cabrio	168	31,095
325Ci	SE cabrio	192	30,540
325Ci	M Sport cabrio	192	32,865
330Ci	SE cabrio	231	33,585
330Ci	M Sport cabrio	231	35,560
M3	Cabrio	343	45,195
320Cd	SE cabrio	150	29,020
320Cd	M Sport cabrio	150	29,020
330Cd	SE cabrio	204	34,020
330Cd	M Sport cabrio	204	35,985
523i	SE	171	27,455
523i	M Sport	171	30,615
525i	SE	218	29,085
525i	M Sport	218	32,245
530i	SE	254	33,040
530i	M Sport	254	35,890
540i	SE	301	37,465
540i	M Sport	301	40,090
550i	SE	361	44,110
550i	M Sport	361	46,310
M5		507	63,495
520d		158	25,925
520d	SE	158	26,235
520d	SE auto	158	26,235
520d	M Sport	158	29,345
525d	SE	174	29,535
525d	M Sport	174	32,695
530d	SE	227	33,545
530d	M Sport	227	36,395
535d	SE	268	37,790
535d	M Sport	268	40,420
523i	SE Touring	171	29,480
525i	SE Touring	218	31,110
525i	M Sport Touring	218	34,270
530i	SE Touring	254	35,065
530i	M Sport Touring	254	37,915
550i	SE Touring	361	46,135
520d	Touring	158	27,925
525d	SE Touring	177	31,635
530d	SE Touring	227	35,620
530d	M Sport Touring	227	38,470
535d	SE Touring	268	39,815
630i		254	47,050
630i	Sport	254	49,250
650i		361	53,020
650i	Sport	361	54,870
M6		500	81,760
630i	Cabrio	254	25,650
630i	Sport cabrio	254	54,850
650i	Cabrio	367	58,420
650i	Sport cabrio	367	60,270
M6	Cabrio	500	87,000
730i	SE	254	52,270
730i	Sport	254	55,895
730	Li	254	52,720
730	Li SE	254	54,870
740i		301	56,595
740i	Sport	301	60,225
740	Li	301	59,345
750i		361	61,045

Model	Derivative	BHP	UK price
750i	Sport	361	64,675
750	Li	361	63,770
760i		445	81,605
760	Li	445	83,730
730d	SE	227	50,875
730	Ld SE	227	53,475
730d	Sport	227	54,505
X3	2.0i	150	25,285
X3	2.0i SE	150	26,435
X3	2.0i Sport	150	27,485
X3	2.0i M Sport	150	28,725
X3	2.5si SE	192	29,725
X3	2.5si Sport	192	30,775
X3	2.5si M Sport	192	32,015
X3	3.0i SE	228	33,205
X3	3.0i Sport	228	34,205
X3	3.0i M Sport	228	35,445
X3	2.0d	150	27,235
X3	2.0d SE	150	28,385
X3	2.0d Sport	150	39,435
X3	2.0d M Sport	150	30,675
X3	3.0d SE	218	32,285
X3	3.0d Sport	218	33,285
X3	3.0d M Sport	218	34,525
X5	3.0i SE	231	36,775
X5	3.0i Sport	231	38,725
X5	4.4i SE auto	360	49,395
X5	4.4i Sport auto	360	50,070
X5	4.8is	360	59,945
X5	3.0d SE	218	37,160
X5	3.0d Sport	218	39,110
Z4	Roadster 2.0i	150	22,945
Z4	Roadster 2.0i SE	150	23,655
Z4	Roadster 2.0i Sport	150	26,240
Z4	Roadster 2.5i SE	174	25,675
Z4	Roadster 2.5i Sport	174	28,260
Z4	Roadster 2.5si SE	218	28,390
Z4	Roadster 2.5si Sport	218	30,750
Z4	Roadster 3.0si SE	261	32,765
Z4	Roadster 3.0si Sport	261	34,195
Z4	M Roadster	338	42,795
Z4	Coupé 3.0si SE	265	31,400
Z4	Coupé 3.0si Sport	265	32,925
Z4	M Coupé	343	41,285
BROOKE			
Double R	2.0 200	200	27,995
Double R	2.3 260	260	31,995
Double R	2.0 300	300	36,995
CADILLAC			
BLS	2.0 T SE	173	20,728
BLS	2.0 T Luxury	173	24,278
BLS	2.0 T Luxury	207	25,678
BLS	2.8 V6 Sport Luxury	252	30,998
BLS	1.9D SE	148	21,473
BLS	1.9D Luxury	148	25,073
CTS	2.8 V6 Elegance	215	24,850
CTS	2.8 V6 Sport Luxury	215	27,350
CTS	3.6 V6 Sport Luxury	257	29,850
CATERHAM			
CSR	200 Roadster	200	31,000
CSR	260 Roadster	260	37,000
CSR	1.4 Class	105	15,450
CSR	1.6 Roadsport	115	18,495
CSR	1.6 SV Roadsport	120	19,995
CSR	1.8 Roadsport	140	19,495
CSR	1.8 Roadsport 140	140	20,495
CSR	1.8 Roadsport 160	165	21,495
CSR	1.8 SV Superlight	140	23,950
CSR	1.8 R300	160	26,250

Model	Derivative	BHP	UK price
CHEVROLET			
Matiz	0.8 S	50	6,145
Matiz	0.8 SE	50	7,145
Matiz	1.0 SE	64	6,595
Matiz	1.0 SE+	64	6,595
Kalos	1.2 S	71	7,095
Kalos	1.2 SE	71	7,595
Kalos	1.4 SX 3dr	93	8,595
Kalos	1.4 SX 5dr	93	8,995
Kalso	1.4 Sport	93	9,995
Lacetti	1.4 SE 5dr	93	9,595
Lacetti	1.4 SE Plus 5dr	93	8,995
Lacetti	1.6 SX 5dr	108	10,595
Lacetti	1.8 Sport 5dr	120	12,595
Lacetti	1.6 SX saloon	121	10,995
Lacetti	1.8 CDX saloon	121	11,995
Lacetti	1.6 SX estate	108	11,095
Lacetti	1.8 Sport estate	120	12,995
Tacuma	1.6 SX	103	10,995
Tacuma	2.0 CDX	119	11,995
CHRYSLER			
PT Cruiser	2.4 Classic	141	12,995
PT Cruiser	2.4 Touring	141	14,550
PT Cruiser	2.4 Limited	141	16,050
PT Cruiser	2.2 CRD Classic	148	14,225
PT Cruiser	2.2 CRD Touring	148	15,725
PT Cruiser	2.2 CRD Limited	148	17,225
PT Cruiser	Cabrio 2.4 Limited	141	18,150
PT Cruiser	Cabrio 2.4i Touring	148	16,650
300 C	3.5i V6	249	25,795
300 C	5.7 V8 Hemi	340	33,040
300 C	SRT-8	425	39,040
300 C	3.0 CRD	218	25,775
300 C	Touring 3.5i V6	249	27,295
300 C	Touring 5.7 V8 Hemi	340	34,290
300 C	Touring 3.0 CRD	218	27,275
Crossfire	3.2i V6 coupé	215	24,995
Crossfire	3.2i V6 coupé SRT-6	330	34,385
Crossfire	3.2i V6 roadster	215	25,995
Crossfire	3.2i V6 roadster SRT-6	330	35,385
Voyager	2.4 SE	145	18,750
Voyager	2.5 CRD SE	141	19,980
Voyager	2.8 CRD LX	150	23,495
Grand Voyager	3.3 Limited	172	30,995
Grand Voyager	2.8 CRD LX	150	25,995
CITROEN			
C1	1.0 Vibe 3dr	67	6,795
C1	1.0 Vibe 5dr	67	7,145
C1	1.0 Rhythm 3dr	55	7,375
C1	1.0 Rhythm 5dr	55	7,725
C1	1.4 HDi Rhythm 5dr	55	8,725
C2	1.1 L	61	8,190
C2	1.1 Design	61	8,490
C2	1.1 SX	61	9,390
C2	1.1 Furio	61	9,190
C2	1.4 Design	75	9,040
C2	1.4 SX	75	9,890
C2	1.4 Stop & Start	75	10,690
C2	1.4 Furio	75	9,690
C2	1.6 VTR Sensodrive	110	11,395
C2	1.6 VTS	123	12,195
C2	1.4 HDi L	70	9,360
C2	1.4 HDi Design	70	9,710
C2	1.4 HDi SX	70	9,710
C2	1.4 HDi Furio	70	10,560
C3	1.1 L	60	9,190
C3	1.1 Desire	60	9,990
C3	1.4 Desire	74	10,490
C3	1.4 SX	74	10,940
C3	1.4 Stop & Start	74	11,540
C3	1.6 SX auto	110	12,295
C3	1.6 VTR	110	12,295
C3	1.6 Exclusive Sensodrive	110	12,840
C3	1.4 HDi L	69	10,460
C3	1.4 HDi Desire	69	11,210
C3	1.6 HDi SX	91	12,260
C3	1.6 HDi Exclusive	91	12,960
C3	1.6 HDi VTR	110	13,260
C3	XTR 1.4 Sensodrive	88	12,040
C3	XTR 1.6 HDi	91	12,960
C3	Pluriel 1.4	75	12,495
C3	Pluriel 1.4 Cote d-Azur	75	12,745
C3	Pluriel 1.4 Exclusive	75	13,895
C3	Pluriel 1.6 Sensodrive	110	14,095
C3	Pluriel 1.4 HDi	110	13,290
C4	1.4 VT coupé	90	11,495
C4	1.4 VTR coupé	90	12,695
C4	1.6 VTR coupé	110	13,295
C4	1.6 VTR Plus coupé	110	14,195
C4	2.0 VTR Plus coupé	178	15,295
C4	2.0 VTS 180 coupé	178	17,620
C4	1.6 HDi VTR coupé	91	14,090
C4	1.6 HDi VTR Plus coupé	108	15,940
C4	2.0 HDi VTS coupé	136	18,090
C4	1.4 LX 5dr	90	11,895
C4	1.6 SX 5dr	110	13,695
C4	2.0 VTR Plus 5dr	141	15,695
C4	2.0 Exclusive auto 5dr	141	15,820
C4	1.6 HDi LX	91	13,290
C4	1.6 HDi SX	108	15,440
C4	2.0 HDi VTR Plus	136	17,190
C4	2.0 HDi Exclusive	136	18,490
C5	1.8 LX	115	15,495
C5	1.8 Design	115	15,495
C5	1.8 VTR	115	16,095
C5	2.0 VTR	141	16,695
C5	2.0 Exclusive auto	141	20,320
C5	3.0 V6 Exclusive	207	21,940
C5	1.6 HDi VTX Plus	108	15,090
C5	1.6 HDi LX	108	15,990
C5	1.6 HDi Design	108	16,590
C5	1.6 HDi VTR	108	17,190
C5	2.0 HDi VTR	136	18,395
C5	2.0 HDi Exclusive	136	20,695
C5	1.8 LX estate	115	16,595
C5	1.8 Design estate	115	17,195
C5	2.0 VTR estate	141	18,120
C5	3.0 V6 Exclusive estate	207	23,040
C5	1.6 HDi LX estate	108	17,090
C5	1.6 HDi Design estate	108	17,090
C5	1.6 HDi VTR estate	108	17,690
C5	2.0 HDi VTR estate	136	18,290
C5	2.0 HDi Exclusive estate	136	21,795
C6	3.0 V6	212	29,545
C6	3.0 V6 Lignage	212	32,645
C6	3.0 V6 Exclusive	212	35,845
C6	2.7 HDi V6	205	31,545
C6	2.7 HDi V6 Lignage	205	34,645
C6	2.7 HDi V6 Exclusive	205	37,845
Berlingo	1.4 Forte	75	10,215
Berlingo	1.4 XTR	75	10,515
Berlingo	1.6 Forte	110	10,715
Berlingo	1.6 XTR	110	11,015
Berlingo	1.6 HDi Forte	75	11,010
Berlingo	1.6 HDi XTR	75	11,310
Berlingo	1.6 HDi Desire	75	11,610
Berlingo	1.6 HDi Forte	92	11,560
Berlingo	1.6 HDi XTR	92	11,860

Model	Derivative	BHP	UK price
Berlingo	1.6 HDi Desire	92	12,160
Xsara Picasso	1.6 LX	110	13,595
Xsara Picasso	1.6 Desire	110	14,695
Xsara Picasso	1.6 VTX	110	11,250
Xsara Picasso	1.6 Exclusive	110	15,495
Xsara Picasso	2.0 Desire auto	137	16,620
Xsara Picasso	2.0 VTX auto	137	13,150
Xsara Picasso	2.0 Exclusive auto	137	17,420
Xsara Picasso	1.6 HDi LX	92	14,640
Xsara Picasso	1.6 HDi Desire	92	15,740
Xsara Picasso	1.6 HDi VTX	92	11,650
Xsara Picasso	1.6 HDi Exclusive	92	16,540
Xsara Picasso	1.6 HDi Desire	108	16,790
Xsara Picasso	1.6 HDi Exclusive	108	17,590
C8	2.0 LX	141	19,535
C8	2.0 SX	141	20,695
C8	2.0 Exclusive auto	141	24,140
C8	2.0 HDi SX auto	110	23,435
C8	2.0 HDi Exclusive auto	110	23,435
C8	2.0 HDi LX	120	23,435
C8	2.0 HDi SX	120	23,435
C8	2.0 HDi SX	134	23,435
C8	2.0 HDi Exclusive	134	23,435
CORVETTE			
Corvette	C6	400	45,850
Corvette	C6 Convertible	400	51,850
Corvette	Z06	505	59,895
DAIHATSU			
Charade	1.0 EL 3dr	58	6,460
Charade	1.0 EL 5dr	58	6,460
Sirion	1.0 S	68	7,460
Sirion	1.3 S	86	8,090
Sirion	1.3 SE	86	8,690
Terios	1.5 S	103	12,995
Terios	1.5 SX	103	14,295
Terios	1.5 SE	103	14,995
Copen	0.7	67	13,495
DODGE			
Caliber	1.8 S	148	11,495
Caliber	1.8 SE	148	11,990
Caliber	1.8 SXT	148	13,790
Caliber	2.0 SXT	154	13,790
Caliber	2.0 SXT Sport	154	13,790
Caliber	2.0 CRD S	138	13,495
Caliber	2.0 CRD SE	138	13,990
Caliber	2.0 CRD SXT	138	15,290
Caliber	2.0 CRD SXT Sport	138	15,430
Viper	SRT-10 coupé	500	69,990
Viper	SRT-10 cabrio	500	69,990
FERRARI			
F430		483	122,775
F430	F1	483	128,275
F430	Spider	483	130,825
F430	F1 Spider	483	135,300
599	GTB Fiorano	611	171,825
612	Scaglietti	532	175,725
612	Scaglietti F1	532	181,225
FIAT			
Panda	1.1 Active	54	6,790
Panda	1.2 Dynamic	60	7,190
Panda	1.2 Dynamic air-con	60	7,740
Panda	1.2 Dynamic SkyDome	60	8,390
Panda	1.2 Alessi	60	8,995
Panda	1.2 4x4	60	9,395
Panda	1.3 Multijet Dynamic	70	8,060
Panda	1.3 Multijet Sporting	70	9,160
Punto	1.2 Active 3dr	60	7,590
Punto	1.2 Active 5dr	60	8,090
Grande Punto	1.2 Active 3dr	65	7,989

Model	Derivative	BHP	UK price
Grande Punto	1.2 Active 5dr	65	8,595
Grande Punto	1.2 Dynamic 3dr	65	8,895
Grande Punto	1.2 Dynamic 5dr	65	9,495
Grande Punto	1.4 Active Sport 3dr	77	8,895
Grande Punto	1.4 Dynamic 3dr	77	9,195
Grande Punto	1.4 Dynamic 5dr	77	9,795
Grande Punto	1.4 Sporting	95	10,695
Grande Punto	1.4 Eleganza	95	10,895
Grande Punto	1.3 Multijet Active 3dr	75	8,895
Grande Punto	1.3 Multijet Active 5dr	75	9,495
Grande Punto	1.3 Multijet Dynamic 3dr	90	10,595
Grande Punto	1.3 Multijet Dynamic 3dr	90	11,195
Grande Punto	1.9 Multijet Eleganza	120	12,695
Grande Punto	1.9 Multijet Sporting	130	12,295
Stilo	1.4 Active 5dr	95	11,250
Stilo	1.4 Dynamic 5dr	95	12,250
Stilo	1.4 Active Sport 3dr	95	11,261
Stilo	1.9 Multijet Active 3dr	120	12,595
Stilo	1.9 Multijet Active 5dr	120	13,095
Stilo	1.9 Multijet Dynamic 5dr	120	14,095
Stilo	1.9 Multijet Sporting	120	13,626
Stilo	1.9 Multijet Sporting	150	14,736
Stilo	1.9 Multijet Active	120	13,995
Stilo	1.9 Multijet Dynamic	120	15,095
Croma	1.8 Dynamic	140	14,995
Croma	1.8 Eleganza	140	16,145
Croma	2.2 Dynamic	147	15,770
Croma	2.2 Eleganza	147	16,920
Croma	2.2 Prestigio	147	18,270
Croma	1.9 Multijet Dynamic	120	15,995
Croma	1.9 Multijet Eleganza	120	17,145
Croma	1.9 Multijet Eleganza	148	18,145
Croma	1.9 Multijet Prestigio	148	19,495
Croma	2.4 Multijet Prestigio	200	22,170
Doblò	1.4 Active	77	9,595
Doblò	1.4 Dynamic	77	10,495
Doblò	1.3 Multijet Active	85	10,590
Doblò	1.3 Multijet Family	85	11,390
Doblò	1.9 Multijet Active	105	10,895
Doblò	1.9 Multijet Dynamic	105	11,795
Doblò	1.9 Multijet Active	120	11,295
Doblò	1.9 Multijet Family	120	12,095
Doblò	1.9 Multijet Dynamic	120	12,195
Sedici	1.6 Dynamic	107	12,495
Sedici	1.6 Eleganza	107	13,495
Sedici	1.9 Multijet Dynamic	120	14,495
Sedici	1.9 Multijet Eleganza	120	15,495
Idea	1.4 Active	95	10,295
Idea	1.4 Dynamic	95	11,745
Idea	1.4 Eleganza	95	13,195
Idea	1.3 Multijet Active	70	11,090
Idea	1.3 Multijet Dynamic	70	12,990
Multipla	1.6 Dynamic Dynamic Family	103	13,370
Multipla	1.9 JTD Dynamic Family	120	14,645
Multipla	1.9 JTD Dynamic Plus	120	16,245
Multipla	1.9 JTD Eleganza	120	17,245
FORD			
Ka	1.3	69	7,095
Ka	1.3 Style	69	7,595
Ka	1.3 Collection	69	8,595
Ka	1.3 Luxury	69	10,295
Sportka	1.6	94	10,300
Sportka	1.6 SE	94	11,300
Fiesta	1.25 Freedom 3dr	75	10,190
Fiesta	1.25 Freedom 5dr	75	10,790
Fiesta	1.25 Studio 3dr	75	8,390
Fiesta	1.25 Studio 5dr	75	8,990
Fiesta	1.25 Style 3dr	75	8,990
Fiesta	1.25 Style 5dr	75	9,590

Model	Derivative	BHP	UK price
Fiesta	1.25 Style Climate 3dr	75	9,595
Fiesta	1.25 Style Climate 5dr	75	10,190
Fiesta	1.25 Zetec 3dr	75	9,595
Fiesta	1.25 Zetec 5dr	75	10,190
Fiesta	1.25 Zetec Climate 3dr	75	10,190
Fiesta	1.25 Zetec Climate 5dr	75	10,790
Fiesta	1.4 Freedom 3dr	79	10,490
Fiesta	1.4 Freedom 5dr	79	11,090
Fiesta	1.4 Style 3dr	79	9,290
Fiesta	1.4 Style 5dr	79	9,890
Fiesta	1.4 Style Climate 3dr	79	9,890
Fiesta	1.4 Style Climate 5dr	79	10,490
Fiesta	1.4 Zetec 3dr	79	9,890
Fiesta	1.4 Zetec 5dr	79	10,490
Fiesta	1.4 Zetec Climate 3dr	79	10,490
Fiesta	1.4 Zetec Climate 5dr	79	11,090
Fiesta	1.4 Ghia 3dr	79	11,340
Fiesta	1.4 Ghia 5dr	79	11,940
Fiesta	1.6 Style 3dr	98	10,895
Fiesta	1.6 Style 5dr	98	11,495
Fiesta	1.6 Style Climate 3dr	98	11,495
Fiesta	1.6 Style Climate 5dr	98	12,095
Fiesta	1.6 Ghia 5dr	98	12,545
Fiesta	1.6 Zetec-S 3dr	98	11,595
Fiesta	ST	148	13,595
Fiesta	1.4 TDCi Studio 3dr	67	9,260
Fiesta	1.4 TDCi Style 3dr	67	9,860
Fiesta	1.4 TDCi Style 5dr	67	10,460
Fiesta	1.4 TDCi Style Climate 3dr	67	10,460
Fiesta	1.4 TDCi Style Climate 5dr	67	11,060
Fiesta	1.4 TDCi Zetec 3dr	67	10,460
Fiesta	1.4 TDCi Zetec 5dr	67	11,060
Fiesta	1.4 TDCi Zetec Climate 3dr	67	11,060
Fiesta	1.4 TDCi Zetec Climate 5dr	67	11,660
Fiesta	1.4 TDCi Ghia 5dr	67	12,510
Fiesta	1.6 TDCi Zetec Climate 3dr	89	11,660
Fiesta	1.6 TDCi Zetec Climate 5dr	89	12,260
Fiesta	1.6 TDCi Ghia 5dr	89	13,110
Fiesta	1.6 TDCi Zetec-S 3dr	89	12,460
Fusion	1.4 Style	78	10,645
Fusion	1.4 Style Climate	78	11,245
Fusion	1.4 Zetec	78	11,245
Fusion	1.4 Zetec Climate	78	11,845
Fusion	1.4 +	78	12,445
Fusion	1.6 Zetec	99	11,845
Fusion	1.6 Zetec Climate	99	12,445
Fusion	1.6 +	99	13,045
Fusion	1.4 TDCi Style	67	11,240
Fusion	1.4 TDCi Style Climate	67	11,840
Fusion	1.4 TDCi Zetec	67	11,840
Fusion	1.4 TDCi Zetec Climate	67	12,440
Fusion	1.4 TDCi +	67	13,040
Fusion	1.6 TDCi Zetec	89	12,410
Fusion	1.6 TDCi Zetec Climate	89	13,010
Fusion	1.6 TDCi +	89	13,610
Focus	1.4 Studio 3dr	79	11,395
Focus	1.4 Studio 5dr	79	11,995
Focus	1.4 LX 3dr	79	12,445
Focus	1.4 LX 5dr	79	13,045
Focus	1.4 Sport 3dr	79	12,445
Focus	1.4 Sport 5dr	79	12,895
Focus	1.6 LX 3dr	79	12,945
Focus	1.6 LX 5dr	79	13,545
Focus	1.6 Sport 3dr	79	13,395
Focus	1.6 Sport 5dr	79	13,995
Focus	1.6 Sport 3dr	79	13,595
Focus	1.6 Zetec 5dr	79	14,195
Focus	1.6 Ghia 5dr	79	15,170
Focus	1.6 Ti-VCT LX 5dr	113	13,795
Focus	1.6 Ti-VCT Sport 5dr	113	14,245
Focus	1.6 Ti-VCT Zetec 3dr	113	13,845
Focus	1.6 Ti-VCT Zetec 5dr	113	14,445
Focus	1.6 Ti-VCT Ghia 5dr	113	15,425
Focus	1.6 Ti-VCT Titanium 3dr	113	15,420
Focus	1.6 Ti-VCT Titanium 5dr	113	16,025
Focus	1.8 LX 5dr	123	14,045
Focus	1.8 Sport 5dr	123	14,495
Focus	1.8 Zetec 3dr	123	14,095
Focus	1.8 Zetec 5dr	123	14,695
Focus	1.8 Ghia 5dr	123	15,670
Focus	1.8 Titanium 3dr	123	15,675
Focus	1.8 Titanium 5dr	123	16,275
Focus	2.0 Zetec 3dr	143	14,595
Focus	2.0 Zetec 5dr	143	15,195
Focus	2.0 Ghia 5dr	143	16,170
Focus	2.0 Titanium 3dr	143	16,175
Focus	2.0 Titanium 5dr	143	16,775
Focus	ST 3dr	222	17,495
Focus	ST 5dr	222	18,095
Focus	ST 2 3dr	222	18,495
Focus	ST 2 5dr	222	19,095
Focus	ST 3 3dr	222	19,495
Focus	ST 3 5dr	222	20,095
Focus	1.6 TDCi Studio 5dr	89	13,495
Focus	1.6 TDCi LX 5dr	89	14,545
Focus	1.6 TDCi Sport 5dr	89	14,995
Focus	1.8 TDCi LX 5dr	89	15,045
Focus	1.8 TDCi Sport 5dr	89	15,495
Focus	1.8 TDCi Sport 3dr	89	15,095
Focus	1.8 TDCi Sport 5dr	89	15,695
Focus	1.8 TDCi Zetec 3dr	89	15,095
Focus	1.8 TDCi Zetec 5dr	89	15,695
Focus	1.8 TDCi Ghia 5dr	89	16,670
Focus	1.8 TDCi Titanium 3dr	89	16,675
Focus	1.8 TDCi Titanium 5dr	89	17,275
Focus	2.0 TDCi Ghia 5dr	134	17,420
Focus	2.0 TDCi Titanium 3dr	134	17,425
Focus	2.0 TDCi Titanium 5dr	134	18,025
Focus	1.6 Ghia saloon	99	15,170
Focus	1.6 Ti-VCT Ghia saloon	113	15,420
Focus	2.0 Ghia saloon	143	16,170
Focus	1.8 TDCi Ghia saloon	113	16,670
Focus	1.8 TDCi Titanium saloon	113	17,275
Focus	2.0 TDCi Ghia saloon	134	17,420
Focus	2.0 TDCi Titanium saloon	134	18,025
Focus	1.6 Studio estate	99	13,345
Focus	1.6 LX estate	99	14,395
Focus	1.6 Sport estate	99	14,845
Focus	1.6 Zetec estate	99	15,045
Focus	1.6 Ghia estate	99	16,020
Focus	1.6 Ti-VCT LX estate	113	14,645
Focus	1.6 Ti-VCT Sport estate	113	15,095
Focus	1.6 Ti-VCT Zetec estate	113	15,295
Focus	1.6 Ti-VCT Ghia estate	113	16,270
Focus	1.6 Ti-VCT Titanium estate	113	16,875
Focus	1.8 Zetec estate	143	15,545
Focus	1.8 Ghia estate	143	16,520
Focus	1.8 Titanium estate	143	17,125
Focus	2.0 Zetec estate	143	16,045
Focus	2.0 Ghia estate	143	17,020
Focus	2.0 Titanium estate	143	17,625
Focus	1.6 TDCi Studio estate	89	14,345
Focus	1.6 TDCi LX estate	89	15,395
Focus	1.6 TDCi Sport estate	89	15,845
Focus	1.8 TDCi LX estate	113	15,895
Focus	1.8 TDCi Sport estate	113	16,345
Focus	1.8 TDCi Zetec estate	113	16,545
Focus	1.8 TDCi Ghia estate	113	17,520

Model	Derivative	BHP	UK price
Focus	1.8 TDCi Titanium estate	113	17,125
Focus	2.0 TDCi Ghia estate	134	18,270
Focus	2.0 TDCi Titanium estate	134	18,875
Focus	1.6 Coupé-cabrio CC-1	99	16,795
Focus	2.0 16v Coupé-cabrio CC-2	143	17,795
Focus	2.0 TDCi Coupé-cabrio CC-3	134	20,270
Focus C-MAX	1.6 Studio 5dr	99	13,695
Focus C-MAX	1.6 LX 5dr	99	14,195
Focus C-MAX	1.6 Zetec 5dr	99	15,270
Focus C-MAX	1.6 Ti-VCT LX	113	14,445
Focus C-MAX	1.6 Ti-VCT Zetec	113	14,445
Focus C-MAX	1.8 LX	118	14,695
Focus C-MAX	1.8 Zetec	118	15,770
Focus C-MAX	1.8 Ghia	118	16,795
Focus C-MAX	2.0 Zetec	143	16,270
Focus C-MAX	2.0 Ghia	143	17,295
Focus C-MAX	1.6 TDCi LX	89	15,195
Focus C-MAX	1.6 TDCi Zetec	89	16,270
Focus C-MAX	1.8 TDCi LX	113	16,195
Focus C-MAX	1.8 TDCi Zetec	113	17,270
Focus C-MAX	1.8 TDCi Ghia	113	18,295
Focus C-MAX	2.0 TDCi Zetec	134	18,020
Focus C-MAX	2.0 TDCi Ghia	134	19,045
Mondeo	1.8 LX 5dr	123	15,995
Mondeo	1.8 Zetec 5dr	123	16,995
Mondeo	1.8 SCi Ghia 5dr	128	18,495
Mondeo	1.8 SCi Ghia X 5dr	128	20,495
Mondeo	2.0 LX 5dr	145	16,495
Mondeo	2.0 Zetec 5dr	145	17,495
Mondeo	2.0 Ghia 5dr	145	18,495
Mondeo	2.0 Ghia X 5dr	145	20,495
Mondeo	2.0 Titanium 5dr	145	18,495
Mondeo	2.0 Titanium X 5dr	145	20,495
Mondeo	2.5 Ghia X auto 5dr	168	22,995
Mondeo	2.5 Titanium X auto 5dr	168	22,995
Mondeo	3.0 Ghia X 5dr	217	22,245
Mondeo	3.0 Titanium X 5dr	217	22,245
Mondeo	ST220 5dr	217	24,495
Mondeo	2.0 TDCi LX 5dr	89	16,495
Mondeo	2.0 TDCi LX 5dr	113	16,995
Mondeo	2.0 TDCi Zetec 5dr	113	17,995
Mondeo	2.0 TDCi Ghia 5dr	113	18,995
Mondeo	2.0 TDCi Titanium 5dr	113	18,995
Mondeo	2.0 TDCi LX 5dr	128	17,495
Mondeo	2.0 TDCi Zetec 5dr	128	18,495
Mondeo	2.0 TDCi Ghia 5dr	128	19,495
Mondeo	2.0 TDCi Ghia X 5dr	128	21,495
Mondeo	2.0 TDCi Titanium 5dr	128	19,495
Mondeo	2.0 TDCi Titanium X 5dr	128	21,495
Mondeo	2.2 TDCi Zetec 5dr	153	18,995
Mondeo	2.2 TDCi Ghia 5dr	153	19,995
Mondeo	2.2 TDCi Ghia X 5dr	153	21,995
Mondeo	2.2 TDCi Titanium 5dr	153	19,995
Mondeo	2.2 TDCi Titanium X 5dr	153	21,995
Mondeo	2.2 TDCi ST 5dr	153	22,795
Mondeo	1.8 LX saloon	123	15,995
Mondeo	1.8 Zetec saloon	123	16,995
Mondeo	1.8 SCi Ghia saloon	128	18,495
Mondeo	1.8 SCi Ghia X saloon	128	20,495
Mondeo	2.0 LX saloon	145	16,495
Mondeo	2.0 Zetec saloon	145	17,495
Mondeo	2.0 Ghia saloon	145	18,495
Mondeo	2.0 Ghia X saloon	145	20,495
Mondeo	2.0 Titanium saloon	145	18,495
Mondeo	2.0 Titanium X saloon	145	20,495
Mondeo	2.5 Ghia X auto saloon	168	22,995
Mondeo	2.5 Titanium X auto saloon	168	22,995
Mondeo	3.0 Ghia X saloon	217	22,245
Mondeo	3.0 Titanium X saloon	217	22,245
Mondeo	ST220 saloon	217	24,495
Mondeo	2.0 TDCi LX saloon	89	16,495
Mondeo	2.0 TDCi LX saloon	113	16,995
Mondeo	2.0 TDCi Zetec saloon	113	17,995
Mondeo	2.0 TDCi Ghia saloon	113	18,995
Mondeo	2.0 TDCi Titanium saloon	113	18,995
Mondeo	2.0 TDCi LX saloon	128	17,495
Mondeo	2.0 TDCi Zetec saloon	128	18,495
Mondeo	2.0 TDCi Ghia saloon	128	19,495
Mondeo	2.0 TDCi Ghia X saloon	128	21,495
Mondeo	2.0 TDCi Titanium saloon	128	19,495
Mondeo	2.0 TDCi Titanium X saloon	128	21,495
Mondeo	2.2 TDCi Zetec saloon	153	18,995
Mondeo	2.2 TDCi Ghia saloon	153	19,995
Mondeo	2.2 TDCi Ghia X saloon	153	21,995
Mondeo	2.2 TDCi Titanium saloon	153	19,995
Mondeo	2.2 TDCi Titanium X saloon	153	21,995
Mondeo	2.2 TDCi ST saloon	153	22,795
Mondeo	1.8 LX estate	123	15,995
Mondeo	1.8 Zetec estate	123	16,995
Mondeo	1.8 SCi Ghia estate	128	18,495
Mondeo	1.8 SCi Ghia X estate	128	20,495
Mondeo	2.0 LX estate	145	16,495
Mondeo	2.0 Zetec estate	145	17,495
Mondeo	2.0 Ghia estate	145	18,495
Mondeo	2.0 Ghia X estate	145	20,495
Mondeo	2.0 Titanium estate	145	18,495
Mondeo	2.0 Titanium X estate	145	20,495
Mondeo	2.5 Ghia X auto estate	168	22,995
Mondeo	2.5 Titanium X auto estate	168	22,995
Mondeo	3.0 Ghia X estate	217	22,245
Mondeo	3.0 Titanium X estate	217	22,245
Mondeo	ST220 estate	217	24,495
Mondeo	2.0 TDCi LX estate	89	17,495
Mondeo	2.0 TDCi LX estate	113	17,995
Mondeo	2.0 TDCi Zetec estate	113	18,995
Mondeo	2.0 TDCi Ghia estate	113	19,995
Mondeo	2.0 TDCi Titanium estate	113	19,995
Mondeo	2.0 TDCi LX estate	128	18,495
Mondeo	2.0 TDCi Zetec estate	128	19,495
Mondeo	2.0 TDCi Ghia estate	128	20,495
Mondeo	2.0 TDCi Ghia X estate	128	22,495
Mondeo	2.0 TDCi Titanium estate	128	20,495
Mondeo	2.0 TDCi Titanium X estate	128	22,495
Mondeo	2.2 TDCi Zetec estate	153	19,995
Mondeo	2.2 TDCi Ghia estate	153	20,995
Mondeo	2.2 TDCi Ghia X estate	153	22,995
Mondeo	2.2 TDCi Titanium estate	153	20,995
Mondeo	2.2 TDCi Titanium X estate	153	22,995
Mondeo	2.2 TDCi ST estate	153	22,795
Galaxy	2.0 LX	143	19,495
Galaxy	2.0 Zetec	143	21,495
Galaxy	2.0 Ghia	143	22,495
Galaxy	1.8 TDCi LX	99	19,495
Galaxy	1.8 TDCi LX 5-speed	123	20,295
Galaxy	1.8 TDCi LX 6-speed	123	20,495
Galaxy	1.8 TDCi Zetec 5-speed	123	22,295
Galaxy	1.8 TDCi Zetec 6-speed	123	22,495
Galaxy	1.8 TDCi Zetec	123	22,295
Galaxy	1.8 TDCi Ghia	123	23,495
Galaxy	2.0 TDCi LX	138	20,995
Galaxy	2.0 TDCi Zetec	138	22,995
Galaxy	2.0 TDCi Ghia	138	23,995
S-MAX	2.0 LX	143	16,995
S-MAX	2.0 Zetec	143	18,995
S-MAX	2.0 Titanium	143	19,995
S-MAX	2.5 Zetec	217	20,495
S-MAX	2.5 Titanium	217	21,995
S-MAX	1.8 TDCi LX 5-speed	123	17,795

Model	Derivative	BHP	UK price
S-MAX	1.8 TDCi Zetec 5-speed	123	19,295
S-MAX	1.8 TDCi Titanium 5-speed	123	20,795
S-MAX	1.8 TDCi LX 6-speed	123	17,995
S-MAX	1.8 TDCi Zetec 6-speed	123	19,495
S-MAX	1.8 TDCi Titanium 6-speed	123	20,995
S-MAX	2.0 TDCi LX	138	18,495
S-MAX	2.0 TDCi Zetec	138	19,995
S-MAX	2.0 TDCi Titanium	138	21,495
HONDA			
Jazz	1.2	76	8,795
Jazz	1.4 SE	82	10,695
Jazz	1.4 Sport	82	11,695
Civic	1.4 S	82	12,930
Civic	1.4 SE	82	13,995
Civic	1.8 ES	138	15,650
Civic	1.8 EX	138	16,850
Civic	1.8 S	138	13,785
Civic	1.8 SE	138	14,650
Civic	1.8 Sport	138	15,350
Civic	2.2 i-CTDi ES	138	16,895
Civic	2.2 i-CTDi EX	138	18,095
Civic	2.2 i-CTDi S	138	15,030
Civic	2.2 i-CTDi SE	138	15,895
Civic	2.2 i-CTDi Sport	138	16,595
Civic	1.3 hybrid	113	16,265
Accord	2.0 SE	153	17,430
Accord	2.0 Type-S	153	19,055
Accord	2.0 EX	153	20,155
Accord	2.4 Type-S	187	19,955
Accord	2.4 EX	187	21,055
Accord	2.2 i-CTDi Sport	138	19,320
Accord	2.2 i-CTDi EX	138	21,125
Accord	Tourer 2.0i SE	153	18,655
Accord	Tourer 2.0i EX	153	21,355
Accord	Tourer 2.4i Type-S	187	21,175
Accord	Tourer 2.4i EX	187	22,275
Accord	Tourer 2.2 i-CTDi Sport	138	20,525
Accord	Tourer 2.2 i-CTDi EX	138	22,330
Legend	3.5	291	36,250
S2000		237	27,295
S2000	GT	237	27,845
FR-V	1.7 SE	126	15,390
FR-V	2.0 SE	148	16,415
FR-V	2.0 Sport	148	17,115
FR-V	2.2 i-CDTi SE	138	17,590
FR-V	2.2 i-CDTi Sport	138	18,290
CR-V	2.0i SE	148	17,725
CR-V	2.0i Sport	148	19,225
CR-V	2.0i Executive	148	21,925
CR-V	2.2 i-CDTi SE	138	18,900
CR-V	2.2 i-CDTi Sport	138	20,400
CR-V	2.2 i-CDTi Executive	138	23,100
HYUNDAI			
Amica	1.1 GSi 5dr	62	5,990
Getz	1.1 GSi 3dr	66	7,490
Getz	1.1 CDX 5dr	66	8,590
Getz	1.4 GSi 3dr	95	8,090
Getz	1.4 CDX 5dr	95	9,340
Getz	1.5 CRTD GSi 5dr	87	9,210
Getz	1.5 CRTD CDX+ 3dr	87	10,060
Matrix	1.6 GSi	102	10,995
Matrix	1.8 CDX	121	12,220
Matrix	1.5 CRDi VGT	81	11,690
Coupé	1.6 S	103	15,145
Coupé	2.0 SE	141	17,170
Coupé	2.7 V6	165	19,190
Sonata	2.0 CDX	143	16,995
Sonata	3.3 V6 CDX	232	19,995
Sonata	2.0 CRTD CDX	138	17,995

Model	Derivative	BHP	UK price
Tucson	2.0 GSi	140	14,820
Tucson	2.0 CDX	140	17,170
Tucson	2.7 CDX	173	19,590
Tucson	2.0 CRTD GSi	111	16,820
Tucson	2.0 CRTD CDX	111	18,170
Santa Fe	2.7 CDX 5-seater	186	23,840
Santa Fe	2.7 CDX 7-seater	186	24,840
Santa Fe	2.7 CDX+ 5-seater	186	25,040
Santa Fe	2.7 CDX+ 7-seater	186	26,040
Santa Fe	2.2 CRTD GSi 5-seater	148	20,995
Santa Fe	2.2 CRTD GSi 7-seater	148	22,020
Santa Fe	2.2 CRTD CDX 5-seater	148	22,820
Santa Fe	2.2 CRTD CDX 7-seater	148	23,820
Santa Fe	2.2 CRTD CDX+ 5-seater	148	24,020
Santa Fe	2.2 CRTD CDX+ 7-seater	148	25,020
Terracan	2.9 CRTD	160	19,370
Trajet	2.0 GSi	139	15,520
Trajet	2.0 CRTD GSi	111	16,520
INVICTA			
S1	320	320	106,000
S1	420	420	120,000
S1	600	600	150,000
JAGUAR			
X-type	2.5 S	191	22,815
X-type	2.5 Sport	191	23,815
X-type	2.5 SE	191	26,815
X-type	3.0 Sport Premium	228	30,040
X-type	3.0 Sovereign	228	30,040
X-type	2.0d Classic	128	19,990
X-type	2.0d S	128	20,990
X-type	2.0d Sport	128	21,990
X-type	2.2d S	152	21,995
X-type	2.2d SE	152	25,995
X-type	2.2d Sovereign	152	28,495
X-type	2.5 S estate	191	23,940
X-type	2.5 SE estate	191	27,940
X-type	3.0 Sport Premium estate	228	31,165
X-type	2.0d S estate	126	22,165
X-type	2.0d SE estate	126	26,165
X-type	2.2d S estate	152	23,165
X-type	2.2d SE estate	152	27,165
X-type	2.2d Sovereign estate	152	29,665
S-type	3.0 R	240	28,045
S-type	3.0 S	240	30,040
S-type	3.0 SE	240	33,040
S-type	3.0 Sport	240	33,040
S-type	4.2 V8 SE	300	38,540
S-type	4.2 V8 Sport	300	39,640
S-type	R	400	50,040
S-type	2.7d	206	28,895
S-type	2.7d S	206	30,895
S-type	2.7d SE	206	34,020
S-type	2.7d Sport	206	33,995
XJ6	3.0 Executive	240	42,040
XJ6	3.0 Sovereign	240	48,040
XJ8	3.5 Sport Premium	262	50,040
XJ8	4.2 Sovereign	300	56,540
XJ8	4.2 Sovereign LWB	300	62,040
XJR		400	62,040
XJ8	4.2 Super V8 LWB	400	75,040
XJ6	2.7D Executive	206	44,020
XJ6	2.7D Sport Premium	206	50,020
XJ6	2.7D Sovereign	206	50,020
XK	4.2	300	59,000
XK	4.2 Convertible	300	65,000
XKR	4.2	420	67,495
XKR	4.2 Convertible	420	73,495

Model	Derivative	BHP	UK price
JEEP			
Wrangler	4.0 Sport	174	16,150
Wrangler	4.0 Sahara	174	19,400
Cherokee	3.7 Limited	201	22,535
Cherokee	2.8 CRD Sport	161	19,935
Cherokee	2.8 CRD Sport auto	161	20,935
Cherokee	2.8 CRD Limited	161	22,535
Cherokee	2.8 CRD Limited auto	161	23,535
Grand Cherokee	5.7 Limited	322	34,535
Grand Cherokee	SRT-8	425	40,585
Grand Cherokee	3.0 CRD Overland	215	33,535
Grand Cherokee	3.0 CRD Limited	215	31,035
Commander	5.7 Hemi	322	34,535
Commander	3.0 CRD Predator	215	27,490
Commander	3.0 CRD Limited	215	31,035
KIA			
Picanto	1.0 S	64	5,895
Picanto	1.0 GS	64	6,395
Picanto	1.1 LX	64	7,195
Picanto	1.1 SE+	64	7,795
Rio	1.4 GS	96	8,495
Rio	1.4 LX	96	9,495
Rio	1.5 CRDi GS	109	9,295
Rio	1.5 CRDi LX	109	10,295
Cerato	1.6 GS 5dr	104	10,295
Cerato	1.6 LX 5dr	104	10,995
Cerato	1.5 CRDi GS 5dr	109	10,995
Cerato	1.5 CRDi LX 5dr	109	11,695
Cerato	1.6 LX saloon	104	10,995
Cerato	2.0 SE saloon	141	12,495
Cerato	1.5 CRDi LX saloon	109	11,695
Magentis	2.0 GS	142	14,495
Magentis	2.7 LS	185	17,495
Magentis	2.0 CRDi GS	138	15,495
Carens	2.0 GS	136	10,495
Carens	2.0 CRDi LX	111	11,495
Carens	2.0 CRDi LE	111	12,495
Sedona	2.9 CRDi GS	182	17,495
Sedona	2.9 CRDi LS	182	19,495
Sedona	2.9 CRDi TS	182	21,495
Sportage	2.0 XE	140	15,295
Sportage	2.0 XS	140	16,695
Sportage	2.7 XS	173	19,295
Sportage	2.0 CRDi XE	111	16,495
Sportage	2.0 CRDi XS	111	18,195
Sorento	3.3 XS	192	23,995
Sorento	3.3 XT	192	25,995
Sorento	2.5 CRDi XE	168	19,995
Sorento	2.5 CRDi XS	168	22,995
Sorento	2.5 CRDi XT	168	24,995
LAMBORGHINI			
Gallardo	5.0	492	117,000
Gallardo	5.0 SE	520	134,000
Murciélago	6.2	570	175,000
Murciélago	Roadster	570	189,950
Murciélago	LP640	631	190,000
LAND ROVER			
Defender	90 TD5 hard top 3dr	122	18,795
Defender	90 TD5 station wagon 3dr	122	20,495
Defender	90 TD5 County hard top 3dr	122	20,195
Defender	90 TD5 County 3dr	122	21,995
Defender	90 TD5 XS 3dr	122	25,595
Defender	110 TD5 hard top 5dr	122	20,395
Defender	110 TD5 station wagon 5dr	122	22,995
Defender	110 TD5 County hard top 5dr	122	21,695
Defender	110 TD5 County 5dr	122	24,495
Defender	110 TD5 XS 5dr	122	27,995
Freelander	3.2 GS	230	26,490
Freelander	3.2 XS	230	28,540

Model	Derivative	BHP	UK price
Freelander	3.2 SE	230	31,540
Freelander	3.2 HSE	230	33,990
Freelander	TD4 S	160	20,935
Freelander	TD4 GS	160	23,435
Freelander	TD4 XS	160	25,485
Freelander	TD4 SE	160	28,485
Freelander	TD4 HSE	160	30,935
Discovery	4.4 V8 S	295	38,040
Discovery	4.4 V8 SE	295	43,040
Discovery	4.4 V8 HSE	295	48,540
Discovery	TDV6 5-seater	193	27,040
Discovery	TDV6 7-seater	193	29,040
Discovery	TDV6 S	193	32,040
Discovery	TDV6 SE	193	37,040
Discovery	TDV6 HSE	193	43,540
Range Rover	Sport V8 SE	295	45,545
Range Rover	Sport V8 HSE	295	50,545
Range Rover	Sport V8 Supercharged	385	58,045
Range Rover	Sport TDV6 S	188	35,545
Range Rover	Sport TDV6 SE	188	40,545
Range Rover	Sport TDV6 HSE	188	44,545
Range Rover	Sport TDV8 HSE	268	53,120
Range Rover	V8 HSE	305	55,075
Range Rover	V8 Vogue	305	61,825
Range Rover	V8 Vogue SE	305	69,875
Range Rover	V8 Supercharged Vogue SE	400	74,795
Range Rover	TDV8 HSE	272	53,995
Range Rover	TDV8 Vogue	272	61,825
Range Rover	TDV8 Vogue SE	272	68,825
LEXUS			
IS 250	″	204	22,488
IS 250	SE	204	25,488
IS 250	SE-L	204	28,088
IS 250	Sport	204	26,588
IS 220d		175	22,243
IS 220d	SE	175	25,243
IS 220d	SE-L	175	27,843
IS 220d	Sport	175	26,988
GS 300		245	30,848
GS 300	SE	245	36,348
GS 300	SE-L	245	38,448
GS 430		279	47,203
GS 450h		292	38,058
GS 450h	SE	292	43,963
GS 450h	SE-L	292	46,808
RX 350		272	31,933
RX 350	SE	272	36,083
RX 350	SE-L	272	42,548
RX 400h		269	36,393
RX 400h	SE	269	40,288
RX 400h	SE-L	269	45,258
SC 430		282	54,778
LOTUS			
Elise	S	134	23,995
Elise	R	189	28,995
Exige		189	30,945
Exige	S	218	34,895
Europa	S	197	33,895
MARCOS			
TSO	GT2	475	49,950
Marcasite	TS250	180	29,950
Marcasite	TS500	320	34,950
MASERATI			
Coupé	GT	390	56,650
Coupé	Gransport	395	66,645
Spyder	Gransport	390	69,040
Quattroporte	4.2	400	74,595
Quattroporte	4.2 Sport GT	400	80,595
Quattroporte	4.2 Executive GT	400	83,195

Model	Derivative	BHP	UK price
MAYBACH			
Maybach	57	543	256,465
Maybach	57 S	612	293,135
Maybach	62	543	298,900
MAZDA			
2	1.25 S	74	8,700
2	1.4 S auto	79	9,600
2	1.4 Antares	79	9,200
2	1.4 Capella	79	10,100
2	1.6 Capella	100	10,600
2	1.4 D S	68	9,730
2	1.4 D Antares	68	9,730
2	1.4 D Capella	68	10,630
3	1.4 S 5dr	83	11,400
3	1.4 TS 5dr	83	12,700
3	1.6 TS 5dr	104	13,300
3	1.6 TS2 5dr	104	14,260
3	2.0 Sport 5dr	148	16,330
3	MPS	260	17,000
3	1.6 D S	89	12,900
3	1.6 D TS	89	14,800
3	1.6 D TS2	89	15,700
3	1.6 TS saloon	104	13,300
3	1.6 TS2 saloon	104	14,260
3	2.0 Sport saloon	148	16,330
3	1.6 D TS2 saloon	107	15,700
5	1.8 TS	113	14,350
5	1.8 TS2	113	15,150
5	2.0 Sport	143	16,350
5	2.0 D TS	108	15,950
5	2.0 D TS2	108	16,750
6	1.8 S 5dr	118	14,150
6	2.0 TS 5dr	145	15,650
6	2.0 TS2 5dr	145	17,150
6	2.3 Sport 5dr	164	18,650
6	2.0 D S 5dr	119	15,250
6	2.0 D TS 5dr	119	16,250
6	2.0 D TS 5dr	141	16,750
6	2.0 D TS2 5dr	141	18,250
6	2.0 D Sport 5dr	141	19,250
6	1.8 TS saloon	118	15,150
6	2.0 TS saloon	145	15,650
6	2.0 TS2 saloon	145	17,150
6	MPS saloon	256	23,995
6	2.0 D TS saloon	141	16,750
6	2.0 D TS2 saloon	141	18,250
6	2.0 S estate	145	15,650
6	2.0 TS estate	145	16,650
6	2.0 TS2 estate	145	18,150
6	2.0 D S estate	119	16,250
6	2.0 D TS estate	141	17,750
6	2.0 D TS2 estate	141	19,250
MX-5	1.8	125	15,650
MX-5	2.0	158	17,450
MX-5	2.0 Sport	158	18,950
MX-5	1.8 Roadster-Coupé	93	18,210
MX-5	2.0 Roadster-Coupé	118	19,210
MX-5	2.0 Sport Roadster-Coupé	118	20,710
RX-8		189	21,400
RX-8		228	22,900
MERCEDES-BENZ			
A	150 Classic 3dr	95	13,770
A	150 Classic 5dr	95	14,520
A	150 Classic SE 3dr	95	14,070
A	150 Classic SE 5dr	95	14,820
A	150 Elegance SE 3dr	95	15,701
A	150 Elegance SE 5dr	95	16,320
A	150 Avantgarde SE 3dr	95	15,765
A	150 Avantgarde SE 5dr	95	16,615

Model	Derivative	BHP	UK price
A	170 Classic 3dr	116	15,020
A	170 Classic 5dr	116	15,770
A	170 Classic SE 3dr	116	15,320
A	170 Classic SE 5dr	116	16,070
A	170 Elegance SE 3dr	116	16,820
A	170 Elegance SE 5dr	116	17,570
A	170 Avantgarde SE 3dr	116	17,015
A	170 Avantgarde SE 5dr	116	17,765
A	200 Classic 3dr	134	16,245
A	200 Classic 5dr	134	16,995
A	200 Classic SE 3dr	134	16,545
A	200 Classic SE 5dr	134	17,295
A	200 Elegance SE 3dr	134	18,045
A	200 Elegance SE 5dr	134	18,795
A	200 Avantgarde SE 3dr	134	18,240
A	200 Avantgarde SE 5dr	134	18,990
A	200 Turbo 3dr	190	20,785
A	200 Turbo 5dr	190	21,535
A	160 CDI Classic 3dr	82	14,560
A	160 CDI Classic 5dr	82	15,310
A	160 CDI Classic SE 3dr	82	14,860
A	160 CDI Classic SE 5dr	82	15,610
A	160 CDI Elegance SE 3dr	82	16,360
A	160 CDI Elegance SE 5dr	82	17,110
A	160 CDI Avantgarde SE 3dr	82	16,555
A	160 CDI Avantgarde SE 5dr	82	17,305
A	180 CDI Classic 3dr	108	15,830
A	180 CDI Classic 5dr	108	16,580
A	180 CDI Classic SE 3dr	108	16,130
A	180 CDI Classic SE 5dr	108	16,880
A	180 CDI Elegance SE 3dr	108	17,630
A	180 CDI Elegance SE 5dr	108	18,380
A	180 CDI Avantgarde SE 3dr	108	17,825
A	180 CDI Avantgarde SE 5dr	108	18,575
A	200 CDI Elegance SE 3dr	140	19,510
A	200 CDI Elegance SE 5dr	140	20,260
A	200 CDI Avantgarde SE 3dr	140	19,705
A	200 CDI Avantgarde SE 5dr	140	20,455
B	150	95	17,235
B	150 SE	95	18,185
B	170	116	18,485
B	170 SE	116	19,195
B	200 SE	134	20,445
B	200 Turbo SE	190	22,795
B	180 CDI	108	18,995
B	180 CDI SE	108	19,945
B	200 CDI SE	140	21,575
C	160 Sportcoupé	122	19,520
C	160 SE Sportcoupé	122	20,220
C	160 Evolution Panorama Sportcoupé	122	21,970
C	160 Sport Sportcoupé	122	21,350
C	180 Kompressor Sportcoupé	143	20,670
C	180 Kompressor SE Sportcoupé	143	21,370
C	180 Kompressor Evolution Sportcoupé	143	19,995
C	180 K Evolution Panorama Sportcoupé	143	23,120
C	180 Kompressor Sport Sportcoupé	143	22,500
C	200 Kompressor Sportcoupé	163	22,215
C	200 Kompressor SE Sportcoupé	163	22,915
C	200 K Evolution Panorama Sportcoupé	163	24,665
C	200 Kompressor Sport Sportcoupé	163	24,045
C	230 SE Sportcoupé	204	24,975
C	230 Evolution Panorama Sportcoupé	204	26,725
C	230 Sport Sportcoupé	204	26,805
C	350 SE Sportcoupé	268	27,975
C	350 Evolution Panorama Sportcoupé	268	29,725
C	350 Sport Sportcoupé	268	29,805
C	200 CDI Sportcoupé	122	22,225
C	200 CDI SE Sportcoupé	122	22,925
C	200 CDI Evolution Panorama Sportcoupé	122	24,675

Model	Derivative	BHP	UK price
C	200 CDI Sport Sportcoupé	122	24,055
C	220 CDI Sportcoupé	150	23,265
C	220 CDI SE Sportcoupé	150	23,965
C	220 CDI Evolution S Sportcoupé	150	22,295
C	220 CDI Evolution Panorama Sportcoupé	150	25,715
C	220 CDI Sport Sportcoupé	150	25,095
C	180 Kompressor Classic	143	21,550
C	180 Kompressor Classic SE	143	22,250
C	180 Kompressor Elegance SE	143	22,750
C	180 Kompressor Avantgarde SE	143	22,750
C	180 Kompressor Sport	143	23,325
C	200 Kompressor Classic	163	23,300
C	200 Kompressor Classic SE	163	24,000
C	200 Kompressor Elegance SE	163	24,500
C	200 Kompressor Avantgarde SE	163	24,500
C	200 Kompressor Sport	163	25,130
C	230 Classic	204	25,590
C	230 Classic SE	204	26,290
C	230 Elegance SE	204	26,790
C	230 Avantgarde SE	204	26,790
C	230 Sport	204	27,420
C	280 Classic	228	27,400
C	280 Classic SE	228	28,100
C	280 Elegance SE	228	28,600
C	280 Avantgarde SE	228	28,600
C	280 Sport	228	29,230
C	350 Elegance SE	268	33,275
C	350 Avantgarde SE	268	33,275
C	350 Sport	268	35,105
C	55 AMG	362	48,790
C	200 CDI Classic	122	23,435
C	200 CDI Classic SE	122	24,135
C	200 CDI Elegance SE	122	24,635
C	200 CDI Avantgarde SE	122	24,635
C	200 CDI Sport	122	25,265
C	220 CDI Classic	150	24,500
C	220 CDI Classic SE	150	25,200
C	220 CDI Elegance SE	150	25,700
C	220 CDI Elegance SE	150	25,700
C	220 CDI Sport	150	26,330
C	320 CDI Elegance SE	224	31,045
C	320 CDI Avantgarde SE	224	31,045
C	320 CDI Sport	224	32,875
C	180 Kompressor Classic estate	143	22,500
C	180 Kompressor Classic SE estate	143	23,200
C	180 Kompressor Elegance SE estate	143	23,700
C	180 Kompressor Avantgarde SE estate	143	23,700
C	180 Kompressor Sport estate	143	24,330
C	200 Kompressor Classic estate	163	24,250
C	200 Kompressor Classic SE estate	163	24,950
C	200 Kompressor Elegance SE estate	163	25,450
C	200 Kompressor Avantgarde SE estate	163	25,450
C	200 Kompressor Sport estate	163	26,080
C	230 Classic estate	204	26,540
C	230 Classic SE estate	204	27,240
C	230 Elegance SE estate	204	27,740
C	230 Avantgarde SE estate	204	27,740
C	230 Sport estate	204	28,370
C	280 Classic estate	228	28,350
C	280 Classic SE estate	228	29,050
C	280 Elegance SE estate	228	29,550
C	280 Avantgarde SE estate	228	29,550
C	280 Sport estate	228	30,180
C	350 Elegance SE estate	268	34,225
C	350 Avantgarde SE estate	268	34,225
C	350 Sport estate	268	36,055
C	55 AMG estate	355	49,740
C	200 CDI Classic estate	122	24,395
C	200 CDI Classic SE estate	122	25,095
C	200 CDI Elegance SE estate	122	25,595
C	200 CDI Avantgarde SE estate	122	25,595
C	200 CDI Sport estate	122	26,225
C	220 CDI Classic estate	150	25,460
C	220 CDI Classic SE estate	150	26,160
C	220 CDI Elegance SE estate	150	26,660
C	220 CDI Avantgarde SE estate	150	26,660
C	220 CDI Sport estate	150	27,290
C	320 CDI Elegance SE estate	224	31,995
C	320 CDI Avantgarde SE estate	224	31,995
C	320 CDI Sport estate	224	33,825
E	200 Kompressor Classic	184	27,520
E	200 Kompressor Elegance	184	29,620
E	200 Kompressor Avantgarde	184	30,120
E	200 Kompressor Sport	184	31,090
E	280 Classic	231	31,770
E	280 Elegance	231	36,990
E	280 Avantgarde	231	34,370
E	280 Sport	231	35,340
E	350 Elegance	272	36,990
E	350 Avantgarde	272	37,440
E	350 Sport	272	38,460
E	500 Elegance	388	47,135
E	500 Avantgarde	388	47,635
E	500 Sport	388	48,605
E	63 AMG	503	66,545
E	220 CDI Classic	170	28,965
E	220 CDI Elegance	170	31,065
E	220 CDI Avantgarde	170	31,565
E	280 CDI Classic	190	32,650
E	280 CDI Elegance	190	34,750
E	280 CDI Avantgarde	190	35,250
E	280 CDI Sport	190	36,220
E	320 CDI Elegance	224	36,895
E	320 CDI Avantgarde	224	37,395
E	320 CDI Sport	224	38,365
E	200 Kompressor Classic estate	184	29,320
E	200 Kompressor Elegance estate	184	31,420
E	200 Kompressor Avantgarde estate	184	31,920
E	200 Kompressor Sport estate	184	32,890
E	280 Classic estate	231	33,590
E	280 Elegance estate	231	35,690
E	280 Avantgarde estate	231	36,190
E	280 Sport estate	231	37,160
E	350 Elegance estate	272	38,790
E	350 Avantgarde estate	272	39,290
E	350 Sport estate	272	40,260
E	500 Elegance estate	388	48,635
E	500 Avantgarde estate	388	49,135
E	500 Sport estate	388	50,105
E	63 AMG estate	514	68,045
E	220 CDI Classic estate	170	30,800
E	220 CDI Elegance estate	170	32,900
E	220 CDI Avantgarde estate	170	33,400
E	280 CDI Classic estate	190	34,450
E	280 CDI Elegance estate	190	36,550
E	280 CDI Avantgarde estate	190	37,050
E	280 CDI Sport estate	190	38,020
E	320 CDI Elegance estate	224	38,695
E	320 CDI Avantgarde estate	224	39,195
E	320 CDI Sport estate	224	40,165
CLS	350	268	43,440
CLS	500	306	52,145
CLS	63 AMG	503	72,995
CLS	320 CDI	221	43,000
S	350	268	56,720
S	500	382	69,770
S	600	517	102,000
S	65 AMG	604	145,365

Model	Derivative	BHP	UK price
S	320 CDI	232	54,975
R	350	268	38,515
R	350 L	268	40,015
R	350 SE	268	41,465
R	350 L SE	268	42,965
R	350 Sport	268	41,465
R	350 L Sport	268	42,965
R	500 SE	382	50,035
R	500 L SE	382	51,535
R	63 L AMG	510	74,115
R	280 CDI	188	36,420
R	280 CDI SE	188	39,370
R	280 CDI Sport	188	39,370
R	320 CDI	221	38,520
R	320 L CDI	221	40,020
R	320 CDI SE	221	41,420
R	320 CDI Sport	221	41,420
CLK	200 Kompressor Elegance	161	29,475
CLK	200 Kompressor Avantgarde	161	29,475
CLK	200 Kompressor Sport	161	31,975
CLK	280 Elegance	228	33,290
CLK	280 Avantgarde	228	33,290
CLK	280 Sport	228	35,790
CLK	350 Elegance	272	37,570
CLK	350 Avantgarde	272	37,570
CLK	350 Sport	272	40,070
CLK	55 AMG	362	60,465
CLK	63 AMG	474	65,215
CLK	220 CDI Elegance	150	29,975
CLK	220 CDI Avantgarde	150	29,975
CLK	220 CDI Sport	150	32,475
CLK	320 CDI Elegance	221	34,130
CLK	320 CDI Avantgarde	221	34,130
CLK	320 CDI Sport	221	36,630
CLK	200 Kompressor Elegance cabrio	163	33,075
CLK	200 Kompressor Avantgarde cabrio	163	33,075
CLK	200 Kompressor Sport cabrio	163	35,575
CLK	280 Elegance cabrio	228	36,890
CLK	280 Avantgarde cabrio	228	36,890
CLK	280 Sport cabrio	228	39,390
CLK	350 Elegance cabrio	272	41,170
CLK	350 Avantgarde cabrio	272	41,170
CLK	350 Sport cabrio	272	43,670
CLK	500 Elegance cabrio	383	51,090
CLK	500 Avantgarde cabrio	383	51,090
CLK	500 Sport cabrio	302	51,090
CLK	500 Sport cabrio	383	52,385
CLK	55 AMG cabrio	362	64,065
CLK	63 AMG cabrio	474	68,815
CL	500	388	79,550
CL	600	517	106,565
SLR	McLaren	460	313,665
SLK	200 Kompressor	161	28,070
SLK	280	228	31,000
SLK	350	268	34,955
SLK	55 AMG	355	50,555
SL	350	272	62,885
SL	500	388	75,880
SL	600	517	101,220
SL	55 AMG	500	97,265
SL	65 AMG	612	147,960
ML	350	268	37,215
ML	350 SE	268	39,965
ML	350 Sport	268	39,965
ML	500 SE	302	50,430
ML	500 Sport	302	50,430
ML	63 AMG	503	73,965
ML	280 CDI	188	35,370
ML	280 CDI SE	188	38,120

Model	Derivative	BHP	UK price
ML	280 CDI Sport	188	38,120
ML	320 CDI	221	37,220
ML	320 CDI SE	221	39,970
ML	320 CDI Sport	221	39,970
ML	420 CDI	302	50,435
GL	500	383	65,720
GL	320 CDI	221	51,675
GL	420 CDI	302	63,075

MINI

Model	Derivative	BHP	UK price
Mini	One	90	10,995
Mini	1.4D	88	12,220
Mini	Cooper	115	12,395
Mini	Cooper S	170	15,520
Mini	Cooper S Works GP	215	22,000
Mini	One Cabrio	90	13,595
Mini	Cooper Cabrio	115	14,925
Mini	Cooper S Cabrio	170	17,960

MITSUBISHI

Model	Derivative	BHP	UK price
Colt	1.1 CZ1 3dr	74	7,494
Colt	1.1 CZ1 5dr	74	7,994
Colt	1.3 CZ2 3dr	95	8,994
Colt	1.3 CZ2 5dr	95	9,494
Colt	1.5 CZ3 3dr	107	10,494
Colt	1.5 CZ3 5dr	107	10,994
Colt	1.5 CZT 3dr	147	12,999
Colt	1.5 DI-D CZ2 3dr	95	10,494
Colt	1.5 DI-D CZ3 5dr	95	10,994
Colt	CZC 1.5	107	13,999
Colt	CZC 1.5 Turbo	147	15,999
Lancer	1.6 Equippe saloon	96	9,999
Lancer	1.6 Elegance saloon	96	10,749
Lancer	1.6 Equippe estate	96	10,499
Lancer	1.6 Elegance estate	96	11,249
Lancer	2.0 Sport estate	133	11,999
Lancer	Evolution IX FQ-300	305	28,039
Lancer	Evolution IX FQ-320	326	30,039
Lancer	Evolution IX FQ-340	345	33,039
Lancer	Evolution IX FQ-360	366	35,504
Grandis	2.4 Classic	162	18,499
Grandis	2.4 Equippe	162	20,499
Grandis	2.4 Warrior	162	22,499
Grandis	2.0 DI-D Classic	134	19,699
Grandis	2.0 DI-D Elegance	134	23,099
Grandis	2.0 DI-D Warrior	134	23,699
Outlander	2.4 Equippe	158	16,999
Outlander	2.4 Sport	158	18,249
Outlander	2.4 Sport SE	158	18,999
Shogun Sport	3.0 Elegance	168	21,999
Shogun Sport	3.0 Warrior	168	21,999
Shogun Sport	2.5 TD Classic	98	16,999
Shogun Sport	2.5 TD Equippe	98	19,999
Shogun Sport	2.5 TD Warrior	98	20,999
Shogun	3.5 GDI Warrior 3dr	200	27,999
Shogun	3.5 GDI Warrior 5dr	200	31,499
Shogun	3.5 GDI Elegance 5dr	200	31,999
Shogun	3.2 DI-D Classic 3dr	162	21,499
Shogun	3.2 DI-D Equippe 3dr	162	22,999
Shogun	3.2 DI-D Elegance 3dr	162	26,499
Shogun	3.2 DI-D Warrior 3dr	162	27,499
Shogun	3.2 DI-D Classic 5dr	162	25,749
Shogun	3.2 DI-D Equippe 5dr	162	26,999
Shogun	3.2 DI-D Elegance 5dr	162	30,499
Shogun	3.2 DI-D Warrior 5dr	162	30,999

MORGAN

Model	Derivative	BHP	UK price
4/4	1.8 2-seater	125	24,323
Plus 4	2.0 2-seater	145	29,081

Model	Derivative	BHP	UK price
Plus 4	2.0 4-seater	145	32,018
Roadster	3.0 V6 2-seater	223	36,190
Roadster	3.0 V6 4-seater	223	39,127
Aero 8		325	62,500
NISSAN			
Micra	1.2 Initia 3dr	79	8,995
Micra	1.2 Initia 5dr	79	9,645
Micra	1.2 Spirita 3dr	79	9,995
Micra	1.2 Spirita 5dr	79	10,645
Micra	1.2 Sport 3dr	79	10,495
Micra	1.2 Sport 5dr	79	11,145
Micra	1.4 Spirita 3dr	87	10,295
Micra	1.4 Spirita 5dr	87	10,945
Micra	1.4 Sport 3dr	87	10,795
Micra	1.4 Sport 5dr	87	11,445
Micra	1.6 Sport SR 3dr	108	10,995
Micra	1.6 Sport SR 5dr	108	11,645
Micra	1.5 dCi Initia 3dr	85	10,095
Micra	1.5 dCi Initia 5dr	85	10,745
Micra	1.5 dCi Spirita 3dr	85	11,095
Micra	1.5 dCi Spirita 5dr	85	11,745
Micra	1.5 dCi Sport 3dr	85	11,595
Micra	1.5 dCi Sport 5dr	85	12,245
Micra C+C	1.4 Urbis	87	13,250
Micra C+C	1.6 Sport	108	13,995
Micra C+C	1.6 Essenza	108	15,250
Note	1.4 S	87	9,990
Note	1.4 SE	87	10,990
Note	1.6 S	108	10,695
Note	1.6 SE	108	11,695
Note	1.6 SVE	108	12,695
Note	1.5 dCi S	85	10,990
Note	1.5 dCi SE	85	11,990
Note	1.5 dCi SVE	85	12,990
Almera	1.5 Flare 3dr	97	8,995
Almera	1.5 S 3dr	97	10,600
Almera	1.5 S 5dr	97	11,200
Almera	1.5 SE 3dr	97	11,350
Almera	1.5 SE 5dr	97	11,950
Almera	1.5 SX 5dr	97	12,300
Almera	1.5 SVE 3dr	97	12,950
Almera	1.5 SVE 5dr	97	13,550
Primera	1.8 Flare 5dr	114	12,795
Primera	1.8 S 5dr	114	15,495
Primera	1.8 SX 5dr	114	16,695
Primera	1.8 SVE 5dr	114	18,195
Primera	1.8 S estate	114	16,595
Primera	1.8 SX estate	114	17,795
Primera	1.8 SVE estate	114	19,295
350Z	-	296	26,345
350Z	GT	296	28,845
350Z	Roadster	300	27,845
350Z	GT Roadster	300	30,345
X-Trail	2.0 SE	138	16,825
X-Trail	2.5 Columbia	163	20,345
X-Trail	2.5 Aventura	163	22,345
X-Trail	2.2 dCi SE 2WD	134	18,425
X-Trail	2.2 dCi SE 4WD	134	19,925
X-Trail	2.2 dCi Columbia	134	21,325
X-Trail	2.2 dCi Aventura	134	23,325
Murano	3.5	231	29,995
Terrano	2.7 TDi SE	123	18,945
Terrano	3.0 TDi SE	154	22,345
Patrol GR	3.0 TD S	160	26,040
Patrol GR	3.0 TD SVE	160	31,540
Pathfinder	4.0 V6 Aventura	270	30,895
Pathfinder	2.5 dCi Trek	171	22,995
Pathfinder	2.5 dCi Sport	171	25,595
Pathfinder	2.5 dCi Aventura	171	28,595

Model	Derivative	BHP	UK price
NOBLE			
M400		425	55,995
PAGANI			
Zonda	S	555	285,000
Zonda	F	594	390,000
PERODUA			
Kelisa	1.0 GXi SE	54	5,592
Kelisa	1.0 GXi SE	54	6,505
Kenari	1.0 GX	54	6,223
Kenari	1.0 EZi	54	7,037
PEUGEOT			
107	1.0 Urban 3dr	67	7,345
107	1.0 Urban 5dr	67	7,695
1007	1.4 8v Dolce	75	10,850
1007	1.4 Sport 2-Tronic	75	12,095
1007	1.4 16v Sport	90	11,850
1007	1.6 Dolce 2-Tronic	110	11,850
1007	1.6 Sport 2-Tronic	110	12,600
1007	1.4 HDi Dolce	70	11,545
1007	1.4 HDi Sport	70	12,295
Partner	2.0 HDi Escapade	90	11,795
206	1.4 Urban 3dr	75	8,345
206	1.4 Urban 5dr	75	9,445
206	1.4 Verve 3dr	75	9,445
206	1.4 Verve 5dr	75	10,045
206	1.6 Sport 3dr	110	10,695
206	1.6 Sport 5dr	110	11,295
206	1.4 HDi Urban 3dr	68	8,860
206	1.4 HDi Urban 5dr	68	9,960
206	1.4 HDi Verve 3dr	68	9,960
206	1.4 HDi Verve 5dr	68	10,560
206	1.6 HDi Sport 3dr	110	11,890
206	1.6 HDi Sport 5dr	110	12,490
206	SW 1.4 Verve	75	10,545
206	SW 1.4 HDi Verve	68	11,060
206	SW 1.6 HDi Verve	110	12,390
206	CC 1.6 Sport	110	14,145
206	CC 1.6 Allure	110	15,145
206	CC 2.0 Allure	138	15,870
206	CC 1.6 HDi Sport	110	14,840
206	CC 1.6 HDi Allure	110	15,840
207	1.4 Urban 3dr	75	8,995
207	1.4 Urban 5dr	75	9,595
207	1.4 S 3dr	75	9,345
207	1.4 S 5dr	75	9,945
207	1.4 S 16v 3dr	87	9,745
207	1.4 S 16v 5dr	87	10,345
207	1.4 Sport 3dr	87	10,895
207	1.4 Sport 5dr	87	11,495
207	1.6 Sport 3dr	110	11,395
207	1.6 Sport 5dr	110	11,995
207	1.6 SE 5dr	110	12,195
207	1.6 T 150 GT 3dr	150	14,345
207	1.4 HDi Urban 3dr	70	9,895
207	1.4 HDi Urban 5dr	70	10,495
207	1.4 HDi S 3dr	70	10,245
207	1.4 HDi S 5dr	70	10,845
207	1.6 HDi S 3dr	90	11,395
207	1.6 HDi S 5dr	90	11,995
207	1.6 HDi Sport 3dr	90	11,995
207	1.6 HDi Sport 5dr	90	12,595
207	1.6 HDi Sport 3dr	110	12,695
207	1.6 HDi Sport 5dr	110	13,295
207	1.6 SE 5dr	110	13,495
207	1.6 HDi GT 3dr	110	14,745
207	1.6 HDi GT 5dr	110	15,345
307	1.4 E 3dr	90	11,550
307	1.4 E 5dr	90	12,150
307	1.4 Urban 3dr	90	11,900

Model	Derivative	BHP	UK price
307	1.4 Urban 5dr	90	12,500
307	1.4 S 3dr	90	12,600
307	1.4 S 5dr	90	13,200
307	1.6 S 3dr	110	13,200
307	1.6 S 5dr	110	13,800
307	1.6 Sport 3dr	110	14,600
307	1.6 Sport 5dr	110	15,200
307	2.0 Sport 5dr	140	16,500
307	2.0 GT 3dr	180	17,000
307	2.0 GT 5dr	180	17,600
307	1.6 HDi Urban 5dr	90	13,900
307	1.6 HDi S 3dr	90	14,000
307	1.6 HDi S 5dr	90	14,600
307	1.6 HDi S 3dr	110	14,900
307	1.6 HDi S 5dr	110	15,500
307	1.6 HDi Sport 3dr	110	16,300
307	1.6 HDi Sport 5dr	110	16,900
307	2.0 HDi GT 3dr	136	17,500
307	2.0 HDi GT 5dr	136	18,100
307	1.6 S estate	110	14,400
307	1.6 HDi Urban estate	90	14,500
307	1.6 HDi S estate	90	15,200
307	1.6 HDi S estate	110	16,100
307	SW 1.6 S	110	14,800
307	SW 1.6 SE	110	15,600
307	SW 1.6 HDi S	90	15,600
307	SW 1.6 HDi SE	90	16,400
307	SW 1.6 HDi S	110	16,500
307	SW 1.6 HDi SE	110	17,300
307	SW 2.0 HDi SE	136	18,300
307	CC 1.6 S	110	17,350
307	CC 2.0 S	138	18,975
307	CC 2.0 Sport	138	20,375
307	CC 2.0 Sport	180	21,575
307	CC 2.0 HDi Sport	136	21,550
407	1.8 S	117	15,500
407	2.0 SE	138	17,175
407	2.2 Sport	163	19,125
407	3.0 Executive	211	24,245
407	1.6 HDi S	110	16,345
407	1.6 HDi SE	110	17,345
407	2.0 HDi S	136	17,250
407	2.0 HDi SE	136	18,250
407	2.0 HDi Sport	136	19,600
407	2.0 HDi Executive	136	21,900
407	2.2 HDi Sport	170	21,100
407	2.7 V6 HDi Executive	205	25,725
407	SW 1.8 S	117	16,725
407	SW 2.0 SE	138	18,375
407	SW 2.2 Sport	163	20,325
407	SW 3.0 Executive	211	25,445
407	SW 1.6 HDi S	110	17,545
407	SW 1.6 HDi SE	110	18,545
407	SW 2.0 HDi S	136	18,450
407	SW 2.0 HDi SE	136	19,450
407	SW 2.0 HDi Sport	136	20,800
407	SW 2.0 HDi Executive	136	23,100
407	SW 2.2 HDi Sport	170	22,300
407	SW 2.7 HDi Executive	205	26,945
407	Coupé 2.2 S	163	21,925
407	Coupé 2.2 SE	163	24,225
407	Coupé 3.0 V6 SE	211	26,745
407	Coupé 3.0 V6 GT	211	28,445
407	Coupé 2.7 V6 HDi SE	205	29,245
407	Coupé 2.7 V6 HDi GT	205	30,945
607	3.0 V6 Executive	211	29,040
607	2.0 HDi Executive	136	24,995
607	2.2 HDi Executive	170	26,495
807	2.0 S	140	19,295
807	2.0 SE	140	21,035
807	2.0 HDi S	110	20,795
807	2.0 HDi SE	110	22,535
807	2.0 HDi Executive	110	23,405
807	2.0 HDi S	120	21,000
807	2.0 HDi SE	120	22,790
807	2.0 HDi Executive	120	24,160
807	2.0 HDi SE	136	23,655
807	2.0 HDi Executive	136	24,995
807	2.2 HDi SE	136	23,365
807	2.2 HDi Executive	136	24,705

PORSCHE

Model	Derivative	BHP	UK price
Boxster		241	33,170
Boxster	S	291	39,850
Cayman		245	36,220
Cayman	S	291	43,930
911	Carrera	321	59,070
911	Carrera 4	321	62,930
911	Carrera 4 Targa	325	70,320
911	Carrera S	350	65,860
911	Carrera 4S	350	69,900
911	Carrera 4S Targa	355	77,370
911	Carrera GT3	409	79,540
911	Carrera GT3 RS	409	94,280
911	Turbo	473	97,840
911	Carrera cabrio	321	65,260
911	Carrera 4 cabrio	321	69,900
911	Carrera S cabrio	350	72,230
911	Carrera 4S cabrio	350	76,880
Cayenne	V6	250	35,560
Cayenne	S	340	44,900
Cayenne	Turbo	450	70,870
Cayenne	Turbo S	521	81,565

PROTON

Model	Derivative	BHP	UK price
Savvy	1.2 Street	75	5,995
Savvy	1.2 Style	75	6,995
Impian	1.6 GLS	102	10,995
Impian	1.6 GSX	102	11,995
Gen-2	1.3 GLS	74	8,795
Gen-2	1.6 GLS	110	9,595
Gen-2	1.6 GSX	110	10,595

RENAULT

Model	Derivative	BHP	UK price
Kangoo	1.2 Authentique	75	9910
Kangoo	1.2 Expression	75	10510
Kangoo	1.6 Authentique	94	11010
Kangoo	1.6 Expression	94	11350
Kangoo	1.5 dCi Authentique	68	10,910
Kangoo	1.5 dCi Expression	68	11,510
Kangoo	1.5 dCi Venture	84	11,625
Clio Campus	1.2	60	7,935
Clio Campus	1.2 16v Sport	75	8,635
Clio Campus	1.5 dCi	68	9,035
Clio Campus	1.5 dCi Sport	68	9,535
Clio	1.2 Extreme 3dr	75	8,995
Clio	1.2 Authentique 5dr	75	9,225
Clio	1.2 Expression 3dr	75	9,610
Clio	1.2 Expression 5dr	75	10,780
Clio	1.4 Expression 3dr	98	10,110
Clio	1.4 Expression 5dr	98	10,780
Clio	1.4 Dynamique 3dr	98	11,089
Clio	1.4 Dynamique 5dr	98	11,542
Clio	1.4 Dynamique S 3dr	98	10,710
Clio	1.4 Privilege 5dr	98	11,980
Clio	1.6 Expression 3dr auto	113	11,710
Clio	1.6 Expression 5dr auto	113	12,380
Clio	1.6 Dynamique 3dr auto	113	12,010
Clio	1.6 Dynamique 5dr	113	11,580
Clio	1.6 Privilege 5dr	113	12,480
Clio	1.6 Initiale 5dr	113	14,100

Model	Derivative	BHP	UK price
Clio	Renaultsport 197	194	15,995
Clio	1.5 dCi Extreme 3dr	68	9,995
Clio	1.5 dCi Authentique 5dr	68	10,225
Clio	1.5 dCi Expression 3dr	68	10,610
Clio	1.5 dCi Expression 5dr	68	11,280
Clio	1.5 dCi Expression 3dr	85	11,110
Clio	1.5 dCi Expression 5dr	85	11,780
Clio	1.5 dCi Dynamique 3dr	85	11,410
Clio	1.5 dCi Dynamique 5dr	85	12,080
Clio	1.5 dCi Dynamique S 3dr	85	11,710
Clio	1.5 dCi Privilege 5dr	85	12,980
Clio	1.5 dCi Dynamique 3dr	105	12,590
Clio	1.5 dCi Dynamique 5dr	105	13,102
Clio	1.5 dCi Privilege 5dr	105	13,730
Clio	1.5 dCi Initiale 5dr	105	15,430
Modus	1.2 Authentique	75	9,205
Modus	1.2 Expression	75	10,260
Modus	1.2 Oasis	75	10,870
Modus	1.4 Expression	98	10,760
Modus	1.4 Oasis	98	11,370
Modus	1.4 Dynamique	98	11,060
Modus	1.4 Privilege	98	11,960
Modus	1.6 Dynamique	113	11,560
Modus	1.6 Privilege	113	12,460
Modus	1.6 Initiale	113	14,160
Modus	1.5 dCi Authentique	68	10,205
Modus	1.5 dCi Expression	68	11,260
Modus	1.5 dCi Oasis	68	11,870
Modus	1.5 dCi Expression	85	11,760
Modus	1.5 dCi Oasis	85	12,370
Modus	1.5 dCi Dynamique	85	12,060
Modus	1.5 dCi Privilege	85	12,960
Modus	1.5 dCi Initiale	85	14,660
Modus	1.5 dCi Dynamique	105	13,335
Modus	1.5 dCi Privilege	105	13,710
Modus	1.5 dCi Initiale	105	15,410
Mégane	1.4 Extreme 3dr	98	11,670
Mégane	1.4 Authentique 5dr	98	11,670
Mégane	1.4 Dynamique 3dr	98	12,970
Mégane	1.4 Dynamique 5dr	98	13,470
Mégane	1.4 Expression 5dr	98	12,970
Mégane	1.6 Authentique 5dr	115	12,170
Mégane	1.6 Dynamique 3dr	115	13,470
Mégane	1.6 Dynamique 5dr	115	13,970
Mégane	1.6 Expression 5dr	115	13,970
Mégane	1.6 Privilege 5dr	115	13,470
Mégane	2.0 Dynamique 3dr	136	14,470
Mégane	2.0 Dynamique 5dr	136	14,970
Mégane	2.0 Privilege 5dr	136	15,970
Mégane	2.0 T Dynamique 3dr	165	15,670
Mégane	2.0 T Dynamique 5dr	165	16,170
Mégane	2.0 T Privilege 5dr	165	17,170
Mégane	Renaultsport 225 5dr	222	20,000
Mégane	Renaultsport 225 Cup 3dr	222	18,600
Mégane	1.5 dCi Extreme 3dr	85	12,970
Mégane	1.5 dCi Authentique 5dr	85	12,470
Mégane	1.5 dCi Expression 5dr	85	13,770
Mégane	1.5 dCi Dynamique 3dr	85	13,770
Mégane	1.5 dCi Dynamique 5dr	85	14,270
Mégane	1.5 dCi Expression 5dr	105	14,470
Mégane	1.5 dCi Dynamique 3dr	105	14,470
Mégane	1.5 dCi Dynamique 5dr	105	14,970
Mégane	1.5 dCi Privilege 5dr	105	15,970
Mégane	1.9 dCi Dynamique 3dr	128	15,670
Mégane	1.9 dCi Dynamique 5dr	128	16,170
Mégane	1.9 dCi Expression 5dr	128	15,670
Mégane	1.9 dCi Privilege 5dr	128	17,170
Mégane	2.0 dCi Dynamique 3dr	150	16,670
Mégane	2.0 dCi Dynamique 5dr	150	17,170
Mégane	2.0 dCi Dynamique 5dr	150	18,170
Mégane	1.4 Expression saloon	98	13,650
Mégane	1.4 Dynamique saloon	98	14,150
Mégane	1.6 Expression saloon	114	14,150
Mégane	1.6 Dynamique saloon	114	14,650
Mégane	1.6 Privilege saloon	114	15,650
Mégane	2.0 Dynamique saloon	134	15,650
Mégane	2.0 Privilege saloon	134	16,650
Mégane	1.5 dCi Expression saloon	85	14,450
Mégane	1.5 dCi Dynamique saloon	85	14,950
Mégane	1.5 dCi Expression saloon	105	15,150
Mégane	1.5 dCi Dynamique saloon	105	15,650
Mégane	1.5 dCi Privilege saloon	105	16,650
Mégane	1.9 dCi Expression saloon	128	16,350
Mégane	1.9 dCi Dynamique saloon	128	16,850
Mégane	1.9 dCi Privilege saloon	128	17,850
Mégane	2.0 dCi Dynamique saloon	150	17,850
Mégane	2.0 dCi Privilege saloon	150	18,850
Mégane	1.4 Expression Sport Tourer	98	13,900
Mégane	1.4 Dynamique Sport Tourer	98	14,400
Mégane	1.6 Expression Sport Tourer	110	14,400
Mégane	1.6 Dynamique Sport Tourer	110	14,900
Mégane	1.6 Privilege Sport Tourer	110	15,900
Mégane	2.0 Dynamique Sport Tourer	134	15,900
Mégane	2.0 Privilege Sport Tourer	134	16,900
Mégane	1.5 dCi Expression Sport Tourer	85	14,700
Mégane	1.5 dCi Dynamique Sport Tourer	85	15,200
Mégane	1.5 dCi Expression Sport Tourer	105	15,400
Mégane	1.5 dCi Dynamique Sport Tourer	105	15,900
Mégane	1.5 dCi Privilege Sport Tourer	105	16,900
Mégane	1.9 dCi Expression Sport Tourer	128	16,600
Mégane	1.9 dCi Dynamique Sport Tourer	128	17,100
Mégane	1.9 dCi Privilege Sport Tourer	128	18,100
Mégane	2.0 dCi Dynamique Sport Tourer	110	18,100
Mégane	2.0 dCi Privilege Sport Tourer	110	19,100
Mégane	1.6 Extreme C-C	115	17,810
Mégane	1.6 Dynamique C-C	115	18,310
Mégane	1.6 Privilege C-C	115	19,310
Mégane	2.0 Dynamique C-C	136	19,310
Mégane	2.0 Privilege C-C	136	20,310
Mégane	2.0 T Dynamique C-C	165	20,510
Mégane	2.0 T Privilege C-C	165	21,510
Mégane	1.9 dCi Dynamique C-C	128	20,510
Mégane	1.9 dCi Privilege C-C	128	21,510
Scénic	1.4 Authentique	97	13,915
Scénic	1.4 Expression	97	15,215
Scénic	1.4 Dynamique	97	14,415
Scénic	1.6 Expression	114	15,715
Scénic	1.6 Oasis	114	16,015
Scénic	1.6 Dynamique	114	16,215
Scénic	1.6 Privilege	114	17,215
Scénic	2.0 Dynamique	134	17,215
Scénic	2.0 Privilege	134	18,215
Scénic	2.0 T Dynamique	165	18,410
Scénic	2.0 T Dynamique	165	19,410
Scénic	1.5 dCi Authentique	85	14,715
Scénic	1.5 dCi Expression	85	16,015
Scénic	1.5 dCi Oasis	85	16,315
Scénic	1.5 dCi Dynamique	85	16,515
Scénic	1.5 dCi Expression	104	16,715
Scénic	1.5 dCi Oasis	104	17,015
Scénic	1.5 dCi Dynamique	104	17,215
Scénic	1.9 dCi Expression	128	17,915
Scénic	1.9 dCi Oasis	128	18,215
Scénic	1.9 dCi Dynamique	128	18,415
Scénic	1.9 dCi Privilege	128	19,415
Grand Scénic	1.6 Authentique	114	15,415
Grand Scénic	1.6 Expression	114	16,715
Grand Scénic	1.6 Oasis	114	17,015

Model	Derivative	BHP	UK price
Grand Scénic	1.6 Dynamique	114	17,215
Grand Scénic	1.6 Privilege	114	18,215
Grand Scénic	2.0 Dynamique	134	18,215
Grand Scénic	2.0 Privilege	134	19,215
Grand Scénic	2.0 T Dynamique	165	19,410
Grand Scénic	2.0 T Privilege	165	20,410
Grand Scénic	1.5 dCi Expression	106	17,715
Grand Scénic	1.5 dCi Oasis	106	18,015
Grand Scénic	1.5 dCi Dynamique	106	18,215
Grand Scénic	1.9 dCi Expression	96	18,915
Grand Scénic	1.9 dCi Oasis	96	19,215
Grand Scénic	1.9 dCi Dynamique	96	19,415
Grand Scénic	1.9 dCi Privilege	96	20,415
Laguna	2.0 Extreme	133	16,425
Laguna	2.0 Expression	133	16,225
Laguna	2.0 Expression Navigation	133	16,775
Laguna	2.0 Dynamique	133	17,325
Laguna	2.0 Dynamique Navigation	133	17,875
Laguna	2.0 Privilege	133	18,575
Laguna	2.0 Initiale	133	21,075
Laguna	2.0 T Dynamique	165	18,425
Laguna	2.0 T Privilege	165	19,675
Laguna	2.0 T Initiale	165	22,175
Laguna	2.0 T GT205	202	21,825
Laguna	3.0 V6 Initiale	207	23,995
Laguna	1.9 dCi Expression	95	16,350
Laguna	1.9 dCi Extreme	128	17,400
Laguna	1.9 dCi Expression	128	17,200
Laguna	1.9 dCi Expression Navigation	128	17,750
Laguna	1.9 dCi Dynamique	128	18,300
Laguna	1.9 dCi Dynamique Navigation	128	18,850
Laguna	1.9 dCi Privilege	128	19,550
Laguna	1.9 dCi Initiale	128	22,050
Laguna	2.0 dCi Extreme	150	18,500
Laguna	2.0 dCi Expression	150	18,300
Laguna	2.0 dCi Dynamique	150	19,400
Laguna	2.0 dCi Dynamique Navigation	150	19,950
Laguna	2.0 dCi Privilege	150	20,650
Laguna	2.0 dCi Initiale	150	23,150
Laguna	2.0 dCi GT175	175	22,550
Laguna	2.2 dCi Dynamique	138	20,525
Laguna	2.2 dCi Privilege	138	21,775
Laguna	2.2 dCi Initiale	138	24,275
Laguna	2.0 Extreme Sport Tourer	133	17,525
Laguna	2.0 Expression Sport Tourer	133	17,325
Laguna	2.0 Expression Navigation Sport Tourer	133	17,875
Laguna	2.0 Dynamique Sport Tourer	133	18,425
Laguna	2.0 Dynamique Navigation Sport Tourer	133	18,975
Laguna	2.0 Privilege Sport Tourer	133	19,675
Laguna	2.0 Initiale Sport Tourer	133	22,175
Laguna	2.0 T Dynamique Sport Tourer	165	19,525
Laguna	2.0 T Privilege Sport Tourer	165	20,775
Laguna	2.0 T Initiale Sport Tourer	165	23,275
Laguna	2.0 T GT205 Sport Tourer	202	22,925
Laguna	3.0 V6 Initiale Sport Tourer	207	25,095
Laguna	1.9 dCi Expression Sport Tourer	95	17,450
Laguna	1.9 dCi Extreme Sport Tourer	128	18,500
Laguna	1.9 dCi Expression Sport Tourer	128	18,300
Laguna	1.9 dCi Expression Nav Sport Tourer	128	18,850
Laguna	1.9 dCi Dynamique Sport Tourer	128	19,400
Laguna	1.9 dCi Dynamique Nav Sport Tourer	128	19,950
Laguna	1.9 dCi Privilege Sport Tourer	128	20,650
Laguna	1.9 dCi Initiale Sport Tourer	128	23,150
Laguna	2.0 dCi Extreme Sport Tourer	150	19,600
Laguna	2.0 dCi Expression Sport Tourer	150	19,400
Laguna	2.0 dCi Dynamique Sport Tourer	150	20,500
Laguna	2.0 dCi Dynamique Nav Sport Tourer	150	21,050
Laguna	2.0 dCi Privilege Sport Tourer	150	21,750
Laguna	2.0 dCi Initiale Sport Tourer	150	24,250

Model	Derivative	BHP	UK price
Laguna	2.0 dCi GT175 Sport Tourer	175	23,650
Laguna	2.2 dCi Dynamique Sport Tourer	138	21,625
Laguna	2.2 dCi Privilege Sport Tourer	138	22,875
Laguna	2.2 dCi Initiale Sport Tourer	138	25,375
Espace	2.0 Rush	140	18,995
Espace	2.0 Authentique	140	19,825
Espace	2.0 Expression	140	21,975
Espace	2.0 T Dynamique	165	23,945
Espace	2.0 T Privilege	165	25,295
Espace	1.9 dCi Rush	118	19,995
Espace	1.9 dCi Authentique	118	20,800
Espace	1.9 dCi Expression	118	22,950
Espace	1.9 dCi Dynamique	118	23,900
Espace	2.0 dCi Dynamique	173	26,775
Espace	2.0 dCi Privilege	173	28,125
Espace	2.2 dCi Expression	148	24,475
Espace	2.2 dCi Dynamique	148	25,425
Espace	2.2 dCi Privilege	148	26,775
Grand Espace	2.0 Turbo Expression	165	24,195
Grand Espace	2.0 Turbo Dynamique	165	25,145
Grand Espace	2.0 Turbo Privilege	165	26,495
Grand Espace	3.5 V6 Initiale	245	35,545
Grand Espace	2.0 dCi Dynamique	173	27,975
Grand Espace	2.0 dCi Dynamique	173	29,325
Grand Espace	2.0 dCi Initiale	173	33,275
Grand Espace	2.2 dCi Expression	148	25,675
Grand Espace	2.2 dCi Dynamique	148	26,625
Grand Espace	2.2 dCi Privilege	148	27,975
Grand Espace	2.2 dCi Initiale	148	31,925
Grand Espace	3.0 dCi Initiale	180	31,775

ROLLS ROYCE

Model	Derivative	BHP	UK price
Phantom		453	216,950

SAAB

Model	Derivative	BHP	UK price
9-3	1.8i	122	16,995
9-3	1.8i Linear	122	18,770
9-3	1.8i Linear Sport	122	19,770
9-3	1.8i Vector	122	20,620
9-3	1.8i Vector Sport	122	21,270
9-3	1.8t Linear	150	20,205
9-3	1.8t Linear Sport	150	21,205
9-3	1.8t Vector	150	22,055
9-3	1.8t Vector Sport	150	22,705
9-3	2.0t Linear	175	21,345
9-3	2.0t Linear Sport	175	22,345
9-3	2.0t Vector	175	23,205
9-3	2.0t Vector Sport	175	23,855
9-3	2.0 T Aero	210	24,995
9-3	2.8 T V6 Aero	250	27,525
9-3	1.9 TiD Linear	120	19,640
9-3	1.9 TiD Linear Sport	120	20,640
9-3	1.9 TiD Vector	120	21,490
9-3	1.9 TiD Vector Sport	120	22,140
9-3	1.9 TiD Linear	150	20,665
9-3	1.9 TiD Linear Sport	150	21,665
9-3	1.9 TiD Vector	150	22,515
9-3	1.9 TiD Vector Sport	150	23,205
9-3	1.8i Sport Wagon	122	17,995
9-3	1.8i Linear Sport Wagon	122	19,770
9-3	1.8i Linear Sport Sport Wagon	122	20,770
9-3	1.8i Vector Sport Wagon	122	19,770
9-3	1.8i Vector Sport Sport Wagon	122	20,770
9-3	1.8t Linear Sport Wagon	150	21,245
9-3	1.8t Linear Sport Sport Wagon	150	22,245
9-3	1.8t Vector Sport Wagon	150	23,095
9-3	1.8t Vector Sport Sport Wagon	150	23,745
9-3	2.0t Linear Sport Wagon	175	23,205
9-3	2.0t Linear Sport Sport Wagon	175	23,345
9-3	2.0t Vector Sport Wagon	175	24,205
9-3	2.0t Vector Sport Sport Wagon	175	24,855

Model	Derivative	BHP	UK price
9-3	2.0 T Aero Sport Wagon	210	25,995
9-3	2.8 T Aero Sport Wagon	247	28,525
9-3	1.9 TiD Linear Sport Wagon	120	20,640
9-3	1.9 TiD Linear Sport Sport Wagon	120	21,640
9-3	1.9 TiD Vector Sport Wagon	120	22,490
9-3	1.9 TiD Vector Sport Sport Wagon	120	23,140
9-3	1.9 TiD Linear Sport Wagon	150	21,665
9-3	1.9 TiD Linear Sport Sport Wagon	150	22,665
9-3	1.9 TiD Vector Sport Wagon	150	23,515
9-3	1.9 TiD Vector Sport Sport Wagon	150	24,165
9-3	1.8t Linear cabrio	150	24,995
9-3	1.8t Vector cabrio	150	27,489
9-3	2.0t Linear cabrio	175	26,489
9-3	2.0t Vector cabrio	175	28,589
9-3	2.0 T Aero cabrio	210	30,874
9-3	2.8 T V6 Aero cabrio	247	33,194
9-3	1.9 TiD Linear cabrio	150	25,450
9-3	1.9 TiD Vector cabrio	150	27,919
9-5	2.0t Linear	150	21,267
9-5	2.0t Linear Sport	150	22,267
9-5	2.0t Vector	150	23,642
9-5	2.0t Vector Sport	150	24,492
9-5	2.3t Linear	185	22,467
9-5	2.3t Linear Sport	185	23,467
9-5	2.3t Vector	185	24,842
9-5	2.3t Vector Sport	185	25,692
9-5	2.3 Aero	260	28,336
9-5	2.3 HOT Aero	260	28,552
9-5	1.9 TiD Linear	150	21,696
9-5	1.9 TiD Linear Sport	150	22,696
9-5	1.9 TiD Vector	150	24,706
9-5	1.9 TiD Vector Sport	150	25,556
9-5	2.0t Linear estate	150	22,467
9-5	2.0t Linear Sport estate	150	23,467
9-5	2.0t Vector estate	150	24,842
9-5	2.0t Vector Sport estate	150	25,692
9-5	2.3t Linear estate	185	23,667
9-5	2.3t Linear Sport estate	185	24,667
9-5	2.3t Vector estate	185	26,042
9-5	2.3t Vector Sport estate	185	26,892
9-5	2.3 HOT Aero estate	260	29,752
9-5	1.9 TiD Linear estate	150	22,296
9-5	1.9 TiD Linear Sport estate	150	23,296
9-5	1.9 TiD Vector estate	150	25,306
9-5	1.9 TiD Vector Sport estate	150	26,156
SEAT			
Ibiza	1.2 Reference 3dr	63	7,545
Ibiza	1.2 Reference 5dr	63	8,145
Ibiza	1.4 Stylance 3dr	74	8,995
Ibiza	1.4 Stylance 5dr	74	9,595
Ibiza	1.4 Sport 3dr	74	8,995
Ibiza	1.4 Sport 5dr	74	9,595
Ibiza	1.8 20VT FR 3dr	148	11,975
Ibiza	1.8 20VT FR 5dr	148	12,575
Ibiza	1.8 20VT Cupra	178	14,425
Ibiza	1.4 TDi Reference 3dr	79	9,570
Ibiza	1.4 TDi Reference 5dr	79	10,170
Ibiza	1.9 TDi Sport 3dr	99	10,790
Ibiza	1.9 TDi Sport 5dr	99	11,390
Ibiza	1.9 TDi FR 3dr	128	13,120
Ibiza	1.9 TDi FR 5dr	128	13,720
Ibiza	1.9 TDi Cupra	158	15,370
Leon	1.6 Essence	101	11,495
Leon	1.6 Reference	101	12,195
Leon	1.6 Stylance	101	13,295
Leon	2.0 FSI Reference Sport	150	14,495
Leon	2.0 FSI Stylance	150	15,695
Leon	2.0 TFSI FR 5dr	197	16,995
Leon	2.0 TFSI F2 3dr	197	16,995

Model	Derivative	BHP	UK price
Leon	1.9 TDi Reference	105	13,195
Leon	1.9 TDi Stylance	105	14,295
Leon	2.0 TDi Reference Sport	140	15,195
Leon	2.0 TDi Stylance	140	16,395
Leon	2.0 TDi FR	168	17,495
Altea	1.6 Essence	101	11,865
Altea	1.6 Reference	101	12,365
Altea	1.6 Reference Sport	101	12,665
Altea	1.6 Stylance	101	13,365
Altea	2.0 FSI Stylance	147	16,495
Altea	2.0 TFSI FR	197	17,295
Altea	1.9 TDi Reference	103	13,365
Altea	1.9 TDi Reference Sport	103	13,665
Altea	1.9 TDi Stylance	103	14,365
Altea	2.0 TDi FR	168	17,795
Toledo	1.6 Reference	101	12,520
Toledo	1.6 Stylance	101	13,520
Toledo	2.0 FSI Sport	150	16,320
Toledo	1.9 TDi Reference	104	13,490
Toledo	1.9 TDi Stylance	104	14,490
Toledo	2.0 TDi Sport	140	16,995
Alhambra	2.0 Reference	113	16,265
Alhambra	1.9 TDi Stylance	113	21,595
Alhambra	2.0 TDi Reference	138	18,495
Alhambra	2.0 TDi Stylance	138	21,120
SKODA			
Fabia	1.2 6v Classic	54	7,570
Fabia	1.2 12v Classic	64	8,075
Fabia	1.2 Ambiente	64	8,735
Fabia	1.2 Sport	64	8,985
Fabia	1.4 Classic auto	75	10,040
Fabia	1.4 Ambiente auto	75	10,700
Fabia	1.4 Sport	75	9,990
Fabia	1.4 Elegance auto	75	11,470
Fabia	1.4 Ambiente	100	9,980
Fabia	1.4 Elegance	100	10,750
Fabia	2.0 Elegance	115	11,825
Fabia	1.4 TDI Classic	70	9,425
Fabia	1.4 TDI Ambiente	70	10,085
Fabia	1.4 TDI Classic	75	9,695
Fabia	1.4 TDI Ambiente	75	10,355
Fabia	1.4 TDI Classic	80	9,840
Fabia	1.4 TDI Ambiente	80	10,500
Fabia	1.9 SDI Classic	64	9,190
Fabia	1.9 SDI Ambiente	64	9,850
Fabia	1.9 TDI Ambiente	100	11,125
Fabia	1.9 TDI Elegance	100	11,895
Fabia	1.9 TDI RS	130	12,375
Fabia	1.4 auto saloon	75	10,485
Fabia	1.4 saloon	100	9,750
Fabia	1.9 SDi saloon	64	9,635
Fabia	1.2 Classic estate	64	8,775
Fabia	1.2 Ambiente estate	64	9,435
Fabia	1.4 Classic auto estate	75	10,740
Fabia	1.4 Bohemia estate	75	10,300
Fabia	1.4 Ambiente auto estate	75	11,400
Fabia	1.4 Elegance auto estate	75	12,170
Fabia	1.4 Ambiente estate	100	10,680
Fabia	1.4 Elegance estate	100	11,450
Fabia	2.0 Elegance estate	115	12,565
Fabia	1.4 TDI Classic estate	70	10,125
Fabia	1.4 TDI Ambiente estate	70	10,785
Fabia	1.4 TDI Classic estate	75	10,395
Fabia	1.4 TDI Bohemia estate	75	10,905
Fabia	1.4 TDI Ambiente estate	75	11,055
Fabia	1.4 TDI Classic estate	80	10,540
Fabia	1.4 TDI Ambiente estate	80	11,200
Fabia	1.9 SDI Classic estate	64	9,890
Fabia	1.9 SDI Ambiente estate	64	10,550

Model	Derivative	BHP	UK price
Fabia	1.9 TDI Ambiente estate	100	11,825
Fabia	1.9 TDI Elegance estate	100	12,595
Roomster	1.4 Level 1	85	10,505
Roomster	1.4 Level 2	85	11,505
Roomster	1.4 Level 3	85	12,505
Roomster	1.6 Level 2	105	11,855
Roomster	1.6 Level 3	105	12,855
Roomster	1.4 TDI Level 1	70	11,020
Roomster	1.4 TDI Level 2	80	12,450
Roomster	1.4 TDI Level 3	80	13,450
Roomster	1.9 TDI Level 2	105	13,050
Roomster	1.9 TDI Level 3	105	14,050
Octavia	1.4 Classic	75	10,990
Octavia	1.6 FSI Classic	115	11,990
Octavia	1.6 FSI Ambiente	115	12,990
Octavia	1.6 FSI Elegance	115	13,990
Octavia	1.6 FSI L&K	115	15,475
Octavia	2.0 FSI Ambiente	148	14,335
Octavia	2.0 FSI Sport	148	15,800
Octavia	2.0 FSI Elegance	148	15,335
Octavia	2.0 FSI L&K	148	16,820
Octavia	2.0 TFSI RS	197	17,525
Octavia	1.9 TDI Classic	105	13,450
Octavia	1.9 TDI Ambiente	105	14,450
Octavia	1.9 TDI L&K	105	16,935
Octavia	2.0 TDI Ambiente	140	15,925
Octavia	2.0 TDI Sport	140	17,390
Octavia	2.0 TDI Elegance	140	16,925
Octavia	2.0 TDI L&K	140	18,410
Octavia	2.0 TDI RS	168	18,370
Octavia	1.6 FSI Classic estate	115	12,840
Octavia	1.6 FSI Ambiente estate	115	13,840
Octavia	1.6 FSI Elegance estate	115	14,840
Octavia	1.6 FSI L&K estate	115	16,325
Octavia	2.0 FSI Ambiente estate	148	15,185
Octavia	2.0 FSI Elegance estate	148	16,185
Octavia	2.0 FSI L&K estate	148	17,670
Octavia	2.0 FSI estate 4x4	148	16,585
Octavia	2.0 TFSI RS estate	197	18,375
Octavia	1.9 TDI Classic estate	105	14,305
Octavia	1.9 TDI Ambience estate	105	15,300
Octavia	1.9 TDI Elegant estate	105	16,300
Octavia	1.9 TDI L&K estate	105	17,785
Octavia	1.9 TDI estate 4x4	105	16,730
Octavia	2.0 TDI Ambiente estate	140	16,775
Octavia	2.0 TDI Elegance estate	140	16,775
Octavia	2.0 TDI L&K estate	140	19,260
Octavia	2.0 TDI RS estate	168	19,220
Superb	2.0 Classic	114	13,925
Superb	1.8 T Classic	148	15,180
Superb	1.8 T Comfort	148	16,580
Superb	2.8 V6 Elegance	190	21,290
Superb	1.9 TDI Classic	100	14,700
Superb	1.9 TDI Classic	105	14,850
Superb	1.9 TDI Comfort	105	16,250
Superb	1.9 TDI Classic	129	15,400
Superb	1.9 TDI Comfort	129	17,000
Superb	1.9 TDI Elegance	129	19,700
Superb	2.0 TDI Classic	140	15,990
Superb	2.0 TDI Comfort	140	17,390
Superb	2.0 TDI Elegance	140	20,090
Superb	2.5 V6 TDI Classic	160	17,615
Superb	2.5 V6 TDI Comfort	160	19,015
Superb	2.5 V6 TDI Elegance	160	21,330
SMART			
Fortwo	Pure Coupé	50	6,775
Fortwo	Pure Coupé	61	7,130
Fortwo	Pulse Coupé	61	8,030
Fortwo	Passion Coupé	61	8,230

Model	Derivative	BHP	UK price
Fortwo	Coupé Brabus	74	12,770
Fortwo	Pure cabrio	61	8,930
Fortwo	Pulse cabrio	61	9,830
Fortwo	Passion cabrio	61	10,030
Fortwo	Cabrio Brabus	74	14,615
Forfour	1.0 Purestyle	64	7,290
Forfour	1.0 Coolstyle	64	8,590
Forfour	1.1 Pulse	75	8,990
Forfour	1.1 Black	75	8,995
Forfour	1.1 Passion	75	10,365
Forfour	1.3 Pulse	95	9,990
Forfour	1.3 Passion	95	11,365
Forfour	1.5 Pulse	109	10,990
Forfour	1.5 Passion	109	12,365
Forfour	1.5 Brabus	177	17,195
Forfour	1.5 CDi Pulse	68	9,990
Forfour	1.5 CDi Passion	68	11,365
Forfour	1.5 CDi Pulse	95	10,990
Forfour	1.5 CDi Passion	95	12,365
Roadster	Brabus	101	16,690
Roadster	Coupés	80	14,515
Roadster	Coupé Brabus	101	17,290
SPYKER			
C8		400	185,000
SSANGYONG			
Rexton	2.7D S 5-SEATER	163	18,995
Rexton	2.7D S 7-SEATER	163	19,495
Rexton	2.7D SE 5-SEATER	163	20,995
Rexton	2.7D SE 7-SEATER	163	21,495
Rexton	2.7D SX 5-SEATER	163	22,995
Rexton	2.7D SX 7-SEATER	163	23,495
Kyron	2.0 S 2WD	141	16,995
Kyron	2.0 S 4WD	141	17,995
Kyron	2.0 SE 4WD	141	18,995
Kyron	2.0 SX 4WD	141	22,495
Rodius	S	163	14,995
Rodius	SE	163	15,995
Rodius	SX	163	19,995
SUBARU			
Impreza	1.5R	104	12,495
Impreza	2.0R	157	16,225
Impreza	2.5 WRX	227	21,445
Impreza	2.5 WRX STi	276	27,000
Impreza	2.5 WRX CZS	282	23,950
Legacy	2.0R	163	17,020
Legacy	2.0RE	163	19,020
Legacy	3.0R spec. B	241	26,945
Legacy	2.0R estate	163	18,020
Legacy	2.0RE estate	163	20,020
Legacy	3.0R spec. B estate	241	27,945
Outback	2.5i S	162	20,625
Outback	2.5i SE	162	22,925
Outback	3.0R	241	26,945
Outback	3.0Rn	241	28,445
Forester	2.0 X	156	17,620
Forester	2.0 X Plus	156	18,120
Forester	2.0 XE	156	20,520
Forester	2.5 XT	208	22,040
Forester	2.5 XTE	208	23,640
Forester	2.5 XTEn	208	24,840
B9 Tribeca	3.0 S5	242	28,995
B9 Tribeca	3.0 SE5	242	31,995
B9 Tribeca	3.0 SE7	242	33,995
SUZUKI			
Alto	1.1 GL	62	5,999
Wagon R+	1.2 GL	102	9,999
Swift	1.3 GL 3dr	91	7,599
Swift	1.3 GL 5dr	91	7,899
Swift	1.5 GLX 3dr	91	8,699

Model	Derivative	BHP	UK price
Swift	1.5 GLX 5dr	91	8,999
Swift	1.3 DDiS	68	9,799
Ignis	1.3 GL	83	7,699
Ignis	1.5 GLX auto	99	8,999
Ignis	1.5 4GRIP GLX	99	9,699
SX4	1.6 GL	106	9,999
SX4	1.6 GLX	106	10,999
SX4	1.6 4GRIP	106	12,999
SX4	1.9 DDiS	120	12,799
Liana	1.6 GL saloon	105	9,999
Liana	1.6 GLX saloon	105	10,999
Liana	1.6 GL 5dr	102	9,999
Liana	1.6 GLX 5dr	102	10,999
Jimny	JLX	84	9,999
Jimny	JLX+	84	10,499
Grand Vitara	1.6 VVT	105	12,875
Grand Vitara	1.6 VVT+	105	13,475
Grand Vitara	2.0	138	15,675
Grand Vitara	1.9 DDiS 5d	127	17,025
TATA			
Safari	2.0 TDi	89	13,995
Safari	2.0 TDi EX	89	14,995
TOYOTA			
Aygo	1.0 VVT-i 3dr	67	6,730
Aygo	1.0 VVT-i 5dr	67	6,980
Aygo	1.0 VVT-i+ 3dr	67	7,230
Aygo	1.0 VVT-i+ 5dr	67	7,480
Aygo	1.0 VVT-i Sport 3dr	67	7,730
Aygo	1.0 VVT-i Sport 5dr	67	7,980
Aygo	1.0 VVT-i Black 3dr	67	7,730
Aygo	1.0 VVT-i Black 5dr	67	7,980
Aygo	1.4D + 3dr	54	8,330
Aygo	1.4D + 5dr	54	8,580
Aygo	1.4D Sport 3dr	54	8,830
Aygo	1.4D Sport 5dr	54	9,080
Yaris	1.0 Ion 3dr	67	7,995
Yaris	1.0 Ion 5dr	67	8,495
Yaris	1.0 T2 3dr	67	8,610
Yaris	1.0 T2 5dr	67	9,110
Yaris	1.0 T3 3dr	67	9,810
Yaris	1.0 T3 5dr	67	10,310
Yaris	1.3 T3 3dr	86	10,310
Yaris	1.3 T3 5dr	86	10,810
Yaris	1.3 T-Spirit 3dr	86	11,310
Yaris	1.3 T-Spirit 5dr	86	11,810
Yaris	1.4 D-4D T2 3dr	89	10,080
Yaris	1.4 D-4D T2 5dr	89	10,580
Yaris	1.4 D-4D T3 3dr	89	11,280
Yaris	1.4 D-4D T3 5dr	89	11,780
Yaris	1.4 D-4D T-Spirit 3dr	89	12,280
Yaris	1.4 D-4D T-Spirit 5dr	89	12,780
Corolla	1.4 T2 3dr	95	11,895
Corolla	1.4 T2 5dr	95	12,395
Corolla	1.4 T3 3dr	95	12,595
Corolla	1.4 T3 5dr	95	13,195
Corolla	1.4 Colour Collection 3dr	95	11,295
Corolla	1.4 Colour Collection 5dr	95	11,895
Corolla	1.4 T-Spirit 5dr	95	14,095
Corolla	1.6 T2 5dr	109	12,900
Corolla	1.6 T3 3dr	109	13,100
Corolla	1.6 T3 5dr	109	13,700
Corolla	1.6 Colour Collection 3dr	109	11,795
Corolla	1.6 Colour Collection 5dr	109	12,395
Corolla	1.6 T-Spirit 5dr	109	14,600
Corolla	1.6 SR 5dr	109	13,295
Corolla	1.8 T Sport Compressor	215	20,040
Corolla	1.4 D-4D T2 3dr	89	12,890
Corolla	1.4 D-4D T2 5dr	89	13,390
Corolla	1.4 D-4D T3 3dr	89	13,590

Model	Derivative	BHP	UK price
Corolla	1.4 D-4D T3 5dr	89	14,090
Corolla	1.4 D-4D Colour Collection 3dr	89	12,290
Corolla	1.4 D-4D Colour Collection 5dr	89	12,790
Corolla	2.0 D-4D T2 5dr	114	14,395
Corolla	2.0 D-4D T3 3dr	114	15,195
Corolla	2.0 D-4D Colour Collection 5dr	114	13,895
Corolla	2.0 D-4D T-Spirit 5dr	114	16,095
Corolla	2.0 D-4D SR 5dr	114	14,795
Corolla	1.4 T2 saloon	95	12,395
Corolla	1.4 T3 saloon	95	13,095
Corolla	1.6 T2 saloon	109	12,900
Corolla	1.6 T3 saloon	109	13,600
Corolla	1.4 D-4D T2 saloon	89	13,390
Corolla	1.4 D-4D T3 saloon	89	14,090
Corolla	1.6 T2 estate	109	13,900
Corolla	1.6 T3 estate	109	14,600
Corolla	2.0 D-4D T2 estate	114	15,395
Corolla	2.0 D-4D T2 estate	114	16,095
Corolla	Verso 1.6 T2	109	14,015
Corolla	Verso 1.8 T2	127	15,020
Corolla	Verso 1.8 T3	127	17,020
Corolla	Verso 1.8 TR	127	16,765
Corolla	Verso 1.8 T-Spirit	127	18,820
Corolla	Verso 2.0 D-4D T2	134	16,120
Corolla	Verso 2.0 D-4D T3	134	18,120
Corolla	Verso 2.0 D-4D TR	134	17,865
Corolla	Verso 2.0 D-4D T-Spirit	134	19,920
Corolla	Verso 2.0 D-4D T180	175	20,920
Avensis	1.8 Colour Collection	127	13,995
Avensis	1.8 T2	127	15,515
Avensis	1.8 T3-S	127	17,015
Avensis	1.8 T3-X	127	17,015
Avensis	2.0 T4	145	19,515
Avensis	2.0 T-Spirit	145	21,015
Avensis	2.0 D-4D T2	124	16,015
Avensis	2.0 D-4D T3-S	124	17,515
Avensis	2.0 D-4D T3-X	124	17,515
Avensis	2.2 D-4D T3-S	148	18,015
Avensis	2.2 D-4D T3-X	148	18,015
Avensis	2.2 D-4D T4	148	19,515
Avensis	2.2 D-4D T-Spirit	148	21,015
Avensis	2.2 D-4D T180	148	21,515
Avensis	1.8 Colour Collection saloon	127	13,995
Avensis	1.8 T2 saloon	127	15,515
Avensis	1.8 T3-S saloon	127	17,015
Avensis	1.8 T3-X saloon	127	17,015
Avensis	2.0 T4 saloon	145	19,515
Avensis	2.0 T-Spirit saloon	145	20,015
Avensis	2.0 D-4D T2 saloon	124	16,015
Avensis	2.0 D-4D T3-S saloon	124	17,515
Avensis	2.0 D-4D T3-X saloon	124	17,515
Avensis	2.2 D-4D T3-S saloon	148	18,015
Avensis	2.2 D-4D T3-X saloon	148	18,015
Avensis	2.2 D-4D T4 saloon	148	19,515
Avensis	2.2 D-4D T-Spirit saloon	148	21,015
Avensis	1.8 T3-S estate	127	18,015
Avensis	1.8 T3-X estate	127	18,015
Avensis	2.0 T4 estate	145	20,515
Avensis	2.0 T-Spirit estate	145	22,015
Avensis	2.0 D-4D T2 estate	124	17,015
Avensis	2.0 D-4D T3-S estate	124	18,515
Avensis	2.0 D-4D T3-X estate	124	18,515
Avensis	2.2 D-4D T3-S estate	148	19,015
Avensis	2.2 D-4D T3-X estate	148	19,015
Avensis	2.2 D-4D T4 estate	148	20,515
Avensis	2.2 D-4D T-Spirit estate	148	22,015
Avensis	2.2 D-4D T180 estate	148	22,515
Prius	T3	76	17,780
Prius	T4	76	18,580

Model	Derivative	BHP	UK price
Prius	T-Spirit	76	20,280
RAV4	2.0 XT3	150	19,040
RAV4	2.0 XT4	150	21,540
RAV4	2.0 XT5	150	24,540
RAV4	2.2 D-4D XT3	134	20,315
RAV4	2.2 D-4D XT4	134	22,815
RAV4	2.2 D-4D XT5	134	25,815
Land Cruiser	4.0 V6 LC4	245	34,415
Land Cruiser	4.0 V6 LC5	245	38,315
Land Cruiser	3.0 D-4D LC3 3d	164	27,415
Land Cruiser	3.0 D-4D LC3 5d	164	28,915
Land Cruiser	3.0 D-4D LC4 5d	164	32,715
Land Cruiser	3.0 D-4D LC5 5d	164	36,615
Amazon	4.7	235	50,840
Amazon	4.2 D-4D	201	48,160
MR2	1.8	138	17,150
MR2	1.8 TF300	138	18,015
TVR			
Tuscan	3.6 Targa	350	39,850
Tuscan	4.0 Targa S	400	49,995
Tuscan	3.6 convertible	350	41,950
Tuscan	4.0 convertible	400	51,995
Tamora	3.6	350	36,425
T350	3.6	350	38,775
T400	4.0	400	70,193
T400	4.0 440	440	75,193
Sagaris	4.0	400	49,350
VAUXHALL			
Agila	1.0 Expression	59	6,495
Agila	1.2 Enjoy	79	8,590
Agila	1.2 Design	79	8,995
Corsa	1.0 Expression 3dr	60	6,995
Corsa	1.0 Life 3dr	60	8,910
Corsa	1.0 Life 5dr	60	9,570
Corsa	1.0 ECO Easytronic 3dr	60	9,430
Corsa	1.0 ECO Easytronic 5dr	60	10,090
Corsa	1.2 Life 3dr	79	9,680
Corsa	1.2 Life 5dr	79	10,340
Corsa	1.2 Design 3dr	79	10,670
Corsa	1.2 Design 5dr	79	11,330
Corsa	1.2 SXi 3dr	79	10,355
Corsa	1.2 SXi 5dr	79	11,015
Corsa	1.2 SXi+ 3dr	79	10,405
Corsa	1.2 SXi+ 5dr	79	11,065
Corsa	1.4 Design 3dr	89	11,790
Corsa	1.4 Design 5dr	89	12,175
Corsa	1.4 SXi 3dr	89	10,815
Corsa	1.4 SXi 5dr	89	11,475
Corsa	1.4 SXi+ 3dr	89	10,865
Corsa	1.4 SXi+ 5dr	89	11,525
Corsa	1.3 CDTi Expression 3dr	69	8,600
Corsa	1.3 CDTi Life 3dr	69	10,440
Corsa	1.3 CDTi Life 5dr	69	11,100
Corsa	1.3 CDTi Design 3dr	69	11,430
Corsa	1.3 CDTi Design 5dr	69	12,090
Corsa	1.3 CDTi SXi 3dr	69	11,115
Corsa	1.3 CDTi SXi 5dr	69	11,775
Corsa	1.3 CDTi SXi+ 3dr	69	11,165
Corsa	1.3 CDTi SXi+ 5dr	69	11,825
Tigra	1.4	90	13,995
Tigra	1.4 Sport	90	14,975
Tigra	1.4 Twinport Exclusive	88	14,975
Tigra	1.8 Sport	125	15,825
Tigra	1.8 Exclusive	123	15,825
Tigra	1.3 CDTi	69	14,840
Tigra	1.3 CDTi Sport	69	15,820
Meriva	1.4 Expression	89	9,995
Meriva	1.4 Life	89	11,495
Meriva	1.4 Club	89	13,195

Model	Derivative	BHP	UK price
Meriva	1.4 Design	89	13,375
Meriva	1.6 Life	99	12,195
Meriva	1.6 Club	99	13,895
Meriva	1.6 Design	99	14,075
Meriva	1.8 VXR	178	16,520
Meriva	1.3 CDTi Expression	74	11,085
Meriva	1.3 CDTi Life	74	12,790
Meriva	1.3 CDTi Club	74	14,490
Meriva	1.7 CDTi Life	99	13,540
Meriva	1.7 CDTi Club	99	15,240
Meriva	1.7 CDTi Design	99	15,420
Astra	1.4 Expression	90	10,995
Astra	1.4 Life	90	12,775
Astra	1.4 Club	90	13,775
Astra	1.4 SXi	90	14,275
Astra	1.6 Life	105	13,275
Astra	1.6 Club	105	14,275
Astra	1.6 Design	105	15,125
Astra	1.6 Elite	105	16,175
Astra	1.6 SXi	105	14,775
Astra	1.8 Life	125	13,775
Astra	1.8 Club	125	14,775
Astra	1.8 Design	125	15,625
Astra	1.8 Elite	125	16,675
Astra	1.8 SRi	125	16,000
Astra	2.0 T Design	170	18,300
Astra	2.0 T SRi	170	18,000
Astra	2.0 T SRi	197	18,950
Astra	1.3 CDTi Life	89	14,370
Astra	1.3 CDTi Club	89	15,370
Astra	1.7 CDTi Life	99	15,220
Astra	1.7 CDTi Club	99	15,720
Astra	1.7 CDTi Design	99	16,570
Astra	1.7 CDTi Elite	99	17,620
Astra	1.7 CDTi SXi	99	16,220
Astra	1.7 CDTi SRi	99	16,920
Astra	1.9 CDTi Design	120	17,425
Astra	1.9 CDTi Elite	120	18,475
Astra	1.9 CDTi SRi	120	17,475
Astra	1.9 CDTi Design	149	18,275
Astra	1.9 CDTi SRi	149	17,975
Astra	1.4 Life estate	90	13,525
Astra	1.4 Club estate	90	14,525
Astra	1.4 SXi estate	90	15,025
Astra	1.6 Life estate	105	14,025
Astra	1.6 Club estate	105	15,025
Astra	1.6 Design estate	105	15,875
Astra	1.6 SXi estate	105	15,525
Astra	1.8 Life estate	125	14,550
Astra	1.8 Club estate	125	15,550
Astra	1.8 Design estate	125	16,400
Astra	1.8 SRi estate	125	16,750
Astra	2.0 T SRi estate	170	18,750
Astra	2.0 T Design estate	170	19,050
Astra	2.0 T SRi estate	197	19,720
Astra	1.3 CDTi Life estate	89	15,120
Astra	1.3 CDTi Club estate	89	16,120
Astra	1.7 CDTi Life estate	99	15,970
Astra	1.7 CDTi Club estate	99	16,470
Astra	1.7 CDTi Design estate	99	17,320
Astra	1.7 CDTi SXi estate	99	16,970
Astra	1.7 CDTi SRi estate	99	17,670
Astra	1.9 CDTi Design estate	120	18,175
Astra	1.9 CDTi SRi estate	120	18,225
Astra	1.9 CDTi Design estate	150	19,025
Astra	1.9 CDTi SRi estate	150	18,725
Astra	1.4 SXi Sporthatch	90	14,275
Astra	1.6 Design Sporthatch	105	15,125
Astra	1.6 SXi Sporthatch	105	14,775

Model	Derivative	BHP	UK price
Astra	1.8 Design Sporthatch	125	15,625
Astra	1.8 SRi Sporthatch	125	16,000
Astra	2.0 T Design Sporthatch	170	18,300
Astra	2.0 T SRi Sporthatch	170	18,000
Astra	VXR	237	19,120
Astra	1.7 CDTi Design Sporthatch	99	16,570
Astra	1.7 CDTi SXi Sporthatch	99	16,220
Astra	1.7 CDTi SRi Sporthatch	99	16,920
Astra	1.9 CDTi Design Sporthatch	120	17,425
Astra	1.9 CDTi SRi Sporthatch	120	17,475
Astra	1.9 CDTi Design Sporthatch	149	18,275
Astra	1.9 CDTi SRi Sporthatch	149	17,975
Astra	TwinTop 1.6	103	16,995
Astra	TwinTop 1.6 Sport	103	17,795
Astra	TwinTop 1.8 Sport	138	18,295
Astra	TwinTop 1.8 Design	138	18,995
Astra	TwinTop 2.0 T Design	197	20,740
Astra	TwinTop 1.9 CDTi Sport	148	19,995
Astra	TwinTop 1.9 CDTi Design	148	20,695
Zafira	1.6 Expression	104	12,995
Zafira	1.6 Life	104	14,600
Zafira	1.6 Club	104	15,300
Zafira	1.8 Life	138	15,825
Zafira	1.8 Club	138	16,525
Zafira	1.8 Design	138	17,725
Zafira	1.8 SRi	138	17,925
Zafira	2.2 Life	146	16,975
Zafira	2.2 Club	146	17,675
Zafira	2.2 Design	146	19,125
Zafira	2.2 SRi	146	18,675
Zafira	2.0 T Design	197	20,595
Zafira	2.0 T SRi	197	20,145
Zafira	VXR	237	22,145
Zafira	1.9 CDTi Life	118	17,100
Zafira	1.9 CDTi Club	118	17,800
Zafira	1.9 CDTi Design	118	19,000
Zafira	1.9 CDTi SRi	118	19,200
Zafira	1.9 CDTi Design	148	20,150
Zafira	1.9 CDTi SRi	148	19,700
Vectra	1.8 Life	120	16,125
Vectra	1.8 Club	120	16,035
Vectra	1.8 Design	120	17,545
Vectra	1.8 SRi	120	16,945
Vectra	2.0 T SRi	173	18,010
Vectra	2.2 Design	154	18,140
Vectra	2.2 Elite	154	20,850
Vectra	2.2 SRi	154	17,535
Vectra	2.8 T Elite	227	23,695
Vectra	VXR	252	24,180
Vectra	1.9 CDTi Life	120	17,570
Vectra	1.9 CDTi Club	120	17,480
Vectra	1.9 CDTi Exclusive	120	15,775
Vectra	1.9 CDTi Design	120	18,990
Vectra	1.9 CDTi SRi	120	18,385
Vectra	1.9 CDTi Life	150	18,070
Vectra	1.9 CDTi Club	150	17,980
Vectra	1.9 CDTi Exclusive	150	16,275
Vectra	1.9 CDTi Design	150	19,490
Vectra	1.9 CDTi Elite	150	22,200
Vectra	1.9 CDTi SRi	150	18,885
Vectra	1.8 Life saloon	120	16,125
Vectra	1.8 Club saloon	120	16,035
Vectra	1.8 Design saloon	120	17,545
Vectra	2.2 Design saloon	154	18,140
Vectra	1.9 CDTi Life saloon	120	17,570
Vectra	1.9 CDTi Club saloon	120	17,480
Vectra	1.9 CDTi Design saloon	120	18,990
Vectra	1.9 CDTi Life saloon	150	18,070
Vectra	1.9 CDTi Club saloon	150	17,980
Vectra	1.9 CDTi Design saloon	150	19,490
Vectra	1.8 Life estate	120	17,125
Vectra	1.8 Club estate	120	17,035
Vectra	1.8 Design estate	120	18,545
Vectra	1.8 SRi estate	120	17,945
Vectra	2.0 T SRi estate	173	19,010
Vectra	2.2 Design estate	154	19,165
Vectra	2.2 Elite estate	154	21,875
Vectra	2.2 SRi estate	154	18,560
Vectra	2.8 T Elite estate	227	24,695
Vectra	VXR estate	252	25,180
Vectra	1.9 CDTi Life estate	120	18,870
Vectra	1.9 CDTi Club estate	120	18,780
Vectra	1.9 CDTi Exclusive estate	120	17,075
Vectra	1.9 CDTi Design estate	120	20,290
Vectra	1.9 CDTi SRi estate	120	19,685
Vectra	1.9 CDTi Life estate	150	19,370
Vectra	1.9 CDTi Club estate	150	19,280
Vectra	1.9 CDTi Exclusive estate	150	17,575
Vectra	1.9 CDTi Design estate	150	20,790
Vectra	1.9 CDTi Elite estate	150	23,500
Vectra	1.9 CDTi SRi estate	150	20,185
Vectra	3.0 CDTi Elite estate	174	26,125
Vectra	3.0 CDTi SRi estate	174	22,810
Signum	1.8 Exclusive	138	18,020
Signum	2.0 T Elegance	173	20,010
Signum	2.0 T Design	173	20,615
Signum	2.0 T Elite	173	23,125
Signum	2.2 Elegance	154	19,505
Signum	2.2 Exclusive	154	18,645
Signum	2.2 Design	154	20,165
Signum	2.2 Elite	154	22,675
Signum	2.8 T Design	227	21,685
Signum	2.8 T Elite	227	24,195
Signum	1.9 CDTi Elegance	120	20,685
Signum	1.9 CDTi Exclusive	120	20,020
Signum	1.9 CDTi Design	120	21,290
Signum	1.9 CDTi Elegance	150	21,185
Signum	1.9 CDTi Exclusive	150	21,185
Signum	1.9 CDTi Design	150	21,185
Signum	1.9 CDTi Elite	150	21,185
Signum	3.0 CDTi Design	174	24,415
Signum	3.0 CDTi Elite	174	26,925

VOLKSWAGEN

Model	Derivative	BHP	UK price
Fox	1.2	54	6,590
Fox	1.2 Urban	54	7,190
Fox	1.4	74	7,395
Fox	1.4 Urban	74	7,995
Polo	1.2 E 3dr	54	7,490
Polo	1.2 E 5dr	54	8,090
Polo	1.2 S 3dr	54	9,090
Polo	1.2 S 5dr	54	9,690
Polo	1.2 E 3dr	63	8,105
Polo	1.2 E 5dr	63	8,705
Polo	1.2 S 3dr	63	9,090
Polo	1.2 S 5dr	63	10,090
Polo	1.4 S 3dr	79	9,800
Polo	1.4 S 5dr	79	10,400
Polo	1.4 SE 3dr	79	10,480
Polo	1.4 SE 5dr	79	11,080
Polo	1.4 Dune	74	12,645
Polo	1.6 Sport 3dr	104	12,535
Polo	1.6 Sport 5dr	104	13,135
Polo	GTI 3dr	150	14,810
Polo	GTI 5dr	150	15,410
Polo	1.4 S TDI 3dr	69	10,645
Polo	1.4 S TDI 5dr	69	11,245
Polo	1.4 SE TDI 3dr	79	11,645
Polo	1.4 SE TDI 5dr	79	12,245

Model	Derivative	BHP	UK price
Polo	1.4 TDI Dune	70	13,490
Polo	1.9 TDI Sport 3dr	99	13,475
Polo	1.9 TDI Sport 5dr	99	14,075
Golf	1.4 S 3dr	79	11,995
Golf	1.4 S 5dr	79	12,495
Golf	1.4 TSI Sport 3dr	138	15,995
Golf	1.4 TSI Sport 5dr	138	16,495
Golf	1.4 TSI Sport 3dr	168	18,095
Golf	1.4 TSI Sport 5dr	168	18,595
Golf	1.6 FSI S 3dr	113	13,895
Golf	1.6 FSI S 5dr	113	14,395
Golf	1.6 FSI SE 5dr	113	15,375
Golf	2.0 FSI GTI 3dr	197	20,360
Golf	2.0 FSI GTI 5dr	197	20,860
Golf	R32 3dr	250	24,240
Golf	R32 5dr	250	24,740
Golf	2.0 SDI S 3dr	74	12,670
Golf	2.0 SDI S 5dr	74	13,170
Golf	1.9 TDI S 3dr	104	14,780
Golf	1.9 TDI S 5dr	104	15,280
Golf	1.9 TDI SE 5dr	104	16,265
Golf	1.9 TDI Sport 3dr	104	16,025
Golf	1.9 TDI Sport 5dr	104	16,525
Golf	2.0 TDI GT 3dr	138	17,995
Golf	2.0 TDI GT 5dr	138	18,495
Golf	2.0 TDI Sport 3dr	138	17,320
Golf	2.0 TDI Sport 5dr	138	17,820
Golf	2.0 TDI Sport 4Motion 5dr	138	18,870
Golf	GT TDI 3dr	168	19,095
Golf	GT TDI 5dr	168	19,595
Golf Plus	1.4 Luna	79	12,995
Golf Plus	1.4 TSI Sport	138	17,215
Golf Plus	1.6 FSI Luna	113	15,010
Golf Plus	1.9 TDI Luna	89	14,880
Golf Plus	1.9 TDI SE	105	16,725
Golf Plus	2.0 TDI Sport	138	18,540
Touran	1.4 TSI SE	138	17,995
Touran	1.4 TSI Sport	138	19,475
Touran	1.6 S	101	14,520
Touran	1.6 FSI SE	113	17,390
Touran	1.9 TDI S	89	15,545
Touran	1.9 TDI S	104	16,050
Touran	1.9 TDI SE	104	17,675
Touran	2.0 TDI SE	138	18,975
Touran	2.0 TDI Sport	138	20,455
Touran	2.0 TDI Sport	168	21,580
Jetta	1.6 FSI S	113	14,635
Jetta	1.6 FSI SE	113	15,625
Jetta	2.0 FSI SE	150	16,650
Jetta	2.0 FSI Sport	150	17,340
Jetta	2.0 TFSI Sport	197	18,815
Jetta	1.9 TDI S	103	15,325
Jetta	1.9 TDI SE	103	16,290
Jetta	2.0 TDI SE	138	17,525
Jetta	2.0 TDI Sport	138	18,015
New Beetle	1.4 Luna	74	11,395
New Beetle	1.6 Luna	102	12,335
New Beetle	2.0	115	14,775
New Beetle	1.8 T	150	15,995
New Beetle	1.9 TDI	99	14,745
New Beetle	1.4 Luna cabrio	74	14,195
New Beetle	1.6 Luna cabrio	102	15,650
New Beetle	2.0 cabrio	113	18,590
New Beetle	1.8 T cabrio	150	19,440
New Beetle	1.9 TDI cabrio	100	18,600
Eos	1.6 FSI	113	19,370
Eos	2.0 FSI	148	20,790
Eos	2.0 FSI Sport	148	21,735
Eos	2.0 TFSI Sport	197	23,315

Model	Derivative	BHP	UK price
Eos	2.0 TDI	138	21,360
Eos	2.0 TDI Sport	138	22,305
Passat	1.6 FSI	113	15,325
Passat	2.0 FSI S	150	16,765
Passat	2.0 FSI SE	150	18,055
Passat	2.0 TFSI Sport	197	20,895
Passat	3.2 4Motion	249	25,860
Passat	1.9 TDI S	104	16,170
Passat	1.9 TDI SE	104	17,460
Passat	2.0 TDI S	138	17,475
Passat	2.0 TDI SE	138	18,765
Passat	2.0 TDI Sport	138	20,205
Passat	2.0 TDI Sport	168	21,010
Passat	2.0 TDI SEL	168	21,735
Passat	1.6 FSI estate	113	16,465
Passat	2.0 FSI S estate	150	17,860
Passat	2.0 FSI SE estate	150	19,150
Passat	2.0 TFSI Sport estate	197	21,990
Passat	3.2 4Motion estate	249	26,955
Passat	1.9 TDI S estate	104	17,265
Passat	1.9 TDI SE estate	104	18,555
Passat	2.0 TDI S estate	138	18,570
Passat	2.0 TDI SE estate	138	19,860
Passat	2.0 TDI Sport estate	138	21,300
Passat	2.0 TDI Sport estate	168	22,130
Passat	2.0 TDI SEL estate	168	22,855
Phaeton	3.2 V6 4Motion	238	44,090
Phaeton	3.2 V6 4Motion LWB	238	46,360
Phaeton	4.2 V8 4Motion LWB	330	55,500
Phaeton	6.0 W12 4Motion LWB	444	73,330
Phaeton	3.0 V6 4Motion	222	42,220
Phaeton	5.0 V10 TDI 4Motion LWB	308	61,660
Touareg	3.6 V6 SE	276	35,915
Touareg	3.6 V6 Altitude	276	38,680
Touareg	2.5 TDI	172	28,600
Touareg	2.5 TDI SE	172	31,865
Touareg	2.5 TDI Altitude	172	34,630
Touareg	3.0 V6 TDI	222	31,825
Touareg	3.0 V6 TDI SE	222	35,090
Touareg	3.0 V6 TDI Altitude	222	37,855
Touareg	5.0 V10 TDI SE	309	53,285
Touareg	5.0 V10 TDI Altitude	309	56,050
Sharan	2.0 S	115	17,940
Sharan	2.0 SE	115	19,315
Sharan	1.8 T Sport	150	23,195
Sharan	1.9 TDI S	113	19,485
Sharan	1.9 TDI SE	113	20,625
Sharan	2.0 TDI S	138	20,235
Sharan	2.0 TDI SE	138	21,375
Sharan	2.0 TDI Sport	138	23,890
VOLVO			
C30	1.6 S	99	14,750
C30	1.6 SE	99	16,250
C30	1.6 Sport	99	17,750
C30	1.8 S	124	15,995
C30	1.8 SE	124	17,495
C30	1.8 SE Sport	124	18,995
C30	1.8 SE Lux	124	18,995
C30	2.0 S	143	16,995
C30	2.0 SE	143	18,495
C30	2.0 SE Sport	143	18,995
C30	2.0 SE Lux	143	18,995
C30	2.4 S	168	17,995
C30	2.4 SE	168	19,495
C30	2.4 SE Sport	168	19,995
C30	2.4 SE Lux	168	19,995
C30	T5 SE	220	21,495
C30	T5 SE Sport	220	22,995
C30	T5 SE Lux	220	22,995

Model	Derivative	BHP	UK price
C30	1.6 D S	108	16,795
C30	1.6 D SE	108	18,295
C30	1.6 D SE Sport	108	19,795
C30	2.0 D S	134	17,795
C30	2.0 D SE	134	19,295
C30	2.0 D SE Sport	134	20,795
C30	2.0 D SE Lux	134	20,795
C30	D5 Geartronic SE	180	22,295
C30	D5 Geartronic SE Sport	180	23,795
C30	D5 Geartronic SE Lux	180	23,795
S40	1.6 S	99	15,730
S40	1.6 SE	99	18,080
S40	1.8 S	123	16,605
S40	1.8 Sport	123	18,255
S40	1.8 SE	123	18,955
S40	1.8 SE Sport	123	20,155
S40	2.0 S	143	17,605
S40	2.0 Sport	143	19,255
S40	2.0 SE	143	19,955
S40	2.0 SE Sport	143	21,155
S40	2.4 S	168	18,895
S40	2.4 Sport	168	20,545
S40	2.4 SE	168	22,445
S40	2.4 SE Sport	168	18,895
S40	T5 Sport	217	23,195
S40	T5 SE	217	23,895
S40	T5 SE Sport	217	25,095
S40	1.6 D S	108	17,265
S40	1.6 D SE	108	19,615
S40	2.0 D S	134	18,290
S40	2.0 D Sport	134	19,940
S40	2.0 D SE	134	20,640
S40	2.0 D SE Sport	134	21,840
S40	D5 Sport	178	23,205
S40	D5 SE	178	23,915
S40	D5 SE Sport	178	25,115
V50	1.8 S	123	17,955
V50	1.8 Sport	123	19,605
V50	1.8 SE	123	20,205
V50	1.8 SE Sport	123	21,405
V50	2.0 S	143	18,955
V50	2.0 Sport	143	20,605
V50	2.0 SE	143	21,205
V50	2.0 SE Sport	143	22,405
V50	2.4 S	168	20,495
V50	2.4 Sport	168	22,145
V50	2.4 SE	168	22,745
V50	2.4 SE Sport	168	23,945
V50	T5 Sport	217	24,545
V50	T5 SE	217	25,145
V50	T5 SE Sport	217	26,345
V50	2.0 D S	134	19,640
V50	2.0 D Sport	134	21,290
V50	2.0 D SE	134	21,890
V50	2.0 D SE Sport	134	23,090
V50	D5 Sport	178	24,565
V50	D5 SE	178	25,165
V50	D5 SE Sport	178	26,365
S60	2.0T S	177	20,370
S60	2.0T Sport	177	22,220
S60	2.0T SE	177	22,870
S60	2.0T SE Sport	177	24,670
S60	2.0T SE Lux	177	25,120
S60	2.5T S	210	22,810
S60	2.5T Sport	210	24,660
S60	2.5T SE	210	25,310
S60	2.5T SE Sport	210	27,110
S60	2.5T SE Lux	210	25,760
S60	T5 Sport	260	26,745

Model	Derivative	BHP	UK price
S60	T5 SE	250	27,395
S60	T5 SE Sport	260	29,095
S60	T5 SE Lux	250	29,645
S60	T5 R AWD	296	34,965
S60	2.4D S	163	22,395
S60	2.4D Sport	163	24,245
S60	2.4D SE	163	24,895
S60	2.4D SE Sport	163	26,695
S60	2.4D SE Lux	163	27,145
S60	D5 S	185	23,255
S60	D5 Sport	185	25,105
S60	D5 SE	185	25,755
S60	D5 SE Sport	185	27,555
S60	D5 SE Lux	185	28,005
V70	2.4 S	140	23,110
V70	2.4 Sport	140	24,960
V70	2.4 SE	140	25,610
V70	2.4 SE Sport	140	27,410
V70	2.4 S	170	24,510
V70	2.4 Sport	170	26,360
V70	2.4 SE	170	27,010
V70	2.4 SE Sport	170	28,810
V70	2.0T S	180	24,875
V70	2.0T Sport	180	26,725
V70	2.0T SE	180	27,375
V70	2.0T SE Sport	180	29,175
V70	2.0T SE Lux	180	29,625
V70	2.5T S	210	26,710
V70	2.5T Sport	210	28,560
V70	2.5T SE	210	29,210
V70	2.5T SE Sport	210	31,010
V70	2.5T AWD S	210	27,865
V70	2.5T AWD Sport	210	29,715
V70	2.5T AWD SE	210	30,365
V70	2.5T AWD SE Sport	210	32,165
V70	T5 Sport	260	30,480
V70	T5 SE	260	31,130
V70	T5 SE Sport	260	32,930
V70	T5 SE Lux	260	33,380
V70	2.4D S	163	25,370
V70	2.4D Sport	163	27,220
V70	2.4D SE	163	27,870
V70	2.4D SE Sport	163	29,670
V70	D5 S	182	26,315
V70	D5 Sport	182	28,165
V70	D5 SE	182	28,815
V70	D5 SE Sport	182	30,615
V70	D5 AWD S	182	27,485
V70	D5 AWD Sport	182	29,335
V70	D5 AWD SE	182	29,985
V70	D5 AWD SE Sport	182	31,785
XC70	2.5T SE	210	30,320
XC70	2.5T SE Sport	210	30,320
XC70	2.5T SE Lux	210	32,920
XC70	D5 SE	182	30,050
XC70	D5 SE Sport	182	31,700
XC70	D5 SE Lux	182	32,650
C70	2.4 Sport	170	26,225
C70	2.4 SE	170	27,475
C70	2.4 SE Lux	170	29,975
C70	T5 Sport	217	29,500
C70	T5 SE	217	30,750
C70	T5 SE Lux	217	33,250
C70	D5 Sport	178	29,420
C70	D5 SE	178	30,670
C70	D5 SE Lux	178	33,170
S80	2.5T S	197	24,375
S80	2.5T SE	197	26,925
S80	2.5T SE Sport	197	28,925

Model	Derivative	BHP	UK price
S80	2.5T SE Lux	197	29,675
S80	3.2 SE	235	30,955
S80	3.2 SE Sport	235	32,955
S80	3.2 SE Lux	235	33,705
S80	4.4 SE	311	38,975
S80	4.4 SE Sport	311	40,975
S80	4.4 SE Lux	311	41,725
S80	2.4D S	161	24,400
S80	2.4D SE	161	26,950
S80	2.4D SE Sport	161	28,950
S80	2.4D SE Lux	161	29,700
S80	D5 SE	182	28,050
S80	D5 SE Sport	182	30,050
S80	D5 SE Lux	182	30,800
S80	D5 SE Lux Geartronic	182	30,800
XC90	3.2 SE	235	36,328
XC90	3.2 SE Sport	235	38,278
XC90	3.2 SE Lux	235	38,428

Model	Derivative	BHP	UK price
XC90	3.2 Executive	235	46,068
XC90	4.4 SE	311	44,225
XC90	4.4 SE Sport	311	45,950
XC90	4.4 SE Lux	311	46,325
XC90	4.4 Executive	311	53,965
XC90	D5 S	182	32,820
XC90	D5 SE	182	35,320
XC90	D5 SE Sport	182	32,720
XC90	D5 SE Lux	182	37,420
XC90	D5 Executive	182	46,330
WESTFIELD			
XTR2	1.3	178	27,950
XTR4	1.8	192	29,995
Sport	1800	120	15,999
Sport	1800	155	16,999
Sport	2000	192	19,950
Mega Roadster	Megabusa	178	22,999
Seight	3.9 V8	200	24,999